T3-BOB-831

1990

The Supreme Court Review

1990
The

"Judges as persons, or courts as institutions, are entitled to no greater immunity from criticism than other persons or institutions . . . [J]udges must be kept mindful of their limitations and of their ultimate public responsibility by a vigorous stream of criticism expressed with candor however blunt."

—*Felix Frankfurter*

". . . while it is proper that people should find fault when their judges fail, it is only reasonable that they should recognize the difficulties. . . . Let them be severely brought to book, when they go wrong, but by those who will take the trouble to understand them."

—*Learned Hand*

THE LAW SCHOOL

THE UNIVERSITY OF CHICAGO

Supreme Court Review

EDITED BY

GERHARD CASPER

DENNIS J. HUTCHINSON

AND DAVID A. STRAUSS

THE UNIVERSITY OF CHICAGO PRESS

CHICAGO AND LONDON

INTERNATIONAL STANDARD BOOK NUMBER: 0-226-09573-8

LIBRARY OF CONGRESS CATALOG CARD NUMBER: 60-14353

THE UNIVERSITY OF CHICAGO PRESS, CHICAGO 60637

THE UNIVERSITY OF CHICAGO PRESS, LTD., LONDON

PRINTED IN THE UNITED STATES OF AMERICA

The paper used in this publication meets the minimum requirements of American National Standard for Information Sciences—Permanence of Paper for Printed Library Materials, ANSI Z39.48-1984. ♾

TO WILLIAM J. BRENNAN, JR.

for whom justice
is the first business of the law

CONTENTS

DOUGLAS LAYCOCK

THE REMNANTS OF FREE EXERCISE

In two opinions last term, the Supreme Court rewrote the law of free exercise. In *Jimmy Swaggart Ministries v. Board of Equalization*,[1] the Court held that the dissemination of religious messages may be taxed under generally applicable laws. In *Employment Division v. Smith*,[2] the Court held that worship services may be prohibited under generally applicable laws. The Court said that generally applicable laws are neutral, and that neutrality is all the Free Exercise Clause requires.

Swaggart produced only modest reaction; *Smith* produced widespread disbelief and outrage. Anger at the result was compounded by anger at the procedure. The Court sharply changed existing law without an opportunity for briefing or argument, and it issued an opinion claiming that its new rules had been the law for a hundred years. An extraordinary coalition of religious and civil liberties groups has sought to have *Smith* overturned, first by an unsuccessful petition for rehearing and now by proposed legislation.[3]

I share the judgment that *Smith* is the more important of the two cases. State and local governments have already relied on *Smith* for

---

Douglas Laycock holds the Alice McKean Young Regents Chair in Law at the University of Texas at Austin.

AUTHOR'S NOTE: I am grateful to my colleagues at Texas for their helpful reactions to this paper at a faculty colloquium, to David Anderson, Joseph Dodge, L. A. Powe, Michael Sharlot, Jordan Steiker, Teresa Sullivan, and Jay Westbrook for comments on a written draft, and to David Petter for research assistance. Michael McConnell and I wrote on these issues simultaneously, exchanged drafts, and influenced each other throughout. I should disclose that I have participated as an advocate in several of the cases discussed in this article.

[1] 493 U.S. 378 (1990).

[2] 110 S.Ct. 1595 (1990).

[3] H.R. 5377 in the 101st Congress, titled the Religious Freedom Restoration Act of 1990. The bill is described in text at notes 226–27 *infra*.

0-226-09573-8/91/1990-001$02.00

authority to dictate the location of an altar in a Catholic church[4] and to suppress animal sacrifice among Afro-Caribbean immigrants;[5] a trial court applying *Smith* has equated the rights of churches with the rights of pornographic movie theaters.[6] It is entirely foreseeable that women and homosexuals will demand ordination under local civil rights ordinances,[7] and that various interest groups will see *Smith* as an invitation to impose their regulatory agenda on churches. *Smith* may authorize all these things or none of them. It announces a dramatic new rule and a large number of ill-defined exceptions, and the relative scope of rule and exception remains to be litigated.

Taxation and tax exemption raise additional complexities, and full treatment of these subjects would require a separate article. But *Swaggart* deserves more attention than it has received. General taxation of churches would also be a dramatic change in church-state relations, and both opinions treat taxation and regulation as equivalent for free exercise purposes.

Smith has already been subjected to substantial scholarly criticism, and I will not retrace all that ground. Michael McConnell has shown that the understanding of free exercise in the founding generation included exemptions for religiously motivated conduct.[8] Thus, *Smith* is probably wrong as a matter of original intent; certainly no plausible opinion can be written without taking account of the evidence McConnell musters. His work was completed before the Court's decision, and published immediately after. It was not brought to the Court's attention, because no one knew the Court was reconsidering the right to exemptions.

Justice O'Connor's dissent and early scholarly commentary document the obvious: the Court's account of its precedents in *Smith* is

[4]Brief of Defendant-Appellant 34–35, in Society of Jesus v. Boston Landmarks Comm'n, 408 Mass. 38, 564 N.E.2d 571 (1990).

[5]Brief of Appellee in Church of the Lukumi Babalu Aye, Inc. v. City of Hialeah, No. 90-5176, in the United States Court of Appeals for the Eleventh Circuit. For the opinion below, see 723 F. Supp. 1467 (S.D. Fla. 1989).

[6]Cornerstone Bible Church v. City of Hastings, 740 F. Supp. 654, 663 (D. Minn. 1990).

[7]*Cf.* Dignity Twin Cities v. Newman Center & Chapel, No. 87204-RE-9 (Minneapolis Comm'n on Civil Rights 1990) (Catholic student center must allocate office and meeting space, but not the use of its chapel, without regard to sexual orientation; impact of *Smith* not considered); Gay Rights Coalition v. Georgetown Univ., 536 A.2d 1 (D.C. App. 1987) (Jesuit university must provide services and facilities to student organizations, but not official recognition as university groups, without regard to sexual orientation); Walker v. First Presbyterian Church, 22 Fair Empl. Prac. 762 (Cal. Super. Ct. 1980) (upholding church's right to discharge homosexual organist).

[8]McConnell, The Origins and Historical Understanding of Free Exercise of Religion, 103 Harv. L. Rev. 1409, 1466–73 (1990).

transparently dishonest.[9] Perhaps the point is made most effectively by quoting Justice Scalia, in a pair of opinions fourteen months apart. Here is Scalia in 1989:

> In such cases as *Sherbert v. Verner*, *Wisconsin v. Yoder*, *Thomas v. Review Bd. of Indiana Employment Security Div.*, and *Hobbie v. Unemployment Appeals Comm'n of Fla.*, we held that the free exercise clause of the First Amendment *required* religious beliefs to be accommodated by granting religion-specific exemptions from otherwise applicable laws.[10]

And here is Scalia in 1990, for the Court in *Smith*:

> We have never held that an individual's religious beliefs excuse him from compliance with an otherwise valid law prohibiting conduct that the State is free to regulate.[11]

He was right the first time.

The early published reactions to *Smith* also make the point that the decision is inconsistent with the apparent meaning of the constitutional text.[12] The Court concedes that religious conduct is the exercise of religion,[13] and it accurately describes the law at issue as a "criminal prohibition" of this religious exercise.[14] On its face, such a law would seem to be a "law prohibiting the free exercise thereof." The Court does not really dispute the point; it says only that this is not the only "permissible" meaning of the text.[15]

When a decision is dubious or demonstrably wrong as a matter of text, precedent, and original intent, it must be based on something else. In this article, I will examine first the theoretical conceptions revealed by *Swaggart*, *Smith*, and the scholarly supporters of the approach taken in *Smith*,[16] and why I think those conceptions are mis-

---

[9] *Smith*, 110 S.Ct. at 1609–12 (O'Connor, J., dissenting); Laycock, The Supreme Court's Assault on Free Exercise and the Amicus Brief That Was Never Filed, 8 J.L. & Religion —— —— (1990); McConnell, Free Exercise Revisionism and the Smith Decision, 57 U. Chi. L. Rev. 1109 (1990); The Supreme Court 1989 Term, 104 Harv. L. Rev. 129, 204–5 (1990).

[10] Texas Monthly, Inc. v. Bullock, 489 U.S. 1, 38 (1989) (Scalia, J., dissenting) (emphasis in original) (citations omitted).

[11] *Smith*, 110 S.Ct. at 1600.

[12] *Id.* at 1608 (O'Connor, J., dissenting); McConnell, note 9 *supra*, at 1114–16; Laycock, note 9 *supra*, at——.

[13] 110 S.Ct. at 1599.

[14] *Id.* at 1603.

[15] *Id.* at 1599–1600.

[16] Marshall, The Case Against the Constitutionally Compelled Free Exercise Exemption, 40 Case Western L. Rev. 357 (1989–90); Tushnet, "Of Church and State and the Supreme Court": Kurland Revisited, 1989 Supreme Court Review 373; West, The Case Against a Right to Religion-based Exemptions, 4 Notre Dame J.L., Ethics, & Pub. Pol'y 591 (1990).

conceptions. I will consider the Court's conception of religious neutrality,[17] its apparent conception of religion, its crucial distinction between religious belief and religious practice, and its conception of the judicial role.

Second, I will consider the doctrinal and practical impact of these cases. The Free Exercise Clause is now principally a special case of equal protection, forbidding religious discrimination. It also survives as an adjunct to the Free Speech Clause, and to the unenumerated right of parents to direct the education of their children. But the Free Exercise Clause itself now has little independent substantive content.

The practical impact may be limited or enormous, depending on the ultimate content of the various exceptions and limitations in the opinion. A rule against express religious discrimination provides more protection for minority faiths than most governments have provided through most of human history. The Court's announced rule should mean that neither criminal punishment nor civil disabilities can be inflicted on religious minorities identified by name, doctrine, or ritual.

But the obvious forms of persecution are not the ones a contemporary American majority is likely to use. The scope of regulation in the modern administrative state creates ample opportunity for facially neutral religious oppression. Such oppressive laws may be enacted through hostility, sheer indifference, or ignorance of minority faiths. If the Court intends to defer to any formally neutral law restricting religion, then it has created a legal framework for persecution, and persecutions will result. I do not use that word hyperbolically or rhetorically. I mean it quite literally, and I will defend the usage.

I. The Cases

A. SWAGGART AND THE TAXATION OF CHURCHES

The *Swaggart* case arose out of California's attempt to collect sales and use tax on Swaggart's distribution of religious books, tapes, and records to Californians. Some of these items were sold in California at evangelistic services that Swaggart called crusades. Most were sold by mail from Swaggart's headquarters in Louisiana. California

[17] See also Laycock, Formal, Substantive, and Disaggregated Neutrality Toward Religion, 39 DePaul L. Rev. 993 (1990).

imposed a 6 percent sales tax on the items sold in California, and a 6 percent use tax on the items sold by mail and used in California.

California demanded that Swaggart collect and remit its use tax, asserting that Swaggart's crusades in California created sufficient jurisdictional contacts to support that demand.[18] Swaggart argued that these contacts were not jurisdictionally sufficient, but the Court held that this claim had not been preserved. Swaggart also argued that the jurisdictional holding penalized the protected decision to hold a church service in California. The cost of entering the state for a crusade was liability to collect and remit use tax on a much larger volume of mail order transactions that would otherwise have been beyond the reach of California law. The Court ignored this argument; in an earlier pair of free speech cases, it had rejected a somewhat similar challenge to judicial jurisdiction based on distribution of a few copies of a publication.[19]

Swaggart did collect and remit the sales tax on items described in the opinion as "nonreligious merchandise,"[20] but perhaps better described as religious memorabilia. These items included T-shirts, mugs, bowls, plates, communion cups, and replicas of Christ's crown of thorns and the ark of the covenant. Many of these items embodied or were marked with religious symbols; they were designed in part to proclaim or reinforce faith. They illustrate the force of the Court's observation that a constitutional tax immunity for religious activities would present non-trivial line-drawing issues.[21]

Swaggart objected to the collection of sales and use tax on books and audio recordings containing explicitly religious messages. The claim was very simple: a tax on the distribution of a book of sermons, or a recording of gospel hymns, was a tax on dissemination of the

[18]Compare National Geographic v. California Equalization Bd., 430 U.S. 551, 556 (1977) (mail order seller must collect use tax on sales to California, where seller maintains two offices in California), with National Bellas Hess, Inc. v. Illinois Revenue Dept., 386 U.S. 753, 756–60 (1967) (mail order seller cannot be required to collect use tax on sales to Illinois, where seller has no offices, property, or agents in Illinois).

[19]Calder v. Jones, 465 U.S. 783, 790–91 (1984); Keeton v. Hustler Magazine, Inc., 465 U.S. 770, 780 n.12 (1984). These cases are suggestive, but they do not control Swaggart's claim. In *Calder* and *Keeton*, publication in the state conferred jurisdiction to decide a dispute that could have been decided elsewhere. In *Swaggart*, the crusades conferred jurisdiction to impose a substantive obligation to collect and remit tax, an obligation that could not otherwise be imposed at all by any governmental unit. Indeed, the Court in *Calder* distinguished substantive protections from procedural rules. See 465 U.S. at 790–91.

[20]*Swaggart*, 110 S.Ct. 688, 692.

[21]*Id.* at 699.

faith. A tax on dissemination of the faith was forbidden by *Murdock v. Pennsylvania*[22] and *Follett v. McCormick*.[23]

Murdock and *Follett* struck down peddler's taxes as applied to sales of religious literature by Jehovah's Witness proselytizers. The Witnesses charged for their literature, but the Court said that was irrelevant. A religious organization must pay the expenses of distributing its message, and an "evangelist. . . . does not become a mere book agent by selling the Bible or religious tracts to help defray his expenses or to sustain him."[24] The Court noted that Thomas Paine had charged for his revolutionary pamphlets.

Swaggart confined *Murdock* and *Follett* to their facts, announcing that they prohibited only "flat license taxes that operated as a prior restraint."[25] A plurality of three had suggested this distinction a year before, in a case striking down a tax exemption that discriminated among publications on the basis of content.[26] Three dissenters had charged that such a distinction "trivializes the holdings" of *Murdock* and *Follett*.[27] But in *Swaggart* the Court accepted the distinction unanimously.

The Court also emphasized other features of California's tax: it was "not a flat tax," it represented "only a small fraction of any retail sale," and it applied "neutrally to all retail sales of tangible personal property."[28]

> Thus, the sales and use tax is not a tax on the right to disseminate religious information, ideas, or beliefs per se; rather, it is a tax on the privilege of making retail sales of tangible personal property and on the storage, use, or other consumption of tangible personal property in California.[29]

The Court's distinction of *Murdock* on the ground that it involved a license tax has some basis in the *Murdock* opinion.[30] The broader notion of formal neutrality has none. *Murdock* rejected formal neutrality as "immaterial." It was not enough that the state "classifies the privi-

---

[22] 319 U.S. 105 (1943).

[23] 321 U.S. 573 (1944).

[24] *Murdock*, 319 U.S. at 111.

[25] *Swaggart*, 110 S.Ct. at 694.

[26] Texas Monthly, Inc. v. Bullock, 489 U.S. 1, 21–25 (1989) (plurality opinion).

[27] *Id.* at 41 (Scalia, J., dissenting).

[28] *Swaggart*, 110 S.Ct. at 695.

[29] *Id.* at 695–96.

[30] *Murdock*, 319 U.S. at 112–15.

leges protected by the First Amendment along with the wares and merchandise of hucksters and peddlers and treats them all alike."[31] But formal neutrality was critical in *Swaggart*: states may now tax religion so long as they do not do so "per se."

B. SMITH AND THE REGULATION OF RELIGIOUS CONDUCT

Smith began as another in a series of unemployment compensation cases, arguably routine in principle,[32] but with facts that could have been made up for a law school exam: two counselors in a drug and alcohol abuse clinic were fired for taking peyote at a worship service of the Native American Church. One was Native American; one was white. By the time the Supreme Court finished with the case, it was no longer an unemployment compensation case, it was certainly not routine, and the facts had become utterly irrelevant.

Peyote is an hallucinogenic drug produced by a small cactus in the southwestern United States and northern Mexico. It is an illegal drug, but it has never been an important recreational drug. One takes peyote by eating the buds of the cactus plant. The buds are tough, bitter, difficult to chew, and frequently cause nausea or vomiting.[33] Peyote appears to be much safer than the synthetic hallucinogenics that are illegally produced and more widely abused;[34] adverse reactions are only very occasionally reported.[35]

There is no dispute that peyote worship is an ancient and bona fide Native American religion, now infused with elements of Christianity.[36] To the believer, peyote is a sacramental substance, an object of worship, and a source of divine protection. The central event at a worship service, or "meeting," is the consumption of peyote in a

---

[31] *Id.* at 115.

[32] See Frazee v. Illinois Dept. of Employment Security, 489 U.S. 829 (1989); Hobbie v. Unemployment Appeals Comm'n, 480 U.S. 136 (1987); Thomas v. Review Bd., 450 U.S. 707 (1981); Sherbert v. Verner, 374 U.S. 398 (1963) (all holding that Free Exercise Clause forbids states to deny unemployment compensation to employees who lose their job because of conflict between job and religious practice).

[33] Anderson, Peyote: The Divine Cactus 161 (1980); Slotkin, The Peyote Way 98 (1956).

[34] Julien, A Primer of Drug Action 152 (4th ed. 1985); Bergman, Navajo Peyote Use: Its Apparent Safety, 128 Am. J. Psych. 695 (1971).

[35] Bergman, note 34 *supra*, at 697 (describing five possible cases in author's clinical experience, crudely estimating one bad reaction in 70,000 ingestions, and describing that as "probably overestimating").

[36] For accounts by anthropologists, see LeBarre, The Peyote Cult (rev. ed. 1964); Slotkin, note 33 *supra*.

highly structured ritual.[37] Federal drug laws and many state drug laws exempt religious use by the Native American Church,[38] and federal drug authorities issue licenses to grow peyote for religious use. There is substantial evidence that on balance the religion is a positive influence on its members, and especially on recovering alcoholics.[39] The irony of drug counselors fired for peyote worship may be more apparent than real; the peyote religion teaches total abstinence from all other drugs, and from recreational use of peyote, emphatically and with some success. But no religious practice is uniform for all believers, and Oregon cited reports that peyote use is not always so structured and constrained as more sympathetic accounts would suggest.[40]

The case that reached the Supreme Court arose on a simple claim for unemployment compensation. In its first encounter with the case, the Court announced that it wanted to decide whether Oregon could criminally punish peyote use, an issue it considered logically prior to the unemployment compensation issue.[41] The Court remanded the case, asking the Oregon Supreme Court to determine whether sacramental peyote use violated Oregon criminal laws. When the case returned to the Court (after an affirmative answer from the Oregon Supreme Court) both sides briefed the criminal law issue under the prevailing standard: would criminal punishment of religious peyote use serve a compelling interest by the least restrictive means?

The Supreme Court rejected the compelling interest standard and announced a fundamentally different standard, without notice to the parties that it was reconsidering the standard. The Court's new standard required no attention to the facts of the case or to any of the issues argued by the parties:

> [I]f prohibiting the exercise of religion . . . is not the object of [a tax or regulation] but merely the incidental effect of a generally applicable and otherwise valid provision, the First Amendment has not been offended. . . . [T]he right of free exercise does not

[37] For descriptions of the meeting, see People v. Woody, 61 Cal. 2d 716, 721, 40 Cal. Rptr. 69, 73, 394 P.2d 813, 817 (1964); Bergman, note 34 *supra* , at 695–96.

[38] 21 C.F.R. §1307.31 (1990). The state exemptions are collected in Smith v. Employment Div., 307 Or. 68, 73 n.2, 763 P.2d 146, 148 n.2 (1988).

[39] Bergman, note 34 *supra*, at 698; Pascarosa & Futterman, Ethnopsychedelic Therapy for Alcoholics: Observations in the Peyote Ritual of the Native American Church, 8 J. Psychedelic Drugs 215 (1976).

[40] Reply Brief for Petitioners 11–14, in *Smith*.

[41] Employment Div. v. Smith, 485 U.S. 660, 672 (1988).

> relieve an individual of the obligation to comply with a "valid and neutral law of general applicability."[42]

Because Oregon's prohibition of peyote is generally applicable, the peyote worship service is not constitutionally protected.

The scope of this new principle is not clear. It applies to religious conduct, but apparently not to religious belief and profession of faith.[43] Even with respect to conduct, the Court recognized exceptions for "hybrid" cases that involve free exercise and some other constitutional right—freedom of speech or press, or the unenumerated right of parents "to direct the education of their children."[44] This last category preserved *Wisconsin v. Yoder*,[45] which exempted Amish children from the first two years of high school. There is either an exception, or an explication of the requirement that laws be neutral and generally applicable, that preserves from overruling the Court's earlier unemployment compensation cases.[46] But this proviso did not apply to *Smith* itself, even though it was an unemployment compensation case.

These exceptions and limitations rest on ill-defined principles and have ill-defined borders. Their most obvious feature is this: although the Court distorted the rationale of its precedents beyond recognition, the exceptions and limitations to its new principle preserved all its prior results. We may be told in the next case that these results were really undermined by *Smith* and that they must now be overruled after all. But the distortions are inexplicable unless someone in the majority wishes to preserve these precedents. Part of the task in future cases is to search for principled lines between what the Court has preserved and what it has rejected.

The lines to be drawn apparently depend on definitional categories. Belief is protected, but conduct generally is not; speech and parental control are protected, but other conduct generally is not; even conduct is protected against non-neutral laws, but not against laws that are neutral and generally applicable. To apply these rules, courts must sort cases into the various categories: belief or conduct; speech, parental control, or something else; neutral or not neutral.

---

[42] *Smith*, 110 S.Ct. at 1600, quoting United States v. Lee, 455 U.S. 252, 263 n.3 (1982) (Stevens, J., concurring).

[43] *Smith*, 110 S.Ct. at 1599.

[44] *Id.* at 1601–2.

[45] 406 U.S. 205 (1972).

[46] *Smith*, 110 S.Ct. at 1603. This proviso is considered in text at notes 199–209 *infra*.

The lines to be drawn do not depend on any balance of competing interests. On the Court's approach, it makes no difference what the state's policy is or what the religious practice is. It is important to understand that the alleged dangers of peyote are irrelevant to the holding in *Smith*. It makes no difference whether peyote is deadly or harmless, or whether peyote worship is infrequent, structured, and disciplined or constant, casual, and dissipated. It makes no difference whether Oregon has forbidden peyote, or wine, or unleavened bread. In Justice Scalia's example, it makes no difference whether the prohibited religious practice is "throwing rice at church weddings" or "getting married in church."[47] Indeed, the Court's principal ground of decision was precisely that courts should not assess the importance of either government interests or religious practices.[48]

The point is underscored by the religious practice at issue. However unfamiliar, deviant, or even dangerous the peyote ritual may seem from a majoritarian perspective, it is also the central religious ritual of an ancient faith. The Court held that Oregon can suppress a worship service, and so long as that is the incidental effect of a generally applicable law, Oregon need have no reason for refusing a religious exemption.

II. Four Misconceptions

A. The Court's Conception of Neutrality

1. *Formal neutrality and majoritarianism*. *Swaggart* and *Smith* make formal neutrality the dominant principle of the Court's free exercise jurisprudence. Instead of a substantive right to be left alone by government, churches and believers now get a right to equal protection. Instead of an exemption from taxation and regulation, churches and believers get the right to be taxed or regulated no more heavily than secular institutions. But in the modern regulatory state, secular institutions are pervasively taxed and regulated. Religious exercise is not free when it is pervasively taxed and regulated.

Eleven years before, in *Jones v. Wolf*,[49] the Court made the same move in another free exercise context, the resolution of internal church disputes in secular courts. *Jones* held that state courts may ap-

[47] *Smith*, 110 S.Ct. at 1605 n.4.

[48] *Id*. at 1604–6.

[49] 443 U.S. 595 (1979).

ply "neutral principles of law" to such disputes, interpreting deeds to church property, corporate charters and trust instruments, and even church constitutions, provided only that secular courts do not decide questions of religious doctrine. This created an alternative to the earlier rule of deference to the highest church authority to decide the dispute.[50] Instead of a right to settle their own disputes, churches got a right to have their disputes resolved by the same rules and procedures applicable to secular institutions.

In each of these contexts, the Court has chosen an equal protection rule instead of an exemption rule. More important, in applying the equal protection rule, the unique features of religion do not require that religion be distinguished from any other human activity. In the Court's view, religious use of peyote, or of wine, is no more protected by the Constitution than is recreational use. A soldier who believes he must cover his head before an omnipresent God is constitutionally indistinguishable from a soldier who wants to wear a Budweiser gimme cap.[51] That is, the Free Exercise Clause has been read to require only religion-blind equal protection. In earlier work, I have called this approach "formal neutrality,"[52] and I will use that term here.

The Court says that churches and believers are entitled to at least formal neutrality, but that government may sometimes give them more. Government may grant religious exemptions from regulation,[53] and secular courts may defer to religious authorities in religious disputes.[54] In these contexts, exemptions are permitted but not required. With respect to taxation, formal neutrality in theory is both the minimum and the maximum. Government may not exempt religious income, property, or activity from taxation, except as part of some larger exempt class defined in secular terms.[55] But in prac-

[50]For the earlier rule, see Serbian E. Orthodox Diocese v. Milivojevich, 426 U.S. 696 (1976); Kreshik v. Saint Nicholas Cathedral, 363 U.S. 190 (1960) (per curiam); Kedroff v. Saint Nicholas Cathedral, 344 U.S. 94 (1952); Watson v. Jones, 80 U.S. (13 Wall.) 679 (1871) (federal common law).

[51]*Cf.* Goldman v. Weinberger, 475 U.S. 503 (1986) (Air Force officer disciplined for wearing yarmulke). The result in *Goldman* was changed by statute. 10 U.S.C. §774 (1988).

[52]Laycock, note 17 *supra*, at 999.

[53]*Smith*, 110 S.Ct. at 1606; Corporation of the Presiding Bishop v. Amos, 483 U.S. 327 (1987).

[54]Jones v. Wolf, 443 U.S. 595, 602 (1979). If the religious dispute involves an issue of theology or religious doctrine, the secular court must defer to religious authority, a form of required exemption that apparently survives *Smith*. See 110 S.Ct. at 1599.

[55]Texas Monthly, Inc. v. Bullock, 489 U.S. 1 (1989).

tice, legislatures exempt from taxation most church income and property, and the Court is unlikely to rigorously scrutinize the boundaries of the secular exemptions that are said to include religion.[56]

The basic pattern is that religious liberty is entitled only to formal neutrality but may get more favorable treatment from the political branches. This is in fact a move to majoritarianism; the Court is getting out of the business of enforcing the religion clauses. Legislatures and enforcement agencies choose when to provide only formal neutrality and when to grant exemptions. Favored religions can be exempted from the rules that burden them, while disfavored religions are denied exemptions from the rules that burden them. The Court somewhat euphemistically concedes that this allocation of responsibility "will place at a relative disadvantage those religious practices that are not widely engaged in."[57] But the Court sees no constitutional issue, because even the worst treated religions get the protections of formal neutrality.

The Court has said remarkably little to defend this proposition. In *Swaggart*, the Court simply assumed it:

> At the outset, it is undeniable that a generally applicable tax has a secular purpose and neither advances nor inhibits religion, for the very essence of such a tax is that it is neutral and nondiscriminatory on questions of religious belief.[58]

The majority in *Smith* defended the proposition by arguing, somewhat circularly, that it would be anomalous to let some people violate the law while others were required to obey it. The Court said that strict scrutiny of racial classifications produces "equality of treatment," which is a "constitutional norm," but that strict scrutiny in *Smith* would produce "a private right to ignore generally applicable laws," which is "a constitutional anomaly."[59] But the Court simply assumed that the group to be exempted was similarly situated with the group not exempted.

Although formal neutrality has become dominant, neither the Court nor individual justices have been consistent about it. Four justices found religion-blindness undeniably neutral in the context of

---

[56]See Walz v. Tax Comm'n, 397 U.S. 664 (1970) (upholding property tax exemptions for "religious, educational, and charitable" organizations).

[57]*Smith*, 110 S.Ct. at 1606.

[58]*Swaggart*, 110 S.Ct. at 698.

[59]*Smith*, 110 S.Ct. at 1604.

taxation, but oppressive in the context of regulation.[60] *Swaggart*'s claim that formally neutral taxation "neither advances nor inhibits religion" invokes the language of the cases on government payments to church-sponsored schools, but it is inconsistent with the substance of those cases. When government pays money to church-sponsored schools, the Court says the benefit advances religion; it is irrelevant that government spends comparable sums on secular schools.[61] But when government takes money from churches, the "burden is not constitutionally significant," and it is dispositive that government takes comparable sums from secular taxpayers.[62]

The Court may resolve this particular inconsistency by permitting formal neutrality under the Establishment Clause as well. But whether applied consistently or inconsistently, formal neutrality is an incorrect interpretation of the religion clauses, and especially of the Free Exercise Clause. It is incorrect for several closely related reasons.

2. *Substantive entitlements and substantive neutrality.* Most directly, the Free Exercise Clause creates a substantive right, and the Court has reduced it to a mere equality right.[63] The Free Exercise Clause does not say that Congress shall make no law discriminating against religion, or that no state shall deny to any religion within its jurisdiction the equal protection of the laws. Rather, it says that Congress shall make no law prohibiting the free exercise of religion. Congress may prohibit many things, but it may not prohibit religious exercise. On its face, this is a substantive entitlement, and not merely a pledge of non-discrimination.

The extreme case of substituting equality rights for substantive rights would be total suppression of all religions. There would be perfect equality, but no religious liberty. No one is proposing that, and no reading of the Court's opinion would permit that, but the ex-

---

[60] *Id.* at 1606–14 (O'Connor, J., concurring, joined by Brennan, J., Marshall, J., and Blackmun, J.). Each of these justices joined Justice O'Connor's unanimous opinion in *Swaggart.*

[61] See Aguilar v. Felton, 473 U.S. 402 (1985) (invalidating federal funding of remedial education for low income children in public and private schools, as applied to instruction provided on premises of religiously affiliated schools); School Dist. v. Ball, 473 U.S. 373 (1985) (invalidating remedial and enrichment courses taught by public school teachers in religiously affiliated schools, although same courses were taught in public schools); but see Bowen v. Kendrick, 487 U.S. 589 (1988) (relying on formal neutrality to uphold grants to religiously affiliated organizations); Mueller v. Allen, 463 U.S. 388 (1983) (relying on formal neutrality to uphold tax deductions for payments to religious schools).

[62] *Swaggart*, 110 S.Ct. at 696. This point is elaborated in Laycock, note 17 *supra*, at 1009–10.

[63] On the distinction, see Simons, Equality as a Comparative Right, 65 B.U. L. Rev. 387 (1985).

treme case highlights the error of taking the substantive entitlement out of the Free Exercise Clause.

Some judges and commentators do indeed appeal to the equality of across-the-board repression in the context of exemptions for religious conduct. In any exemption case, one can imagine, and often identify in the real world, a religion with an analogous practice so disruptive or dangerous that few judges would require an exemption. Justice Stevens concludes from this that if we cannot exempt every minority faith, we should not exempt any.[64] Thus, if courts would not require the military to tolerate saffron robes in combat, they should not require the military to tolerate yarmulkes on a stateside Air Force base. The resulting burden on observant Jews may seem arbitrary and irrational when considered in isolation. But in Justice Stevens' view, it is justified because it avoids any appearance of discrimination against the wearers of saffron robes, and it avoids the necessity of judicial distinctions among religions. He prefers even-handed repression to imperfect liberty.

Mark Tushnet makes a similar point, complaining that "Christians sometimes win but non-Christians never do."[65] Better, therefore, to repress Christian minorities as well. In fact, there have been judicial wins for non-Christians,[66] and many of the Christian wins are achieved by small and highly unconventional Christian sects, such as the Amish, Jehovah's Witnesses, and Seventh Day Adventists. Tushnet's instinct is sound: judges are more likely to respond sympathetically to religious claims that are familiar, easily understood, and unthreatening. But that problem cannot be solved by judicial abdica-

---

[64]Goldman v. Weinberger, 475 U.S. 503, 512–13 (1986) (Stevens, J., concurring); United States v. Lee, 455 U.S. 252, 263 (1982) (Stevens, J., concurring).

[65]Tushnet, note 16 *supra*, at 381.

[66]See Larson v. Valente, 456 U.S. 228 (1982) (invoking Establishment Clause to protect Unification Church from discriminatory regulation); United States v. Ballard, 322 U.S. 78 (1944) (holding that jury in prosecution for mail fraud could not determine truth or falsity of religious beliefs of the I Am movement). In Bowen v. Roy, 476 U.S. 693 (1986), there were five votes for the proposition that, if the case survived a mootness challenge, the government could not require Native Americans to use social security numbers in violation of their religious beliefs. *Id.* at 715–16 (Blackmun, J., concurring); *id.* at 726–33 (O'Connor, J., joined by Brennan, J. & Marshall, J., concurring); *id.* at 733 (White, J., dissenting). For illustrative cases in the lower courts, see Benjamin v. Coughlin, 905 F.2d 571 (2d Cir.) (invalidating prison rule requiring Rastafarians to cut their hair), cert. denied, 111 S.Ct. 372 (1990); Islamic Center, Inc. v. City of Starkville, 840 F.2d 293 (5th Cir. 1988) (protecting Islamic student center from discriminatory zoning decisions); Kahane v. Carlson, 527 F.2d 492 (2d Cir. 1975) (requiring prison to provide Kosher food for observant Jewish prisoners). Most cases striking down government sponsored religious observances and displays have struck down Christian observances and displays. Most notably, see County of Allegheny v. American Civil Liberties Union Greater Pittsburgh Chapter, 492 U.S. 573 (1989) (striking down Christian creche but permitting Jewish menorah).

tion, because legislators are even more likely to favor familiar faiths with enough adherents to matter at the polls. Constitutionally adjudicated exemptions for small or unpopular religious minorities merely match the legislative exemptions commonly granted to larger or more accepted faiths.[67] Even if the Court were to forbid legislated exemptions, the majority would rarely be required to violate its deeply held beliefs, because the majority's deeply held beliefs will normally be reflected in legislation without an exemption.

With or without constitutional exemptions, some religions will be burdened by law more than others. Without constitutional exemptions, the line will be drawn between those faiths that can prevail in the legislature and those that cannot. With constitutional exemptions, the line will be between those faiths that can prevail either in the legislature or in the courts, and those that cannot prevail in either place. It is clear that a rule of constitutional exemptions would produce more religious liberty, because it gives religious liberty claims two chances to prevail.

It is not clear why anyone thinks such a rule would produce more discrimination among religious faiths. Why should we expect legislatures to draw more principled lines than courts? Legislators are under no obligation to be principled. Subject only to their oath to uphold the Constitution, they are free to reflect majority prejudices, to respond to the squeakiest wheel among minorities, to trade votes and make compromises, and to ignore problems that have no votes in them. This political freedom is good for many things, but it is not good for achieving even-handed treatment of many small, disparate, and sometimes odd or obnoxious religious minorities.

Judges are far from perfect, but they are sworn to do equal justice to all, to decide every case presented to them, and to treat like cases alike. They are obliged by precedent and accepted judicial norms to give principled reasons for their decisions. Justice Blackmun argued that the state's obligation to treat all religions equally "is fulfilled by the uniform application of the 'compelling interest' *test* to all free exercise claims, not by reaching uniform *results* as to all claims."[68] Judges cannot achieve the ideal of "uniform application," but even so, a line based on compelling interest is likely to be more principled than a line based on who can get the sympathetic attention of enough

[67] Pepper, Taking the Free Exercise Clause Seriously, 1986 BYU L. Rev. 299, 312–16; Galanter, Religious Freedoms in the United States: A Turning Point? 1966 Wis. L. Rev. 217, 291.

[68] *Smith*, 110 S.Ct. at 1621 (Blackmun, J., dissenting).

legislators. The goal of neutrality among faiths is not a reason to reject the substantive entitlement in the Free Exercise Clause.

There is a separate concern about neutrality between religion and non-religion. The Free Exercise Clause comes paired with the Establishment Clause, and government neutrality toward religion is an important part of the combined mandate of the two clauses. But if the two clauses also create substantive entitlements defined in terms of religion, then formal religion-blind neutrality must not be the kind of neutrality they mandate. Neutrality requires that like things be treated alike, but also that unlike things be appropriately distinguished.

Religion is unlike other human activities, or at least the founders thought so. The proper relation between religion and government was a subject of great debate in the founding generation,[69] and the Constitution includes two clauses that apply to religion and do not apply to anything else. This debate and these clauses presuppose that religion is in some way a special human activity, requiring special rules applicable only to it. To distinguish between a yarmulke and a gimme cap is not to discriminate between indistinguishable head coverings, but to distinguish a constitutionally protected activity—religious exercise—from an activity not mentioned in the Constitution.

The neutrality mandated by the Constitution is not formal neutrality, but substantive neutrality. By substantive neutrality, I mean that government should "minimize the extent to which it either encourages or discourages religious belief or disbelief, practice or nonpractice, observance or nonobservance."[70] So defined, substantive neutrality is consistent with the substantive entitlement created by the text of the Free Exercise Clause.

To consider the claim that religious exemptions are substantively neutral, one must consider the incentive effects of denying exemptions and of granting them. It is clear that criminal punishment of religious practice discourages believers from practicing their faith.

---

[69]For historical accounts of these debates, see Curry, The First Freedoms: Church and State in America to the Passage of the First Amendment (1986); Buckley, Church and State in Revolutionary Virginia, 1776–1787 (1977). For legal analyses of these debates, see McConnell, note 8 *supra*; Laycock, "Nonpreferential" Aid to Religion: A False Claim about Original Intent, 27 William & Mary L. Rev. 875 (1986); Smith, Separation and the "Secular": Reconstructing the Disestablishment Doctrine, 67 Tex. L. Rev. 955 (1989). I briefly consider the source of my disagreement with Stephen Smith in Laycock, Original Intent and the Constitution Today, in the First Freedom: Religion and the Bill of Rights 87, 92–93, 103–4 (Wood, ed., 1990).

[70]Laycock, note 17 *supra*, at 1001.

But in most contexts, an exemption for religious practice does not encourage non-believers to join the faith. Much religious activity is self-restraining, burdensome, or meaningless to non-believers. Gentile soldiers will not wear yarmulkes just because it is permitted, and there is no evidence that drug abusers are switching to peyote in states where peyote worship is permitted. The magnitude of encouragement incident to an exemption is generally smaller than the magnitude of discouragement incident to criminalization, and so exemption comes closer to substantive neutrality.[71]

In some contexts, such as conscientious objection to military service, religious duty may coincide with self-interest. When that happens, exemptions may tempt non-believers to belief—sometimes to true belief and not merely to false claims of belief. Substantive neutrality then becomes unachievable. Granting exemptions encourages religion, refusing exemptions discourages religion, and both effects are large.[72] Whatever the proper solution in such difficult cases, the difficulty does not arise in the run of cases. In most contexts, the substantive entitlement to exercise religion is consistent with the government's duty of substantive neutrality toward religion.

3. *Free exercise and other constitutional doctrine.* Understanding free exercise as a substantive right eliminates some alleged anomalies identified in *Smith.* The Court analogized formally neutral laws that prohibit religious exercise to formally neutral laws that disproportionately burden racial minorities.[73] The disproportionate racial impact of a formally neutral law does not raise any special issue under the Equal Protection Clause.[74] Critics have argued that the Court is simply wrong about racial impact;[75] on this view, the Court has ended the anomaly by getting the religion cases wrong as well. But even if the Court is right about racial impact, there would be no anomaly in protecting conscientious objectors under the Free Exercise Clause.

---

[71]For an economic version of this argument, see McConnell & Posner, An Economic Approach to Issues of Religious Freedom, 56 U. Chi. L. Rev. 1, 32–54 (1989).

[72]For further analysis, see Laycock, note 17 *supra*, at 1017–18.

[73]*Smith*, 110 S.Ct. at 1604 n. 3.

[74]Washington v. Davis, 426 U.S. 229 (1976). Similarly, a law that merely has a disproportionate impact on religious minorities raised no special issue under the Free Exercise Clause even before *Smith*. See Braunfeld v. Brown, 366 U.S. 599, 606 (1961).

[75]See, *e.g.*, Binion, Intent and Equal Protection: A Reconsideration, 1983 Supreme Court Review 397; Eisenberg, Disporportionate Impact and Illicit Motive: Theories of Constitutional Adjudication, 52 NYU L. Rev. 36 (1977); Perry, The Disproportionate Impact Theory of Racial Discrimination, 125 U. Pa. L. Rev. 540 (1977). For comparisons of equal protection and the religion clauses, see Binion at 418–19; Eisenberg at 156–68.

The explanation is that the Equal Protection Clause really is just an equality right. It creates no substantive entitlement to engage in any particular conduct or to be evaluated by any particular criteria. A civil service examination with disparate racial impact does not penalize an activity that the Constitution protects. A law prohibiting peyote worship does prohibit an activity the Constitution protects. Moreover, the victims are given an incentive to avoid the penalty by abandoning their faith. Such a law directly penalizes religious exercise, even if it also has other applications to non-religious uses. The impact on religious users is not a mere statistical association; it is a flat prohibition of their religious exercise. Whatever the proper solution to the problem of statistical disparate impact, that solution does not speak to the issue in *Smith*.

The Court in *Smith* also asserted that "generally applicable laws unconcerned with regulating speech that have the effect of interfering with speech do not thereby become subject to compelling-interest analysis under the First Amendment."[76] Like the Free Exercise Clause, the speech clause creates a substantive right with a neutrality component. If it were true that the Court had rejected all challenges to formally neutral rules that suppress speech, that would support *Smith* by analogy. But it is not true.

The Court has, for example, constitutionally exempted unpopular political parties and movements from statutory duties to disclose their lists of members or contributors.[77] Another example is *Roberts v. United States Jaycees*,[78] which upheld Minnesota's public accommodations law as applied to the Jaycees' exclusion of female members. The law was facially neutral and not directed at speech, but it burdened the Jaycees' right of association. The Court upheld the law because the burden on associational rights was modest, but the Court unambiguously decided the case under the compelling interest test.[79]

Probably the best example is *Hustler Magazine v. Falwell*,[80] which

[76]*Smith*, 110 S.Ct. at 1604 n.3, citing Citizen Publishing Co. v. United States, 394 U.S. 131, 139 (1969). See also *Smith*, 110 S.Ct. at 1600, citing Minneapolis Star & Tribune Co. v. Minnesota Comm'r of Revenue, 460 U.S. 575 (1983). *Citizen Publishing* and *Minneapolis Star*, respectively, upheld the application of facially neutral antitrust and tax laws to commercial media corporations. The commercial context is surely relevant to the holdings.

[77]NAACP v. Alabama, 357 U.S. 449 (1958). See also Brown v. Socialist Workers '74 Campaign Comm. (Ohio), 459 U.S. 87 (1982); Stone & Marshall, Brown v. Socialist Workers: Inequality as a Command of the First Amendment, 1983 Supreme Court Review 583.

[78]468 U.S. 609 (1984).

[79]*Id.* at 623–24.

[80]485 U.S. 46 (1988).

created special defenses to protect speech from the formally neutral tort of intentional infliction of emotional distress. The elements of the tort do not mention speech, and many of its applications do not involve speech at all.[81] When the tort is applied to speech, the speech is typically deceptive, harassing, or both, often merely incidental to conduct such as a practical joke or wrongful discharge of an employee, and thus of limited First Amendment significance.[82] But the Court unanimously agreed that to apply the tort to outrageous speech about a public figure would violate the speech clause.

The rule in *Hustler* is modeled on cases like *New York Times v. Sullivan*,[83] which imposed constitutional limits on defamation liability. The rules of defamation are not formally neutral, because the tort can be committed only by speech. But at a sufficient level of generality, even the law of defamation can be stated in formally neutral terms. Defamation applies to speech the formally neutral principle that underlies all of tort law: one who inflicts harm on another without legal excuse must generally pay compensation. Similarly, defamation is partly exempted from the formally neutral rules of punitive damages, a set of remedial rules that apply to a broad range of torts.

The constitutional defect in unlimited liability for defamation had nothing to do with whether it was conceived as a specific rule about speech or as a neutral application of a broad principle about tortious harm. The defect was that tort liability for speech penalized the exercise of a substantive constitutional right. Because that was the defect, the principle of the defamation cases clearly applied to emotional distress inflicted by speech, and it was irrelevant in *Hustler* that intentional infliction of emotional distress might be more readily conceived of as formally neutral.

The lesson of the defamation cases is applicable to many of the Court's cases protecting speech: The laws were not formally neutral, but if they had been, they would have been struck down anyway. Consider *Schneider v. State*,[84] holding that the state's interest in pre-

---

[81] See Restatement (Second) of Torts §46 (1965) ("One who by extreme and outrageous conduct intentionally or recklessly causes severe emotional distress to another" is liable for damages); Growth Properties I v. Cannon, 282 Ark. 472, 669 S.W.2d 447 (1984) (building temporary access road for heavy equipment over graves); Great Atlantic & Pacific Tea Co. v. Roch, 160 Md. 189, 153 A. 22 (1930) (delivering dead rat in a bread wrapper).

[82] For illustrations, see Keeton, Dobbs, Keeton, & Owen, Prosser and Keeton on the Law of Torts §12 at 57–66 (5th ed. 1984 and Supp. 1988).

[83] 376 U.S. 254 (1964).

[84] 308 U.S. 147 (1939).

venting litter was not sufficient to justify a ban on distributing leaflets. Suppose the law had forbidden any person on a public street to hand to any other person any tangible property not requested by the recipient, and that a leafleteer had been arrested under this law. The result should have been the same. The problem in *Schneider* was not that leaflets were treated more harshly than cigarette samples, but that leaflets were constitutionally protected and cigarette samples were not.

Another example of exemption for speech is *Cantwell v. Connecticut*,[85] protecting religious speech from a formally neutral rule about breach of peace. Justice Scalia in *Smith* treated another part of *Cantwell*, the requirement of a license for religious or charitable solicitation, as an unconstitutional but formally neutral law. And he recognized *Murdock* and *Follett* as exempting religious speech from formally neutral license taxes. These three cases were the basis for his recognition of a hybrid class of free speech and free exercise, protected from formally neutral regulation.[86] But he ignored these cases in his footnote claiming that exemptions from formally neutral laws would be inconsistent with free speech doctrine.

Another arguable example is formally neutral rules restricting symbolic speech, such as draft-card burning and flag burning. The Court said the flag burning laws were motivated by hostility to the messages expressed by flag burning, so that those laws were not neutral even if neutrally worded.[87] The Court refused to consider motive in the draft-card burning prosecution, and upheld the statute under a deferential standard of review.[88] The Court also applies an increasingly deferential standard of review in the time-place-and-manner cases,[89] which typically involve laws that expressly regulate communication but are formally neutral as to content.

---

[85]310 U.S. 296 (1940).

[86]*Smith*, 110 S.Ct. at 1601.

[87]See United States v. Eichman, 110 S.Ct. 2404 (1990); Texas v. Johnson, 491 U.S. 397 (1989).

[88]United States v. O'Brien, 391 U.S. 367 (1968).

[89]See, *e.g.*, United States v. Kokinda, 110 S.Ct. 3115 (1990) (upholding ban on solicitation on sidewalk leading to post office); Ward v. Rock Against Racism, 491 U.S. 781, 791, 799 (1989) (requiring only that law not be motivated by hostility to message, that it serve a "substantial government interest that would be achieved less effectively absent the regulation," and that it leave open ample alternative means of communication); Frisby v. Schultz, 487 U.S. 474 (1988) (upholding ban on picketing a single residence); Boos v. Barry, 485 U.S. 312 (1988) (upholding ban on congregating within five hundred feet of a foreign embassy); Los Angeles City Council v. Taxpayers for Vincent, 466 U.S. 789 (1984) (upholding ban on placing signs on utility poles); Heffron v. International Soc'y for Krishna Consciousness, 452 U.S. 640 (1981) (upholding rule confining all solicitation at state fair to booths).

For better or worse, the Court has never universalized the compelling interest test. A lower standard of review is more defensible in symbolic speech and time-place-and-manner cases; a restriction on a particular means or place of expression is unlikely to entirely suppress a viewpoint in the way that a restriction on a particular means of worship can entirely suppress a religious faith.[90] But the important point here is that the Court has not simply refused to review the burden on speech in these cases. Mere formal neutrality does not put restrictions on speech beyond challenge in the way that formally neutral restrictions on religious practice now appear to be beyond challenge.[91]

The detail required to explore these inconsistent claims in the Court's opinion should not be allowed to obscure the main point. The Court's formal conception of neutrality ignores the substantive content of the Free Exercise Clause, and it begs the question of what kind of neutrality such a substantive clause requires.

B. THE COURT'S CONCEPTION OF BELIEF AND PRACTICE

The second key conception in the *Smith* opinion is a distinction between belief and practice. The Court says that religious "belief and profession" is protected "first and foremost."[92] Belief and profession appear to be protected even from formally neutral regulation, although the Court waffles on that.[93]

The Court concedes that religious conduct is also the exercise of religion,[94] but it says that religious conduct is protected only from formally discriminatory regulation. And religious conduct is broadly defined to include doing or not doing any "physical acts," with a list of examples that goes to the heart of religious practice: "assembling with others for a worship service, participating in sacramental use of

---

[90]*Cf.* Stone, Constitutionally Compelled Exemptions and the Free Exercise Clause, 27 Wm. & Mary L. Rev. 985, 990–93 (1986).

[91]For further analysis and additional cases, see Stone, Content-Neutral Restrictions, 54 U. Chi. L. Rev. 46, 105–14 (1987). The Court has agreed to review two recent decisions protecting expressive activity from formally neutral laws. Cohen v. Cowles Media Co., 457 N.W.2d 199 (Minn.) (rejecting claims of fraud, breach of contract, and promissory estoppel for newspaper's breach of reporter's promise to conceal identity of source), cert. granted, 111 S.Ct. 578 (1990); Miller v. Civil City of South Bend, 904 F.2d 1081 (7th Cir.) (refusing to apply public indecency law to nude dancing offered as entertainment), cert. granted *sub nom.* Barnes v. Glen Theatre Inc., 111 S.Ct. 38 (1990).

[92]*Smith*, 110 S.Ct. at 1599.

[93]See text at notes 182–85 *infra*.

[94]*Smith*, 110 S.Ct. at 1599.

bread and wine, proselytizing, abstaining from certain foods or certain modes of transportation."[95]

The Court draws its sharp line between belief and practice where Oliver Cromwell drew it, with worship on the unprotected side. Cromwell said to the Catholics of Ireland:

> For that which you mention concerning liberty of conscience, I meddle not with any man's conscience. But if by liberty of conscience you mean a liberty to exercise the mass, I judge it best to use plain dealing, and to let you know, where the Parliament of England have power, that will not be allowed of.[96]

In similar fashion, Oregon and the Court have said that the peyote worshipers of Oregon can believe their religion but not practice it. The only difference between Scalia's definition of religious liberty and Cromwell's is that Scalia requires formal neutrality. Scalia would not let Cromwell expressly forbid Catholic worship services while permitting Puritan worship services. But Scalia has permitted Oregon to achieve that result with respect to peyote worship, and his test would permit Cromwell to achieve it with respect to the Mass. Cromwell could forbid the consumption of wine, or forbid the consumption of wine in any public place where children are present. Either provision would be facially neutral, and either would preclude the Mass as it has been practiced for centuries. It is unclear whether Scalia would let a court inquire into Cromwell's motive for such a law.[97]

Of course no state today is likely to suppress the Mass, and despite virulent anti-Catholicism in the founders' generation, no American government in 1791 was likely to do so either. But Protestant-Catholic conflict was the most important source of religious persecution known to the founders. The purpose that we can most confidently attribute to the religion clauses is that the two centuries of religious conflict in the wake of the Reformation were not to be repeated here.[98] Surely the founders did not intend a Free Exercise Clause capable of giving constitutional legitimacy to Cromwellian persecutions—a clause that would permit the Protestant winners of a religious civil war to lawfully suppress the Mass.

---

[95] *Ibid.*

[96] Hill, God's Englishman 121 (1970).

[97] See text at notes 210–12 *infra*.

[98] See Laycock, Text, Intent, and the Religious Clauses, 4 Notre Dame J.L. Ethics & Pub. Pol'y 683, 691–93 (1990).

To invoke the shade of Cromwell is to invite the response that one does not do constitutional law by imagining impossible cases. But what makes the Cromwellian example seem impossible is that Catholics are part of the social and political mainstream, and there is no danger that lingering anti-Catholic prejudices will break out into open persecution. Both history and present experience reveal ample danger for religions outside the mainstream.[99]

C. THE COURT'S CONCEPTION OF RELIGION

Swaggart and *Smith* say little explicit about the Court's conception of religion, but they imply much. I should probably say here that I know little about the personal religiosity of the justices, which is none of my business. They are protected by both the Free Exercise Clause and the Test Oath Clause. Their personal religious conceptions may be quite different from the conceptions implicit in their opinions. They may have accepted convenient arguments to reach a legal result without considering the extent to which those arguments implied a conception of religion. But whatever they consciously thought about, a conception of the Free Exercise Clause inevitably implies a conception of religion.

1. *Religion as obeying the rules.* Parts of the *Swaggart* opinion experiment dangerously with a narrow conception of religion as obeying the rules. This implication appears most strongly in the free exercise holding. *Swaggart* appears to assume that the Free Exercise Clause protects conscientious objection claims, but not church autonomy claims.[100]

As to conscientious objection, *Swaggart* clearly assumed that if a specific doctrinal tenet forbids a church or its believers to comply with a particular law, then the Free Exercise Clause requires an exemption, subject to the compelling interest standard. This assumption was rejected three months later in *Smith*, but *Swaggart* does not appear to anticipate that development. Justice O'Connor wrote *Swaggart*, and she wrote separately in *Smith* to reject the Court's doctrinal shift. If *Swaggart* implies a limit on free exercise, it is a limit independent of what followed in *Smith*.

As to church autonomy, *Swaggart* assumes that there is little or no

---

[99]See text at notes 228–74 *infra*.

[100]I distinguish between these kinds of claims in Laycock, Towards a General Theory of the Religion Clauses: The Case of Church Labor Relations and the Right to Church Autonomy, 81 Colum. L. Rev. 1373, 1388–90 (1981).

free exercise restraint on government's power to regulate and burden religious practice and religious institutions, so long as government does not require violation of specific doctrinal tenets. The Court held open only the possibility that a free exercise issue might be raised if a generally applicable tax were heavy enough to "effectively choke off an adherent's religious practices."[101]

Thus, the Court rejected the free exercise claim because the Swaggart organization did not allege that "the mere act of paying the tax, by itself, violates its sincere religious beliefs," and because the burden of paying the tax was "not constitutionally significant." The economic cost of the tax was like the economic cost of "other generally applicable laws and regulations." Churches must comply with such laws unless their religious beliefs "mandated" noncompliance.[102]

This emphasis on what is required or mandated is not the whole of the opinion, but it is an important part of the opinion.[103] Before trying to parse out how far the holding depends on this view, I want to explore what is at stake. What would follow if the Court were committed to the position that the Free Exercise Clause protects only the right to obey a religion's mandatory teachings?

This position implies a wholly negative view of religion. It assumes that religions lay down certain binding rules, and that the exercise of religion consists only of obeying the rules. It is as though all of religious experience were reduced to the Book of Leviticus. It is the view of religion held by many secularized adults, who left the church in their youth after hearing much preaching about sin and failing to experience any benefits.

Those who stay in the church are those who do experience benefits. In the view of religion as obeying the rules, all the affirmative, communal, and spiritual aspects of religion are assumed away, placed outside the protection of the Free Exercise Clause. Practices that merely grow out of religious experience, or out of the traditions and

---

[101]*Swaggart*, 110 S.Ct. at 697.

[102]*Id.* at 696–97.

[103]The Boston Landmarks Commission cited *Swaggart* for the proposition that state control of the location of altars is of no First Amendment significance unless a church's specific religious beliefs forbid it to put the altar where the state wants it. Brief of Defendant-Appellant 28, 36–37, in Society of Jesus v. Boston Landmarks Comm'n, 408 Mass. 38, 564 N.E.2d 571 (1990) (decided for church on state constitutional grounds). See also Rector of St. Bartholomew's Church v. City of New York, 914 F.2d 348, 355 (2d Cir. 1990) (citing *Swaggart* for proposition that regulatory burdens on churches, without more, are of no constitutional significance), cert. denied, 111 S.Ct. 1103 (1991).

interactions of a religious community, are constitutionally unprotected unless they are mandated by binding doctrine.

Lower courts have taken this conception of religion to astonishing lengths, upholding even discriminatory burdens on non-mandatory religious exercise. Thus, courts have held that rules excluding student prayer groups from campuses raise no free exercise issue, because Christians are not required to pray at any particular time or place.[104] The Second Circuit suggested that Islamic prayer might be different, because Islamic prayer is required at particular times, and those times might fall within the school day.[105] The Sixth Circuit held that there is no burden on religion when the public school requires children to read books that undermine their religious faith, so long as the school does not require them to believe what they read.[106]

A trial court, in a statutory employment discrimination case, held that leading a group of Catholic and Episcopalian laypeople is not protected religious practice, because it is not "required" by the faith.[107] On that standard, the ministry is not protected religious practice either, because most members do not become ministers. A state supreme court has so held! A blind ministry student, denied vocational training benefits that would have been available for any secular occupation, argued that he was entitled to benefits under the Free Exercise Clause. The court held that he had no claim, because he had not lost benefits "because of conduct mandated by religious belief."[108] The court had already held that paying the benefits would violate the state Establishment Clause; perhaps the free exercise reasoning is confined to its facts. The Supreme Court of the United States has sensibly held that the ministry is protected free exercise, although it could not agree on a majority opinion.[109]

---

[104]Brandon v. Board of Educ., 635 F.2d 971, 977 (2d Cir. 1980), cert. denied, 454 U.S. 1123 (1981); Chess v. Widmar, 480 F. Supp. 907, 917 (W.D. Mo. 1979), rev'd on other grounds, 635 F.2d 1310 (8th Cir. 1980), aff'd *sub nom.* Widmar v. Vincent, 454 U.S. 263 (1981). The result, but not the free exercise reasoning, was changed by the Equal Access Act, 20 U.S.C. §4071 et seq. (1988), upheld in Board of Education v. Mergens, 110 S.Ct. 2356 (1990).

[105]*Brandon*, 635 F.2d at 977.

[106]Mozert v. Hawkins County Public Schools, 827 F.2d 1058, 1063–68 (6th Cir. 1987), cert. denied, 484 U.S. 1066 (1988).

[107]The unreported opinion is described and reversed in Dorr v. First Kentucky Nat'l Corp., 41 Fair Empl. Prac. Cases 421, 423–24 (6th Cir.), vacated and rehearing en banc granted, 42 Fair Empl. Prac. Cases 64 (6th Cir. 1986). No further proceedings are reported.

[108]Witters v. State Comm'n for the Blind, 112 Wash. 2d 363, 371, 771 P.2d 1119, 1123 (quoting Thomas v. Review Bd., 450 U.S. 707, 718 (1981)), cert. denied, 110 S.Ct. 147 (1989).

[109]McDaniel v. Paty, 435 U.S. 618 (1978).

It is probably the case that most religious practice is religiously motivated but not religiously mandated. Most religions have some unambiguous requirements, and in some religions, compliance with a distinctive set of rules is one of the central and defining characteristics of the faith. But for many believers, the attempt to distinguish what is required from what grows organically out of the religious experience is an utterly alien question, perhaps a nonsensical and unanswerable question, certainly a question that reflects failure to comprehend much of their faith and experience. In most faiths, serious believers rarely concentrate their efforts on identifying the minimum that God requires. The most widely shared religion in the United States is not such a legalistic faith; consider Christ's denunciation of "lawyers and Pharisees, hypocrites," in part for their legalisms.[110]

It is true that the interest in free exercise is at a maximum when government prohibits what faith unambiguously requires, or requires what faith prohibits. These are the conflicts that present the greatest potential for suffering and persecution, and the burden of justification on government should also be at a maximum. But these cases are only a small part of religious practice, and they should be only a small part of what the Free Exercise Clause protects. Otherwise, no free exercise issue would be raised by a People's Bureau for the Management and Supervision of Non-Mandatory Aspects of Religious Practice. The category of mandatory rules does not even exhaust the core of religious exercise, as illustrated by the examples of prayer and the ministry.[111]

Perhaps the Court's emphasis on specific doctrinal tenets was not intended to exhaust the meaning of the Free Exercise Clause, but only to exhaust the scope of the *Sherbert-Yoder* line of conscientious objection cases. But such a reading might improve the opinion only a little. Perhaps the Court meant something like this: Swaggart's dissemination of his religious messages is a religious practice, but California has not forbidden that. The dissemination of messages is

---

[110]Matthew 23 (New English Bible; in several other translations the denunciation is of "scribes and Pharisees"). See also 2 Corinthians 3:6 (God's new covenant is "expressed not in a written document, but in a spiritual bond; for the written law condemns to death, but the Spirit gives life.").

[111]For further criticism of the emphasis on what the faith requires, see Gedicks, Toward a Constitutional Jurisprudence of Religious Group Rights, 1989 Wis. L. Rev. 99, 142–44; Laycock, note 100 *supra*, at 1390–91. For arguments supporting that emphasis, see Choper, Defining "Religion" in the First Amendment, 1982 U. Ill. L. Rev. 579; Stone, note 90 *supra*, at 993.

burdened, but burdens are permitted unless they are formally discriminatory, or unless they "effectively choke off" religious practice. Refusing to pay tax is forbidden and not merely burdened, but refusing to pay tax is not a religious practice unless it is mandated by religious teachings. So if the dissemination of the messages is not unconstitutionally burdened, there is no independent free exercise objection to payment of the tax.

There may be further clues in the Court's Establishment Clause holding. Swaggart challenged the sales and use tax as an excessive church-state entanglement under the Establishment Clause. It is strange to think of taxing churches as an establishment of religion, but the Court's current doctrine made the claim plausible. The Court rejected this claim in terms that also imply a narrow view of religion, but not quite so narrow as religion-as-obeying-the-rules. The Court rejected the entanglement claim because collection of the tax did not require "on-site" supervision of "day-to-day operations," or inquiry "into religious content of the items or the religious motivation for selling or purchasing the items." And "assuming that the tax imposes substantial administrative burdens," such burdens are not "constitutionally significant."[112]

At least here the Court recognizes religious motivations in terms that are not limited to compulsion. But again the focus is on specifically religious content and choices. There is little recognition of a general church interest in managing its own institutions. Government can apparently regulate the day to day operations of a church so long as it does not supervise them on site. That implication under the Establishment Clause is consistent with the Court's implication under the Free Exercise Clause that non-mandatory religious practice is protected from discrimination or crushing burdens, but not from burdens that fail to choke off the practice.

In the Establishment Clause part of the *Swaggart* opinion, the Court said it was already settled that churches are subject to regulation, and so it followed that they are subject to taxation.[113] In fact it was not settled under either clause that churches are subject to regulation. In *NLRB v. Catholic Bishop*,[114] the Court held the National Labor Relations Act inapplicable to parochial school teachers, because to apply it would raise grave questions under the religion

---

[112]*Swaggart*, 110 S.Ct. at 696, 698, 699.

[113]*Id.* at 698–99.

[114]440 U.S. 490 (1979).

clauses. The constitutional problem was not that collective bargaining might violate Catholic doctrine, which has long supported the moral right of workers to organize.[115] Rather, *Catholic Bishop* contemplated a right of religious institutions to be free of regulation that intrudes into their internal affairs, and the Court stretched the statute to avoid deciding that issue. Similarly, the Court had held that secular courts could not resolve internal church disputes, even on administrative matters.[116] Some scholars have argued that these cases should point the way to a general right to church autonomy; other scholars have argued against such a right.[117]

Swaggart's brief relied heavily on these church autonomy cases, and hardly at all on the *Sherbert-Yoder* cases. But the Court ignored the church autonomy issue and the cases that posed it, and decided the *Sherbert-Yoder* issue instead. Without ever actually considering the question, *Swaggart* assumed that churches have at most a very narrow right to autonomous control of their internal affairs. If that assumption holds, it will be a very great loss to religious liberty, for reasons I have discussed at length elsewhere.[118] It would not permit a single Bureau for the Supervision of Religion—that would be discriminatory. Instead, it would permit something that may be far worse: it would permit every government bureau to supervise religion in the neutral pursuit of its own bureaucratic agenda.

This aspect of *Swaggart* may be moot after *Smith*'s holding that mandatory religious practice is equally subject to regulation. But even the holding may not be moot, and the implicit view of religion is certainly not moot. *Smith* has narrow boundaries. It does not apply to belief and profession, to hybrid cases, or to laws that are not neutral and generally applicable. Outside those boundaries, *Swaggart*'s conception of religion may remain relevant.

2. *Religion as a preference. Smith* depends on another belief about religion in contemporary America. This belief is not mentioned explicitly, and no particular sentence or paragraph implies it, but I suspect that it is critical to the whole opinion. The Court believes

---

[115] Centesimus Annus (1991); Laborum Exercens (1981); Rerum Novarum (1891).

[116] Serbian E. Orthodox Diocese v. Milivojevich, 426 U.S. 696, 710, 720–24 (1976); Kedroff v. Saint Nicholas Cathedral, 344 U.S. 94, 116 (1952).

[117] Compare Esbeck, Establishment Clause Limits on Governmental Interference with Religious Organizations, 41 Wash. & Lee L. Rev. 347 (1984) and Laycock, note 100 *supra*, with Lupu, Free Exercise Exemption and Religious Institutions: The Case of Employment Discrimination, 67 B.U. L. Rev. 391 (1987); and Marshall & Blomgren, Regulating Religious Organizations Under the Establishment Clause, 47 Ohio St. L.J. 293 (1986).

[118] Laycock, note 100 *supra*.

that religious minorities will give up their faith without a fuss if the law says they must. The Court believed it was deciding that strange people must modify their strange religions to conform to the legitimate demands of a modern society.

The Court probably did not believe it was deciding that these strange people should be forced to practice their religion underground, in the modern equivalent of catacombs. The Court almost certainly did not believe it was deciding that all these people should be imprisoned for their faith. I doubt the Court thought about enforcement at all, in part because there was no real criminal prosecution before it.

If enforcement problems did cross the mind of any justice in the majority, he surely assumed that there are not many potential martyrs in modern America. In a secular society where most people profess a religion but few let it inconvenience them, suppressing a faith would not be a problem. Religion is a preference like any other, and faced with a threat of enforcement, believers would change their preference. No persecutions would be necessary, because the threat of persecution would suffice.[119]

For some faiths and some believers, the Court is surely right. For others, it is likely to be wrong. The Mormons eventually gave up polygamy, but only after half a century of sometimes bloody conflict, the legal dissolution of their church, and the seizure of all its property. A few did not give it up; Mormon polygamy survives among underground groups who consider themselves the true faithful, and a polygamy case is pending in the Utah Supreme Court.[120] The Jehovah's Witnesses did not give up their conscientious objection to wartime alternative service, and five thousand of them spent part of World War II in federal prison.[121]

The secularization of society is not universal. There are still those among us who experience or think they experience divine instructions, and who are willing to suffer for their faith. There are un-

---

[119]For elaboration of this theme, see Carter, Evolutionism, Creationism, and Treating Religion as a Hobby, 1987 Duke L.J. 977.

[120]In re Adoption of W.A.T., 1991 WL42632 (Utah 1991) (polygamous parents may adopt children if adoption will promote the children's interests). See also Cleveland v. United States, 329 U.S. 14 (1946) (criminal prosecution for polygamy); Potter v. Murray City, 760 F.2d 1065 (10th Cir.) (police officer discharged for polygamy), cert. denied, 474 U.S. 849 (1985); Barlow v. Blackburn, 165 Ariz. 351, 798 P.2d 1360 (App. 1990) (same); Driggs, After the Manifesto: Modern Polygamy and Fundamentalist Mormons, 32 J. Church & State 367 (1990).

[121]See Sibley & Jacob, Conscription of Conscience: The American State and the Conscientious Objector, 1940–1947, at 34, 84, 355–58 (1952).

familiar faiths arriving by immigration from all corners of the world, and many of them may have practices that will offend some local code. There are religious traditions among us that have survived hundreds or thousands of years of official hostility and intermittent persecution, and we should not expect them to suddenly conform to secular demands after reviewing *Smith* and the statute book. If the Court thought its opinion could be implemented without suffering, without religious resistance, without difficult choices about the means to overcome that resistance—in short, without a whole cluster of evils that the Free Exercise Clause was designed to avoid—it was almost certainly mistaken.

But suppose the Court were right, and minority faiths comply with little resistance. Some may convert to Christianity or some other accepted faith; others may modify their own practice to eliminate any conflict with the law. The result will be that government has importantly determined religious faith and practice, terminating the existence of minority faiths or changing their central content. Suppression of a faith is no less suppression when the victims go quietly.

D. THE COURT'S CONCEPTION OF JUDICIAL ROLE

Smith importantly depends on a particular conception of the judicial role: judges are not to balance competing interests. A right to religious exemptions from regulation cannot be absolute; the state must be able to override it for sufficiently compelling reasons. But if such a right is judicially enforceable, then judges must apply the compelling interest test, balancing the government's need for regulation against the believer's right to practice his faith.

That, the Court assures us, would be "horrible." "[I]t is horrible to contemplate that federal judges will regularly balance against the importance of general laws the significance of religious practice." Suppression of religious minorities "must be preferred to a system . . . in which judges weigh the social importance of all laws against the centrality of all religious beliefs."[122] The Court says that its list of cases in which religious practice requires exemption from secular law is a parade of procedural horribles: These cases are horrible not because of their possible results, but because they would require judges to make judgments.

My reactions to this basis for the Court's holding come from two

[122] *Smith*, 110 S.Ct. at 1606 & n.5.

different perspectives. First, I think the Court is just wrong to be afraid of balancing, and that it has exaggerated both the difficulties and the uniqueness of balancing in the free exercise context. Second, from the Court's own perspective, it is caught in contradiction. It has used astonishingly activist methods in pursuit of its non-activist agenda.

1. *The ubiquity of balancing.* If the Court is serious about getting federal judges out of the business of balancing, then a wholesale revolution in constitutional law is imminent. Balancing is absolutely central to the constitutional method adopted by the modern Court.[123] This is no accident; the sweeping imperatives of the Constitution's individual rights provisions, sometimes conflicting with the government's urgent need for exceptions, inherently require some sort of balancing.[124]

There is little reason to believe that *Smith* heralds a serious renunciation of balancing, although a changing Court may tilt the constitutional balance more and more in favor of the government. At one point in *Smith*, the Court recognizes that the compelling interest test is "familiar from other fields."[125] Elsewhere, it inconsistently claims that its aversion to balancing is general, and that it never balances with a variable on each side.

> It is no more appropriate for judges to determine the "centrality" of religious beliefs before applying a "compelling interest" test in the free exercise field, than it would be for them to determine the "importance" of ideas before applying the "compelling interest" test in the free speech field.[126]

There is a problem with both halves of this comparison. I begin with the speech side, where the argument comes close to plain silliness. The Court has "long recognized that not all speech is of equal First Amendment importance."[127] It holds that political speech is more important than commercial speech,[128] that criticism of public

[123]See Aleinikoff, Constitutional Law in the Age of Balancing, 96 Yale L.J. 943 (1987).

[124]See Laycock, Notes on the Role of Judicial Review, the Expansion of Federal Power, and the Structure of Constitutional Rights, 99 Yale L.J. 1711, 1743–47 (1990).

[125]*Smith*, 110 S.Ct. at 1604.

[126]*Ibid.*

[127]Hustler Magazine, Inc. v. Falwell, 485 U.S. 46, 56 (1988), quoting Dun & Bradstreet, Inc. v. Greenmoss Builders, Inc., 472 U.S. 749, 758 (1985). For an extensive review of variations in the protection accorded different kinds of speech, see Young v. American Mini Theatres, Inc., 427 U.S. 50, 63–71 (1976) (plurality opinion).

[128]See, *e.g.*, Posadas de Puerto Rico Assoc. v. Tourism Co., 478 U.S. 328, 340 (1986); Central Hudson Gas & Elec. Corp. v. Public Serv. Comm'n, 447 U.S. 557, 561–63 (1980); Friedman v. Rogers, 440 U.S. 1, 10 (1979).

figures is more important than criticism of private figures,[129] that pornography has limited value[130] and obscenity has almost no value,[131] and that some speech is not of public concern.[132] The day after *Smith*, four of the five justices in the majority routinely balanced the "exceedingly modest" interest in possessing child pornography against the state's compelling interest in preventing "the exploitative use of children."[133] They did not find it necessary to explain away their statement of the day before.

The first half of the quoted comparison is part of the Court's attempt to show that balancing is uniquely difficult in free exercise cases. The Court considers and rejects the possibility that only "central" religious practices should be protected. A threshold requirement of centrality would indeed be a mistake, both under-inclusive and unworkable. It would be under-inclusive because all religious practices are part of free exercise, and not just those the Court finds central. It would be unworkable because religious centrality is a continuous variable. It cannot be converted into a dichotomous variable, controlling a discontinuous leap from no protection at all to the compelling interest test, without producing distortion, error, and indefensible differences in result.

The opinion's talk of centrality as a threshold requirement is thus a manufactured difficulty. But the Court is right that any balancing in the free exercise context must consider the burden on religious exercise as well as the threat to government's compelling interests. The Court says it would be unworkable to deny that point, for to deny it would require "the same degree of 'compelling state interest' to impede the practice of throwing rice at church weddings as to impede the practice of getting married in church."[134] But of course no one ever denied the point, and the Court's reductio ad absurdum boomerangs. The majority appears to say it would be "horrible" and inappropriate for judges to recognize the difference between throwing rice and getting married in church. I think they could handle it.

---

[129]Compare Gertz v. Welch, 418 U.S. 323 (1974) (private figure suing for defamation need show only negligence), with New York Times Co. v. Sullivan, 376 U.S. 254 (1964) (public figure suing for defamation must show actual malice).

[130]Young v. American Mini Theatres, Inc., 427 U.S. 50, 70–71 (1976) (plurality opinion).

[131]Miller v. California, 413 U.S. 15, 20, 34–36 (1973).

[132]See Estlund, Speech on Matters of Public Concern: The Perils of an Emerging First Amendment Category, 56 Geo. Wash. L. Rev. 1 (1990).

[133]Osborne v. Ohio, 110 S.Ct. 1691, 1695, 1696 (1990).

[134]*Smith*, 110 S.Ct. at 1605 n.4.

Of course there would be hard cases as well as easy cases. But free exercise exemption cases are not uniquely unmanageable. Many free exercise cases fall into categories in which the balance is largely determined by the category.[135] The degree of unconstrained judicial discretion would be further reduced if courts would take the compelling interest test literally and seriously. The question should not be whether it would be better on the whole to deny the exemption, but whether a particular religious exercise is doing such severe and tangible harm that the Court can imply from necessity an exception to a textually absolute constitutional right.[136]

2. *Judicial activism in pursuit of judicial minimalism.* When I say that the Court pursued its minimalist agenda with activist methods, I do not mean merely that it demolished twenty-seven years of precedent. That is not irrelevant; precedent should not be overruled lightly, or disingenuously. Rewriting the rationale of all those cases is an activist technique, but it is not inherently illegitimate. No reasoned understanding of precedent says that libertarian judges can overrule majoritarian precedents but not vice versa.

Some of what the Court did in *Smith* does seem to be at the borders of jurisprudential legitimacy, and some of it crosses over. The Court artificially created a broad issue by an extraordinary procedure, and then decided that issue with substantive premises that come from outside the Constitution.

a) The procedure that created the issue. A state administrative agency denied unemployment compensation because it found that Smith and Black had been discharged for misconduct as defined by the employer. The state courts reversed.[137] The Oregon Supreme Court said that the state's deference to employers' definitions of misconduct was religiously neutral, and thus permissible under the state constitution. But it found federal law clearly to the contrary. Smith and Black had been discharged for practicing their religion, and to withhold unemployment compensation in those circumstances would violate the Free Exercise Clause as interpreted in *Sherbert v. Verner*[138] and similar cases.

---

[135] The point is elaborated in McConnell, note 9 *supra*, at 1144–49.

[136] See Laycock, note 124 *supra*, at 1745–46.

[137] Black v. Employment Div., 75 Or. App. 735, 707 P.2d 1274 (1985), aff'd as modified, 301 Or. 221, 721 P.2d 451 (1986), vacated, 485 U.S. 660 (1988); Smith v. Employment Div., 75 Or. App. 764, 709 P.2d 246 (1985), aff'd as modified, 301 Or. 209, 721 P.2d 445 (1986), vacated, 485 U.S. 660 (1988).

[138] 374 U.S. 398 (1963).

The Oregon court expressly held that the state's interest in enforcing its drug laws was irrelevant to an unemployment compensation case.[139] The United States Supreme Court granted certiorari and vacated the judgment, holding that Oregon's criminal law was relevant after all.[140] If religious use of peyote violated Oregon's criminal law, and if that criminal law were constitutional, then Oregon could send Smith and Black to prison. A fortiori it could withhold their unemployment compensation. The Court remanded for a determination whether Smith and Black had violated the criminal law of Oregon.

This does seem to be a case in which the greater power would properly include the lesser. If it is constitutional to impose a large (criminal) penalty, it must surely be constitutional to impose a small (loss-of-benefits) penalty for the very same conduct. But it is not clear why this reasoning required a remand. It should be constitutional to impose the loss-of-benefits penalty even in a state that chooses not to impose the criminal penalty. The proposition that the greater power includes the lesser would not seem to depend on whether the greater power is actually exercised.

The problem is not with the Court's reasoning that the greater power includes the lesser, but with the unexamined consequences of applying that reasoning in this context. Surely Oregon can waive or disclaim its criminal law interests, and that may have happened here. So far as one can tell from the published opinions, the prosecutor had no intention of prosecuting, Smith and Black were not deterred by fear of prosecution, and the state's highest court had said the state's criminal law interests were irrelevant. The state Attorney General made no move to prosecute, but he did insist that criminal law policies were relevant to the unemployment compensation issue.

The Court could have denied certiorari, or it could have decided the case as the Oregon court presented it. Instead, the Court reached out for the criminal law issue that it considered logically antecedent to the issue actually presented. This raised substantive, jurisdictional, and prudential questions that the Court appeared not to notice. The substantive question was whether a restriction on a constitutional right could be justified by a state interest not considered by the legislature when it enacted the challenged law.[141] The

[139]Smith v. Employment Div., 301 Or. 209, 219, 721 P.2d 445, 450 (1986).

[140]Employment Div. v. Smith, 485 U.S. 660 (1988).

[141]Compare Mississippi Univ. for Women v. Hogan, 458 U.S. 718, 730 & n.16 (1982); Weinberger v. Wiesenfeld, 420 U.S. 636, 648 & n.16 (1975); Jimenez v. Weinberger, 417 U.S. 628, 634 (1974); United States Dept. of Agric. v. Moreno, 413 U.S. 528, 536–37 (1973); Eisenstadt

jurisdictional question was whether the dispute over the relevance of Oregon's criminal law policy went to the federal question of constitutional justification, or to the state question of the meaning of the unemployment compensation laws. The prudential question was whether the Court should decide the constitutionality of a criminal law in a case in which no criminal prosecution was pending, threatened, or feared, on an administrative record so skimpy that the state court had taken most of its facts from a California precedent decided twenty years before.[142] Justices Rehnquist, White, O'Connor, and Scalia voted to decide the criminal law issue in this posture. In any other context, it seems doubtful that they would have considered the constitutionality of a criminal law in such an abstract posture.[143]

The fifth vote came from Justice Stevens, who wrote the opinion. He has argued in other contexts that the Court should not even review state court judgments upholding federal claims against states. He has said that if a state court provided more protection than the Constitution requires, this "outcome of the state processes offended no federal interest whatever."[144] He has found it "extraordinary" and wholly unjustified for the Supreme Court to uphold a state statute on "a rational basis that the highest court of the State has expressly rejected."[145] If a state court substituted its judgment for the legislature's, that was a "matter of indifference" to federal courts. That was in search and seizure, commerce clause, and equal protection cases. For Justice Stevens, free exercise cases are different.[146]

On remand, the Supreme Court of Oregon dutifully answered the questions posed to it, while making clear its view that it had been asked for an advisory opinion.[147] The Oregon court said that there

---

v. Baird, 405 U.S. 438, 450 (1972) (all suggesting a negative answer); with United States R.R. Retirement Bd. v. Fritz, 449 U.S. 166, 179 (1980); Hampton v. Mow Sun Wong, 426 U.S. 88, 103–5 (1976); and Flemming v. Nestor, 363 U.S. 603, 612 (1960) (all suggesting an affirmative answer).

[142]Black v. Employment Div., 301 Or. 221, 225–27, 721 P.2d 451, 453–54 (1986), quoting at length from People v. Woody, 61 Cal. 2d 716, 40 Cal. Rptr. 69, 394 P.2d 813 (1964).

[143]See, *e.g.*, City of Los Angeles v. Lyons, 461 U.S. 95 (1983); Younger v. Harris, 401 U.S. 37, 41–42 (1971) (no case or controversy where no genuine threat of prosecution).

[144]Michigan v. Long, 463 U.S. 1032, 1068 (1983) (Stevens, J., dissenting); see *id.* at 1068–70.

[145]Minnesota v. Clover Leaf Creamery, 449 U.S. 456, 482 (1981) (Stevens, J., dissenting); see *id.* at 477–89.

[146]On Justice Stevens' apparent hostility to religion, see Laycock, note 17 *supra*, at 1010.

[147]Smith v. Employment Div., 307 Or. 68, 73, n.3, 763 P.2d 146, 148 n.3 (1988) (departing from its usual practice of considering the state constitution first, because "no criminal case is before us").

was no exemption for religious use in the Oregon drug laws, but that criminal punishment of the peyote service would violate the federal Free Exercise Clause as interpreted by Congress. Congress had repeatedly indicated its view that the regulatory exemption for peyote worship is constitutionally required.[148] These views had been expressed only in legislative history and not in statutory text, but the Oregon court accepted them as an authoritative exercise of Congressional power, under section 5 of the Fourteenth Amendment, to "protect against state infringement what it believes to be the free exercise of religion protected under the First Amendment."[149]

The state again successfully petitioned for certiorari. The case had now been converted into a proxy for a criminal prosecution, but the focus remained on peyote. The parties argued about its dangers, about the patterns of religious use, about whether a religious exemption would undermine all drug laws. Both sides agreed on the constitutional standard: Smith and Black were entitled to practice their religion unless the state had a compelling reason to prevent them. The only issue was whether Oregon's interest was compelling.

The Court did not decide that issue. Instead it decided that no justification was required where the law was neutral and generally applicable. The alleged dangers of peyote were irrelevant to that issue; the facts and record were irrelevant; nothing mattered except the formal neutrality of the Oregon drug laws. Once again the question identified by the Court was logically antecedent to the question presented by the parties. But this time, neither side urged the relevance of the antecedent question, and neither side had any reason to suspect that the antecedent question might really be at issue.

In other cases where the Court has decided to reconsider important issues not briefed by the parties, it has announced its attention and set the case for new briefs and new argument.[150] It did not take that step in *Smith*. It fundamentally changed the law of free exercise without briefs or argument, in an abstract case created by the Court. The extraordinarily activist procedure contrasts sharply with the professed goals of minimizing judicial power.

---

[148] *Id.* at 74–75, 763 P.2d at 149, citing committee reports on the Drug Abuse Control Amendments of 1965 and the American Indian Religious Freedom Act of 1978.

[149] Smith v. Employment Div., 307 Or. 68, 75, 763 P.2d 146, 149 (1988).

[150] See, *e.g.*, Patterson v. McLean Credit Union, 485 U.S. 617 (1988); Garcia v. San Antonio Metro. Transit Auth., 468 U.S. 1213 (1984); Illinois v. Gates, 459 U.S. 1028 (1982); Alfred Dunhill, Inc. v. Republic of Cuba, 422 U.S. 1005 (1975); Brown v. Board of Educ., 347 U.S. 483, 495–96 (1954); Brown v. Board of Education, 345 U.S. 972 (1953).

b) Extra-constitutional substantive premises. Smith's strange procedural history may be idiosyncratic to the particular case, but the Court's substantive premises appear to be generally applicable. I start with the Court's treatment of *Wisconsin v. Yoder.*[151] The Court said in *Smith* that *Yoder* would be illegitimate if decided under the Free Exercise Clause alone, but that it is legitimate as a hybrid case of free exercise and "the right of parents to direct the education of their children."[152]

Of course the Constitution nowhere expressly mentions any right of parents or any right to direct education or anything about children. If there is a parental right to direct the education of children, it is an unenumerated right, protected only by the Ninth Amendment, or as the Court would presumably have it, by substantive due process.[153] Especially in the wake of the Bork nomination and his inkblot theory of the Ninth Amendment,[154] I am delighted to see Justices Scalia, Rehnquist, Kennedy, and White unambiguously endorse unenumerated rights in an opinion for the Court. I hope they mean it.

But I find it illegitimate to make unenumerated rights superior to the enumerated ones. Why is the Court willing to balance the state's interest against parental preference on behalf of the unenumerated right of parental control, but not on behalf of the explicit right to free exercise of religion? If the Court feels free to enforce the unenumerated rights it likes, and to strip nearly all independent meaning from the enumerated rights it does not like, it is hard to see how the existence of a written Constitution affects its decisions. The point of enumerating certain rights was to ensure that at least those rights get enforced.

The answer to this puzzle may be that the Court's explanation of *Yoder* was made up for this day only, and we should not pay any attention to it. But the distinction also fits with the Court's fears that free exercise exemptions discriminate in favor of persons with religious motivations. Religion should be broadly defined for purposes of free exercise exemptions,[155] but no plausible definition will make all

[151]406 U.S. 205 (1972).

[152]*Smith*, 110 S.Ct. at 1601 (citation omitted).

[153]See Pierce v. Society of Sisters, 268 U.S. 510, 533–35 (1925) (finding right to send children to private schools in Due Process Clause); Roe v. Wade, 410 U.S. 113, 153 (1972) (preferring to find right to abortion in Fourteenth Amendment rather than Ninth).

[154]See Bork, The Tempting of America 166 (1990).

[155]See Laycock, note 17 *supra*, at 1002; *cf.* Welsh v. United States, 398 U.S. 333, 344 (1970)

claims religious. A parental right to control education can be asserted by any parent, and so is more neutral than a free exercise right to control religious education.

Whatever the merits of a parental right to control education, the Court cannot legitimately reject free exercise claims on the ground that the clause protects only the exercise of religion. There is unambiguously in the Constitution a clause that protects only the exercise of religion. To reject claims under that clause because it does not fit the Court's conception of neutrality is to unabashedly substitute the Court's preferences for the text of the Constitution. And that is precisely what the opponents of judicial activism say they most fear.

The same activist error occurs in more general terms in the Court's hostility to balancing. The Court agrees that plaintiffs are engaged in religious exercise and that Oregon is prohibiting that exercise. But the Court says it is not required to read the text in this straightforward way, and that it will not do so because that would require judicial balancing, which would be horrible. How does the Court know it would be horrible? Where in the Constitution does it say that? The horror of balancing is the Court's own preference, injected into the Constitution without a basis in the text, in this case at the cost of stripping most of the meaning out of an express part of the text.

The constitutional text is absolute, but everyone recognizes that some exceptions are required. The Court's emphasis on formal neutrality is an attempt to limit the absolute text in a way that avoids balancing. But formal neutrality completely misfits the policies of the clause. It fits neither the interests of the government nor the interests of religion. It fails to protect core religious functions, and it often infringes religious liberty where the government has no real need to do so. It limits the text in a way that does not plausibly serve the purposes of the text.

The need for limitations on the absolute text is an implication from necessity, and the Court will interpret the text most faithfully if it directly addresses the question of when implied exceptions are necessary. The combination of express substantive right and the necessity of implied exceptions leads directly to a certain kind of balancing. The Court cannot just say that such a clause is inconsistent with its conception of the judicial role. The judicial role is defined by the Constitution; the Constitution is not defined by changing concep-

(interpreting conscientious objector provisions of Selective Service Act to protect non-theistic objectors).

tions of the judicial role. To refuse to enforce rights that are in the Constitution is as mistaken as enforcing rights that are not in the Constitution.

III. The Practical Impact: What Is Left of Free Exercise?

A. TAXATION OF CHURCHES

The doctrinal change with respect to taxation is reasonably clear. Most tax statutes exempt churches, and that has not changed. *Murdock* struck down a minor tax on proselytizing, and created a plausible constitutional argument for more general church tax immunity. But the scope of constitutional tax immunity was never clear, and the issue was rarely litigated, because the statutory exemptions sufficed.

Swaggart unambiguously eliminates most constitutional claims to tax exemption. The real choices are now up to legislatures and tax authorities, where the impact is likely to be marginal. The Court's new rule is that churches are constitutionally immune only from a flat tax that acts as a prior restraint. The boundaries of this category are not wholly unambiguous—what about a flat tax collected after the taxed activity is completed, or a proportionate tax that must be estimated and paid in advance, or a franchise tax on the existence of the religious organization, proportioned to some measure of size or activity and collected at the end of the year? But these are marginal questions, because license taxes of any form are a minor source of revenue.

The important change is that churches may now be subjected to all but a tiny percentage of the taxes in a modern society. All the major taxes—sales tax, use tax, income tax, and property tax—and most minor taxes, including gross receipts taxes and most excise taxes and transfer taxes, are formally neutral, generally applicable, and not a flat license tax collected in advance. All would seem to be authorized by the opinion in *Swaggart*.

Whether these taxes will in fact be levied is up to the political branches and to state and local governments. *Texas Monthly v. Bullock* says that taxing authorities may not exempt religious organizations or activity as such, but *Texas Monthly* reaffirms that taxing authorities may include churches in broader categories of tax exempt organizations, such as charitable organizations or not-for-profit organizations.[156]

---

[156] 489 U.S. 1, 11–13 (1989). See Walz v. Tax Comm'n, 397 U.S. 664 (1970).

There is little reason to expect a wholesale movement to repeal traditional tax exemptions. But increased taxation about the margins is inevitable. Governments in need of revenue will be more aggressive about taxing marginal church properties near the borders of the statutory exemptions, more aggressive about collecting tax on taxable activities that were formerly ignored or assumed to be exempt, and more aggressive about demanding "voluntary" contributions in lieu of taxes. Most churches will be burdened; some economically marginal churches will lose properties or abandon ministries. The fixed compliance costs of an interstate ministry are substantial, with scores of local jurisdictions adding their various levies to the basic state sales and use tax. The Court relied on these compliance costs when it held that the Commerce Clause exempts mail order sellers from collecting tax for their buyers' home states.[157] But if entering a state to hold a worship service is a permanent submission to the state's taxing jurisdiction, the Commerce Clause rule is of no benefit to a traveling ministry.

Churches responding to new demands for revenue have lost their biggest bargaining chip; with no constitutional defense possible, they can never threaten constitutional litigation. We may reasonably expect political battles in tax-writing committees over proposals to limit or repeal various exemptions that include religion. Whether these developments are good or bad, and how they comport with a more general understanding of the religion clauses, I leave for another day.

I note only one point, which frames the issue and explains why it must await another day. Even if the result in *Swaggart* is defensible, the reasoning is not. The Court holds that the burden of taxation is constitutionally insignificant, but that cannot be right. Nor is it the case that tax exemption, considered alone, is a subsidy. Government does not subsidize a church by leaving it alone.

If churches may be taxed, it is because they receive some (but not all) government services, and because government services to a tax exempt body are a form of subsidy. The question is whether government services plus tax exemption is a greater departure from neutrality than the burdens of taxation. The answer may depend on the tax. A tax on unrelated business income is very different from a tax on dissemination of religious messages or on property essential to worship, or a tax that can be triggered by a sermon identifying

[157]See National Bellas Hess, Inc. v. Department of Revenue, 386 U.S. 753, 759–60 (1967).

political candidates whose views of public policy do not violate the church's views of morality.[158] Waiving a fee for specific services, like postage stamps, looks much more like a direct subsidy than exemption from taxes that go into general revenues. Both burden and subsidy may vary with context, and some cases may be hard. But the answer is not to dismiss the serious burdens of taxation as constitutionally insignificant. Religion is not free when the government charges for its exercise.

B. REGULATION OF RELIGIOUS PRACTICE

The impact of regulation on religious practice is much less clear. This impact may be sweeping or limited, depending on how the Court interprets all the boundaries and exceptions to its opinion. *Smith* announces a general rule of devastating sweep, but it also announces six overlapping exceptions and limitations, and *Swaggart* recognizes a seventh. The Free Exercise Clause never requires exemptions from formally neutral regulations of conduct, but:

1. This rule does not apply to regulation of religious belief and profession.[159]
2. This rule does not apply to religious speech.[160]
3. This rule does not apply to parental control of children's education.[161]
4. This rule does not apply to unemployment compensation cases.[162]
5. This rule does not apply to regulatory schemes that require an "individualized governmental assessment of the reasons for the relevant conduct."[163]
6. This rule does not apply to laws that are not formally neutral and generally applicable.
7. There may be some protection for religious practice under the Establishment Clause.[164]

---

[158]See Gaffney, On Not Rendering to Caesar: the Unconstitutionality of Tax Regulation of Activities of Religious Organizations Relating to Politics, 40 DePaul L. Rev. 1 (1990); Caron & Dessingue, IRC §501(c)(3): Practical and Constitutional Implications of "Political" Activity Restrictions, 2 J.L. & Pol. 169 (1985).

[159]*Smith*, 110 S.Ct. at 1599.

[160]*Id*. at 1601–2. The Court distinguishes "profession" from "speech" without explanation. See text at notes 182–84 *infra*.

[161]*Smith*, 110 S.Ct. at 1601.

[162]*Id*. at 1602–3.

[163]*Id*. at 1603.

[164]*Swaggart*, 110 S.Ct. at 698–99.

If the Court means to defer to the political branches on questions of formal neutrality and the scope of the exceptions to *Smith*, then very little is left of judicially enforceable free exercise. There are many religious practices that conflict with the regulatory agenda of one or another interest group, and there are few burdens on religion that cannot be conceptualized in formally neutral terms. But if the Court is serious about requiring at least formal neutrality, and if it is serious about its list of cases in which the Constitution still requires exemptions, then much religious exercise can still claim judicial protection. A serious requirement of formal neutrality must consider legislative motive, religious gerrymanders, exceptions, exemptions, defenses, gaps in coverage, actual or potential bias in enforcement, and whether the state regulates comparable secular conduct or pursues its alleged interests in secular contexts.

In the remainder of this section, I examine each of the exceptions and limitations in turn, reading them optimistically from the perspective of religious liberty.

1. *Belief and profession*. The Court begins its analysis by distinguishing "belief and profession" from "physical acts."[165] It does not explicitly say that belief and profession are protected even from formally neutral regulation, but that is implied by the structure of the opinion and by the cases cited. The Court says that government cannot "punish the expression of religious doctrines it believes to be false," citing *United States v. Ballard*.[166] *Ballard* was a mail fraud prosecution against an evangelist who promised divine intervention on behalf of his contributors. The mail fraud law is formally neutral, but its application to claims of religious faith would plainly restrict religious exercise, and *Ballard* created a constitutional exemption.

Similarly, the Court says that government cannot "lend its power to one or the other side in controversies over religious authority or dogma," citing cases on secular resolution of disputes arising out of church schisms.[167] The Court does not cite *Jones v. Wolf*,[168] which moved this body of law considerably closer to the formal neutrality model. But even after *Jones*, some formally neutral rules remain un-

[165] *Smith*, 110 S.Ct. at 1599.

[166] *Ibid*., citing 322 U.S. 78, 86–88 (1944).

[167] Serbian E. Orthodox Diocese v. Milivojevich, 426 U.S. 696, 708–25 (1976); Presbyterian Church v. Mary Elizabeth Blue Hull Presbyterian Church, 393 U.S. 440, 445–52 (1969); Kedroff v. St. Nicholas Cathedral, 344 U.S. 94, 95–119 (1952).

[168] 443 U.S. 595 (1979).

constitutional. Courts cannot apply to churches a formally neutral rule that when a private association splits into competing factions, the right to the original association's name and property goes to the faction that adheres most closely to the original goals, purposes, or rules of the association.[169] The Court's brief reference to these cases in *Smith* implies that even formally neutral laws cannot interfere with internal church disputes, at least with respect to "religious authority or dogma."[170]

This restriction could provide substantial protection against a potent source of formally neutral intrusions into churches: the whole body of modern labor law, including discrimination laws, collective bargaining laws, and wrongful discharge law. These laws provide few exceptions for churches, but courts have generally refused to apply them to ministers and other religious teaching personnel.[171] There is no exception in the employment discrimination laws for sex discrimination by churches.[172] Must religious schools employ unwed mothers as school teachers?[173] Must faiths that teach a moral duty of mothers to care for small children in the home employ mothers of small children in paid work for the church outside the home?[174] Must the Roman Catholic Church ordain women priests?[175] Must churches employ or ordain practicing homosexuals under local gay rights ordinances?[176] Can courts review the church's reasons for discharging a parochial school teacher,[177] a pastor,[178] or a

[169]Jones v. Wolf, 443 U.S. 595, 599–600, 602, 609 (1979); Presbyterian Church v. Mary Elizabeth Blue Hull Memorial Presbyterian Church, 393 U.S. 440 (1968).

[170]*Smith*, 110 S.Ct. at 1599.

[171]The cases are collected in Laycock & Waelbroeck, Academic Freedom and the Free Exercise of Religion, 66 Tex. L. Rev. 1455, 1462 nn.27–30.

[172]42 U.S.C. §2000e-1 and e-2 (1988).

[173]See Dolter v. Wahlert High School, 483 F. Supp. 266 (N.D. Iowa 1980) (holding that school is constitutionally protected if it acted for religious reasons and did so consistently).

[174]See Ohio Civil Rights Comm'n v. Dayton Christian Schools, Inc., 477 U.S. 619 (1986) (failing to decide the issue); McLeod v. Providence Christian School, 408 N.W.2d 146 (Mich. App. 1987) (reinstating teacher).

[175]See Comment, 13 Colum. J.L. & Soc. Probs. 257 (1977) (implausibly finding the issue close before *Smith*, but concluding that state's interest was not compelling).

[176]See Walker v. First Presbyterian Church, 22 Fair Empl. Prac. Cases 762 (Cal. Super. Ct. 1980) (upholding discharge of homosexual organist); *cf.* Gay Rights Coalition v. Georgetown Univ., 536 A.2d 1 (D.C. App. 1987) (refusing to order Catholic university to grant official recognition to gay rights organization).

[177]See Miller v. Catholic Diocese, 728 P.2d 794 (Mont. 1986) (refusing to review discharge of school teacher).

[178]See, *e.g.*, Hutchison v. Thomas, 789 F.2d 392 (6th Cir.) (refusing to review forced retirement of Methodist minister), cert. denied, 479 U.S. 885 (1986).

bishop?[179] All of these cases present an internal dispute between the employee and the church, and often there is a reform faction that supports the employee's position and an entrenched faction that resists it. If government cannot interfere in "controversies over religious authority," then courts should continue to dismiss most of these cases.

Similarly, there is no express exception for churches in the National Labor Relations Act. The Supreme Court implied one in *NLRB v. Catholic Bishop*,[180] holding that the bishop did not have to bargain collectively with unions of parochial school teachers. Some state labor boards have stepped into the resulting gap and successfully asserted jurisdiction.[181] Does *Smith* validate these state labor board cases? Is there now no constitutional barrier to unionized parochial schools? What about convents and monasteries? Because it is almost inevitable that the union represents one contending faction within the church, and that unionization will affect future decisions about teaching personnel, *Catholic Bishop* may survive as a case about interference with internal church disputes. Alternatively, it may survive as a hybrid case about free exercise and parental control of education.

2. *Speech.* The Court in *Smith* appeared to say that religious speech is still protected even from formally neutral laws. The Court discussed speech in four different places, with no cross-references. First, the Court said that "belief and profession" are protected, citing *Ballard*, a religious speech case.[182] Second, the Court said that proselytizing and assembling for worship are conduct, even though they would seem to be speech and profession.[183] Third, the Court recognized a right to constitutional exemptions from generally applicable laws in hybrid cases involving free exercise and speech, citing *Cantwell*, *Murdock*, and *Follett*, all religious speech cases.[184] So religious speech would seem to be protected as a hybrid claim, even if it is characterized as conduct. Finally, the Court said that the compelling

---

[179]See Serbian E. Orthodox Diocese v. Milivojevich, 426 U.S. 696 (1976) (refusing to let civil court review decision to remove bishop and appoint a successor).

[180]440 U.S. 490 (1979).

[181]Catholic High School Ass'n v. Culvert, 753 F.2d 1161 (2d Cir. 1985) (state labor board can assert jurisdiction over religious schools, except where sponsoring church has doctrinal objection to collective bargaining).

[182]*Smith*, 110 S.Ct. at 1599.

[183]*Ibid.*

[184]*Id.* at 1601.

interest test does not apply to "generally applicable laws unconcerned with regulating speech that have the effect of interfering with speech," citing an antitrust case.[185]

This fourth passage is misleading as a description of the Court's precedents, and in any event applies only to those laws that are formally neutral as between speech and non-expressive conduct. By its terms, this passage does not apply to laws that restrict speech but are formally neutral as between religious and secular speech. The passage appears in a footnote responding to the dissent, and it surely should not be taken as rejecting the Court's approving citations, in text, of *Ballard*, *Cantwell*, *Murdock*, and *Follett*. Despite the ambiguity of four separate discussions, it appears that religious speech is still protected even from formally neutral laws.

An exception for speech should have many applications, some of them familiar. Religious speech has been and still is protected by the Speech Clause.[186] The Free Exercise Clause stands as textual evidence that religious speech is central to the First Amendment, like fully protected political speech and not like commercial speech, obscenity, or other categories of speech with only limited constitutional protection. Presumably the Court's category of "hybrid" free speech and free exercise cases recognizes this fully protected status.

Continued protection for religious speech is key to the many suits for fraud and intentional infliction of emotional distress now pending against high-demand religions.[187] These suits are typically brought by disgruntled members and their families; they often produce multi-million dollar verdicts that threaten the very existence of the defendant religion.[188] The trials of these cases are generally charac-

---

[185]*Id.* at 1604 n.3.

[186]See, *e.g.*, Airport Comm'rs v. Jews for Jesus, Inc., 482 U.S. 569 (1987) (religious solicitation in airport); Heffron v. International Soc'y for Krishna Consciousness, Inc., 452 U.S. 640 (1981) (religious solicitation at state fair, held properly regulated under same rules as secular solicitation at state fair); Widmar v. Vincent, 454 U.S. 263 (1981) (religious student groups on university campus); Fowler v. Rhode Island, 345 U.S. 67 (1953) (religious service in park).

[187]See, *e.g.*, Molko v. Holy Spirit Ass'n, 46 Cal. 3d 1092, 762 P.2d 46, 252 Cal. Rptr. 122 (1988), cert. denied, 109 S.Ct. 2110 (1989); Christofferson v. Church of Scientology, 57 Or. App. 203, 644 P.2d 577, review denied, 293 Or. 456, 650 P.2d 928 (1982), cert. denied, 459 U.S. 1206 (1983). A high-demand religion is one that demands much of its adherents: strict moral codes that are enforced and not merely encouraged, significant lifestyle changes, dietary restrictions, conspicuous dress, and the like.

[188]George v. International Soc'y for Krishna Consciousness, No. D007153 (Cal. App. 4th Dist. 1989) ($32.7 million verdict reduced to $3 million), vacated, 111 S.Ct. 1299 (1991); Wollersheim v. Church of Scientology, 212 Cal. App. 3d 872, 260 Cal. Rptr. 331 (1989) ($30 million verdict reduced to $2.5 million), vacated, 111 S.Ct. 1298 (1991); Church Universal & Triumphant, Inc. v. Witt, No. B021187 (Cal. App. 2d Dist. 1989) ($1.5 million), cert. denied,

terized by attempts to incite the jury to fear and hatred of a strange faith. But the liability rules of fraud and emotional distress are formally neutral.

Religious speech requires the protection of the *Ballard* rule against fraud claims; jurors should not be allowed to decide whether claims of religious faith are true or false. *Ballard* does not and should not protect fraudulent claims about empirical matters that are verifiable in this world.

Religious speech also requires protections analogous to those accorded the media in defamation[189] and emotional distress cases.[190] The Court recently vacated two judgments affirming large awards of punitive damages against religious bodies for intentional infliction of emotional distress.[191] The Court decided no First Amendment issue; it remanded for consideration in light of its resolution of an insurance company's claim that standardless awards of punitive damages violate the Due Process Clause.[192] If religious speech is still protected from burdensome but formally neutral rules, then the Court cannot assume that the rule it creates for insurers is automatically adequate for churches.

If religious speech is protected and religious conduct is not, litigants will claim that much conduct that previously would have been protected under the Free Exercise Clause is now protected as speech. Some of these claims may be strained, but many will be quite legitimate. William Marshall, who urged the Court to do what it did in *Smith*, has also written that most religious conduct can be protected as speech.[193] Certainly all claims to control ministers, teachers, and others who speak for the church may plausibly be presented as speech claims. Challenges to regulation of religious ritual and to landmarking of sacred architecture might plausibly be brought as speech claims. Surely the Boston Jesuits' desire to relocate their altar

---

110 S.Ct. 839 (1990); O'Neil v. Schuckardt, 112 Idaho 472, 733 P.2d 693 (1986) ($1 million against priest; $250,000 affirmed; new trial granted on the rest because damages for invasion of privacy could not be separated from damages for alienation of affections, a tort not recognized in Idaho); Christofferson v. Church of Scientology, 5 Religious Freedom Rptr. 126 (Or. Cir. Ct. Multnomah County 1985) ($39 million); Guinn v. Church of Christ, 775 P.2d 766 (Okla. 1989) ($390,000 against local congregation).

[189] New York Times Co. v. Sullivan, 376 U.S. 254 (1964).

[190] Hustler Magazine, Inc. v. Falwell, 485 U.S. 46 (1988).

[191] *George* and *Wollersheim*, both cited in note 188 *supra*.

[192] Pacific Mutual Life Ins. Co. v. Haslip, 111 S.Ct. 1032 (1991).

[193] Cf. Marshall, note 16 *supra*, with Marshall, Solving the Free Exercise Dilemma: Free Exercise as Expression, 67 Minn. L. Rev. 545 (1983).

in accord with the liturgical reforms of the Second Vatican Council is a case of symbolic speech.

3. *Parental control of education.* The Court's exception for the unenumerated right of parents to control their children's education would appear to make *Smith* inapplicable to a large body of litigation, mostly in the state courts, about conflicts between religion and state educational systems. The issues in these cases include intrusive regulation of religious schools,[194] home schooling,[195] and exemptions from public school curricula that undermine religious faith.[196] Even without *Smith* the states have been winning most of these cases in the lower courts, but the states have lost some, and they have lost the cases decided on the merits in the Supreme Court.[197] Most of these issues remain open at the Supreme Court level, and apparently they remain subject to the compelling interest test.

4. *Unemployment compensation cases.* The Court's exception for the unemployment compensation cases is the most cryptic of all. At one point, it seems to be an arbitrary exception for unemployment compensation only, based on nothing but precedent, like the distinction between baseball and football in antitrust law. The Court says: "Even if we were inclined to breathe into *Sherbert* some life beyond the unemployment compensation field, we would not apply it to require exemptions from a generally applicable criminal law."[198] If these two categories overlap—as in *Smith*, in which the employee was discharged for violating a generally applicable criminal law—the criminal-law category controls.

---

[194] Cases upholding such regulation are collected in New Life Baptist Church Academy v. Town of E. Longmeadow, 885 F.2d 940, 950 (1st Cir. 1989), cert. denied, 110 S.Ct. 1782 (1990). For cases limiting such regulation, see Farrington v. Tokushige, 273 U.S. 284 (1927); Kentucky State Bd. for Elementary & Secondary Educ. v. Rudasill, 589 S.W.2d 877 (Ky. 1979), cert. denied, 446 U.S. 938 (1980); State v. Whisner, 47 Ohio St. 2d 181, 351 N.E.2d 750 (1976); see also State v. Emmanuel Baptist Preschool, 434 Mich. 380, 455 N.W.2d 1 (1990) (limiting regulation of church day care center).

[195] Cases upholding restrictions on home schooling are collected in New Life Baptist Church Academy v. Town of E. Longmeadow, 885 F.2d 940, 950–51 (1st Cir. 1989), cert. denied, 110 S.Ct. 1752 (1990). The home schooling movement has been politically strong enough to get substantial legislative accommodation in many states. For a collection of statutes, see Comment, The Constitutionality of Home Education Statutes, 55 UMKC L. Rev. 69 (1986). See also Wisconsin v. Yoder, 406 U.S. 205 (1972) (finding constitutional right to home schooling for Amish children in ninth and tenth grade).

[196] Mozert v. Hawkins County Public Schools, 827 F.2d 1058 (6th Cir. 1987), cert. denied, 484 U.S. 1066 (1988).

[197] Wisconsin v. Yoder, 406 U.S. 205 (1972); Farrington v. Tokushige, 273 U.S. 284 (1927); Pierce v. Society of Sisters, 268 U.S. 510 (1925).

[198] *Smith*, 110 S.Ct. at 1603.

But the Court does offer a reason for the unemployment compensation exception, and the reason appears to have other applications. Indeed, the reason appears to have many applications, and to be a special case of the general requirement of neutrality. It requires separate treatment.

5. *"Individualized governmental assessment of the reasons for the relevant conduct."* The Court says that the unemployment compensation cases provide for "individualized governmental assessment of the reasons for the relevant conduct," and that "where the State has in place a system of individual exemptions, it may not refuse to extend that system to cases of 'religious hardship' without compelling reason."[199] There are two points run together here. One is individualized assessment, and the other is non-religious exemptions. They will often appear together, but as a matter of logic and policy, they have independent force.

The Court does not explain why individualized assessment cases are to be treated differently, but the reason must be that individualized decisionmaking provides ample opportunity for discrimination against religion in general or unpopular faiths in particular. Courts cannot assume that an individualized decisionmaking process was religion-blind just because the underlying statute or legal principle is religion-blind. For example, part of the problem in the fraud and intentional infliction of emotional distress suits against high-demand religions is that the jury can readily vent its hostility to strange religions in the guise of enforcing a supposedly neutral common law rule.

This is also true, of, for example, zoning, landmarking, and condemnation decisions. Zoning boards restrict the location of new churches,[200] and what is far worse, restrict the ministries of existing churches.[201] They sometimes discriminate against minority

[199]Both quotations appear *id.* at 1603, citing Bowen v. Roy, 476 U.S. 693, 708 (1986) (plurality opinion).

[200]See, *e.g.*, Love Church v. City of Evanston, 896 F.2d 1082 (7th Cir. 1989) (city code required special use permit for any new church; claim dismissed for lack of standing), cert. denied, 111 S.Ct. 252 (1990); Lakewood, Ohio Congregation of Jehovah's Witnesses, Inc. v. City of Lakewood, 699 F.2d 303 (6th Cir. 1983) (zoning decision forbidding church to build on its land, upheld), cert. denied, 464 U.S. 815 (1983). A majority of courts hold, often on grounds other than free exercise, that churches cannot be excluded from residential zones. Reynolds, Zoning the Church: The Police Power Versus the First Amendment, 64 B.U. L. Rev. 767, 776–77 (1985).

[201]See, *e.g.*, Havurah v. Zoning Bd. of Appeals, 177 Conn. 440, 418 A.2d 82 (1979) (zoning decision forbidding use of church for overnight accommodations, struck down); Burlington Assembly of God Church v. Zoning Bd. of Adjustment, 238 N.J. Super. 634, 570 A.2d 495

faiths.[202] The administration of landmarking laws has burdened churches at rates many times higher than any other class of property.[203] Older religious institutions with open space are sometimes special targets of eminent domain, because it is cheaper to buy open space than to destroy buildings and restore it.[204] These land use cases are readily subject to analysis under the *Smith* exception for individualized assessments.

In such individualized decisionmaking processes, the Court's explanation of its unemployment compensation cases would seem to require that religion get something analogous to most-favored nation status. Religious speech should be treated as well as political speech, religious land uses should be treated as well as any other land use of comparable intensity, and so forth. Alleged distinctions—explanations that a proposed religious use will cause more problems than

(1989) (refusal of variance for church radio tower, struck down); St. John's Evangelical Lutheran Church v. Hoboken, 195 N.J. Super. 414, 479 A.2d 935 (1983) (zoning decision forbidding church to shelter homeless, struck down); Westchester Reform Temple v. Brown, 22 N.Y.2d 488, 239 N.E.2d 891, 293 N.Y.S.2d 297 (1968) (setback rules imposing financial hardship on expansion of synagogue, struck down); see also Grosz v. City of Miami Beach, 721 F.2d 729 (11th Cir. 1983) (zoning decision forbidding meetings of prayer group in private home, upheld), cert. denied, 469 U.S. 827 (1984). For analysis and more cases, see Reynolds, note 200 *supra*, at 810–17.

[202] Islamic Center, Inc. v. City of Starkville, 840 F.2d 293 (5th Cir. 1988) (series of zoning decisions refusing to allow Moslems to meet in university neighborhood where no Christian church had ever been denied zoning, struck down); Moore v. Trippe, 743 F. Supp. 201 (S.D.N.Y. 1990) (repeated citations against Buddhist temple, and zoning amendment requiring special use permit for any change to property); Reynolds, note 200 *supra*, at 770–71 & n.20.

[203] L'Heureux, Ministry v. Mortar: A Landmark Conflict, in Kelley, Government Intervention in Religious Affairs 2, at 164, 168 (1986) (stating that religious buildings are less than 1/3 of one percent of buildings in New York City, but more than fourteen percent of buildings designated as landmarks in New York City). For further analysis, see Carmella, Houses of Worship and Religious Liberty: Constitutional Limits to Landmark Preservation and Architectural Review, 36 Vill. L. Rev. ——— (1991); Greenawalt, Church and State: Some Constitutional Questions in Landmarking of Church-owned Properties, in Historic Preservation Law 465 (Robinson, ed., 1982). For illustrative cases, see Church of St. Paul and St. Andrew v. Barwick, 67 N.Y.2d 510, 496 N.E.2d 183, 505 N.Y.S.2d 24, cert. denied, 479 U.S. 985 (1986); First Covenant Church v. City of Seattle, 114 Wash. 2d 392, 787 P.2d 1352, vacated for reconsideration in light of *Smith*, 111 S.Ct. 1097 (1991). For an application of *Smith*, see Rector of St. Bartholomew's Church v. City of New York, 914 F.2d 348, 354–55 (2d Cir. 1990) (finding a landmarking ordinance neutral and generally applicable, and finding discretionary application to individual churches of "no constitutional relevance"), cert. denied, 111 S.Ct. 1103 (1991).

[204] For a reported example, see Yonkers Racing Corp. v. City of Yonkers, 858 F.2d 855, 871 (2d Cir. 1988), cert. denied, 489 U.S. 1077 (1989); Other condemnations with devastating consequences can be avoided only by an exemption. See Pillar of Fire v. Denver Urban Renewal Auth., 181 Colo. 411, 509 P.2d 1250 (1973), where a thirty-three block urban renewal project included a denomination's first church, which had great historical and symbolic significance. The court conditioned the condemnation on proof of "a substantial interest without a reasonable alternative means of accomplishment." *Id*. at 417, 509 P.2d at 1253.

some other use already approved—should be subject to strict scrutiny.

The other point in the Court's explanation of its unemployment compensation cases is secular exemptions. If the state grants exemptions from its law for secular reasons, then it must grant comparable exemptions for religious reasons. But this is part of the requirement of formal neutrality or general applicability, and nothing should turn on whether the secular exemptions are "individualized." If the potential for an individualized secular exemption requires religious exemptions, then a fortiori a whole class of secular exemptions should require religious exemptions.

In general, the allowance of any exemption is substantial evidence that religious exemptions would not threaten the statutory scheme. The state may conceivably have a compelling reason for denying some claims to religious exemption even though it grants other exemptions, but such cases should be quite rare. An example is *Gillette v. United States*,[205] holding that Congress could exempt from the military draft conscientious objectors who objected to war in any form, without exempting the much more numerous group who objected to unjust wars.

The requirement that religious conduct get the benefit of secular exemptions is a requirement of broad potential application. American statutes are riddled with exceptions and exemptions for various special interests, small businesses, private citizens, and government agencies. The federal employment discrimination laws do not apply to Congress or to employers with fewer than fifteen employees.[206] The law penalizing employers of illegal aliens does not apply to employers of household help.[207] The Florida humane slaughter law exempts any person slaughtering and selling "not more than 20 head of cattle nor more than 35 head of hogs per week."[208] And so on.

Exemptions for secular interests without exemptions for religious practice reflect a hostile indifference to religion. It is not that the legislature was consciously trying to harm religion when it failed

---

[205] 401 U.S. 437 (1971).

[206] 42 U.S.C. §2000e (1988).

[207] But see Intercommunity Center for Justice & Peace v. Immigration & Naturalization Serv., 910 F.2d 42, 45 (2d Cir. 1990), finding this exception irrelevant to a free exercise claim. It is not clear from the opinion whether plaintiffs urged that the exception in the statute triggered an exception to *Smith*. In any event, the court found that the government's interest was compelling.

[208] Fla. Stat. Ann. §828.24(3) (1976).

to create a religious exemption. Rather, it is that such a discriminatory pattern of exemptions shows that the legislature's goals do not require universal application, and that the legislature values the exempted secular activities more highly than the constitutionally protected religious activities. This pattern of exemptions reflects a legislative judgment that the free exercise of religion is less important than the demands of some special interest group of no constitutional significance. But that is a judgment inconsistent with the constitutional guarantee.

A set of exemptions so institutionalized and generalized that they do not even seem to be exemptions is the scheduling of government functions on the Christian calendar. The Court is so accustomed to this calendar that it appears to think of persons desiring to observe minority holy days as asking for special treatment.[209] Consider a Jewish student who asks to make up an examination administered on Yom Kippur. Such a student is not seeking special treatment; he is seeking an accommodation equal to that already extended to Christians. The school's calendar is not formally neutral just because it never mentions religion. School never meets on Sunday; it never meets on Easter; there is a long break at Christmas, even in schools where the Christmas break falls at an awkward time near the end of the semester. School is the clearest example, but the point is general. Operating on a Christian calendar is a sensible accommodation to the Christian majority, but there is nothing neutral about it. Calendar exemptions for minority religious observance should be required, even after *Smith*, because the calendar is not neutral.

6. *Formal neutrality.* The Court in *Smith* never defines neutrality. But the Court does implicitly recognize the obvious dangers of evasion and abuse.

Consider first the case of formally neutral laws enacted for the purpose of suppressing a minority faith. Recall the hypothetical of a law banning consumption of wine in public places where children are present. The Court says that a law is neutral if prohibiting the exercise of religion "is not the object of the [law] but merely the incidental effect."[210] This language would seem to recognize that even a facially neutral law enacted with bad motive—for the "object" of suppressing a religion—is unconstitutional. That inference is sup-

---

[209]See Ansonia Bd. of Education v. Philbrook, 479 U.S. 60 (1986); *id*. at 79 (Stevens, J., dissenting in part).

[210]*Smith*, 110 S.Ct. at 1600.

ported by the Court's immediate citation to *Grosjean v. American Press Co.*[211]

The "incidental effect" language might also mean that a law is not neutral if its anti-religious applications are such a major part of the total applications that the anti-religious effect cannot be characterized as "incidental." Consider a facially neutral ban on the sale of unleavened bread. It is hard to imagine any motive for such a law other than hostility to Jews and to those Christians who use unleavened bread in the Eucharist. But suppose the state proves that its actual motive was legitimate—for example, to help the depressed local leaven industry. Still, because there are virtually no secular uses of unleavened bread to be affected by this law, the anti-religious effect would not be incidental, but overwhelmingly dominant. Such a law would not satisfy the Court's "incidental effect" requirement. It would be unconstitutional unless it served a compelling interest by the least restrictive means, which is surely impossible in this example.[212]

Consider also religious gerrymanders—laws carefully crafted to burden or benefit a particular religious practice without affecting similar secular practices or similar practices by another religion. Bad motives may be hidden in people's heads, but a gerrymander is visible on the face of the statute book. Examples are a law forbidding any person wearing a saffron robe to appear on the streets with a shaved head, or a law forbidding the consumption of unleavened bread and bitter herbs at the same meal. Semester break at Christmas is more benign religious gerrymander, but a gerrymander nonetheless.

A statute that appears neutral in isolation may be obviously not neutral when one considers the jurisdiction's treatment of similar matters. If the state permits the same conduct for secular reasons that it forbids for religious reasons, or if it permits the infliction of the same harm for secular reasons that it forbids when inflicted for religious reasons, its regulation is neither neutral nor generally appli-

[211] 297 U.S. 223, 250–51 (1936), cited in *Smith*, 110 S.Ct. at 1600. *Grosjean* struck down a Louisiana tax on all newspapers with circulation greater than 20,000. With only one exception, drawing the line at 20,000 taxed all the urban papers that opposed Huey Long, and exempted all the small town papers that supported him. For analysis of *Grosjean*, see Powe, The Fourth Estate and the Constitution 222 (1991).

[212] Compare the Court's example of an "obviously" unconstitutional law making it a crime to bow down before a golden calf. *Smith*, 110 S. Ct. at 1599.

cable. Even under *Smith*, it must have a compelling reason for treating the religious conduct less favorably than the secular conduct.

7. *The Establishment Clause.* Finally, there is the surviving protection for religious exercise in the Establishment Clause. For twenty years the Court has summarized the Establishment Clause in its three-part *Lemon* test, stating that a law violates the Establishment Clause if it lacks a secular purpose, if it has the primary effect of either advancing or inhibiting religion, or if it excessively entangles the state in religious affairs.[213] The Court has entertained claims by churches that burdensome regulations violate the inhibiting or entanglement prongs of the Establishment Clause, most recently in *Swaggart*.[214] With *Smith* apparently taking away much of the protection previously found in the Free Exercise Clause, churches will increasingly turn to whatever protections may be found in the Establishment Clause.

I find it implausible that a burden on religion might violate the Establishment Clause,[215] and especially so in the only case that matters—when it does not also violate the Free Exercise Clause. Carl Esbeck has argued, however, that the Establishment Clause regulates the institutional relationship between the state and organized churches, and that the proper institutional relationship is one of separation and mutual independence.[216] Thus, a law that reduces the mutual independence of church and state presents an Establishment Clause issue, and it is irrelevant whether the law tends to help churches or harm them. Doctrinal tenets of the affected churches and the formal neutrality of the law are also irrelevant.

This argument is not inconsistent with any specific language in *Smith*, but there is no evidence in *Smith* or elsewhere that the Court will give more than minimal scope to the Establishment Clause in cases not involving arguable aid to religion. The Court has never ruled that a burden on religion violates either the inhibiting or entanglement prongs of its Establishment Clause doctrine. The Court

---

213 Lemon v. Kurtzman, 403 U.S. 602, 612–13 (1971).

214 *Swaggart*, 110 S.Ct. at 697–99; Tony and Susan Alamo Foundation v. Secretary of Labor, 471 U.S. 290, 305–6 (1985).

215 Laycock, note 100 *supra*, at 1378–86.

216 Esbeck, Towards a General Theory of Church-State Relations and the First Amendment, 4 Pub. L.F. 325 (1985); Esbeck, Establishment Clause Limits on Governmental Interference with Religious Organizations, 41 Wash. & Lee L. Rev. 347 (1984).

has found violations of the entanglemen t doctrine only from programs in which there was a benefit to religion,[217] and it rejected the entanglement claim in *Swaggart*. This last exception to *Smith* may also be least.

IV. The Legal Framework for Persecution

Smith announces a general rule that the Free Exercise Clause provides no substantive protection for religious conduct. It also notes enough exceptions and limitations to swallow most of its new rule. Everything seems to depend on judicial willingness to enforce the exceptions and police the neutrality requirement. The previous section assumed that *Smith*'s exceptions and limitations are to be given full scope in the protection of religious liberty. This section assumes the opposite.

The Court in *Smith* was evidently seeking to get religious exemption cases out of the courts and to leave to the political branches the messy task of balancing the competing interests in religious exercise and government regulation. If the Court pursues that goal, it is unlikely to be vigorous about checking for bad motive or religious gerrymander. It may be myopic or deferential in considering claims that analogous secular behavior has gone unregulated. It is unlikely to expand the exceptions it created; it may let them wither away.

The early decisions applying *Smith* in the lower courts give little content to the exceptions or even to the requirement of neutrality.[218]

---

[217]See, *e.g.*, Aguilar v. Felton, 473 U.S. 402, 408–14 (1985) (remedial instruction in math and reading for impoverished students attending religious schools); Larkin v. Grendel's Den, Inc., 459 U.S. 116, 126–27 (1982) (partial delegation of zoning power to churches). The Court did find an Establishment Clause violation in Larson v. Valente, 456 U.S. 228 (1982), which struck down a burdensome regulation that had been designed to regulate the Unification Church without affecting more mainstream faiths. This was based not on any prong of the *Lemon* test, but on a separate principle that the Establishment Clause forbids discrimination among faiths. *Larson*'s requirement of denominational neutrality under the Establishment Clause corresponds to *Smith*'s requirement of denominational neutrality under the Free Exercise Clause.

[218]See Salvation Army v. Department of Community Affairs, 919 F.2d 183, 199–200 (3d Cir. 1990) (hybrid freedom of association claim adds nothing to free exercise claim); Rector of St. Bartholomew's Church v. City of New York, 914 F.2d 348, 354–55 (2d Cir. 1990) (landmark ordinance is neutral because it potentially applies to all buildings; irrelevant that designation process is individualized), cert. denied, 111 S.Ct. 1103 (1991); Intercommunity Center for Justice v. Immigration & Naturalization Serv., 910 F.2d 42, 45 (2d Cir. 1990) (secular exemptions irrelevant to claim for religious exemption); Cornerstone Bible Church v. City of Hastings, 740 F. Supp. 654 (D. Minn. 1990) (upholding exclusion of churches from commercial zone, finding the ordinance neutral despite its express reference to churches, holding that hybrid free speech claim added nothing to the free exercise claim, holding it irrelevant that church could find nowhere else in city to meet, and ignoring individualized decision-making in

If this trend continues, minority religions will effectively be at the mercy of the political branches. Many religions will be burdened, sometimes severely. Just how severely depends on how far the courts withdraw. I consider two doctrinal possibilities.

A. FORMAL NEUTRALITY WITHOUT EXCEPTIONS

First, assume that the courts carefully scrutinize legislative enactments for bad motives, religious gerrymanders, and the like, but that they narrowly interpret the *Smith* exceptions for internal church decisionmaking, speech, and parental control. That is, assume that the courts apply formal neutrality quite generally, but insist that it really be neutral. What results would follow?

One result might be more legislative exemptions for churches and believers. But if legislatures do not provide exemptions—if all the regulatory burdens of the modern state are laid on churches—churches would be severely damaged. The institutional damage to churches would be of two kinds. The first is simply the sheer burden of compliance. Rightly or wrongly, businesses complain about being strangled in red tape. But churches are not businesses; their product cannot be sold at a profit, and they cannot raise the price to cover the cost of regulation. They are largely dependent upon voluntary contributions, much of their cash flow is committed to charity,[219] and a

zoning process). But see You Vang Yang v. Sturner, 750 F. Supp. 558 (D.R.I. 1990) ("regretfully" applying *Smith* to uphold requirement of mandatory autopsy as applied to Hmong accident victim; nothing in opinion indicates any plausible basis for claiming an exception to *Smith*); Montgomery v. County of Clinton, 743 F. Supp. 1253, 1259 (W.D. Mich. 1990) (even with no arguable exception relevant, *Smith* still requires rational basis review). See also State v. Hershberger 462 N.W.2d 393 (Minn. 1990) (rejecting *Smith* in principle and granting religious exemptions under state constitution); State v. French, 460 N.W.2d 2 (Minn. 1990) (same); Society of Jesus v. Boston Landmarks Comm'n, 408 Mass. 38, 564 N.E. 2d 571 (1990) (ignoring *Smith* and granting religious exemptions under state constitution). *Salvation Army*, the first case in this note, may be correctly decided under *Smith*, because freedom of association is itself a derivative right. That is, freedom of religious association is derived from the Free Exercise Clause, and could not plausibly change the free-exercise standard of review. The reasoning in *Salvation Army* should not apply to a true hybrid claim, involving an independent right such as free speech or parental control of education.

[219]Compare Hodgkinson, Weitzman & Kirsch, From Belief to Commitment—the Activities and Finances of Religious Organizations in the United States 49 (1988) (42% of church expenditures go to "non-religious" charitable and cultural activities), with Interfaith Research Comm. of the Comm'n on Private Philanthropy and Public Needs—a Study of Religious Receipts and Expenditures in the United States 402–34 (1977) (15% or less of church expenditures go to purposes that are neither sacramental or educational). The categories in the two studies are not well defined, and the reasons for their strikingly different results are unclear. Contributing factors appear to be that Hodgkinson, Weitzman, & Kirsch treated the cost of church-sponsored schools as charitable, and that they used current operating expenses as the denominator.

building in which to function is a large fixed expense. The demands of the modern regulatory state may severely constrain the religious mission.

Second, churches would frequently find that they simply cannot practice important parts of their faith, even within the enclave of the religious community. They would lose much of their capacity to preserve their distinctive traditions and values; they would gradually be suppressed or forced into assimilation. Theology could remain pluralistic, but religious practice would be pressured toward homogeneity by the sheer pervasiveness of modern regulation. The churches would lose much of their role as mediating institutions and havens for pluralism.

If this sounds alarmist, simply consider the range of regulatory issues mentioned in Part III, and a few additional examples. If churches must share control of their institutions with unions and labor boards; if every church personnel dispute is resolved under secular standards with potential recourse to secular courts; if egalitarian sex roles may be enforced in church employment, or in the church itself as a place of public accommodation; if church schools must conform to secular models of curriculum, student discipline, and academic freedom; if church disciplinary processes are subject to secular standards of due process, or if any church discipline at all risks liability for intentional infliction of emotional distress; if all new ministries require notice to the neighbors and approval from the zoning board; if the Salvation Army cannot continue its ministry to the homeless unless it pays them the minimum wage;[220] if nuns cannot carry the handicapped homeless up a flight of steps because the code requires an elevator;[221] in short, if churches are neutrally subjected to the full range of modern regulation, it is hard to see how they can sustain any distinctive social structure or witness.

The impact would be greatest on the faiths most committed to traditional values and traditional sources of authority and most alienated from modern understandings of liberty and equality. Some will view it as a good thing to drag these "backward" institutions into the

---

[220]See DePalma, Salvation Army Is Told to Pay Minimum Wage, N.Y. Times, Sept. 16, 1990, §1, part 1, at 42, col. 5. See also Salvation Army v. Department of Community Affairs, 919 F.2d 183 (3d Cir. 1990) (rejecting most of Salvation Army's challenge to application of boarding house regulations to its shelters).

[221]See Roberts, Fight City Hall? Nope, Not Even Mother Teresa, N.Y. Times, Sept. 17, 1990, at B1, col. 1 (reporting permanent closure of religious order's shelter for the homeless; elevator was prohibitively expensive and violated religious order's teachings against using modern conveniences).

secular virtues of the post-modern age, but that assumes a dictatorial confidence in contemporary secular values. Believers who want a more libertarian or egalitarian church can find one; those who want no church at all can easily have that. Believers who want a more traditional religious community are entitled to it.

These institutional impacts are in addition to the more widely recognized harm to individual conscientious objectors. Those who believe that God has commanded what the law forbids face an excruciating choice. Formal neutrality permits them no escape.

These are the consequences of formal neutrality without legislative exemptions. Legislative exemptions are often hard to get, and they often require a political battle. They may become harder to get in the wake of *Smith*. An arguable constitutional claim to exemption is also a political argument for exemption. If the Supreme Court says there is no constitutional right to exemption, the political argument for exemption is also weakened.

Legislative exemptions are hard to get because the political dynamic of the modern regulatory state recognizes no natural limits to the pursuit of secular values. New regulatory legislation typically results when some interest group successfully demands it, and when such legislation is successfully enforced, it is either by the interest group on behalf of private litigants or by an agency that is committed to the legislative goals. Both the interest group and the agency tend to be single-mindedly focused on the benefits of their legislation; it is not for them to balance competing interests. Thus, those who initiate and enforce much modern legislation tend to be wholly unsympathetic to claims that religious liberty requires an exemption.

If a church says that the sheer burden of compliance with particular legislation interferes with the religious mission, the interest group is unlikely to see that as an important enough reason to justify an exemption. If a church says that it is conscientiously opposed to compliance, the interest group is likely to see the church as an enemy, as a symbol of resistance to the goals of the legislation, legitimating other resistance by its moral or theological stance. If such a church can be forced to comply, that is an important victory in the larger fight to establish the goals of the interest group as unquestionably good things.

Many of the church landmarking disputes illustrate the first kind of clash. Proponents of landmarking seem genuinely unable to comprehend why churches object to maintaining their houses of worship as permanent architectural museums, at the expense of those who worship there, for the aesthetic pleasure of those who do not. It does not matter to the landmarkers that the building has become liturgically or physically obsolete, that it is designed for a congregation much larger than the one that now worships there, or that maintaining the building may absorb all the resources that might have gone into charity, evangelism, education, or other aspects of the religious mission.[222] The Second Circuit has cited *Swaggart* for the proposition that no constitutional issue is raised by a law that "drastically restricted the Church's ability to raise revenues to carry out its various charitable and ministerial programs."[223]

The conflict over student gay rights organizations at Georgetown University illustrates the second kind of clash.[224] This dispute has so far produced ten published judicial orders and two Acts of Congress. The sums expended on litigation and legislative lobbying far exceeded any economic stake for either side. The stakes were political and symbolic: could gay students force a Catholic university to recognize their equal status, and subsequently, could Congress force the City Council to accept the legitimacy of religious refusals to recognize the gay students' equal status? It is hardly surprising that those who have devoted their time to leading the gay rights movement tend to see only one side to this issue.

For churches and believers to get regulatory exemptions one at a time, statute by statute, requires a whole series of political battles of the magnitude illustrated by the landmarking dispute and the Georgetown gay rights dispute. A perpetual fight for regulatory exemptions will create serious political entanglement between church and state. I do not at all suggest that such political entanglement is unconstitutional,[225] but chronic legislative battles over the proper relationship between church and state are surely an unfortunate development.

The proposed Religious Freedom Restoration Act would avoid these problems by legislating religious exemptions all at once, across the board.[226] The bill would provide that states must exempt

---

[222]See generally Carmella, note 203 *supra*.

[223]Rector of St. Bartholomew's Church v. City of New York, 914 F.2d 348, 355 (2d Cir. 1990), cert. denied, 111 S.Ct. 1103 (1991).

[224]The judicial and legislative history is summarized in Clarke v. United States, 915 F.2d 699 (D.C. Cir. 1990).

[225]For effective criticism of the political entanglement doctrine, see Gaffney, Political Divisiveness Along Religious Lines: The Entanglement of the Court in Sloppy History and Bad Public Policy, 24 St. Louis U.L.J. 205 (1980).

[226]H.R. 5377 in the 101st Congress.

churches and believers from laws that burden religious practice, unless the laws are formally neutral and there is compelling reason to deny the exemption. This part of the bill would be enacted pursuant to Congressional power to enforce the Fourteenth Amendment, which incorporates the free exercise clause. The bill would apply the same rule to federal law as a mandatory rule of construction. Future Congresses could deny exemptions without a compelling interest, but only by express reference to the Religious Freedom Restoration Act. The model here is the Anti-Injunction Act,[227] which forbids federal injunctions against state judicial proceedings except where "expressly authorized" by Act of Congress. The bill gives Congress an opportunity to consider the need for religious exemptions in general terms, without the pressure of a particular problem to be addressed at the behest of a particular competing interest group.

B. FORMAL NEUTRALITY WITHOUT JUDICIAL SCRUTINY

1. *The risk of persecution*. So far I have assumed that even if *Smith*'s exceptions to formal neutrality are allowed to wither, the Court will insist that formal neutrality at least be formally neutral. The equal protection right recognized in *Smith* requires strict scrutiny for its enforcement. The pervasiveness of modern regulation creates ample opportunity to hide hostile legislation in formally neutral terms. To avoid that danger, laws that burden religious practice must be scrutinized for evidence of anti-religious motive, religious gerrymander, or secular exemptions not available to churches or believers. The Court must perform at least this task, and insist that trial judges perform it. If the Court will not do this much, it has created a legal framework for persecution.

I want to be very careful here, to avoid either overstating or understating the dangers. Religious liberty is one of America's great inventions. The extent of religious pluralism in this country, and of legal and political protections for religious minorities, is probably unsurpassed in human experience. I have no desire to deny that achievement. But a counter-tradition also runs through American history. There have been religious persecutions in the American past, and it would be foolish to assume that there will not be religious persecutions in the American future. There are localized religious persecutions in the American present, and if the Court gives those persecutions a way to escape judicial review, they will accelerate.

---

[227] 28 U.S.C. §2283 (1988).

Persecution is a strong term, but it is the word I mean. Still, there are degrees of persecution. This country has never experienced the worst, and I am not predicting the worst. The strongest form of persecution is a systematic effort to kill all persons who believe in a minority faith, or who refuse to profess belief in the established faith. That has happened in other lands, but it has never happened here, and there is no apparent danger that it will happen here.

The next strongest form of persecution is a systematic effort to entirely eliminate the practice of a faith within a jurisdiction. This is what Cromwell did when he suppressed the Mass, and this is what the Court says Oregon may do to suppress peyote worship. There is an important difference between the two cases, but the Court's emphasis on formal neutrality does not capture that difference. From the perspective of the minority whose religion is suppressed, it matters little whether Oregon suppresses all uses of peyote or only religious uses of peyote. The victims may feel worse knowing that Oregon has singled them out for discriminatory legislation, but either way, the dominant fact is that they cannot worship.

From the point of view of the worshipper, what is importantly different between the Oregon situation and Cromwell is that the executive branch in Oregon is not committed to vigorous enforcement efforts. It is not searching out peyote worshippers, prosecuting them, and demanding long prison sentences. The state has invested substantial litigation resources to win a symbolic affirmation of its right to suppress; it has not so far invested enforcement resources to actually suppress. A serious enforcement effort would surely produce a political reaction, and if the peyote worshipers persisted in the face of repeated prosecutions, it seems unlikely that the state would have the political will for persistent enforcement. I do not know the political situation in Oregon, but nothing I have read suggests the degree of hatred needed to fuel serious persecution. The legal framework for persecution is in place, but not the political will.

2. *Past American persecutions*. At times Americans have had the political will for persecution, and in places they have it today. The history of religious tolerance in America reveals a gradually expanding circle of religious groups that are tolerated and even accepted, together with recurrent outbursts of public or private persecution of religions outside that perimeter.

The New England theocracy expelled dissenters, executed Quaker missionaries who returned,[228] and most infamously, perpetrated

[228]Boorstin, The Americans—the Colonial Experience 35–40 (1958).

the Salem witch trials. The political reaction to these trials broke the power of the theocracy in Massachusetts.[229] Colonial Virginia imprisoned Baptist ministers for preaching without a license.[230] But the largest and most important colonial religious persecution is relatively unknown. This was the total suppression of African religion among the slaves, what one historian has called "the African spiritual holocaust."[231]

The best known victims of American religious persecution in the nineteenth century were Catholics and Mormons. Hostility to Catholics fueled successive political movements.[232] The first peaked at mid-century, with mob violence, church burnings, and the anti-Catholic, anti-immigrant Know Nothing Party sweeping elections in eight states.[233] The worst of this was in the form of private violence rather than governmental action. But government was responsible for a de facto Protestant establishment in the public schools.[234]

After the Civil War, there was a nationwide movement to forbid the expenditure of public funds in sectarian schools. This culminated in a proposed constitutional amendment, sponsored by James G. Blaine and defeated by Democrats in the Senate,[235] and a wave of state constitutional amendments forbidding public financing of religious schools.[236] The state constitutional amendments may be defended as a victory for disestablishment and thus for religious liberty, although that view of disestablishment has been disputed.[237] Whatever the ultimate merits of that argument, the historical political movement was targeted at Catholics, who had complained of Protestant instruction in the public schools, and much of the motivation was anti-Catholicism.[238] It was in the context of this controversy

---

[229]See Starkey, The Devil in Massachusetts—a Modern Enquiry into the Salem Witch Trials 248–70 (1961).

[230]See Boorstin, note 228 *supra*, at 136.

[231]Butler, Awash in a Sea of Faith 129–63 (1990).

[232]For general accounts of American anti-Catholicism, see Bennett, The Party of Fear—from Nativist Movements to the New Right in American History (1988); Schwartz, The Persistent Prejudice—Anti-Catholicism in America (1984).

[233]See Bennett, note 232 *supra*, at 27–155; Levy, The Establishment Clause 170 (1986); 1 Stokes, Church and State in the United States 836–37 (1950); 2 *id.* at 67–68.

[234]See Kaestle, Pillars of the Republic 71–103 (1971); Ravitch, The Great School Wars 35, 45, 51–52, 80 (1974); 2 Stokes, note 233 *supra*, at 47–72, 549–51; Zollman, American Church Law §§58–60 at 72–74 (2d ed. 1933).

[235]The proposed amendment is reprinted in 2 Stokes, note 233 *supra*, at 68–69.

[236]*Id.* at 69–70; Zollman, note 234 *supra*, §§62–66 at 75–80.

[237]See McConnell, The Selective Funding Problem: Abortions and Religious Schools Funding, 104 Harv. L. Rev. 989 (1991); McConnell & Posner, note 71 *supra*, at 14–32.

[238]For accounts of the fight over religion and the Protestant Bible in public schools, see

that a Protestant minister endorsed Blaine's campaign for the Presidency on the ground that the Democrats were the party of "rum, Romanism, and rebellion."[239]

A third wave came after World War I, when Oregon enacted a formally neutral law requiring all children to attend public schools.[240] The effect would have been to close all private schools, most of which were Catholic. The Supreme Court invalidated the Oregon law before it could take effect.[241]

The Mormon experience was worse, and government was more fully involved. The Mormons fled from New York, to Ohio, to Missouri, to Illinois, to Utah, which was then in the most isolated reaches of Mexico.[242] They were driven off their lands in Missouri by a combination of armed mobs and state militia.[243] Their prophet, Joseph Smith, was murdered by a mob while in the custody of the state of Illinois.[244]

The federal effort to suppress Mormon polygamy appears to have been a bona fide effort to suppress polygamy and not an effort to destroy Mormonism entirely. But the government was quite willing to destroy Mormonism entirely if that were necessary to suppress polygamy. The government prosecuted "hundreds" of Mormons for polygamy,[245] it imposed test oaths that denied Mormons the right to vote,[246] and it dissolved the Mormon Church and confiscated its property.[247] The Supreme Court upheld all of this.

A less noted aspect of the Mormon persecution is that Congress

---

Glenn, The Myth of the Common School 115–235 (1988); Kaestle, note 234 *supra*, at 158–70; Ravitch, note 234 *supra*, at 27–76. Focusing on Massachusetts, Glenn argues that Catholics and conservative Protestants initially offered similar objections to the liberal Protestantism and Unitarianism that prevailed in Horace Mann's common schools, but that the liberal and conservative Protestant factions united as Catholic immigration increased.

[239]For accounts of the incident, which probably cost Blaine the Presidency, see History of American Presidential Elections 1789–1968 at 1606 (Schlesinger, ed., 1971) (reprinting the story from the New York World, Oct., 30, 1884); Samuel Dickinson Burchard, in 2 Dictionary of American Biography 271 (Johnson & Malone, eds., 1958).

[240]See 2 Stokes, note 233 *supra*, at 737–41.

[241]Pierce v. Society of Sisters, 268 U.S. 510 (1925).

[242]See Arrington & Bitton, The Mormon Experience 44–64 (1979).

[243]*Id.* at 45–46; Arrington, Brigham Young 62–78 (1985); 2 Stokes, note 233 *supra*, at 43–44.

[244]Arrington & Bitton, note 242 *supra*, at 65–82; 2 Stokes, note 233 *supra*, at 46.

[245]Arrington & Bitton, note 242 *supra*, at 280. These prosecutions were upheld in Reynolds v. United States, 98 U.S. 145 (1878).

[246]Davis v. Beason, 133 U.S. 333 (1890).

[247]Late Corporation of the Church of Jesus Christ of Latter Day Saints v. United States, 136 U.S. 1 (1890).

regulated family law directly, taking this traditional authority away from the territorial legislature. Unable to regulate family law directly after statehood, Congress required Utah and several other western states to attempt to disable their state legislatures. The Enabling Acts authorizing creation of these states required that the state constitution ban polygamy in a clause irrevocable without a popular referendum plus the consent of Congress.[248]

The Jehovah's Witness cases that reached the Supreme Court from the late 1930s to the early 1950s arose from the best known twentieth-century outbreak of religious persecution. The Witnesses were persistent and aggressive proselytizers, and their message was offensively intolerant of other faiths, and especially of Catholicism.[249] Towns all over America tried to stop them from proselytizing, enacting a remarkable variety of ordinances, most of which were struck down.[250] The Court's decision in *Minersville School District v. Gobitis*,[251] upholding the requirement that Jehovah's Witnesses salute the flag, triggered a nationwide outburst of private violence against the Witnesses.[252]

The Court in *Smith* relied heavily on *Gobitis* and on one of the Mormon cases, *Reynolds v. United States*.[253] Both of these cases were central to genuine persecutions. *Pierce v. Society of Sisters*,[254] striking down the formally neutral law closing private schools, averted an-

---

[248]See, *e.g.*, Utah Enabling Act, ch. 138, § 3, 28 Stat. 107 (1894); Utah Const. art. III; New Mexico & Arizona Enabling Act, ch. 310, §§2, 36 Stat. 557, 558, *id.* §20 at 569; Ariz. Const. art. XX; Dakota, Montana, and Washington Enabling Act, ch. 180, §4, 25 Stat. 676, 677 (1889). In fact, these "irrevocable" clauses are revocable through ordinary state political processes. Congressional control over state laws and constitutions is unenforceable, because it would violate each state's constitutional right to equal sovereignty. See Coyle v. Smith, 221 U.S. 559 (1911).

[249]See the descriptions of their tactics and message in Douglas v. City of Jeannette, 319 U.S. 157, 166–74 (1943) (Jackson, J., dissenting); Cantwell v. Connecticut, 310 U.S. 296, 301–3 (1940).

[250]The cases are collected in Laycock, A Survey of Religious Liberty in the United States, 47 Ohio St. L.J. 409, 419–20 (1986).

[251]310 U.S. 586 (1940).

[252]See Irons, The Courage of Their Convictions 22–35 (1988).

[253]*Smith*, 110 S.Ct. at 1600. The Court does not cite West Virginia Bd. of Educ. v. Barnette, 319 U.S. 624 (1943), which overruled the result in *Gobitis*. The opinion for the Court in *Barnette* relies on the Free Speech Clause, and holds that no one can be required to salute the flag. It is thus formally consistent with the *Gobitis* holding that religious objectors were not entitled to an exemption from a generally applicable rule. *Id.* at 634–36. I am indebted to my colleague Scot Powe for pointing out that votes essential to the majority filed concurring opinions based on the Free Exercise Clause. *Id.* at 643–44 (Black, J., and Douglas, J., concurring); *id.* at 644–47 (Murphy, J., concurring).

[254]268 U.S. 510 (1925).

other genuine persecution. The connection between religious persecution and formal neutrality interpretations of the Free Exercise Clause is not merely theoretical. It is historical.

3. *Contemporary persecutions.* These historical persecutions have two contemporary counterparts. There may be others, but these are the two I know about sufficiently to describe. One is the treatment of the so-called cults, itself a derogatory term. I mean the unfamiliar, high-demand, proselytizing religions, recently arrived from Asia or recently invented on these shores: the Hare Krishnas, the Unification Church, the Scientologists, and others less well known. Most of them are recent developments, but one, the Hare Krishnas, is generally accepted by Hindus as a bona fide branch of Hinduism.[255]

A loosely organized movement of private citizens is working to destroy these religions.[256] The best known controversy has surrounded the movement's technique of physically abducting and "deprogramming" young adults who have joined high demand religions against the wishes of their families.[257] But the anti-cult movement found a much more powerful weapon in tort suits for emotional distress and punitive damages. These suits have produced verdicts exceeding $30 million. Verdicts as large as $3 million have survived post-trial motions and remittiturs, and some of these verdicts exceed $5 million with accrued interest.[258] Few minority religions can survive more than one such judgment; none can survive several. All Krishna temples and monasteries in the United States are now in receivership, execution proceedings, or subject to lis pendens filings, to secure just one of these judgments. The Supreme Court vacated the judgment for further consideration of the Krishnas' constitutional claims;[259] if those claims are ultimately rejected, the temples and monasteries will be sold. Seizing places of worship is a time honored means of persecution: the Romans destroyed the Jewish Temple, and

[255]See Brief of World Hindu Assembly of North America, et al., as Amicus Curiae, in International Soc'y of Krishna Consciousness v. George, 111 S.Ct. 1299 (1991). For good descriptions and analyses of the Hare Krishnas, Scientologists, and Unification Church, see the essays in The Future of New Religious Movements (Bromley & Hammond, eds., 1987).

[256]The movement is carefully described in Shupe & Bromley, The New Vigilantes (1980). The inference that the movement seeks to destroy these religions is mine, not Shupe & Bromley's, and the inference is based largely on developments subsequent to their book.

[257]See *id.* at 121–67.

[258]See cases cited note 188 *supra*. For the $5 million figure, see Petition for Certiorari 8, in International Soc'y for Krishna Consciousness v. George, 111 S.Ct. 1299 (1991).

[259]International Soc'y for Krishna Consciousness v. George, 111 S.Ct. 1299 (1991).

Henry VIII seized the Catholic monasteries, and both events are remembered centuries later.

These extraordinary judgments have resulted from the application of formally neutral tort rules in decidedly non-neutral ways. The typical plaintiff is a disgruntled former adherent of the faith, often joined by relatives. The torts commonly alleged include intentional infliction of emotional distress, invasion of privacy, fraud and misrepresentation, and false imprisonment based not on alleged physical restraint but only on claims of "brainwashing." The alleged wrongdoing typically consists of a series of communications, many of them communications about religious belief. Most of the sums claimed are punitive damages and compensatory damages for emotional distress, neither of which is measurable by any objective standard.

From beginning to end, these cases consist of subjective and intangible elements. Even with careful and unbiased effort, it is difficult to separate the actionable wrongdoing, where there is any, from protected religious exercise. These cases provide maximum opportunity for juries to act on their prejudices, and minimum opportunity for judges to control juries.

Whatever the merits and demerits of these religions that seem so odd to most Americans, they are, in historical perspective, simply the "cults" of our time. Other "cults" appear throughout the American past.[260] The Baptists, Methodists, Presbyterians, Mormons, and Jehovah's Witnesses all began as unfamiliar, high-demand, proselytizing religions, greeted with deep hostility by more sedate and longer established faiths. Nineteenth-century America spawned many such groups, most of which eventually faded away. Parents of converts reacted in much the same way as modern parents of Krishna or Unification converts, and angry parents found professional help. Today's anti-cult psychiatrists diagnose "coercive persuasion"; the nineteenth-century equivalent was "religious insanity."[261]

The other victim of contemporary religious persecution is the Santeria minority in South Florida. Santeria is an Afro-Caribbean religion with an estimated hundred million adherents in the Western

[260]See Ahlstrom, A Religious History of the American People (1972); Clark, The Small Sects in America (1937); Noyes, Strange Cults and Utopias of 19th-Century America (1966); Pattison & Ness, New Religious Movements in Historical Perspective, in Galanter, Cults and New Religious Movements 43 (1989); 2 Stokes, note 233 *supra*, at 112–20.

[261]Pattison & Ness, note 260 *supra*, at 75–76.

hemisphere.[262] Santeria and similar Afro-Caribbean religions may be the third largest religious group in South Florida, after Christianity and Judaism. An anthropologist who has studied African religion on both sides of the Atlantic reports that Santeria is faithful to its African roots.[263] It is not Voodoo, and it is not Satanism.[264] It is an ancient faith that has not adapted to the mores of modern Western culture.

The essential Santeria rituals involve the sacrifice of animals, usually goats and chickens. A government wishing to suppress the Santeria worship service would pass a law forbidding animal sacrifice. The City of Hialeah has passed four such ordinances, and their constitutionality is now in litigation.[265] Under *Smith*, the threshold issue is whether the ordinances are formally neutral.

It seems to me obvious that the ordinances are not neutral. Hialeah ordinances and Florida law permit people to kill animals for a vast array of secular reasons. Indeed, hunting is a constitutionally protected activity in Florida,[266] the state runs camps to teach children how to hunt,[267] and it is a criminal offense to help an animal escape from a hunter.[268] Florida also expressly permits the slaughter of animals for food,[269] the killing of unwanted pets and animals of "no commercial value,"[270] and the extermination of pests.[271] Indeed, so long as one refrains from torture, it appears that one can legally kill an animal in Florida for any reason except religious sacrifice.

The City responds that all other reasons for killing animals are distinguishable, and that Santeria animal sacrifice falls into several categories that are religiously neutral: all killings of animals in a ritual or ceremony, all unnecessary killings of animals, all killings not pri-

---

[262]Gonzales-Wippler, Santeria: The Religion 9 (1989).

[263]Bastide, African Civilisations in the New World 115 (Green, trans., 1971).

[264]*Id.* at 138.

[265]Church of the Lukumi Babalu Aye, Inc. v. City of Hialeah, 723 F. Supp. 1467 (S.D. Fla. 1989), appeal pending, No. 90-5176 in the Eleventh Circuit. The author is appellate counsel for the church.

[266]Alford v. Finch, 155 So.2d 790, 793 (Fla. 1963); Bell v. Vaughn, 155 Fla. 551, 21 So.2d 31 (1945); Fla. Const. art. 4 §9.

[267]Henderson, Camera-Toting Kids Sought to Infiltrate Hunt, Miami Herald 5B (June 15, 1990).

[268]Fla. Stat. Ann. §372.705 (Supp. 1991).

[269]Fla. Stat. Ann. §§828.22 to 828.26 (1976 & Supp. 1991); Hialeah Ordinances 87-40, 87-52, 87-72.

[270]Fla. Stat. Ann. §828.073(4)(c)2 (Supp. 1991); Hialeah Ordinance 87-40.

[271]Fla. Stat. Ann. §482 (Supp. 1991).

marily for food purposes, all killings for food purposes in a place not zoned for slaughterhouses, and so on.[272]

The ordinances distinguish ritual sacrifice, which is forbidden, from ritual slaughter, which is protected.[273] The legal difference is said to be that ritual slaughter is primarily for food, but ritual sacrifice is primarily for ritual and only secondarily for food. The factual difference is said to be that practitioners of ritual slaughter use a different knife stroke from practitioners of ritual sacrifice.[274] The political difference is that ritual slaughter is conducted by Jews in Kosher slaughterhouses; ritual sacrifice is conducted by Santeria priests in private homes.

A court willing to police gerrymanders, to examine motive, to examine regulation of comparable conduct and comparable harms—a court at all willing to insist that formal neutrality at least be formally neutral—can readily strike these ordinances down. A court willing to defer to the political branches can readily accept one of the City's rationalizations and uphold these ordinances. None of the other common ways of killing animals is exactly like Santeria sacrifice.

Santeria was long suppressed in Cuba, and the Santeria community has adhered to its faith and practice despite generations of social and governmental hostility. It seems clear that many adherents will ignore the ordinances even if they are upheld in court. The real question is whether the anti-Santeria coalition—animal rights activists, Christian fundamentalists, and people who just seem to find animal sacrifice disgusting—will have the strength to demand vigorous and persistent enforcement. If it does, and these ordinances are upheld, there will be a full-scale persecution in South Florida.

I have explored these examples at some length to make a point that is simple to understand but perhaps difficult to accept. Religious persecution can happen, is happening, in the United States, even in 1991. One minority's worship service is now subject to suppression in Oregon, with the blessing of the Supreme Court. If the Hialeah ordinances are upheld, a second minority's worship services will be subject to suppression and may be actively suppressed. If the Hare

---

[272]Each of these classifications appears expressly in one or more of the four ordinances enacted to suppress animal sacrifice. The theory that animal sacrifice is unnecessary also appears in Fla. Atty. Gen'l Opinion 87-56, Annual Report at 146 (1987). The Attorney General failed to see that the necessity of animal sacrifice is a purely theological question.

[273]Compare Hialeah Ordinance 87-40 with Fla. Stat. Ann. §828.22(3) (1976).

[274]Brief of Appellee 40–41, in *Lukumi*, No. 90-5176 in the United States Court of Appeals for the Eleventh Circuit.

Krishna temples and monasteries are sold, a third minority's worship services will have been suppressed. In a nation that sometimes claims to have been founded for religious liberty, it is not supposed to be that way.

V. Conclusion

When the Free Exercise Clause was adopted, religious pluralism in the United States consisted mostly of Protestant pluralism, and the scope of government was minimal. Today, the scope of pluralism and the scope of government are both vastly greater. The occasions on which the normal course of government restricts religious exercise have multiplied manyfold. The need for religious exemptions has multiplied in the same proportion.

The Court seems to see the number of potential requests as a threat to orderly government. But the number of potential requests is also a measure of the cumulative burden on religious exercise. The cumulative weight of government on religious minorities is sometimes crushing. The impact on government programs of exemptions for religious minorities is often quite minor, and almost never crushing. In the exceptional case, government can invoke the compelling interest test.

I would grant most requests for exemption, because I think the text and the purposes of the Free Exercise Clause require that government leave religion as free as can be managed in a complex urban society. Exemptions should be routine and not exceptional. The Court has taken the opposite view: it thinks judicial exemptions should be exceptional at best; it may think exemptions should not exist at all.

Religious liberty is popular in the abstract, but unpopular in its concrete applications. A secular society is far too quick to decide that its interests in uniform application of the law override the needs of religious minorities, or even of the religious mainstream. Religious minorities may seem strange or obnoxious; their objections to the majority's secular notion of what is good and right may seem wrongheaded. One function of judicial review is to protect religious exercise against such hostile or indifferent consequences of the political process. The Court has abandoned that function, at least in substantial part, and perhaps entirely.

MURRAY DRY

FLAG BURNING AND THE CONSTITUTION

Texas v. Johnson,[1] the Supreme Court's decision in 1989 invalidating Texas' flag desecration law, arguably did no more than follow established free speech doctrine. But the decision upset many people. Congress responded by passing the Flag Protection Act[2] which was designed to meet the Supreme Court's objections by omitting any reference to "knowingly offending others" or to "knowingly cast[ing] contempt" upon the flag.[3] Notwithstanding the briefs in support of the law from both Houses of Congress as well as the Justice Department, the Supreme Court invalidated it in *Eichman v. United States*,[4] on the authority of *Johnson* and a number of earlier decisions. This conflict between the judicial interpretation of the law of the Constitution and the understanding of the people and their representatives merits careful examination for two reasons.

First, the controversy forces us to note an important evolution in our understanding of freedom of speech. We enjoy and tolerate more freedom generally, not simply freedom of speech, than we used to. As a result, we have less confidence in what we stand for and look up to as a body politic, as a people in the collective sense. The flag-burning controversy is interesting here because flag burning—a form of symbolic expression—illustrates the blending of freedom

Murray Dry is a professor of Political Science at Middlebury College.

Author's Note: I would like to thank Eve Adler, Eric Davis, Dan Kahan, Jim Stoner, and Barry Sullivan for reading and commenting on earlier drafts of this article.

[1] 109 S.Ct. 2533 (1989).

[2] 103 Stat. 777, 18 U.S.C. §700 (Supp. 1990).

[3] These phrases were in either the Texas law or the then existing federal flag-burning act. Compare *Johnson*, 109 S.Ct. at 2537 n.1 (Texas statute) with United States v. Eichman, 110 S.Ct. 2404, 2407 n.3 (1990) (old and new federal laws). See note 85 *infra* for the text of the new Act.

[4] 110 S.Ct. 2404 (1990).

0-226-09573-8/91/1990-002$02.00

generally with freedom of speech. The First Amendment refers to freedom of speech, but the Court and commentators have used that term interchangeably with freedom of expression. In addition, the flag-burning issue, like other important symbolic expression cases, reveals the following dilemma: without the assistance of criminal law, it is hard to maintain effective restraints on conduct which shocks people's sensibilities. But those shocked sensibilities, present in different ways on both sides of the flag-burning controversy, pose a challenge to our country's continued ability to support equality of rights, which is to say to support our form of government and way of life.

The second and related reason for considering the flag-burning controversy concerns the respective roles of Congress and the courts, especially the Supreme Court, in maintaining our constitutional government. From June 1989 to June 1990 there were extensive Congressional hearings on flag burning, resulting in the legislation to reverse *Johnson*. After *Eichman*, Congress reconsidered a proposed constitutional amendment to protect the American flag, but it failed to gain the necessary two-thirds vote in either house. We can thus learn: (1) how Congress understands and responds to an important Supreme Court decision in constitutional law with which it disagrees; (2) how the Supreme Court responds to a Congressional attempt to revise a constitutional decision by statute; and (3) how Congress understands its constitutional obligations to the Bill of Rights and its powers under the amendatory provisions of Article V.

I. Free Speech: From the Framing of the First Amendment (1789) to "Symbolic Expression" and the First Flag Desecration Cases (1969–1974)

A. THE CONSITUTION AND THE BILL OF RIGHTS

The central questions for the framers of the Constitution concerned a firm national government: whether to have one and if so how to construct it. In the Convention, the major constitutional changes proposed, and eventually adopted, concerned the powers of government, the structure of government, and representation. Very little was said about a bill of rights in the Federal Convention, and except for George Mason's suggestion that liberty of the press should be guaranteed, freedom of speech was not mentioned at all. When the changes were debated in the several state ratification conventions, the Anti-Federal critics contended that election to office in large heterogeneous districts did not guarantee a truly representative legislative branch, that too much power was concentrated in the Senate and executive, and that jury trial in the neighborhood was not guaranteed. The major Anti-Federal proposals for amendment were not limited to the specific protections of individual rights that became our Bill of Rights. And even where states proposed guarantees of freedom of speech, religion, or conscience, there was no discussion of the meaning of these terms.[5]

The Constitution's ratification was made possible when the Massachusetts Federalists proposed recommendatory amendments, to go along with an unqualified ratification, rather than conditional amendments.[6] Subsequent state conventions did likewise. James Madison, who was elected to the first House of Representatives, assumed responsibility for getting a bill of rights passed and succeeded in securing the allegiance of those who feared the loss of trial by jury and other specific rights while conceding nothing to those who wished to weaken the powers of the new national government.[7] There was some debate in the House on the meaning of the religion clauses, but none in connection with the free speech guarantee, perhaps because there was no current free speech controversy. Consequently, until the Alien and Sedition Acts, in 1798, which spurred Madison and Jefferson to write their Virginia and Kentucky Resolutions, respectively, the American founders did not reflect seriously on the purposes or the reach of freedom of speech.[8]

---

[5]The proposed amendments can be found in Schwartz, The Roots of the Bill of Rights, 5 vols. (1980), and Elliot, The Debates of the State Conventions on the Adoption of the Federal Constitution, 5 vols. (1891) (cited below as Elliot's Debates). See also Dry, Federalism and the Constitution: The Founders' Design and Contemporary Constitutional Law, 4 Constitutional Commentary 233, 238–47 (1987); Levy, Emergence of a Free Press ch. VIII (1985). It is likely that there was no debate over the specific meaning of the proposed amendments in the state conventions for the same reason there was little or no debate in Congress: the major issue was ratification, and consequently the proposals were made either to limit the powers of the new government or to make sure that the government would be bound by the same rights provisions that were commonly found in the state constitutions and bills of rights.

[6]See III Elliot, The Debates in the Several State Conventions on the Adoption of the Federal Constitution as Recommended by the General Convention at Philadelphia in 1787 at 176–77 (1791); see also *id.* at 122–25.

[7]See Dry, note 5 *supra*, at 240–41.

[8]Leonard Levy's work, Emergence of a Free Press (1985), is the standard source on this subject. It is a substantial revision of his earlier work, Legacy of Supression (1960). Levy still argues, however, and the evidence supports him, that seditious libel was not called into question, as inconsistent with republican government, until after the passage of the Sedition Act of 1798. I have discussed this further in "Free Speech and Republican Government," 6 Constitutional Commentary 355 (1989).

The Sedition Act of 1798 punished malicious writing, utterances, or publications which might excite the people against the government or government officials or stir up sedition. Madison argued both that the First Amendment removed the subject of free speech entirely from the power of Congress, and that the First Amendment, unlike English common law, did not permit seditious libel to be punished. Madison argued that a citizen's ability to criticize his government was essential to republican government in America, in contrast to England's monarchy, and that the American practice in the states was not "confined to the strict limits of the common law."[9]

By giving special emphasis to speech critical of the government or government officials, Madison's argument reflects what has been called the self-government justification for free speech. It does not necessarily, however, support the claim that the Free Speech Clause is limited to political speech.[10] The founding debate on republican government emphasized the importance of individual liberty; that, together with the presence of the religion clauses in the First Amendment, suggests that the Free Speech Clause protects the private sphere as well as citizen activity.[11]

On the other hand, Madison's argument is not as protective of free speech as the modern doctrine. The Supreme Court's current approach distinguishes between content-based and content-neutral restrictions on speech. Under the Court's approach to content-based restrictions, some categories of speech, such as obscenity, libel (in part), "fighting words," and child pornography, are not protected by the First Amendment; other categories (such as commercial speech and arguably non-obscene offensive speech)[12] are of lower value and receive limited protection. Speech that is not in one of these low-value categories is protected unless the government can meet an extremely high burden.[13] The test for "content-neutral" restrictions—

[9]See Madison's Report on the Virginia Resolutions, in IV Elliot's Debates 546–80, esp. 569–71, 575.

[10]See, *e.g.*, Meiklejohn, Free Speech and Its Relation to Self-Government (1948); Bork, Neutral Principles and Some First Amendment Problems, 47 Ind. L. J. 1, 20–28 (1971).

[11]See Storing, The Consitution and the Bill of Rights, in Harmon, ed., Essays on the Constitution of the United States 32–48, esp. 48 (1978).

[12]See Virginia Pharmacy Board v. Virginia Citizens Consumer Council, 425 U.S. 748 (1976); compare City of Renton v. Playtime Theatres, 475 U.S. 41 (1986), and FCC v. Pacifica Foundation, 438 U.S. 720 (1978), with Sable Communications, Inc. v. FCC, 109 S.Ct. 2829, 2836–39 (1989).

[13]See, *e.g.*, New York Times Co. v. United States, 403 U.S. 713 (1971); Brandenburg v. Ohio, 395 U.S. 444 (1969).

regulations of the time or place at which people may speak—is more flexible and generally requires courts to balance the speaker's interest against the government's.[14]

B. THE SUPREME COURT ON THE FLAG AND FREE SPEECH: THE EARLIEST CASES

The first time the Supreme Court decided a case involving a flag desecration law was in 1907, when it unanimously upheld Nebraska's law and its application to defendants who had placed a representation of the American flag on bottles of beer which they offered for sale.[15] The defendants made an economic liberty argument but said nothing in particular about freedom of speech—perhaps because the action was at best symbolic expression, which had not yet been recognized as speech; perhaps because it was commercial advertising, which also had not been recognized as protected speech; or perhaps because the Supreme Court had not applied the First Amendment to the states via the Fourteenth Amendment's Due Process Clause. The first Justice Harlan, for a unanimous Court, declared:

> [T]o every true American the flag is the symbol of the Nation's power, the emblem of freedom in its truest, best sense. . . . As the statute in question evidently had its origin in a purpose to cultivate a feeling of patriotism among the people of Nebraska, we are unwilling to adjudge that in legislation for that purpose the State erred in duty or has infringed the constitutional right of anyone.[16]

The first full-fledged constitutional controversy over the flag and free speech involved the Jehovah's Witnesses, who were the litigants in five cases that reached the Supreme Court, with two receiving full opinions: *Minersville v. Gobitis*,[17] in 1940, which upheld the flag salute requirement, and *West Virginia State Board of Education v. Barnette*,[18] in 1943, which overturned *Gobitis*. The protesting Witnesses' literal reading of the Biblical commandment against having any other gods and against bowing down to any graven images gave rise to their objection to the State's required participation in the pledge and salute

---

[14]See, *e.g.*, Members of the City Council v. Taxpayers for Vincent, 466 U.S. 789, 808–12 (1984).

[15]Halter v. Nebraska, 205 U.S. 34 (1907).

[16]*Id.* at 43.

[17]310 U.S. 586.

[18]319 U.S. 624.

by all public school pupils. In *Gobitis* the issue was framed as whether the Free Exercise Clause mandated an exception to an otherwise valid secular requirement. Justice Frankfurter wrote an opinion for eight justices, ruling that the constitutional principles of religious freedom do not grant individuals special exemptions from otherwise valid government regulations. In a phrase that could have come from a contemporary communitarian, Justice Frankfurter remarked that "[t]he ultimate foundation of a free society is the binding tie of cohesive sentiment." After noting that "'[W]e live by symbols,'" and that "[t]he flag is the symbol of our national unity," Frankfurter quoted from Justice Harlan's *Halter* opinion.[19] Acknowledging that "for ourselves we might be tempted to say that the deepest patriotism is best engendered by giving unfettered scope to the most crotchety beliefs,"[20] Justice Frankfurter concluded with an abbreviated version of his case for judicial self-restraint:

> Except where the transgression of constitutional liberty is too plain for argument, personal freedom is best maintained—so long as the remedial channels of the democratic process remain open and unobstructed—when it is ingrained in a people's habits and not enforced against popular policy by the coercion of adjudicated law.[21]

Justice Harlan Fiske Stone, the only dissenter in *Gobitis*, referred to the need for an accommodation between "specific constitutional restrictions," such as "freedom of speech and of religion," and the "powers which government normally exercises."[22] Since there were other ways to inculcate patriotism, such as through a required course of study, he thought the required flag salute and pledge must fall before "the freedom of the individual from compulsion as to what he shall think and what he shall say, at least where the compulsion is to bear false witness to his religion."[23] After referring to his footnote in *Carolene Products*, for its emphasis on the need to protect "discrete and insular minorities," Justice Stone concluded by suggesting that the legislation before the Court should be subjected to the same strict scrutiny that the Court had applied where other religious and racial minorities were involved.[24]

Three years later, in 1943, now Chief Justice Stone was a member

---

[19] 310 U.S. at 596.

[20] *Id.* at 598.

[21] *Id.* at 599.

[22] *Id.* at 602, 603.

[23] *Id.* at 604.

[24] *Id.* at 605–7.

of a six-justice majority for overturning *Gobitis* and invalidating the flag salute and pledge requirement in public schools. Justice Jackson's opinion for the Court formulated the issue in terms of freedom of speech and concluded that no one, regardless of the basis of his objection, could be forced to salute the flag and say the pledge of allegiance in order to attend public school. Justice Jackson's opinion included the memorable and widely quoted passage:

> If there is any fixed star in our constitutional constellation, it is that no official, high or petty, can prescribe what shall be orthodox in politics, nationalism, religion, or other matters of opinion or force citizens to confess by word or act their faith therein.[25]

The statement is important for the constitutional law of free speech, because the prohibition on what officials can do introduces what comes to be called "content-neutrality," which can also be called the "anti-orthodoxy" principle. All that is needed is a symbolic expression doctrine, and the ground is laid for a right to burn a flag of one's own.[26]

Much of Justice Frankfurter's *Barnette* dissent, which begins with a striking personal reference,[27] reiterates his *Gobitis* opinion: he argues against special exemptions for religious claimants—an argument that does not address Justice Jackson's free speech rationale—and he argues for a limited judicial power if liberal democracy is to flourish. "Of course patriotism cannot be enforced by the flag salute. But neither can the liberal spirit be enforced by judicial invalidation of illiberal legislation."[28] Notwithstanding his return to symbols ("Symbolism is inescapable. Even the most sophisticated live by symbols"),[29] Justice Frankfurter agreed with Justice Jackson that the school board's inflexibility was foolish; they disagreed about whether the foolishness was also unconstitutional. Justice Jackson's position on symbols was that "a person gets from a symbol the meaning he puts into it, and what is one man's comfort and inspiration is another's jest and scorn."[30]

---

[25]West Virginia State Bd. of Ed. v. Barnette, 319 U.S. 624, 642 (1943).

[26]This is not to suggest that Justice Jackson necessarily would have agreed with the Court on flag burning. I discuss this subject in my conclusion.

[27]"One who belongs to the most vilified and persecuted minority in history is not likely to be insensible to the freedoms guaranteed by our Constitution." *Barnette*, 319 U.S. at 646.

[28]*Id.* at 670.

[29]*Id.* at 662.

[30]*Id.* at 632–33.

C. THE O'BRIEN TEST FOR SYMBOLIC EXPRESSION, THE FLAG DESECRATION CASES OF 1969 TO 1974, AND COHEN V. CALIFORNIA

1. *O'Brien and the symbolic expression test.* The Universal Military Training and Service Act of 1948 provided for Selective Service registration and also required all registrants to keep their certificates in their "personal possession at all times"; the maximum punishment for a knowing violation was a $5,000 fine and five years' imprisonment.[31] Draft card burning became a form of protest against the war in Vietnam in the spring of 1965, and in response to these protests, which did not alarm Selective Service officials,[32] Congress passed an amendment later that year to the 1948 law, making knowing destruction and knowing mutilation additional offenses. The court of appeals invalidated the law on two grounds: since non-possession was already punishable, the amendment served no valid purpose; and "singling out persons engaging in protest for special treatment . . . strikes at the very core of what the First Amendment protects."[33]

In *United States v. O'Brien*,[34] the Supreme Court, reversing the court of appeals, began by stating that the law dealt with conduct, not speech, and that notwithstanding O'Brien's claim to have communicated a message, "we cannot accept the view that an apparently limitless variety of conduct can be labeled 'speech' whenever the person engaging in the conduct intends thereby to express an idea."[35] Having said that, however, the Court went on to acknowledge that O'Brien's conduct came within the First Amendment and then to set out a test for legislation affecting a free speech interest:

> [W]hen "speech" and "non-speech" elements are combined in the same course of conduct, a sufficiently important governmental interest in regulating the non-speech element can justify incidental limitations on First Amendment freedoms. . . . [A] government regulation is sufficiently justified [1] if it is within the constitutional power of the government; [2] if it furthers an important or substantial governmental interest; [3] if the governmental interest is unrelated to the suppression of free expression; and [4] if the incidental restriction on alleged First Amendment

---

[31] See Alfange, Free Speech and Symbolic Compliance: The Draft Card Burning Case, 1968 Supreme Court Review 1, 4.

[32] See *id.* at 4 n.17, quoting a letter from Selective Service Director Hershey to Congressman Saylor, to the effect that "adequate authority exists to enforce compliance with the law either through accelerated induction or by criminal prosecution."

[33] O'Brien v. United States, 376 F.2d. 538, 541 (1st Cir. 1967).

[34] 391 U.S. 367 (1968).

[35] *Id.* at 376.

> freedoms is no greater than is essential to the furtherance of that interest.[36]

The key question turns out to be whether the governmental interest is or is not related to the suppression of free expression. In an important article commenting on the decision, John Hart Ely identified the third part of the test as performing the "switching function": if the governmental interest is related to the suppression of speech, strict scrutiny is given to the statute, which almost always means it is invalidated; if the governmental interest is not related to the suppression of speech, then some form of balancing takes place, and the statute is likely to survive constitutional scrutiny.[37]

The Court's application of the test in *O'Brien* is worth considering, since it was not obviously correct and the controversy over the legislature's motive in that case resembles the controversy over the Flag Protection Act of 1989. Chief Justice Warren's opinion for the Court in *O'Brien* offered three arguments against the reasoning of the court of appeals. First, the substantial governmental interest in the nondestruction provisions (generally, the interest in the efficient administration of the Selective Service system; specifically, the interest in a quick determination of who is available for induction in times of crisis) was not undermined by the preexistence of the non-possession regulations; in the absence of multiple punishment, Congress can provide alternative statutory avenues of prosecution. Second, there were some differences between the old regulations and the new; under the old law, one could possess a mutilated draft card or mutilate or burn someone else's card. And finally, in response to O'Brien's, and the court of appeals', suggestion that Congress' purpose or motive was "to suppress freedom of speech," the Court stated that "under settled principles the purpose of Congress, as O'Brien uses that term, is not a basis for declaring legislation unconstitutional."[38]

2. *The Flag Desecration Cases of 1969 to 1974.* In *Street v. New York*, decided in 1969, appellant had been convicted of violating a statute making it a misdemeanor to "publicly mutilate, deface, defile, trample upon, or cast contempt upon either by words or act any flag of the United States."[39] Hearing that the civil rights leader James Meredith had been shot, Street took an American flag from his apart-

---

[36] *Id.* at 376–77.

[37] Ely, Flag Desecration: A Case Study in the Roles of Categorization and Balancing in First Amendment Analysis, 88 Harv. L. Rev. 1482 (1975).

[38] 391 U.S. at 383.

[39] 394 U.S. at 576, 577–78.

ment outside on a street corner, lit the flag with a match, and dropped it on the pavement. An officer approached a crowd of thirty persons, heard Street say "We don't need no damn flag," and, asking if Street had burned the flag, heard appellant reply: "Yes, that is my flag; I burned it. If they let that happen to Meredith we don't need an American flag."[40] The Court reversed Street's conviction, holding by a five to four vote that the law was unconstitutionally applied in this case since "it permitted [Street] to be punished merely for speaking defiant or contemptuous words about the American flag."[41] The Court therefore did not have to consider whether it would have been constitutional to convict Street simply for flag burning. Justice Black, who prided himself on his "absolutist" approach to freedom of speech but who never was persuaded by the "symbolic speech" concept, wrote in dissent: "It passes my belief that anything in the Federal Constitution bars a State from making the deliberate burning of the American flag an offense."[42] And Justice Fortas argued that the American flag was a special kind of property, "subject to special burdens and responsibilities."[43]

Street suggests that in 1969 the Court was divided on the constitutional status of symbolic expression in general and flag burning in particular. As a result, it was also divided on whether or not it should rush in to confront the issue if there was any way to avoid it. Furthermore, in 1969, as in 1989 and 1990, the division on the Court did not follow simple liberal versus conservative, or judicial activism versus judicial self-restraint, lines: not all usually liberal Justices were willing to embrace communicative conduct as protected expression (Justice Black), and some of those Justices thought that treatment of the flag could be regulated (Justices Fortas and Stevens); on the other hand, certain conservative Justices did think certain forms of the communicative conduct qualified as protected expression (Justices Harlan, Kennedy, and Scalia).[44]

Two cases in 1974 involved flag abuse rather than flag burning. In the first case, *Smith v. Goguen*,[45] appellee Goguen wore a four by six inch cloth version of the flag sewn to the seat of his trousers. He was convicted of violating the provision of Massachusetts flag misuse statute which subjects to criminal liability anyone who "publicly

[40] *Id.* at 579.

[41] *Id.* at 581.

[42] *Id.* at 610.

[43] *Id.* at 617 (dissenting opinion).

[44] See Appendix for chart of the Supreme Court's flag-burning decisions and the votes of the Justices.

[45] 415 U.S. 566.

. . . treats contemptuously the flag of the United States." The Supreme Court ordered the conviction set aside on vagueness grounds. Justice Powell, writing for a six-justice majority, noted that unlike disorderly conduct statutes, there is no reason for broad discretion in the area of flag contempt. "Indeed, because display of the flag is so common and takes so many forms, changing from one generation to the another and often difficult to distinguish in principle, a legislature should define with some care the flag behavior it intends to outlaw."[46] Justice White concurred on First Amendment grounds, not the void for vagueness grounds; he also indicated that he would uphold a straightforward flag desecration law.[47]

Justice Rehnquist dissented, reading the statute to protect the physical integrity of the flag and arguing that such was an important governmental interest unrelated to the suppression of free speech.[48] Justice Blackmun also dissented, disagreeing with the majority that the words "'treats contemptuously' are necessarily directed at protected speech,"[49] and agreeing with Justice Rehnquist that the Massachusetts Supreme Judicial Court had limited the statute to protecting the physical integrity of the flag.

Finally, in *Spence v. Washington*,[50] decided in June 1974, the Supreme Court, in a per curiam opinion, with Chief Justice Burger and Justices White and Rehnquist dissenting, reversed a conviction under Washington's flag misuse statute. In May, 1970, Spence, a college student, hung his American flag from the window of his apartment upside down, with a peace symbol, made of removable tape, attached. He was prosecuted under an "improper use" statute, which among other things prohibited the display of any American flag with anything printed, painted, or attached. He testified that he put the peace symbol on the flag and displayed it in public to protest against the invasion of Cambodia and the killings at Kent State University, events which had occurred a few days prior to his arrest. "I felt that the flag stood for America and I wanted people to know that I thought America stood for peace."[51]

The Court overturned the conviction, observing that the flag was private property, that there was no trespass or breach of the peace, and that appellant engaged in a clear form of communication. The Court's explanation of when symbolic conduct is protected expres-

---

[46] *Id.* at 568–69, 581.

[47] *Id.* at 586–87.

[48] *Id.* at 599–600.

[49] *Id.* at 590.

[50] 418 U.S. 405.

[51] *Id.* at 408.

sion has been adopted in all subsequent cases: "An intent to convey a particularized message was present, and in the surrounding circumstances, the likelihood was great that the message would be understood by those who viewed it."[52]

The rest of the opinion is unclear about the significance of the difference between this form of flag misuse and desecration, or burning. For example, is it of constitutional significance that the message "was not an act of mindless nihilism," and that appellant did not "permanently disfigure the flag or destroy it"?[53] The bare majority of the Court apparently wanted to keep that distinction open, since it concluded that "no interest the State may have in preserving the physical integrity of a privately owned flag was significantly impaired on these facts."[54]

In dissent, Justice Rehnquist, with the *Barnette* case in mind, maintained that the state has a valid interest in preserving the character of the flag, even if that did not mean it could enforce that character with every conceivable means. This may be a valid basis for distinguishing the flag salute requirement from flag misuse statutes, but the *Spence* majority rejected it. Furthermore, if the question is whether a State can withdraw "a unique national symbol from the roster of materials that may be used as a background for communications,"[55] then it seems that the Court's *Spence* decision clearly pointed to its decision in *Texas v. Johnson*, handed down fifteen years later.

3. *Cohen v. California*. In 1971, the Supreme Court overturned a disturbing the peace conviction against a young man named Cohen, who walked into a federal court building wearing a jacket containing the message "Fuck the Draft." In his opinion for the Court, Justice Harlan concluded that the words did not come under the legal definition of obscenity, because they were not erotic, or the definition of fighting words, since they were not addressed to anyone in particular; in addition, since the display did not take place where substantial privacy interests were invaded, and since there was no evidence of a disturbance of the peace, the conviction had to be overturned.[56] The case is thus important for its narrowing of the "fighting words" doctrine to direct personal insults and for effectively ruling that harms to "sensibility" were insufficiently weighty when standing against free speech claims, no matter how crude. The *Cohen* decision on crude

[52] *Id*. at 410–11.

[53] *Id*. at 410, 413.

[54] *Id*. at 415.

[55] *Id*. at 423.

[56] Cohen v. California, 403 U.S. 15 (1971).

expression plus the inclusion of symbolic expression within the First Amendment led to the protection of flag burning.

II. The Supreme Court Strikes Down a Flag Desecration Law: Texas v. Johnson (1989)

Texas' "desecration of venerated objects" statute covered public monuments, places of worship or burial, and state or national flags. It defined "desecrate" as "defac[ing], damag[ing], or otherwise physically mistreat[ing] [any of these objects] in a way that the actor knows will seriously offend one or more persons likely to observe or discover his action." While the Republican National Convention was taking place in Dallas in 1984, and renominating President Reagan, Gregory Lee Johnson participated in a political demonstration which ended in front of Dallas City Hall, where Johnson unfurled the American flag, doused it with kerosene, and set it on fire. While the flag burned, the protestors chanted "America the red, white, and blue, we spit on you."[57] No one was injured or threatened, although many reported being seriously offended by the flag burning.

Johnson was convicted and sentenced to one year in prison and fined $1,000 for this expressive conduct. The Texas Court of Criminal Appeals reversed, on First Amendment grounds, and the Supreme Court affirmed in an opinion by Justice Brennan. Justices Marshall, Blackmun, Kennedy, and Scalia joined; Justices Rehnquist, White, O'Connor, and Stevens dissented.

Justice Brennan had no difficulty using the *Spence* test to demonstrate that the flag burning was expressive conduct. Following *O'Brien*, he then considered whether the governmental interest was unrelated to the suppression of free expression. The state introduced two interests—preventing breaches of the peace and preserving the flag as a symbol of nationhood and national unity. Justice Brennan found that the first interest was not implicated on the facts of the case, since giving serious offense did not satisfy either the Court's incitement test or its "fighting words" test. Justice Brennan found that the second interest was present and, citing *Spence*, that it was also related to speech. "We are thus outside of *O'Brien*'s test altogether."[58]

Justice Brennan next considered whether the state's interest in preserving the flag as a symbol of the nation justified the restriction.

---

[57] Texas v. Johnson, 109 S.Ct. 2533, 2536 (1989).

[58] *Id.* at 2542.

He first showed that "strict scrutiny" applied by demonstrating that the law was "content-based," and not "content-neutral." Johnson "was prosecuted for his expression of dissatisfaction with the policies of this country, expression situated at the core of our First Amendment values."[59] He was prosecuted for burning the flag because he knew that his politically charged expression would cause "'serious offense'," not because the flag "was dirty or torn."[60] Whether Johnson's treatment of the flag violated the Texas law "depended on the likely communicative impact of his expressive conduct." Therefore, Justice Brennan reasoned, "this restriction on Johnson's expression is content-based,"[61] and must be subjected "to the most exacting scrutiny."[62]

In applying strict scrutiny to the Texas statute, Justice Brennan drew substantially on Justice Jackson's *Barnette* opinion and fashioned his own version of the "fixed star in our constitutional constellation": "If there is a bedrock principle underlying the First Amendment, it is that the Government may not prohibit the expression of an idea simply because society finds the idea itself offensive or disagreeable."[63] Justice Brennan concluded his opinion by urging those of us who disagree with the flag burners "to persuade them that they are wrong," to wave our own flag, to "salut[e] the flag that burns," and to give "its remains a respectful burial." "We do not consecrate the flag by punishing its desecration, for in doing so we dilute the freedom that this cherished emblem represents."[64]

In a brief concurrence, Justice Kennedy indicated that his conception of the judicial power and his understanding of "the law and the

---

[59] *Id.* at 2543.

[60] *Ibid.* In this context, he cites Justice Blackmun's dissent in *Goguen*, which I will consider below.

[61] 109 S.Ct. at 2543.

[62] *Id.* at 2543–44. Justice Brennan's treatment of prong three of the *O'Brien* test implied that after a statute is found to be related to the suppression of free expression, it must also be shown to be "content-specific" in order for the "strict scrutiny" test to apply. But a law whose interest is the suppression of speech, as opposed to one which, while furthering other purposes, incidentially limits speech, would be subject to strict scrutiny, even if it were content-neutral. As Ely puts it, the key question for this part of the *O'Brien* test is "whether the harm that the state is seeking to avert is one that grows out of the fact that the defendant is communicating, and more particularly out of the way people can be expected to react to his message. . . . " See Ely, note 37 *supra*, at 1492. Geoffrey Stone appears to take a different position on this matter, in his Flag Burning and the Constitution, 75 Iowa L. Rev. 111 (1989). He says that content-neutral restrictions falling outside of *O'Brien*'s test for purpose do not require "strict scrutiny." But his examples seem to me to qualify as time, place, and manner regulations whose purpose is not related to the suppression of free expression.

[63] *Johnson*, 109 S.Ct. at 2544.

[64] *Id.* at 2547–48.

Constitution" compelled him to decide the case as he did, notwithstanding his "distaste for the result."[65] Chief Justice Rehnquist wrote a long dissenting opinion, which included generous quotations from patriotic poetry to support his contention that the flag is a special symbol of American unity and nationhood. He also stated: "Surely one of the high purposes of a democratic society is to legislate against conduct that is regarded as evil and profoundly offensive to the majority of people, whether it be murder, embezzlement, pollution, or flag burning."[66] Not only does flag burning seem out of place in such company, but in addition to the offensive language on Paul Cohen's jacket, the expressive conduct of the Ku Klux Klan and the American Nazi Party, which comes closer to flag burning than to the other three offenses, has been protected under the First Amendment.[67]

Justice Stevens' dissent argued first that the government's power to prohibit the public desecration of the American flag "is unique." A country's flag is a symbol not just of "nationhood and national unity," but also of "the ideas that characterize the society that has chosen that emblem as well as the special history that has animated the growth and power of those ideas."[68] Disagreeing with the majority's suggestion that this decision would enhance the flag's symbolic importance, Justice Stevens claimed that "sanctioning the public desecration of the flag will tarnish its value—both for those who cherish the ideas for which it waves and for those who desire to don the robes of martyrdom by burning it."[69] He also compared flag burning to posting bulletin boards and graffiti on the Washington Monument, or conveying a political message by spray painting the Lincoln Memorial.[70] But unlike flags, which are many and privately owned, the Memorial and the Monument are each singular and publicly owned objects, and the Government can therefore demonstrate a substantial interest in protecting them which is unrelated to the suppression of speech.

Justice Stevens also argued that the prohibition on flag burning differs significantly from the flag salute requirement of *Barnette*. But, Justice Jackson's principle, that there is no orthodoxy which public

---

[65] *Id.* at 2548.

[66] *Id.* at 2555.

[67] Brandenburg v. Ohio, 395 U.S. 444 (1969); National Socialist Party v. Skokie, 432 U.S. 43 (1977).

[68] *Id.* at 2566.

[69] *Ibid.*

[70] *Id.* at 2567.

officials may enforce, when combined with recognition of symbolic expression, easily develops to protect Spence, and now Johnson, both of whom conveyed distinct political messages.

Finally, Justice Stevens argued that the statute did not violate content neutrality, since "the concept of 'desecration' does not turn on the substance of the message the actor intends to convey, but rather on whether those who view the *act* will take serious offense.[71] But, Justice Stevens' remarks concerning the flag as symbol of country and way of life tell against him here, since that is precisely the message that he thinks the government can protect by prohibiting flag desecration.

The opinions in *Johnson* did not explicitly refer to specific theories of the First Amendment. But the acceptance of "symbolic expression" as part of protected speech, which already had a twenty-year history by 1989, reflects a limited recognition of the "self-fulfillment" or "individual autonomy" arguments for free speech; a clear message must be intentionally communicated, but there is great latitude in the manner of expression. The emphasis on content-neutrality reflects the notion that government has no business enforcing orthodoxy, and this is perhaps the best explanation for the "marketplace of ideas" approach to free speech. Finally, to the extent to which flag burning is clearly political in the core sense of the term, protecting this form of speech is linked to the self-government rationale.

III. Flag Burning and the Constitution After Johnson

President Bush condemned *Johnson*, in a speech at the Iwo Jima Monument, less than a week after it was handed down, and expressed his support for a constitutional amendment. The Senate passed a resolution, 97 to 3, expressing "profound disappointment" that the Court protected "such reprehensible conduct." Both houses of Congress held hearings to consider statutory and constitutional responses to the Court's ruling. Thus, aside from the important free speech issue, the controversy over flag burning reveals an important aspect of the separation of powers: how Congress interprets its constitutional powers in light of a Supreme Court decision that restricts those powers.

---

[71] *Ibid.*

A. THE CONGRESSIONAL HEARINGS OF 1989 AND THE FLAG PROTECTION ACT OF 1989

Both Houses conducted four days of hearings on the flag burning controversy; the House Judiciary Subcommittee on Civil and Constitutional Rights, which met for four days in July, and the Senate Judiciary Committee, which met for two days in August and two more in September.[72] Each committee called roughly the same number and kind of witnesses; they included constitutional specialists such as law school professors, present and former government officials, members of Congress, and spokesmen for interested associations, especially veterans' groups, and some individuals who served with distinction in the armed forces. The options were to pass a law to protect the flag against burning or other forms of mutilation, to pass a constitutional amendment, or to do nothing. Most of the debate centered on the statute versus amendment issue, and much of that took on a lawyer-like technical character: the issues involved the proper reach of the *Johnson* decision, the meaning of the Supreme Court's doctrine on "content neutrality," and, by way of illustration, the consideration of possibly analogous restrictions on free expression.

1. *The politics of flag protection.* The flag had become so embroiled in partisan politics from the 1988 Presidential election, that any Congressional consideration of flag burning was bound to become caught up in that atmosphere. That this happened can be shown with reference to Congressional statements and votes, as well as with some of the expert testimony Congress received.

On July 27, 1989, the full House Judiciary Committee voted 28 to 6 in favor of H.R. 2978.[73] There was no vote on H.J. Res. 350, the

---

[72]Statutory and Constitutional Responses to the Supreme Court Decision in Texas v. Johnson, Hearings before the Subcomm. on Civil and Constitutional Rights, Comm. on the Judiciary, House of Representatives, 101st Cong., 1st Sess., (1989); Hearings on Measures to Protect the Physical Integrity of the American Flag. Hearings on S 1338, H.R. 2978, and S.J. Res. 180 before the Comm. on the Judiciary, United States Senate, 101st Cong., 1st Sess., (1989). Subsequent citations will be to either the House or the Senate Hearings.

[73]This refers to Senator Joseph Biden's (D-De) proposal, which appears in the House Hearings at 18. The critical language was: "(a) Whoever knowingly mutilates, defaces, burns, maintains on the floor or ground, or tramples upon any flag of the United States shall be fined not more than $1,000 or imprisoned for not more than one year, or both." While there was no recorded vote in the printed report, the "Nay" votes came from Representatives John Conyers Jr. (D-Mi), Chuck Douglas (R-NH), Barney Frank (D-Ma), Patricia Schroeder (D-Co), George Crockett Jr. (D-Mi), and Howard Berman (D-Ca). Of these, Mr. Douglas indicated that his opposition was based on his conviction that only a constitutional amendment could protect the flag. On the vote on the House floor, Douglas, Schroeder, Crockett, and Berman voted "no," but Frank voted "yes" and Conyers did not vote or record a preference.

constitutional amendment, either in the committee or in the House. The matter became moot, for the time being, after the Senate failed to pass the amendment on October 19. On September 21, 1989, the Senate Judiciary Committee, in separate votes accompanying separate reports, voted 9 to 5 to report the statute (S1338) favorably and 8 to 6 to report the constitutional amendment (S 180) unfavorably. The fourteen Senators on the committee can thus be identified with one of four possible positions on flag burning.

1. Favor either one: Senators Dennis DeConcini (D-Ar), Howell Heflin (D-Al), Strom Thurmond (R-SC), Alan Simpson (R-Wy)—4 conservatives
2. Oppose both: Senators Edward Kennedy (D-Ma), Howard Metzenbaum (D-Oh), Gordon Humphrey (R-NH)—2 liberals, 1 conservative
3. Favor the law, oppose the amendment : Senators Joseph Biden (D-De), Patrick Leahy (D-Vt), Paul Simon (D-Il), Arlen Specter (R-Pe), Herbert Kohl (D-Wi)—5 liberals
4. Favor the amendment, oppose the law: Senators Orrin Hatch (R-Ut), Charles Grassley (R-Io)—2 conservatives

These two votes show that support for a revision of *Johnson* was stronger in the House than in the Senate. This may have been due to the timing of the hearings; it may also reflect the fact that all Representatives must seek reelection every two years. In addition, those advocating a constitutional amendment were more vocal in the House than the Senate, and those opposing any Congressional response to *Johnson* were more easily identified in the Senate than in the House. When House Minority Leader Robert Michel (R-Il) introduced a proposed constitutional amendment to the House committee, Representative Don Edwards (D-Ca), chairman of the House Subcommittee holding the hearings, asked: "Mr. Michel, you pointed out several times, and I agree with you, that the American flag has a unique place in our nation. Those are your own words. Would you think that the Constitution also has a unique place in our Nation?" Representative Michel replied that the Constitution and the Bill of Rights "are . . . sacred to us . . . as documents," while the flag is sacred as "a physical symbol."[74] Mr. Edwards, who (from his question) would have preferred to take no action, was among the 28 subcommittee members voting for a statutory revision of *Johnson*. Several liberal Senators who also probably favored no action also voted for the statutory approach, although some also voted against it.

[74]House Hearings at 43.

And the votes of the individual committee members were recorded in the Senate Report, while that was not the case in the House Report.

In the midst of political pressure for action, Congress sought expert testimony from constitutional law authorities on the question whether the Supreme Court's *Johnson* decision could be overturned by a carefully drawn statute. Much of the testimony was thoughtful and to the point, but some of the most prominent constitutional scholars and teachers acted more like advocates than instructors.

For example, when Harvard Law Professor Charles Fried, who had been Solicitor General from October 1985 to January 1989, testified before the House committee on July 19, 1989, he took the position that "the *Johnson* case is right, not just as a matter of present constitutional law. It is right in principle."[75] Asked whether the proposed statute's constitutionality was "a reasonably close question," Professor Fried replied, "I really don't think so," although he acknowledged that "as Solicitor General . . . I would have been bound to try to defend it."[76] But Professor Fried had initially submitted written testimony in support of a statute protecting the physical integrity of the flag. Two days later, he submitted contradictory testimony and spoke against the constitutionality as well as the wisdom of such a law.[77]

Professor Fried gave no account of why he initially supported the statute, in written testimony for the Committee, and why he changed his mind abruptly (except to say that his first reply was "prompted by a telephone call to me in the south of France, where I was vacationing" and the atmosphere was not conducive to "sober constitutional reflection"). Perhaps at the last minute Professor Fried decided that he did not want to become a part of the political attempt to hold off the movement for a constitutional amendment by supporting a statute. The committee members who sought his counsel in this matter, many of whom shared his views about the merits of the issue, and who were also feeling the political pressure to do something, would have benefited from a more complete account of his thinking.

Laurence Tribe, also a professor at Harvard Law School and the primary adviser to Senator Biden, the chairman of the Senate Judiciary Committee and chief sponsor of a statutory response to *Johnson*,

[75]House Hearings at 221.

[76]*Id.* at 227.

[77]See House Hearings at 219–35.

confidently testified, before both the House and the Senate Committees, that the proposed flag protection act was constitutional. In his treatise *American Constitutional Law* published first in 1978 and revised in 1988, Professor Tribe anticipated the flag-burning controversy and argued that the kind of statute he was now supporting would be unconstitutional. Several experts testifying in favor of a constitutional amendment took pains to point this out.[78]

There is reason for concern when a scholar contradicts a position he has taken in his scholarly work, at a time when it is very useful to the politicians he supports that he do so. Professor Tribe's best explanation, in his testimony before the House Committee, was that the popular reaction to the controversy changed his mind and that "if you freeze constitutional analysis in time, if you don't open your mind to what's going on in the country and the lessons of experience, you're not a very good constitutional analyst."[79]

If Professor Tribe's change of position reflects the "politics" of the flag burning controversy, in the sense that for supporters of *Johnson* a statutory response is the "lesser of two evils," it has something in common with Professor Fried's change of position, which appears to take the "high moral ground" against political considerations. Neither scholar provided a full account of his change of position and neither acknowledged what could be said for the opposing position. Such an "advocacy" approach to testimony on the part of constitu-

---

[78]See House Hearings at 85–86, 156–57. In his treatise, Professor Tribe distinguished his hypothetical flag-burning law from the draft card burning statute in *O'Brien*, concluding that the flag burning law would require strict scrutiny and thereby be found unconstitutional. He arrived at this conclusion by asking the question, "What is the government's interest in preventing such acts?" Starting with the Court's speculation in *Spence* that interest would be "in preserving the flag as a national symbol capable of mirroring the sentiments of all who view it," Professor Tribe argued that that purpose differs from the purpose which the Court accepted when it upheld the law against draft card durning. In that case, the facilitation of identification in an emergency was thwarted as much by private as by public draft card burning; in the case of the hypothetical flag law, however, "closet" burning of the flag would not implicate the interest in maintaining the flag as national symbol, and this shows that the interest is related to the suppression of speech, since it "arises only when such conduct is perceived by others, and only when the conduct is interpreted in a certain way." Tribe, American Constitutional Law, 801–2 (2d ed. 1988).

[79]House Hearing at 103. In his most recent book, On Reading the Constitution (1991), coauthored with Michael C. Dorf, Professor Tribe writes that the Flag Protection Act of 1989 was "properly struck down." *Id.* at 25. Despite this remark, and an earlier one that the authors "applaud" "the 1989 and 1990 Supreme Court rulings [in *Johnson* and *Eichman*]" (*id.* at 2), the book makes no mention of Professor Tribe's vigorous advocacy of a flag protection bill. The only difference between the bill proposed by Senator Biden and supported by Professor Tribe in 1989 and the Flag Protection Act of 1989 is that the latter added "physically defiles" to the former's "knowingly mutilates, defaces, burns, maintains on the floor or ground, or tramples upon. . . ." Compare Senate Hearings at 45 (S 1338) with 18 U.S.C. 700.

tional law experts and teachers does not enhance Congress' ability to deliberate on important constitutional questions.

2. *The statutory response versus the constitutional amendment.* Critics of the statutory approach contended that both *Spence* and *Johnson* show that no flag protection act can pass prong three of the *O'Brien* test: the requirement that the government's interest be "unrelated to the suppression of free expression." These critics urged that the government's interest in assuring a proper treatment of the flag by protecting it against desecration is due to the flag's symbolizing the nation. Therefore prohibiting acts of destruction of privately owned flags, which acts are clearly intended to convey a negative or critical message about the nation or its government, is necessarily directly related to the suppression of expression.

Defenders of the statute replied that a law which focused "on the physical integrity of the flag itself," and "not on the likely reaction of the audience . . . or on the expressive motive of the actor who attacks the flag," would be content-neutral and not based on a government interest related to the suppression of speech.[80] One defender of the statute contended that "what bothers most people" is not the message conveyed by flag burning but something "much more like sympathy for the intangible thing that's going up in flames. It hurts to see the flag burn."[81] But how can we feel sympathy, or compassion, for an inanimate object? Moreover, why should we be bothered by flag burning unless we are offended by the disrespectful way in which the burner is treating the symbol of our country and way of life?

Protection of the physical integrity of the flag was also likened to protection of gravesites, churches and synagogues, and bald eagles, but these cases can be distinguished: the property probably would not belong to the protester; in addition, the protester would have a harder time passing the *Spence* test for a clear political message that others could be expected to understand; and, finally, the government has a reason for protecting the items which is unrelated to the suppression of expression.

The claim that a statute forbidding flag burning is content-neutral and is not based on a government interest related to the suppression of free expression was also refuted by Congress's treatment of the problem of disposing of soiled or worn-out flags. The Flag Protection

[80] House Hearings at 114.

[81] *Id.* at 104; Senate Hearings at 144.

Act of 1989 specifically exempted burning for this reason from its prohibition. The content-based nature of this distinction is clear: flag burners intend to offend others by publicly destroying the nation's symbol; Boy Scouts and others who ceremoniously destroy soiled flags intend to show respect for that symbol. If we ask why we cannot follow that distinction and pass a constitutional law to protect the flag, the answer is that the *Johnson* decision built on the symbolic expression doctrine, as articulated in *O'Brien* and applied to flags in *Spence*, and the *Cohen v. California* decision of 1970, which recognized the legitimacy of various modes of expression.

3. *The case for doing nothing versus taking action*. The senators supporting a statute and opposing an amendment in 1989 seem to have been "playing for time"; if the law did not pass constitutional muster, they would not be confronted with a straight up or down vote on flag protection until some time in the future, when popular sentiment might not be as strong as it was in the summer of 1989. Apart from such interesting political considerations, different judgments concerning the desirability of constitutional amendments in response to controversial Supreme Court decisions seem to account for the different positions taken by members of Congress and by constitutional scholars who testified. These different positions seem to be based on (1) an assessment of the likelihood that one constitutional amendment would lead to others, which would threaten constitutional stability, and (2) an overall assessment of the constitutional power of the federal courts, especially the Supreme Court. The first point might be correct. On the other hand, one could argue that a statutory response which the Supreme Court honored might well induce a reconsideration of other First Amendment decisions, which formed the basis of the *Johnson* decision, whereas an amendment would single out the flag for special protection and leave First Amendment doctrine on free speech otherwise unaffected.

Furthermore, those who say that a constitutional amendment to protect the flag will "trump the First Amendment" do not state the issue fairly.[82] Even though it may have been better to spell out precisely in the amendment what can be protected, rather than to authorize Congress and the states to act, the intention was to overturn a particular, controversial interpretation of the First Amendment. In-

[82]Professor Dellinger, in his Senate testimony, argued that the proposed amendment either "override[s] or trump[s] the First Amendment and other provisions of the Bill of Rights, or it does nothing." Senate Hearings at 548. The latter point refers to the inexplicitness of the proposal.

deed, four Justices believed that the First Amendment did not protect flag burning. It therefore begs the question to say that the proposed amendment derogated from the First Amendment.

The House first passed a Flag Protection bill on September 12, 1989, 380–38; the opposition consisted mostly of conservative Republicans, who favored the constitutional amendment, and liberal Democrats, who (presumably) favored doing nothing.[83] Then, on October 5, the Senate, after seven hours of debate, passed the House version 91–9, after adding three amendments. First, Senator Pete Wilson (R, Ca) offered an amendment adding the words "physically defiles." Senator Biden, the author of the bill, opposed the amendment on the grounds that the words implied a communicative injury and thus risked judicial invalidation. Senator Biden's motion to table was defeated 31–69; afterward, the amendment passed 76–24. Senator Dole also succeeded in adding the provision prohibiting the flag from being maintained on the floor or ground. Finally, Senator Biden succeeded in amending the provision for expedited review so that the Supreme Court would take the appeal from a district court, but only after that court had ruled on the constitutionality of the measure.[84] The House then approved its bill with the Senate amendments on October 12, by a vote of 371–43, and sent the bill to the President.[85] The next day the President indicated that he would permit the bill to become law without his signature, since he thought a constitutional amendment "is the best way to provide lasting protection for the flag."[86] On October 19, the Senate rejected the proposed constitutional amendment, with 51 voting in favor, 48 against.[87]

B. BACK TO THE COURTS

On October 28, the day the new law went into effect, Mark Haggerty, Jennifer Campbell, Darius Strong, Carlos Garza, and other individuals burned a flag in front of a post office in Seattle, Wash-

---

[83]Cong. Q. 2400 (Sep. 16, 1989).

[84]*Id.* at 2446 (Oct. 7, 1989).

[85]The Act provides: "(a)(l) Whoever knowingly mutilates, defaces, physically defiles, burns, maintains on the floor or ground, or tramples upon any flag of the United States shall be fined under this title or imprisoned for not more than one year, or both.

"(2) This subsection does not prohibit any conduct consisting of the disposal of a flag when it has become worn or soiled.

"(b) As used in this section, the term 'flag of the United States' means any flag of the United States, or any part thereof, made of any substance, of any size, in a form that is commonly displayed." 18 U.S.C. §700 (Supp. 1990).

[86]Cong. Q. 2720 (Oct. 14, 1989).

[87]*Id.* at 2803 (Oct. 21, 1989).

ington. Two days later, on October 30, Shawn Eichman, David Blalock, and Scott Tyler did the same thing in Washington, D.C., on the east steps of the Capitol. The flag burning controversy was back in the courts.

On February 21, 1990, Judge Barbara Rothstein, of the United States District Court for the Western District of Washington, invalidated the new law in the *Haggerty* case. On March 5, 1990, Judge June Green, for the District Court for the District of Columbia, invalidated the law in the *Eichman* case. The opinions of the two district courts were similar, and Judge Green acknowledged her debt to Judge Rothstein's opinion.[88]

Judge Rothstein began with the question whether the conduct involved is protected expression. She answered in the affirmative, with a quotation from *Johnson* on the "overtly political nature" of the conduct and a quotation from a leaflet publicizing the event to show that defendants' conduct was also "intended to convey a political message and thus implicates the First Amendment."[89]

The second question concerned the nature of the government's interest, which determines the applicable standard of scrutiny. *Johnson* relied on *Spence* to hold that the relevant governmental interest—preserving the flag as a symbol of the nation—was directly related to the suppression of expression. Judge Rothstein rejected the argument (advanced not by the Justice Department but in a brief filed by the Senate) that the Flag Protection Act was a content-neutral protection of the physical integrity of the flag and therefore was based on an interest unrelated to freedom of expression. Judge Rothstein replied as follows:

> Unfortunately, the Senate's definition of what constitutes content-neutrality is incorrect, and thus dooms its entire argument. . . . [C]ontent-neutral restrictions on speech are "those that 'are *justified* without reference to the content of the regulated speech.'" [citations omitted] Thus, it is the *reason* for the legislation and not its *scope* which determines content-neutrality. If the justification for protecting the flag is related to the suppression of expression, it is not content-neutral even though the Act on its face is applicable to anyone who engages in certain conduct regardless of the actor's intent or the impact of the conduct.[90]

The Senate also argued that the legislation was not related to the

---

[88]United States v. Haggerty, 731 F. Supp. 415 (W.D. Wash. 1990); United States v. Eichman, 731 F. Supp. 1123 (D.D.C. 1990).

[89]731 F. Supp. at 418 n. 3.

[90]*Id*. at 419–20.

suppression of expression because "Congress is pursuing the affirmative objective of preserving the flag as the embodiment of diverse views and not simply advancing its own view of the flag." Judge Rothstein found this argument to be without merit: "[P]ursuing the affirmative goal of preserving the flag because it represents a nation of diverse views inevitably results in suppressing the views of those who would express their opinion by destroying the flag."[91]

Finally, Judge Rothstein rejected the argument that the Flag Protection Act, unlike the Texas law invalidated in *Johnson*, was an across-the-board prohibition and was therefore constitutional:

> Although the Act does not focus on the actor's motive, the types of conduct proscribed are those generally associated with disrespect for the flag. Other types of conduct which also threaten the physical integrity of the flag but which do not communicate a negative or disrespectful message, like flying the flag in inclement weather or carrying it into battle, are not prohibited. Thus, the Act fails to protect the flag's physical integrity in all circumstances.[92]

Judge Rothstein then reasoned that since the expression is "situated at the core of First Amendment values," the only question was whether there is "a compelling national interest in protecting the flag." To this Judge Rothstein replied that the *Johnson* Court "reaffirmed that the core purpose of the First Amendment is to protect political dissent, and . . . to suppress such criticism in one instance so as to protect the sensibilities of the majority does not strengthen the nation. On the contrary, it erodes our political freedom."[93]

The Flag Protection Act provided for a direct appeal to the Supreme Court of any federal district court decision about its constitutionality and for expedited consideration by the Supreme Court. The two cases were consolidated on expedited appeal to the Supreme Court, which heard oral argument on May 14, 1990, and handed down its decision on June 11, 1990, affirming the District Courts by the same 5–4 vote that decided *Johnson* a year earlier. Justice Brennan again wrote the opinion of the Court and Justice Stevens again wrote a dissent. This time there were no other opinions.

After reviewing the *Johnson* decision and setting out the language of the new law, Justice Brennan took note of an argument made by the

---

[91]*Id.* at 420.

[92]*Id.* at 420 n.6.

[93]*Id.* at 422. Judge Green's comment on this point was that the government can promote this interest by "gentle persuasion." *Eichman*, 731 F. Supp. at 1130.

Solicitor General. This argument relied principally on *New York v. Ferber*,[94] which held that the government may prohibit child pornography, essentially because of the harmful effects of child pornography on the children who are filmed or photographed.

> As decisions such as *Ferber* suggest, the protections of the First Amendment do not apply where (1) the speech (or expressive conduct) is narrowly and precisely defined, (2) whatever value the expression may have to the speaker (or others) is outweighed by its demonstrable destructive effect on society as a whole or on particular overarching social policies [citations omitted], and (3) the speaker has suitable alternative means to express (and others have means to receive) whatever protected expression may be part of the intended message [citations omitted].[95]

Justice Brennan dismissed this argument on the ground that flag burning "enjoy[s] full protection of the First Amendment."[96] Justice Brennan then turned to the question whether the Flag Protection Act, which proscribed all "conduct (other than disposal) that damages or mistreats a flag," was distinguishable from the Texas statute, which was directed at acts which "'the actor knows will seriously offend' onlookers."[97] Justice Brennan's first response was that the Government's interest in preserving the "'physical integrity' of a privately owned flag rests upon a perceived need to preserve the flag's status as a symbol of our Nation and certain national ideals." Therefore, the Government's desire to preserve the flag as a symbol of the nation is not threatened by private acts of destruction but "is implicated 'only when a person's treatment of the flag communicates [a] message' to others that is inconsistent with those ideals."[98] Justice Brennan conceded that "the Government has a legitimate interest in preserving the flag's function as an 'incident of sovereignty'," but he questioned the application of that interest to this case. He reasoned that "the flag-burner's message depends in part on the viewer's ability to make this very association" between the mistreated flag and the United States.[99]

---

[94]458 U.S. 747 (1982). See Brief for the United States in United States v. Eichman, 110 S.Ct. 2404 (1990), at 32–33.

[95]United States v. Eichman, 110 S.Ct. 2404, 2407 (1990).

[96]110 S.Ct. at 2407–8. Justice Brennan added that "we deal here with concededly political speech and have no occasion to pass on the validity of laws regulating commercial exploitation of the image of the United States flag." *Id.* at 2408 n.4.

[97]*Id.* at 2408. This was the key argument in support of a statutory response to *Johnson*, the one which drew on the reference to the limits of the Texas statute, with the accompanying citation to Justice Blackmun's *Goguen* dissent. See *Johnson* at 2543, including note 6.

[98]110 S.Ct. at 2408.

[99]*Id.* at 2408 n.6.

Justice Brennan then stated that except for the prohibition against "burn[ing]" the flag, "each of the special terms" describing the proscribed action, which included "mutilates, defaces, physically defiles, burns, maintains on the floor or ground, or tramples upon," "unmistakably connotes disrespectful treatment of the flag and suggests a focus on those acts likely to damage the flag's symbolic value."[100] Finally, Justice Brennan noted that the specific exemption for disposal of "worn or soiled" flags "protects certain acts traditionally associated with patriotic respect for the flag."[101]

Accordingly, Justice Brennan concluded that the Flag Protection Act "still suffers from the same fundamental flaw" as the Texas law: "it suppresses expression out of concern for its likely communicative impact."[102] "We decline," Justice Brennan wrote for the court, "the Government's invitation to reassess this conclusion in light of Congress' recent recognition of a purported 'national consensus' favoring a prohibition on flag-burning." Regardless of whether such a consensus exists, any suggestion that popular opposition to political expression strengthens the Government's interest in suppressing it "is foreign to the First Amendment."[103]

In the final section of his opinion, Justice Brennan invoked Justice Jackson's *Barnette* opinion, urging that national unity is an end which can be fostered by persuasion and example but not by coercion. He repeated the statement in *Johnson* that the bedrock principle underlying the First Amendment is that "the Government may not prohibit the expression of an idea simply because society finds the idea itself offensive or disagreeable." He concluded that "punishing desecration of the flag dilutes the very freedom that makes this emblem so revered, and worth revering."[104]

Justice Stevens began his dissenting opinion by claiming that "the Court's opinion ends where proper analysis of the issue should begin." He agreed with the majority that the government may not restrict the expression of ideas it does not like. But he offered a three-part test that resembled the test offered in the Solicitor General's brief:

> [C]ertain methods of expression may be prohibited if (a) the pro-

---

[100] *Id.* at 2409.

[101] *Ibid.* A footnote here (note 8) drew on the point made by Judge Rothstein to the effect that the Act did not prohibit other conduct, such as flying a flag in a storm, which might threaten its physical integrity without showing disrespect.

[102] *Id.* at 2409.

[103] *Ibid.*

[104] *Id.* at 2410.

> hibition is supported by a legitimate societal interest that is unrelated to suppression of the ideas the speaker desires to express; (b) the prohibition does not entail any interference with the speaker's freedom to express those ideas by other means; and (c) the interest in allowing the speaker complete freedom of choice among alternative methods of expression is less important than the societal interest supporting the prohibition.[105]

On the first point, Justice Stevens began by identifying two components to the government's interest in the flag: "in times of crisis, it inspires and motivates the average citizen to make personal sacrifices . . . [and] at all times, it serves as a reminder of the paramount importance of pursuing the ideals that characterize our society."[106] Then he considered whether the interest in preserving the value of the flag as symbol of the nation is "unrelated to suppression of the ideas that flag burners are trying to express." Justice Stevens grouped the ideas expressed by flag burning in three categories: first, the burner may intend "to convey hatred, contempt, or sheer opposition" to the United States; second, he may "seek to convey the depth of his personal conviction about some issue [such as opposition to the war in Vietnam] by willingly provoking the use of force against himself"; and third, "a flag burner may intend to make an accusation against the integrity of the American people who disagree with him," that is, he may be burning the flag to charge that the majority has "forsaken" its "commitment to freedom and equality."[107]

Justice Stevens urged that "the Government's legitimate interest in preserving the symbolic value of the flag" is unrelated to any of these messages:

> [T]he flag uniquely symbolizes the ideas of liberty, equality, and tolerance. . . . The flag embodies the spirit of our national commitment to those ideals. The message thereby transmitted does not take a stand upon our disagreements, except to say that those disagreements are best regarded as competing interpretations of shared ideals. It does not judge particular policies, except to say that they command respect when they are enlightened by the spirit of liberty and equality. To the world, the flag is our promise that we will continue to strive for these ideals. To us, the flag is a reminder both that the struggle for liberty and equality is unceasing, and that our obligation of tolerance and respect for all of our fellow citizens encompasses those who disagree with us—indeed, even those whose ideas are disagreeable or offensive.

---

[105] *Ibid.*

[106] *Ibid.*

[107] *Ibid.*

> Thus, the Government may—indeed it should—protect the symbolic value of the flag without regard to the specific content of the flag burners' speech.[108]

Justice Stevens suggested that America's disagreements "are best regarded" as occurring within its fundamental agreement on the principles of equality and freedom. He is not clear on whether this is the most accurate way to regard the differences or whether it is only the most edifying way to regard them. That we may have a problem here is evidenced both by the existence of "offensive" ideas, which are likely not to be reconcilable with our "shared ideals," and by the prevalence of flag burning, which is offensive behavior that is practiced, in part, for that very reason. Justice Stevens' strongest point here is that effective attachment to those shared ideals may require a willingness to show respect, and if necessary, to have that showing of respect enforced by criminal law, for the symbol of our country and its ideals.

Justice Brennan, by contrast, emphasized the clear difference between respectful and disrespectful treatments of the flag as the basis for his conclusion that what appeared to be "content-neutral," and hence unrelated to the suppression of expression, was not. Since disposal of a worn or soiled flag is treated differently from the deliberately offensive political messages conveyed by flag burning, it is clear that even the superficially neutral Flag Protection Act is content-based when it comes to respectful and disrespectful ways of treating the symbol of the country. As long as we recognize content neutrality, symbolic expression, and a variety of modes of expression, and as long as a distinct message is communicated, the existing constitutional doctrines require that we come to the conclusion that the majority of the Court adopted.

In light of the attention that was given to framing a flag protection act that would pass constitutional muster, it is worth noting that each of the Justices voted the same way in *Johnson* and *Eichman* and that none of them apparently thought there was any difference in the issues presented. Justice Blackmun, on whom the advocates of the across-the-board statute relied for the "swing vote," did not change his vote. Likewise, while none of the four dissenting Justices in *Johnson* bowed to precedent (although Justice Stevens acknowledged the claim of *stare decisis*), none of them expressed the view that the issue was any different in *Eichman* than it had been in *Johnson*. If Jus-

---

[108] *Id.* at 2411.

tice Blackmun had written a short concurring opinion in *Johnson*, disavowing his *Goguen* dissent, perhaps the Flag Protection Act of 1989 would not have been passed. But then again, perhaps we would now be in the midst of a ratification debate over a constitutional amendment.

C. A FINAL CONGRESSIONAL CONSIDERATION: THE DEBATE AND VOTE ON THE PROPOSED CONSTITUTIONAL AMENDMENT

On June 13, 1990, two days after the Supreme Court's decision in *Eichman*, the House Judiciary Subcommittee on Civil and Constitutional Rights sent H.J. Res. 350, the proposed constitutional amendment, to the full Judiciary Committee with a negative recommendation. On June 19, that Committee voted 19–17 to send the measure to the Floor with no recommendation, after failing to recommend it to the full House by a 17–19 vote.[109] While the amendment's supporters originally advocated a speedy consideration of the measure, the opponents appear to have been better organized; anticipating the Supreme Court's decision, they had been preparing for another campaign against the amendment. While the supporters objected and sought a delay of at least three days, ostensibly to obtain a report from the Judiciary Committee but actually to enable the veterans' groups supporting the amendment to organize communications to Congress, the opponents succeeded, on a 231–192 vote, in getting the measure considered on June 21.[110] After seven hours of debate on the amendment, it failed to pass when only 254 voted for it and 177 voted against. Five days later, on June 26, the Senate took up the measure, even though the House vote precluded the amendment from going to the states. After attempts at other statutory and amendatory measures failed, S.J. Res. 332, identical to the House resolution, failed to pass, when only 58 senators voted in favor, 42 voted against.[111]

---

[109]Congressional Quarterly, June 23, 1990 at 1963. The full committee vote is given in the Committee markup for H.J. Res. 350 at 147–65.

[110]Apparently some supporters of the amendment, including Jack Brooks (D-Te), chairman of the House Judiciary Committee, got upset with the other supporters' delaying tactics; they voted for the rule. The vote is at Congressional Record H 4004–5. The story is in Congressional Quarterly, June 23, 1990 at 1963.

[111]Cong. Rec. S 8736–7.

VI. Conclusion

During the Senate Hearings, Judge Pollack, who argued in support of "doing nothing," made this statement about and in support of the Supreme Court:

> What the Founders had probably not fully anticipated was that the Supreme Court itself would in the course of its extraordinary institutional development become in effect a vehicle for modifying, liberating, derigidifying the Constitution as occasion called for, but always within the main lines of the principles embodied by the framers in the great charter.[112]

We may quibble with the suggestion that the founders' constitutionalism was inappropriately rigid, but we must agree that the Supreme Court's exercise of the power of judicial review has made it possible for the American Constitution to remain viable as our frame of government and our fundamental law, notwithstanding the significant changes that have taken place in our country's two-hundred-year history.[113]

The lesson of the flag-burning controversy for the separation of powers seems to be that Congress in general recognizes and respects the important contribution of the judiciary and especially the Supreme Court in interpreting the Constitution by developing constitutional law doctrines on a case-by-case basis. The specialized Congressional committees in the House and the Senate did an excellent job of familiarizing themselves with the relevant judicial decisions, constitutional doctrines, and arguments relevant to a statutory response to the Supreme Court's decision in *Johnson*. I should add, however, that all the Committee members needed to support the Flag Protection Act of 1989 was the finding of a plausible argument for its constitutionality, and some who doubted the law's constitutionality voted for it anyhow. The members of Congress not serving on the two Committees were less interested in and confident about their handling of a constitutional issue involving the Bill of Rights.[114] In such matters, as opposed to matters of constitutional structure, Congress seems hesitant to challenge the Court if it requires the ex-

---

[112]Senate Hearings at 286.

[113]I have discussed this point in connection with the enumeration of powers and the Tenth Amendment in Dry, note 5 *supra*, at 233–34, 247–50.

[114]I am grateful to my colleague Eric Davis for suggesting this point.

ercise of its Article V amendment power. The most striking evidence of this came in the remarks of Senate Majority Leader George Mitchell (D-Me) at the end of the Senate debate. After expressing his agreement with the dissenting Justices in *Eichman*, he said: "But, under our system, once the Supreme Court has ruled, that ruling is the law of the land. So even though I disagree with the court's ruling, I accept it."[115]

As for the First Amendment and freedom of speech, the development of the doctrine of symbolic expression and its application to flag burning reflects both continuity and change in American constitutional law. That can be illustrated by comparing the principles of the Declaration of Independence, which refer to the "self-evident truth" of natural equality, with Justice Jackson's "fixed star" argument, which says that in America there is no orthodoxy that officials can enforce. While the two statements differ in their emphasis, the extent of their difference in practice depends mainly on the limits of criminal law. Applying Justice Jackson's argument to the flag-burning controversy, the government is now prevented from protecting the symbol of the country against hostile and destructive forms of expression.

We noted, in connection with Justice Stevens' dissent in *Eichman*, that there are different positions on freedom and tolerance: we have moved, over time, from tolerating tolerant views to tolerating all views, even intolerant ones, out of a respect for dissent and a fear of misuse of government power to restrain intolerant views. For example, Justice Jackson, whose *Barnette* dissent is the linchpin of Justice Brennan's two opinions on flag burning, may not have been persuaded of the necessity of extending the "fixed star" principle that no official can prescribe what is orthodox to protect flag burners. He dissented in two free speech cases involving the danger of physical violence on the public streets from "ideological fighting words" directed against Jews and Catholics. In the first, he warned against converting the "constitutional Bill of Rights into a suicide pact"; in the second he warned that "to blanket hateful and hate-stirring attacks on races and faiths under the protections for freedom of speech" was more likely to "belittle[] great principles of liberty" than to "be a noble innovation."[116] Since Justice Jackson's time, the symbolic ex-

---

[115]Cong. Rec. S8735 (June 26, 1990).

[116]Terminiello v. Chicago 337 U.S. 1, 37 (1949); Kunz v. New York, 340 U.S. 290, 295 (1952). The phrase "ideological fighting words" comes from Harry Kalven, A Worthy Tradition 82, 86 (1988).

pression doctrine, plus an openness to a variety of modes of expression, first established in the offensive words case (*Cohen*), leads to an equal tolerance of flag burning as the equivalent of speech critical of a particular American policy or American government and political life altogether. The only limits concern incitement to violence and the likelihood that violence will occur, or a manifest breach of the peace.

These changes in the law reflect changes in manners and mores as well, and for that reason they must be acknowledged in our constitutional law. But the need to accept such changes, by establishing the "anti-orthodoxy principle," poses a special problem for American government, which Justice Jackson's dissents illustrated. We cannot use the criminal law to prohibit extreme forms of offensive as well as divisive expression, and such expression can affect opinions and then behavior in such a way as to threaten the conditions for securing rights in civil society. The challenge is to find new ways to affirm the principles of liberty and equality without using the criminal law to punish those who wish to engage in offensive conduct which does not rise to the level of an incitement to imminent violence with a clear and present danger of producing such violence. The greater threat is not so much that violence will result before it can legally be restrained; it is that permissiveness will ultimately weaken our freedom as individuals as well as citizens.

Liberal constitutionalism as we know it today, especially in America, gives the individual substantial freedom, including the freedom to act without responsibility. To the extent to which coercion, in the form of the criminal law, is limited, we must put a greater burden on indirect devices, such as the authority of the government as educator and the family. Considering the government as educator, as long as public schools do not prescribe a mindless orthodoxy to their students, faculty, or library officials, authorities may select teachers, librarians, books and other learning materials with a view toward an education appropriate to American citizenship. There is First Amendment case law to support this view. In addition to Justice Jackson's dictum, in *Barnette*, about the appropriateness of requiring civics courses in public school, more recent cases allow public school authorities to make choices regarding courses and books for libraries, and to regulate, to some extent, school assemblies and newspapers.[117] And nothing in the flag-burning cases calls into question

[117]See Board of Education v. Pico, 457 U.S. 853 (1982); Bethel School District No. 403 v. Fraser, 478 U.S. 675 (1986); Hazelwood School District v. Kuhlmeier, 484 U.S. 260 (1988).

the government's authority to support patriotism with flag raising ceremonies or with public monuments and memorials dedicated to statesmen and war heroes. Laws punishing the destruction of government property, including American flags, remain in full force.[118] Attempts to assist parents in child-rearing by means of "family hour" restrictions on indecent but not obscene broadcasts[119] and "fair notice" provisions on movies and records, along with restrictions on minors, are constitutionally permissible.

As we ponder the importance of free expression, be it as a check on the government or in the name of self-development, it is also important to remember the limits of the doctrine of "content-neutrality."Otherwise people may come to conclude that whatever is permitted must have an equal claim to validity and justice with everything else that is permitted. Justice Brennan's suggestion that when we see a flag burning, we salute it, or give it a decent burial,[120] properly understood, means that liberal constitutionalism need not stand for mindless relativism. Just because the criminal law must follow content neutrality when it treats expression, even the symbolic kind, government and public authorities generally are not prevented from cultivating an appreciation that the form and substance of our expression of opinions should reflect, as Justice Stevens put it, "what the flag uniquely symbolizes[,] the ideas of liberty, equality, and tolerance."[121]

---

[118]In the Seattle flag-burning case, after the Supreme Court's decision in *Eichman*, Haggerty and the other defendants—who had burned a flag belonging to the Postal Service, rather than their own flag—pleaded guilty to destruction of federal property. On Oct. 19, 1990, two of the defendants, Strong and Garza, were sentenced to three days incarceration and a $200 fine (plus $25 for court costs) and two others, Haggerty and Campbell, were sentenced to a fine of $75 (plus $25 for court costs).

[119]FCC v. Pacifica, 433 U.S. 726 (1978).

[120]Texas v. Johnson, 109 S.Ct. at 2547.

[121]*Eichman*, 110 S.Ct. at 2411.

APPENDIX

Chart of Justices' Votes in Flag Desecration and Misuse Decisions

	Cases				
Justices	*Street* (5–4) (1969)	*Goguen* (6–3) (1974)	*Spence** (6–3) (1974)	*Johnson* (5–4) (1989)	*Eichman* (5–4) (1990)
Harlan	M**	. . .	. . .	. . .	. . .
Brennan	M	M	M	M**	M**
Marshall	M	M	M	M	M
Stewart	M	M	M	. . .	. . .
Douglas	M	M	M*	. . .	. . .
Warren	D*	. . .	. . .	. . .	. . .
White	D*	M*	D	D	D
Black	D*	. . .	. . .	. . .	. . .
Fortas	D*	. . .	. . .	. . .	. . .
Powell	. . .	M**	M	. . .	. . .
Burger	. . .	D	D*	. . .	. . .
Blackmun	. . .	D*	M	M	M
Rehnquist	. . .	D*	D*	D*	D
O'Connor	. . .	. . .	. . .	D	D
Stevens	. . .	. . .	. . .	D*	D*
Scalia	. . .	. . .	. . .	M	M
Kennedy	. . .	. . .	. . .	M*	M

Note.—M = majority; D = dissent; * = wrote an opinion; ** = wrote majority opinion.
*The Court handed down a per curiam opinion in *Spence*.

JULIAN N. EULE

PROMOTING SPEAKER DIVERSITY: AUSTIN AND METRO BROADCASTING

It happens every couple of years in my First Amendment course. A single student—or a small group of them—threatens to dominate class discussion. The frequency of these students' interjections is punctuated by the protracted nature of their discourse. Recognizing that the class is hearing more and more of fewer and fewer voices, I seek to remedy the situation by ignoring the frantic hand waving of the offending individuals or by cutting short their monologues. Inevitably, some comedian in the class offers a social commentary on my efforts. "Oh Professor," the joker caustically inquires, "aren't you ignoring the fundamental lesson of the First Amendment?"

It certainly appeared so. As the Supreme Court said in *Buckley v. Valeo:* "[T]he concept that government may restrict the speech of some elements of our society in order to enhance the relative voice of others is wholly foreign to the First Amendment."[1] The Court has since repeated that statement many times.[2]

Last term, in two surprising cases, *Austin v. Michigan Chamber of Commerce*[3] and *Metro Broadcasting v. Federal Communications Commis-*

Julian N. Eule is Professor of Law, University of California, Los Angeles

Author's Note: I am grateful to Daniel Brenner, Erwin Chemerinsky, Joel Handler, Kenneth Karst, Matthew Spitzer, and Jonathan Varat for their thoughtful comments and suggestions.

[1] 424 U.S. 1, 48–49 (1976).

[2] Meyer v. Grant, 486 U.S. 414, 426 n.7 (1988); Citizens Against Rent Control v. Berkeley, 454 U.S. 290, 295 (1981); First Nat'l Bank of Boston v. Bellotti, 435 U.S. 765, 790 (1978). See also Powe, Mass Speech and the Newer First Amendment, 1982 Supreme Court Review 243.

[3] 110 S.Ct. 1391 (1990).

0-226-09573-8/91/1990-0006$02.00

sion,[4] the Supreme Court gave its approval to government action designed precisely to "enhance the relative voice" of some members of society at the expense of others. The concept that government may tone down or amplify particular voices in order to promote speaker diversity is no longer a stranger to the First Amendment. I can't wait until next semester.

I. Toning Down Dominant Voices: Austin v. Michigan Chamber of Commerce

In response to the abuses of the Watergate era, Congress enacted the 1974 amendments to the Federal Election Campaign Act of 1971, limiting both contributions to campaigns for political office and independent expenditures in support of a candidate.[5] The defenders of the statute primarily relied on two governmental interests as justification for these limitations. First, they argued that the restrictions were necessary to prevent actual or perceived corruption of elected officials beholden to large campaign donors. In *Buckley v. Valeo*, the Supreme Court accepted this as sufficiently weighty to justify the contribution limits.[6] When it came to the expenditure limitations, however, the "corruption" justification fell short. Independent expenditures, the *Buckley* Court concluded, did not present the same dangers of actual or apparent *quid pro quo* arrangements posed by large contributions.[7]

This forced the Act's defenders to turn to their second justification—"equalization." Expenditure limits, they argued, served "to mute the voices of affluent persons and groups in the election process and thereby to equalize the relative ability of all citizens to affect the outcome of elections."[8] The Court's response was terse—it required only two sentences and one footnote—and it was unequivocal. The First Amendment barred abridging the rights of wealthy persons to

[4] 110 S.Ct. 2997 (1990).

[5] 86 Stat. 3, as amended by the Federal Election Campaign Act Amendments of 1974, 88 Stat. 1263.

[6] 424 U.S. 1, 26–29 (1976).

[7] *Id*. at 45–46. Additionally the Court found that, assuming *arguendo* that large independent expenditures posed as great a risk of actual or perceived corruption as large contributions, the Act—as construed by the Court—only restricted express advocacy of the election or defeat of a candidate and was thus too susceptible of evasion to be effective. *Id*. at 45.

[8] *Id*. at 25–26.

engage in political expression in order to enhance the relative clout of less affluent segments of society.[9] The Court did not inquire whether disparity of wealth in fact enabled certain voices disproportionately to stock the marketplace of ideas. It mattered not. Government could not silence some voices in order to amplify others. More speech, not less, was the only constitutionally acceptable response to dominating voices.

Two years after *Buckley* the Court's stance appeared to waver. In *First National Bank of Boston v. Bellotti*,[10] the Court narrowly struck down a Massachusetts statute forbidding a select group of business corporations from seeking to use political contributions or expenditures to influence the outcome of ballot measures other than those "materially affecting" the corporation's property, business, or assets. Justice Powell's opinion for the five-justice majority contained mixed signals. On the one hand, he reiterated *Buckley*'s unambiguous rejection of the equalization rationale. Justice Powell described the suggestion that government had a valid interest in muting the corporations' dominance of the electoral process, in order to enhance the relative voices of smaller, less influential speakers, as "unsettling" and in contradiction of "basic tenets of First Amendment jurisprudence."[11]

Yet, scarcely two pages earlier, Justice Powell's opinion had a remarkably different tone. Massachusetts' argument that the views of wealthy corporations threatened to drown out other points of view, said Justice Powell, "would merit our consideration" if it "were supported by record or legislative findings."[12] *Bellotti* thus simultaneously rejected the validity of governmental efforts to equalize voices and invited better documentation of speaker domination.

Twelve years of schizophrenia followed. During this period the Court intermittently rejected the equalization rationale;[13] sustained statutes in instances where it was far from evident that the corruption

---

[9]*Id.* at 48–49. Despite this summary rejection of the "equalization" justification, the Court is somewhat more ambiguous in its references to the argument later in the opinion, appearing to question the efficacy of the means more than the validity of the end. See *id.* at 54, 56–57.

[10]435 U.S. 765 (1978).

[11]*Id.* at 791 n.30.

[12]*Id.* at 789. Justice Powell, however, concluded that there was "no showing that the relative voice of corporations has been overwhelming or even significant in influencing referenda in Massachusetts." *Ibid.*

[13]See, *e.g.*, Citizens Against Rent Control v. Berkeley, 454 U.S. 290, 295 (1981).

rationale alone was sufficient to sustain the result;[14] and appeared to hold out the possibility that an equalization rationale might suffice given the right facts.[15] Then last Term, the Court upheld an equalization effort on a record every bit as sparse as the one found wanting in *Bellotti*.

Section 54(1) of the Michigan Campaign Finance Law prohibits corporations from using corporate treasury funds for independent expenditures in support of or in opposition to any candidate for state office.[16] The Michigan statute is modeled on a provision of the Federal Election Campaign Act of 1971.[17] The Michigan State Chamber of Commerce, a nonprofit Michigan corporation, wished to spend general treasury funds for a newspaper advertisement endorsing a candidate for the Michigan House of Representatives. Because section 54(1) made such expenditures a felony, the Chamber brought suit for injunctive relief, contending that the absolute ban violated its First Amendment rights.[18]

Egalitarianism, a concept that *Buckley* and *Bellotti* had labeled "foreign," "intolerable," and "unconvincing," was about to find its place in the sun. By a 6–3 vote, the Court in *Austin v. Michigan Chamber of Commerce* upheld the Michigan ban.[19] For the first time a spending limit was sustained.

The Court in *Austin* accomplished this by blurring the line between the corruption and equalization rationales for campaign finance laws. When the Court in *Buckley* and *Bellotti* spoke of corruption, it clearly meant something akin to bribery. If government sought to regulate campaign finance in order to obviate the reality or appearance of undue influence on individual candidates by

---

[14]See Powe, note 2 *supra*, at 257–61 (placing California Med. Ass'n v. FEC, 453 U.S. 182 (1981) in this category).

[15]See, *e.g.*, FEC v. Massachusetts Citizens for Life, 479 U.S. 238 (1986); FEC v. National Conservative Political Action Committee, 470 U.S. 480 (1985).

[16]Mich. Comp. Laws §169.254(1) (1979).

[17]See Austin v. Michigan Chamber of Commerce, 110 S.Ct. 1391, 1395n.1 (1990).

[18]Although the Michigan law also prohibits corporate contributions, the case before the Supreme Court only involved the expenditure ban. *Ibid.*

[19]110 S.Ct. 1391 (1990). Five opinions were filed. All six members of the majority joined Justice Marshall's opinion for the Court, although Justices Brennan and Stevens both added individual concurrences. Justice Scalia wrote an individual dissent and Justice Kennedy authored a dissent signed by Justices O'Connor and Scalia. This article is not intended to be a full examination of the *Austin* decision. Indeed, there are significant aspects of the case (*e.g.*, the exemption of media corporations from Michigan's ban and the captive shareholder issue that played a prominent a role in Justice Brennan's concurrence) that I will completely ignore. I look at this case, as well as one other from last term, only to explore one facet—the Court's changing attitudes toward government promotion of speaker diversity.

wealthy benefactors, its interest, the Court ruled, was compelling. The corruption addressed in these cases is that of the *legislative* process. Duly elected representatives, who owed an obligation to consider the interests of all those who elected them, would be inclined to disproportionately consider the interests of those who financed their campaign. Or, at least, that was likely to be the public perception.

In *Austin*, Justice Marshall acknowledged that the prevention of corruption, actual or perceived, was the only legitimate, let alone compelling, governmental interest thus far identified for restricting campaign finances.[20] But, he continued, corruption had two facets. One was the type of corruption addressed in *Buckley* and *Bellotti*—which Marshall labeled "financial *quid pro quo*" corruption. Michigan's regulation, however, aimed at a different type of corruption—a corruption of the *electoral* process threatened by the "corrosive and distorting effects of immense aggregations of wealth that are accumulated with the help of the corporate form and have little or no correlation to the public's support for the corporation's political ideas."[21] In other words, corporations spoke too loudly and wielded too much influence on the electorate. Government had a compelling interest in stifling this dominating voice because the volume was disproportionate to public support for the views conveyed.

Nobody ought to be fooled. This is simply a repackaging of the equalization goal. The corporate voice is being contained[22] in order to "equalize the relative ability of all citizens to affect the outcome of elections."[23] Once the definition of corruption is enlarged to encom-

[20]110 S.Ct. at 1397 (citing FEC v. National Conservative Political Action Committee, 470 U.S. 480, 496–97 (1985)).

[21]*Ibid.* Justice Stevens, a member of the six-justice majority in *Austin*, appears to partially disassociate himself from the recognition of this second facet of corruption. Although he joined Justice Marshall's opinion, Justice Stevens wrote separately to reject *Buckley*'s conclusion that independent expenditures pose no significant threat of corrupting officeholders. Justice Stevens reasoned that because corporate expenditures, no less than corporate contributions, create "the danger of either the fact, or the appearance, of *quid pro quo* relationships," the Michigan law could be upheld solely as an effort to address this traditional species of corruption. *Id.* at 1407–8 (Stevens, J., concurring).

Justice Brennan also wrote a separate concurring opinion, focusing more on protecting shareholders from forced expression than on the corrosive influence of money on the electoral process. But Justice Brennan, unlike Justice Stevens, explicitly embraced the majority's expanded definition of corruption. *Id.* at 1403 (Brennan, J., concurring). With Justice Brennan's resignation, Justice Stevens may prove to be the key to the vitality of the concept of electoral corruption.

[22]Because the Michigan law permits corporations to express their political views through separate segregated funds, see Michigan Comp. Laws §169.255(1) (1979), it lessens rather than silences the corporate voice.

[23]Buckley v. Valeo, 424 U.S. at 25–26.

pass the corruption of the electoral process as well as the elected candidate, the distinction between the corruption rationale and the equalization one is obliterated.

Justice Marshall did attempt to deny that he was embracing equalization. The Michigan Act, he asserted, does not seek to equalize; "rather it ensures that expenditures reflect actual public support for the political ideas espoused by corporations."[24] But nobody who ever waved the banner of equalization meant anything else. The defenders of the expenditure limitations in *Buckley* did not argue for some cartoon-like equalization of speech where each person gets ten seconds to state his or her—or its—views. They urged only the equalization of "relative voices," "relative influence," or the "relative ability of all citizens to affect the outcome of elections." And what the citizens' voices, influence, or ability were intended to relate to was the public support for the views offered. Justice Scalia's dissent in *Austin* mockingly described the rationale endorsed by the majority as the "New Corruption," and unmasked it as precisely the same justification "proposed and soundly rejected in *Buckley*."[25] On this point, he is undoubtedly on the mark. But, the Court misstepped in *Buckley* when it characterized the government's goal, and Justice Scalia's reference to the "one-man, one-minute" principle of the *Austin* majority[26] merely compounds the error.

A good deal of confusion results from the terminology. From the outset, the goal behind the imposition of expenditure limitations, like those struck down in *Buckley*, was unfairly labeled "equalization." Not very many persons are going to have $1,000 to spend promoting a single political candidate or $25,000 to spend on behalf of their own congressional candidacy. Fewer still will be the Presidential candidates with $30,000,000 in their campaign coffers. Neither Congress nor Michigan aimed to establish a "one-person, one-minute" rule; both sought the far less ambitious goal of reducing the grossly disparate and distorting impact of dominating voices on the electoral process.

The problem is that the term "equalization," like racial "quotas,"

[24] 110 S.Ct at 1397–98.

[25] *Id.* at 1411 (Scalia, J., dissenting). There certainly appears to be little difference between the government goal endorsed by Justice Marshall in *Austin* and the one which Justice White unsuccessfully invoked in *Buckley*. *See* Buckley v. Valeo, 424 U.S. at 264–66 (White, J., concurring in part and dissenting in part) (Congress entitled to determine that wealth ought to play a less corrupting influence in deciding the outcome of political elections).

[26] 110 S.Ct. at 1411 (Scalia, J., dissenting).

has become a buzz word. Affirmative efforts by government to ensure wider representation of different groups and diverse views in American society deserve more serious consideration than the reflexive invocation of simplistic labels. One might have thought that we had learned the pitfalls of simplistic labeling of government goals from the unfortunate *Lochner* era.[27] For several decades, the Court adhered to the view that unequal bargaining power was not an excuse for legislative intervention. It was, the Court often reminded legislatures, incompatible with liberty of contract to remedy those "inequalities of fortune that are the necessary result of the exercise of those rights."[28] Equalization or redistribution of economic power was therefore an impermissible end of government.

Buckley, like *Lochner*, attempted to identify a category of impermissible ends—and it was not entirely fortuitous that the *Buckley* Court gave this class of illegitimate goals the same primitive label. *Austin* represents a substantial retreat from *Buckley*'s wholesale rejection of equalization or redistribution efforts by representative legislatures. But, as with the early cases which marked *Lochner*'s demise, the Court still feels trapped by the existing legal framework.

Austin is thus marked by a degree of incoherence to be expected in an initial step down a new path.[29] Justice Marshall feels constrained to fit Michigan's ends within the corruption rubric that the earlier cases established. Likewise, he disavows any equalization purpose. As Justice Scalia recognizes, however, the electoral corruption relied upon by the majority is a good deal closer to the government goal *Buckley* spurned than it is to the government interest *Buckley* embraced.

The Court would do well, as it continues to walk away from *Buckley*, to reject both a contortion of the definition of corruption and a return to the emotion-laden label of equalization. What legislation like that at issue in *Buckley* and *Austin* is really after is the promotion

---

[27]The period, generally regarded as beginning in 1897 and concluding in 1937, gets its name from Lochner v. New York, 198 U.S. 45 (1905).

[28]Coppage v. Kansas, 236 U.S. 1, 17 (1915).

[29]Although *Austin* is the initial holding along this new path, the Court had previously revealed its contemplation of such a route, most recently in FEC v. Massachusetts Citizens for Life, 479 U.S. 238 (1986). In his *Austin* dissent, Justice Scalia accuses the majority of acting without precedent in allowing the voice of private corporations to be stifled in order to assure the fairness of elections. 110 S.Ct. at 1408 (Scalia, J., dissenting). Yet, Justice Scalia joined the majority opinion in *Massachusetts Citizens for Life*, in which Justice Brennan specifically acknowledged "the legitimacy of Congress' concern that organizations that amass great wealth in the economic marketplace not gain unfair advantage in the political marketplace. " *Id.* at 257.

of viewpoint and speaker diversity.[30] This does not mean that every voice must be heard equally—or that each voice must be heard in perfect proportion to the support it enjoys in the general population[31]—but it entails an effort at ensuring that the public is exposed to a broad array of views. It is perhaps the height of irony that in the very same sentence in which the *Buckley* Court rejects equalization, it endorses such diversity as a central goal of the First Amendment:[32]

> [T]he concept that government may restrict the speech of some elements of our society in order to enhance the relative voice of others is wholly foreign to the First Amendment, *which was designed "to secure 'the widest possible dissemination of information from diverse and antagonistic sources.'"*

Buckley therefore did not reject the end of promoting diversity. It took issue instead with the government's choice of means. Promoting diversity was perfectly fine so long as voices were not silenced to achieve that goal.[33] By styling the government interest as equalization instead of the promotion of diversity, *Buckley* skirted the real issue. There is often a tension between the two tenets of the First Amendment that are reflected in the *Buckley* quotation—the precept that speech may not be suppressed because of the identity of the speaker and the equally critical demand that the public be exposed to the widest possible diversity of views. *Buckley* assumed that the government neutrality called for by the first would inevitably secure the second. When, however, a speaker—like the over eager student in my classroom or the wealthy Michigan corporation—threatens to monopolize the marketplace of ideas so as to produce a homogeneous flow of information to the public, the assumption is incorrect.[34]

---

[30] *Cf.* Powe, *supra* note 2, at 246 (identifying the government interest asserted in *Buckley* as one of speech enhancement). As in so many realms, my colleague Kenneth Karst was years ahead of me. The validity of campaign-finance regulation, he urged, calls for balancing its likelihood of increasing diversity of political expression against its cost to political freedom. "No slogan—not even Equality—can substitute for such an inquiry." Karst, Equality as a Central Principle in the First Amendment, 43 U. Chi. L. Rev. 20, 64–65 (1976).

[31] Indeed, such a formula would be a dangerous one for it locks in the status quo. *Cf. Austin*, 110 S.Ct. at 1415 (Scalia, J., dissenting) ("To the extent a valid proposition has scant public support, it should have wider rather than narrower public circulation.").

[32] 424 U.S. at 48–49 (citations omitted) (emphasis supplied).

[33] That this indeed was the Court's view in *Buckley* is confirmed by its validation of government subsidies designed to promote a greater diversity of discussion and participation in the electoral process. Such government action, said the Court, furthers rather than abridges First Amendment values. *Id.* at 92–93.

[34] See generally Fiss, Free Speech and Social Structure, 71 Iowa L. Rev. 1405 (1986). On the surface this may appear to be a conflict between a speaker-focused and an audience-focused

Once again, *Lochner* offers an historical analogy. The *Lochner* Court placed great trust in the natural operation of the economic marketplace. In turn we learned, however, both that there was nothing "natural" about the way in which the marketplace operated and that the marketplace was not infallible. The rise of legal realism brought about the first revelation; the Depression brought about the second. *Buckley* manifested an abiding trust in an unregulated marketplace of ideas. *Austin* reveals a loss of faith.

Austin recognized, to begin with, that Michigan's ban on the use of corporate treasury funds is not upsetting the "natural" order of the arena of political debate. The extent to which a well-financed corporate speaker can dominate the "marketplace" has little to do with the persuasiveness of the speech. The Milton-Holmes imagery of government sitting neutrally on the sidelines while truth and falsehood grapple for public acceptance in a free and open encounter is more myth than reality. Government is not neutral. In particular, it grants corporations numerous special economic advantages. "These state-created advantages," Justice Marshall reasoned in *Austin*, "not only allow corporations to play a dominant role in the nation's economy, but also permit them to use 'resources amassed in the economic marketplace' to obtain 'an unfair advantage in the political marketplace.'"[35] Justice Marshall emphasized that "the mere fact that corporations may accumulate large amounts of wealth is not the justification" for Michigan's bar. It is rather that corporations have achieved their position of strength through the intervention of the state.[36] Asking government to be a neutral observer in the political marketplace in the face of inequities that it has brought about in the economic marketplace is unrealistically to subdivide American society.

Austin not only recognizes that the political marketplace has no natural order; it also acknowledges a degree of market failure. For years, legal and political commentators have talked of the threat to

view of the First Amendment—the right to speak versus the right to receive information. Not so. Dominating speakers not only deprive the public of diverse views, but render other speakers ineffectual. *See* Wright, Money and the Pollution of Politics: Is the First Amendment an Obstacle to Political Equality, 82 Colum. L. Rev. 609, 637 (1982). The conflict, therefore, can be viewed as much between speakers as between the speaker and the public.

[35] 110 S.Ct. at 1397 (citations omitted).

[36] *Id.* at 1398. Justice Marshall relies heavily on FEC v Massachusetts Citizens for Life, 479 U.S. 238 (1986) for these conclusions. Justice Scalia's *Austin* dissent condemning Justice Marshall's reasoning, 110 S.Ct. at 1408–10 (Scalia, J., dissenting), virtually ignores this earlier case, an opinion that Justice Scalia remarkably joined without comment.

the electoral process—and thus ultimately to the core of our democratic structure—posed by the pervasive and corrupting influence of money.[37] The Court in *Buckley* would hear none of it. *Quid pro quo* corruption was conceded. Watergate made such possibilities impossible to ignore. But, while individuals could be corrupted, there was no systemic failure. In *Bellotti*, the Court conceded the possibility of corporate monopolization of the political marketplace but called for more legislative evidence. In *Austin*, that proof was not forthcoming. No matter. The Court is now prepared to take judicial notice of the fact that Holmes's marketplace is not in full working order. The wealthy corporation speaks too loudly, distorting the political process and undermining its integrity.[38] Because this distortion is attributable to the government's own doing, it has a compelling justification for toning down the corporate voice.

It is hard to know exactly how far the Court will be willing to go with *Austin*. At the top of the list of unanswered questions is the continued viability of *Buckley* and *Bellotti*. Both have been severely impaired by the Court's willingness to accept, as "compelling," a government objective that those cases appeared to reject as illegitimate. But each of these cases is missing an element that *Austin* used to bolster its conclusion.

Buckley's invalidation of Congress's limitation on political expenditures can be viewed narrowly as applying only to wealthy individuals. The rights of corporations to make political expenditures were not specifically adjudicated in *Buckley*—or so the *Austin* majority implicitly assumed. The Court described *Buckley* as a case about "individual donors";[39] and Justice Stevens, in his concurring opinion,

---

[37]See, *e.g.*, Drew, Politics and Money (1983); Fiss, note 34 *supra*; Chevigny, The Paradox of Campaign Finance, 56 NYU L. Rev. 206 (1981); Lowenstein, Campaign Spending and Ballot Propositions: Recent Experience, Public Choice Theory and the First Amendment, 29 UCLA L. Rev. 505 (1982); Carter, Technology, Democracy, and the Manipulation of Consent (Book Review), 93 Yale L.J. 581 (1984).

[38]In fact, the Court found it sufficient that corporate political expenditures presented the "*potential* for distorting the political process," and created a "*significant possibility*" that the integrity of the process might be undermined. 110 S.Ct. at 1398, 1402 (emphasis supplied). Justice Scalia's dissent took the majority to task for such speculation, warning that the "explicit acceptance of 'potential danger' as adequate to establish narrow tailoring" weakens the First Amendment "even more than its recognition of an insubstantial interest as 'compelling'." *Id.* at 1414 (Scalia, J., dissenting). *Austin*, Justice Scalia asserted, marks "the first time since Justice Holmes left the bench" that the Court has held that "a direct restriction upon speech is narrowly tailored if it extends to speech that has the mere *potential* for producing social harm." *Id.* at 1413–14.

[39]*Id.* at 1397.

described it as having drawn distinctions "between individual expenditures and individual contributions."[40]

If, therefore, *Buckley* is to be seen as surviving *Austin*, it must be on this individual/corporation distinction. But can such a line be supported under the Court's reasoning? An individual billionaire may drown out the voices of others as effectively as the Michigan Chamber of Commerce. And the volume with which such an individual speaks may have no more relationship to the public support for the position espoused than in the case of the corporation. If the corporation's voice may be toned down in the interest of promoting speaker diversity, why not the individual's?

The *Austin* majority's answer that the corporation is unique because it has achieved its position of strength with government assistance is not fully satisfactory. As Justice Scalia pointed out, private individuals are often the beneficiaries of special advantages conferred by the State: tax breaks, contract awards, cash subsidies. Those who get rich, and stay that way, usually owe government a debt of gratitude. On the other hand, there are differences of degree, and the Court might properly make distinctions based on them.[41]

The largest impediment to drawing distinctions between individual and corporate speakers is *Bellotti*. The Court there held that the inherent worth of speech does not depend on its source. Corporate speakers, no less than individual speakers, serve the First Amendment interest of informing the public. The Court thus held that Massachusetts could not ban corporate expenditures directed at influencing the vote on ballot measures. On at least two levels—its rule of parity for corporate speech and its specific holding—the vitality of *Bellotti* is threatened by *Austin*.

Bellotti's holding probably survives *Austin* only if the Court is willing to draw distinctions between independent corporate expenditures on behalf of political candidates and those made respecting

---

[40]*Id.* at 1407 (Stevens, J., concurring). Justice Scalia's dissent took issue with this characterization. The Federal Campaign Act, he pointed out, restricted political expenditures by "persons," not individuals, and the word "persons" was specifically defined to embrace corporations. Furthermore, the *Buckley* plaintiffs included several corporations. Finally, Scalia noted, the *Buckley* opinion often refers to restrictions placed on "individuals and groups." See 110 S.Ct. at 1410 (Scalia, J., dissenting).

[41]Justice Brennan, in his concurrence in *Austin*, identified an additional ground for distinguishing individuals and corporations: a corporation may spend money for political purposes that shareholders object to. No similar argument can be made about individuals.

ballot measures.[42] There are indications that some of the justices believe that the two situations deserve different treatment. The Court's opinion in *Austin* virtually shuns *Bellotti*, making no effort to distinguish it. In his concurring opinion, however, Justice Stevens asserted that "there is a vast difference between lobbying and debating public issues on the one hand, and political campaigns for election to public office on the other."[43]

This difference only makes sense, however, if the government's concern is with *quid pro quo* corruption, which is how Justice Stevens understood the Michigan statute.[44] Once the focus shifts to electoral corruption—or promoting speaker diversity—distinguishing between candidate elections and ballot measure campaigns is unsound. Indeed, Daniel Lowenstein has persuasively demonstrated that speaker domination is more prevalent in ballot measure elections than in candidate contests.[45] Furthermore, without the cues provided by political party identification, speaker domination poses a greater threat to the integrity of ballot measure results.[46] Thus, any empirical differences regarding market failure that might exist between ballot measure and candidate elections would militate in favor of a greater governmental interest in the plebiscitary context.

Beyond the issue of whether *Buckley* and *Bellotti* survived it, *Austin* raised a broader question. Was the Court's new receptivity to government efforts at promoting speaker diversity limited to the electoral context? In one sense, elections are a special case. They are the "bedrock of our political system."[47] Elections are how the majority speaks and we count on voting results to express—however crudely—the will of the people. Nowhere is the consequence of speaker domination greater, for disproportional speaking in the election setting raises the spectre of disproportional representation. But any possibil-

[42]The two cases differ in a more subtle way. The Michigan legislation in *Austin* permits corporations to make political expenditures through segregated funds or political action committees. Only the use of corporate treasury funds is prohibited. The Massachusetts law in *Bellotti*, on the other hand, forecloses all corporate political expenditures for certain ballot measures. For Justice Brennan, at least, this may justify different results. 110 S.Ct. at 1402 & n.1. (Brennan, J., concurring).

[43]*Id.* at 1407 (Stevens, J., concurring).

[44]See note 21 *supra*.

[45]Lowenstein, note 37 *supra*, at 589.

[46]See Eule, Judicial Review of Direct Democracy, 99 Yale L.J. 1503, 1515–19 (1990).

[47]*Cf.* Reynolds v. Sims, 377 U.S. 506, 562 (1964) ("As long as ours is a representative form of government . . . the right to elect legislators in a free and unimpaired fashion is a bedrock of our political system.")

ity that the *Austin* approach was an isolated phenomenon limited to elections was dispelled exactly three months later.

II. Turning Up Diverse Voices: Metro Broadcasting v. Federal Communications Commission

Writing more than a decade ago, Kenneth Karst observed and applauded the Supreme Court's increased use of equal protection analysis in its First Amendment decisions.[48] The parallels between these two areas of constitutional law remain striking. In particular, the relation between formal and substantive equality that Professor Karst identified as a fundamental issue under both provisions continues to plague the justices. The Equal Protection Clause has been the focus of a struggle over whether attainment of racial diversity and racial equality justifies a departure from the norm of government color-blindness. A parallel struggle is evident in the First Amendment debate—reflected in the division of the Court in *Austin*—concerning the merits of abandoning government neutrality in order to secure a more diverse flow of information to the public. In *Metro Broadcasting v. Federal Communications Commission*[49] the two debates came together in the same case.

Although racial minorities constitute more than one-fifth of the population of the United States, relatively few members of minority groups have held broadcast licenses. In 1978, minorities owned less than 1 percent of the Nation's radio and television stations. In May 1978, the Federal Communications Commission (FCC or Commission) adopted a Statement of Policy on Minority Ownership of Broadcasting Facilities. Observing that the views of racial minorities were inadequately represented in the broadcast media, the FCC described the situation as detrimental to the entire viewing and listening public. "Adequate representation of minority viewpoints in programming," the Statement concluded, "serves not only the needs and interests of the minority community but also enriches and educates the non-minority audience."[50] To enhance diversified programming, which it described as a key objective of both the Communications Act of 1934 and the First Amendment, the FCC adopted two minority preference policies.

---

[48]Karst, note 30 *supra*.

[49]110 S.Ct. 2997 (1990).

[50]*Id*. at 3004.

First, the Commission pledged to consider minority ownership as one factor when assessing competing applicants for new broadcast licenses. The Commission's previous six-factor standard was to be supplemented by a minority ownership "plus" factor. Second, the FCC adopted a "distress sale" policy for the transfer of existing licenses. As a general rule, a licensee whose qualifications to continue to hold the license have been called into question by the Commission may not transfer that license prior to a revocation or renewal hearing. The distress sale policy permitted a licensee designated for such a hearing to transfer the license to an FCC-approved minority enterprise at a price not to exceed 75 percent of fair market value.

Each policy was separately challenged under the equal protection component of the Fifth Amendment by broadcasting companies that were not minority owned. Although neither company asserted a violation of its free speech rights, the First Amendment played a prominent role in the Supreme Court's resolution of the consolidated cases. In a departure from recent affirmative action litigation, the racial preferences were not defended solely as a remedy for past discrimination. Instead, the FCC sought to justify its "non-neutrality" in much the same way as Michigan had done in *Austin*—as an effort to secure for the viewing and listening public "the widest possible dissemination of information from diverse and antagonistic sources."[51] By a 5–4 margin, the Court gave the diversity rationale its imprimatur.[52]

In at least two ways, the diversity goal had an easier road to travel in *Metro* than in *Austin*. To begin with, the standard of review adopted in *Metro* was more lenient. Because the *Austin* Court found expressive rights implicated, the Michigan ban had to be justified by a "compelling state interest." In *Metro*, Justice Brennan's opinion for the Court declared that benign racial preferences mandated by Congress[53] are constitutionally permissible so long as they serve "impor-

---

[51]*Id.* at 3010 (citation omitted).

[52]Four opinions were filed. All five members of the majority joined Justice Brennan's opinion for the Court, although Justice Stevens added an individual concurrence. Justice O'Connor filed a dissent joined by Justices Scalia and Kennedy and the Chief Justice. Justice Kennedy filed a separate dissent joined by Justice Scalia. *Metro*, like *Austin*, contains a number of different facets. This article ignores many of these, focusing instead only on the Court's acceptance of the speaker diversity rationale.

[53]Although initially adopted by the FCC, Congress subsequently signaled its approval of the preference policies. When the FCC decided in the mid-1980s to review the policies' validity, Congress attached a rider to FCC appropriation s legislation "prohibiting the Commission from spending any appropriated funds to examine or change its minority ownership policies." 110 S.Ct. at 3006.

tant governmental objectives."[54] He had little difficulty finding this standard satisfied. Devoting only two paragraphs to the "ends" inquiry, Justice Brennan concluded "that the interest in enhancing broadcast diversity is, at the very least, an important governmental objective." "Diversity of views and information on the airwaves," he asserted, "serves important First Amendment values."[55]

The second factor that made the diversity objective easier to sustain in *Metro* was that Justice Brennan had some precedent in his favor. More than twenty years earlier, in *Red Lion Broadcasting Co. v. FCC*,[56] the Court had unanimously upheld FCC rules requiring broadcasters to afford reply time to individuals who were the subject of political editorials or personal attacks. *Red Lion* rested its decision on no fewer than four cornerstones—the enhanced capacity of "new" technology to drown out the free speech of others, the scarcity of available frequencies, the government's role in allocation of these frequencies, and the right of viewers and listeners to be informed.

The Court has consistently refused to extend *Red Lion* in the two decades since it was decided. Five years after the decision, the Court in *Miami Herald Pub. Co. v. Tornillo*[57] unanimously struck down a Florida attempt to impose a similar "right of reply" requirement on newspapers without a single citation to *Red Lion*. And in *Buckley*, the majority rejected the relevance of *Red Lion* to Congress's effort at limiting political expenditures. The broadcast media was different, and *Red Lion*'s conclusions had no part to play in a "traditional free speech case."[58]

Red Lion lives. Although *Austin* does not cite it, several of its cornerstones are very much in evidence in Justice Marshall's opinion there. *Red Lion*'s reasoning that the government's power to grant and deny licenses carries with it a power to restrict their use[59] parallels *Austin*'s conclusion that corporate speech may be more readily restricted because the corporation receives privileges from the state.[60] Similarly, *Red Lion*'s concern with the quasi-monopolistic capacity of

---

[54] *Id.* at 3008–9.

[55] *Id.* at 3010.

[56] 395 U.S. 367 (1969).

[57] 418 U.S. 241 (1974).

[58] 424 U.S. at 49 n.55. See also First Nat'l Bank of Boston v. Bellotti, 435 U.S. at 791 n.30 (*Red Lion* only applies in the special context of limited access to the channels of communication).

[59] 395 U.S. at 389.

[60] 110 S.Ct. at 1397.

broadcasters to snuff out the free speech of others[61] is not unlike *Austin*'s anguish over the corrosive effects of a corporation's large political "war chest."[62]

But it is in *Metro* that *Red Lion* really is rejuvenated—and expanded. The Court in *Metro* emphasized the scarcity of electromagnetic frequencies and the government's unique role in the allocation of those frequencies—with a concomitant power to regulate licensees—and concluded by noting that it is the right of viewers and listeners, not the right of broadcasters that is paramount. For each of these propositions, the principal citation was to *Red Lion*.[63]

The *Red Lion* citation, however, is far too slender to carry the Court's conclusion in *Metro*. First off, the advent of cable and satellite television has rendered *Red Lion*'s scarcity rationale thoroughly obsolete.[64] More important, affording an individual limited access to reply to a personal attack is several steps removed from preferring a minority licensee so that the public will hear a greater diversity of views. Justice O'Connor's dissent is undoubtedly correct when she asserts that the FCC's diversity interest in *Metro* "presents, at the very least, an unsettled First Amendment issue." *Red Lion* was precedent for "limited measures to increase information and views generally," but the Court had "never upheld a broadcasting measure designed to amplify a distinct set of views or the views of a particular class of speakers."[65] Something more is at play here than a mere dusting off of *Red Lion*.

Admittedly, much of what drives the debate in *Metro* is the Court's continuing struggle over the meaning of racial equality and the use of race-conscious remedies to overcome the lingering effects of racial discrimination. The four members of the Court who dissented in *Metro* adhered to their previously announced position that racial

[61] 395 U.S. at 387–92.

[62] 110 S.Ct. at 1397, 1401, 1402.

[63] *Id.* at 3010.

[64] See Spitzer, Seven Dirty Words and Six Other Stories 7–42 (1986); Fowler & Brenner, A Marketplace Approach to Broadcast Regulation, 60 Tex. L. Rev. 207, 221–26 (1982). The diminishing number of cities with competing newspapers and the incidence of multiple ownership in the print media suggest that scarcity of expressional opportunity may not be an issue confined to electronic broadcasting. Indeed, since all resources are scarce, the scarcity rationale for distinguishing between broadcast and other media may not have been valid even at the time of *Red Lion*.

[65] 110 S.Ct. at 3036 (O'Connor, J., dissenting). Indeed, Justice O'Connor goes on to assert that prior decisions of the Court suggest that allocating broadcast licenses to achieve a more diverse mix of views would run afoul of the First Amendment. *Ibid.*

preferences will be tolerable only if narrowly designed to remedy specifically identified past discrimination. In fact, none of the four—O'Connor, Rehnquist, Scalia, and Kennedy—has ever cast a vote in favor of a constitutionally attacked racial preference. Three members of *Metro*'s majority—Brennan, Marshall, and Blackmun—consistently are willing to embrace a broader notion of affirmative action, one that permits its use to remedy historical exclusion and underrepresentation or even to promote a more forward-looking vision of a diverse society. None of these three has ever cast a vote against a benign racial preference. Justices Stevens and White are the wildcards. Both Stevens and White voted to invalidate a minority set-aside program last Term in *City of Richmond v. J.A. Croson Co.*[66] and both joined Justice Brennan's opinion to give him a majority in *Metro*. I do not plan to address here the possible distinctions that induced Justices White and Stevens to treat the two cases differently, although Justice White's authorship of *Red Lion* is a factor worth contemplating. Nor will I address the merits of the majority's resolution of the equal protection issue. I am sure that many trees will be felled in the forthcoming exploration of these questions. It is, instead, the First Amendment implications of the Court's debate that I wish to highlight.

It is easy to lose the First Amendment aspects of *Metro* in the affirmative action milieu. One might well be inclined to discount the significance of a great deal of what Justice Brennan says about speaker diversity because of the setting in which he says it. But, because all five of the *Metro* majority were also in the *Austin* majority,[67] I am prepared to conclude that at least part of what we are observing in *Metro* is part of a new judicial receptivity to governmental sound mixing.

Indeed, the discourses surrounding affirmative action and speech enhancement are fundamentally the same debate. The resistant pleas for color-blindness and speaker-neutrality share a belief that government does best when it does least, a concern that government cures for inequities would be worse than the disease, and a trust that if we only give the private sector enough time the problems of dominance and subordination will eventually work themselves out. Racial discrimination will become a thing of the past and truth will win out in the marketplace of ideas. Government's role is to remain formally

[66]109 S.Ct. 706 (1989).

[67]Except for Chief Justice Rehnquist, who joined the *Austin* majority but dissented in *Metro*, the voting breakdown in the two cases was identical.

neutral and to educate by its neutrality.[68] Justice Brennan's majority opinion in *Metro* implicitly rejects this model of formal neutrality and acknowledges the legitimacy of government's role in remedying existing inequities. And it does so in the name of speaker diversity as well as racial diversity.

Like the majority in *Austin*, the *Metro* majority perceives a market failure. The market alone does not ensure that the needs of the public are met. "[B]roadcast content is not purely market-driven."[69] The range of programming is determined as much by who owns the stations as by public needs. Because of the "barriers encountered by minorities in entering the broadcast industry,"[70] minorities are grossly underrepresented among owners of television and radio stations. Consequently the minority perspective is lacking in program content. The world that television and radio offer their audience is largely a white one.[71]

The *Metro* dissent did not contest this portrait. It did not matter to the dissenters that programming decisions lead to the dominance of the white speaker any more than it mattered to Justice Scalia in *Austin* that wealthy corporations talked too loudly. This was not something that government could correct by "burdening" the dominating voice. Justice O'Connor began her *Metro* dissent by contesting only the "compelling" nature of the diversity goal.[72] But, she was just warming up. Through the course of the opinion, she denied that it is "substantial."[73] By the end, diversity did not even qualify as a "legitimate" end of government.[74] Justice O'Connor is no longer merely denying its validity as a justification for affirmative action. "Even considered as other than a justification for using race classifications," she concluded, "the asserted interest in diversity of views falls short of being weighty enough."[75] We are in the First Amendment now. Justice O'Connor is questioning the validity of amplification of a dis-

[68]For a critique of the use of the model of formal equality to invalidate government efforts at affirmative action, see Karst, Private Discrimination and Public Responsibility: Patterson in Context, 1989 Supreme Court Review 1, 35–46.

[69]110 S.Ct. at 3012.

[70]*Id.* at 3012–13.

[71]*Id.* at 3020–21 (citing findings of Kerner Commission and United States Commission on Civil Rights).

[72]*Id.* at 3034 (O'Connor, J., dissenting).

[73]*Ibid.*

[74]*Id.* at 3036 (O'Connor, J., dissenting).

[75]*Ibid.*

tinct set of views or the views of a class of speakers quite apart from whether such a goal can carry a plan including racial preferences. Justice Kennedy was even harsher in his assessment, labeling the government's claim of a public interest in broadcast diversity as "trivial."[76]

The dissent's resistance to government amplification efforts in *Metro* mirrored Justice Scalia's concerns in *Austin*. First, the dissenters were troubled about the "facade" problem. Because diversity is amorphous and unverifiable, Justice O'Connor remarked, "it will prove impossible to distinguish naked preferences."[77] Justice Scalia's *Austin* dissent was similarly apprehensive. Perhaps the Michigan ban had a "noble" objective, he conceded. Then again, perhaps the Michigan legislature was trying to give unincorporated unions a political advantage over major employers, or perhaps it was acting on the knowledge that incumbent officeholders generally win with "balanced" presentations.[78]

It is easy to see why the dissenters might be troubled by such possibilities. Justice Brennan's assurance that an examination of legislative history will separate benign measures from malevolent ones[79] is not going to be very comforting to a group of justices who eschew inquiries into actual legislative motivation when plausible permissible purposes can be discerned from the face of a statute.[80] Thus, the only way to guarantee that legislatures will not misbehave is by ensuring that they do nothing.

Second, the dissenters in *Metro* were concerned about the selectivity of speaker diversity efforts—the underinclusion problem. Thus, just as Justice Scalia wondered in *Austin* about why rich and powerful newspapers are permitted to continue speaking in the wake of corporate restrictions,[81] Justice O'Connor, in *Metro*, questioned why the FCC has sought to amplify only one kind of diverse viewpoint.[82] Of course, neither Justice Scalia or Justice O'Connor would

---

[76]*Id.* at 3045 (Kennedy, J., dissenting).

[77]*Id.* at 3036 (O'Connor, J., dissenting). See also *id.* at 3046 (Kennedy, J., dissenting) ("Although the majority is 'confident' that it can determine when racial discrimination is benign . . . it offers no explanation as to how it will do so.").

[78]*Id.* at 1415 (Scalia, J., dissenting).

[79]*Metro*, 110 S.Ct. at 3008 n.12.

[80]See, *e.g.*, United States v. O'Brien, 391 U.S. 367 (1968); City of Renton v. Playtime Theaters, 475 U.S. 41, 47–48 (1986); Edwards v. Aguillard, 482 U.S. 578, 636–40 (1987) (Scalia, J., dissenting).

[81]110 S.Ct. at 1414–15 (Scalia, J., dissenting).

[82]*Id.* at 3038 (O'Connor, J., dissenting).

be receptive to greater efforts at promoting speaker diversity: their position is that government ought never to tone down or turn up the volume of particular speakers. The concern they articulate is more accurately one of impossibility—there is no way that anyone could ever achieve a balanced sound mix, so we are best off abandoning the effort.[83]

Third, the dissenters in *Metro* questioned the efficacy of the government's diversity effort. At least, if we are to risk the problems of facades and selectivity, we should be getting something in the bargain. The dissenters doubt that there are any real benefits. Will ownership diversity lead to the program diversity that the agency is after? The majority's response was largely the same it gave in *Austin*. It is adequate here that the "potential" for such diversity exists just as it sufficed in *Austin* that corporate use of treasury funds "potentially" distorted the political process.[84] The *Metro* majority acknowledged the absence of any "ironclad guarantee that each minority owner will contribute to diversity," but concluded that the expectation of Congress and the Commission that "in the aggregate" greater broadcast diversity will result is a logical one. A broadcast industry with greater minority participation "will produce more variation and diversity than will one whose ownership is drawn from a single racially and ethnically homogeneous group."[85]

The problem identified by the dissent here is one that is intrinsic to government sound mixing efforts. The ultimate goal is to expose the public to a broad diversity of speech, but the means used instead promotes a broader range of speakers. There will always, therefore, be the question of linkage. At one point in her *Metro* dissent Justice O'Connor implied that government might be more direct in its efforts. "The FCC," she said, "could directly advance its interest by requiring licensees to provide programming that the FCC believes would add to diversity."[86] But content regulation lies at the core of the First Amendment's prohibitory command, as Justice Brennan noted in his response. Direct control over programming, he admon-

---

[83]Alternatively, their argument might be seen as reflecting a concern about the government's motivation. If there are lots of equally worthy subjects for government sound mixing and the legislature has addressed only one, maybe something less benign than a diversity interest is at work. Justice Scalia's point about Michigan's disparate treatment of powerful labor unions and corporate employers suggests this argument.

[84]See note 38 *supra*.

[85]110 S.Ct. at 3016–17.

[86]110 S.Ct. at 3039 (O'Connor, J., dissenting).

ished, could raise "serious First Amendment issues."[87] One cannot help but have some sympathy with Justice O'Connor's reaction. The FCC and the Court, she observed, are trying to have it both ways. They assert a diversity goal alleged to serve important First Amendment interests and then justify its indirect means of speaker preference by invoking First Amendment impediments to direct programming control. If the First Amendment bars direct government efforts to diversify program content, then doesn't it equally preclude indirect methods of attaining the same goal? Either the end is legitimate or it is not.[88]

Justice O'Connor, however, overlooks the lesson of *Buckley*. Encouraging "the widest possible dissemination of information from diverse and antagonistic sources" is a central aim of the First Amendment. Once that is acknowledged, the fight only revolves around the permissible means.[89] *Buckley* permitted subsidies. It precluded expenditure limitations. *Austin* and *Metro* permit speaker classification in the pursuit of viewpoint diversity. They do not, however, condone viewpoint regulation. If government is to be permitted to encourage the diversity that *Buckley* admits it may seek, it will have to do so by indirectly focusing on the speaker rather than the speech. The crudeness of this proxy will inevitably lead to linkage questions. Will the corporate curbs in *Austin* lead to a more "balanced" presentation of political views? Will minority station owners safeguard the public's right to receive a diversity of views and information?[90] These are legitimate inquiries, but the indirect nature of the government's efforts ought not to condemn them.

A fourth and final objection to the FCC's amplification effort is only hinted at in Justice O'Connor's dissent. Promoting viewpoint diversity, she worried, has "no logical stopping point."[91] Justice Scalia's dissent in *Austin* sounded a similar note of alarm, calling

---

[87] *Id.* at 3019 n.36. Accord: Karst, note 30 *supra*, at 49 (continuing government surveillance over broadcast content presents grave dangers); Shiffrin, Government Speech, 27 UCLA L. Rev. 565, 596 n.162 (1980) (spectre of a Commission order that broadcasters must cover particular issues would surely raise grave constitutional questions).

[88] 110 S.Ct. at 3039 (O'Connor, J., dissenting).

[89] See note 33 *supra* and accompanying text.

[90] A comprehensive—although ultimately inconclusive—empirical examination of this question appears in Spitzer, Justifying Minority Preferences in Broadcasting, 64 So. Cal. L. Rev. 293 (1991).

[91] Although Justice O'Connor initially used this phrase in reference to racial preferences aimed at correcting societal discrimination, 110 S.Ct. at 3035, she later asserted that the interest in broadcast diversity "suffers from the same defects." *Id.* (O'Connor, J., dissenting).

Michigan's corporations the "first object" of Orwellian censorship.[92] These concerns are worthy of attention. A Court that wishes to travel down the road announced in *Austin* and *Metro* ought to give some thought to where it is headed.

III. Cabining the Concept

Justices Scalia and O'Connor raise the spectre of government sound mixing gone wild. First, legislatures restrict the campaign activity of the rich corporation. Is there any reason to stop with corporations? Wealth corrupts the electoral process even when it is individuals that are spending on behalf of political candidates. There is no need, however, to limit our efforts to candidate elections. The outcomes in ballot measure campaigns are also severely distorted by one-sided spending.[93] But, why stop here? Money is not the only resource that is unequally distributed and used to drown out other voices. Professor Sanford Levinson lists celebrity and disposable time as two other possibilities, and asks whether those motivated by egalitarian concerns can limit their attention only to *monetary* inequality affecting the electoral process.[94] And once we restrict the speech of some in order to enhance that of others, is there any reason to focus on the electoral process only? So, it's on to radio and television, and by now we're remedying white and male[95] domination of the electronic marketplace of ideas. Where will it all lead?

Political realism suggests that legislative pursuit of speaker diversity will be rare. The American experience with speech infringements is stocked with attempts to *suppress* dissent, not with efforts to promote it. We have learned to expect the majority's silencing of the unpopular voice. Few will be the instances that legislatures act on behalf of unheard or seldom heard voices and against dominant ones.[96] The feared implications of the view embraced in *Austin* and *Metro* may be more imagined than real. If resistance to efforts at pro-

---

[92] 110 S.Ct. at 1408 (Scalia, J., dissenting).

[93] See Lowenstein, note 37 *supra*.

[94] Levinson, Regulating Campaign Activity: The New Road to Corruption (Book Review), 83 Mich. L. Rev. 939, 948–49, 953 (1985).

[95] The FCC has a gender preference policy mirroring its racial "plus" factor for license applicants. The gender policy, however, was not before the Court in *Metro*. 110 S.Ct. at 3005 n.7.

[96] This political reality should caution us to remain vigilant lest legislation masquerading as protection of minority interests should in fact be something else. See Ely, Democracy and Distrust 172 (1980). Both Justices Scalia and O'Connor fear that the judiciary will be unable to distinguish the truly benign from the masquerade. See text accompanying notes 77–80 *supra*.

moting speaker diversity is to be prompted by a phobia of slippery slopes, the fear must be generated by more than hypothetical slides.

Even were we to acknowledge a substantial risk of legislative abuse of the diversity objective, however, it is not evident why this possibility should cause us to reject any instance of its invocation. This need not be an all-or-nothing proposition.[97] Many of the justices, like Scalia and O'Connor, who opt for "nothing" reveal a lack of faith in the Court's ability to draw boundaries. To a large degree, their concerns prove too much. The persistent fear of First Amendment absolutists that approving a single instant of government speech suppression inevitably leads to untrammeled censorship has not deterred the Court from condoning legislative limitations on obscenity, child pornography, false speech, and the advocacy of illegal action. Neither Justice Scalia nor Justice O'Connor has resisted such bans for fear of judicial inability to articulate a stopping point.

As the preceding pages reveal, the Court no longer views restrictions placed on some speakers in order to enhance the relative voice of others as invariably impermissible. But the concerns of Justices O'Connor and Scalia, as well as those of thoughtful scholars like Scot Powe and Sanford Levinson,[98] suggest the need for a cabining principle. There is no effort in either *Austin* or *Metro* to propose such a stopping point. Indeed, the absence of a single citation to *Austin* in *Metro* hints that the Court either is unaware of the common path it is following in the two opinions or is presently content to endorse such sound mixing on an *ad hoc* basis.[99]

Lack of imagination, limited foresight, a shortage of space and a degree of humility preclude a detailed proposal here of any comprehensive cabining principle. What follows is neither offered as description of what the justices themselves revealed nor as fully embraced normative vision. It does seem to me, however, that if the Court continues along the unpaved route seen this Term, it will be incumbent on all of us in the legal profession to tender some guide-

[97]Accord: Karst, note 30 *supra*, at 48 (absence of obvious stopping-place for claim to access to broadcast media need not prevent the Court from drawing any boundary at all).

[98]See generally Powe, note 2 *supra*; Levinson, note 94 *supra*.

[99]There is admittedly an argument to be made for an *ad hoc* approach. If one is willing to regard the promotion of speaker diversity as a valid end in any case, the government might be permitted to successfully pursue such a goal—assuming the absence of a facade problem—anytime it can [1] make a case for the efficacy of its effort; [2] establish that it has imposed no greater burden on the stifled speaker than is necessary to prevent its domination; and [3] convince the Court that the need for sound mixing outweighs the speech restrictions imposed. Because I believe that categorical lines are less open to manipulation than case-by-case balancing, I am sympathetic to the need for a cabining principle.

posts. I offer Part III of this article as no more than a focal point for beginning to think about the possibilities.

One might well imagine a number of potential cabining principles. The scarcity rationale, invoked to distinguish *Red Lion* from cases like *Tornillo*,[100] *Buckley*,[101] and *Pacific Gas & Electric*,[102] was an early attempt to cabin diversification efforts. It has, however, become technologically antiquated and does not begin to explain *Austin*.

Alternatively, one could seek to confine government sound mixing to situations of market failure. This framework neatly fits both *Austin* and *Metro*. But the questionable ability of courts to identify a "properly functioning marketplace,"[103] and the myriad instances in which legislatures might in good faith be able to point to market failure, suggest that a cabining principle along such lines may not prove terribly cabining.

The most inviting possibility for someone, like myself, who is sympathetic to a "representation-reinforcement" vision of the judicial role[104] might be a multi-tiered approach to speaker classifications. It seems entirely appropriate that judicial resistance to government enhancement efforts should increase in direct response to the relative insularity and unpopularity of the muted speakers. Such an extension of *Carolene Products* footnote 4[105] has already been anticipated and condemned by Scot Powe.[106] His objections merit consideration. Chief among these is his allegation that the specific command of the First Amendment is designed to place the substantive value of uninhibited speech beyond the purview of the ordinary operations of the political process, a position that he contends is embraced by both Justice Stone and John Ely.[107] The notion that our vision of free speech should be informed by other democratic values,

---

[100]418 U.S. 241 (1974). See Powe, Tornillo, 1987 Supreme Court Review 345.

[101]424 U.S. 1, 49 n.55 (1976).

[102]Pacific Gas & Electric Co. v. Public Utilities Comm'n, 106 S.Ct. 903, 908 n.6 (1986).

[103]See Baker, Realizing Self-Realization: Corporate Political Expenditures and Redish's "The Value of Free Speech," 130 U. Pa. L. Rev. 646, 651 & n.21 (1982).

[104]See Eule, *supra* note 46, at 1525 n.91 (1990).

[105]See United States v. Carolene Products, 304 U.S. 144, 152 n.4 (1938) (articulating justifications for departing from presumption of constitutionality ordinarily due legislative enactments).

[106]See Powe, note 2 *supra*, at 282 n.116.

[107]It is not at all clear that Powe correctly captures Ely's position. See Ely, note 96 *supra*, at 93–94 (primary function of First Amendment is to help make our governmental processes work; view that free expression *per se*, without regard to what it means to the process of government, is our preeminent right has highly elitist cast).

however, is not so preposterous as Powe would have us believe. The First Amendment is not a constitutional island. Further, there is substantial dispute over whether the free speech guarantee serves principally as an instrument for the enhancement of the political process[108] or should be imbued with some intrinsic value independent of its role in informing the electorate and checking the governors.[109]

Here is not the place to add my voice to this debate. How one comes out on this dispute may well predetermine the general appeal of a footnote 4 cabining principle. But, at least for one group of speakers—the corporate speaker—it turns out to be largely irrelevant which side of the discourse has the upper hand. The commercial corporation *both* distorts the political process and proves a poor candidate for concerns about self-realization and self-fulfillment.[110]

The framers of the First Amendment could scarcely have anticipated its application to the corporate form. That, of course, ought not to be dispositive. What is compelling, however, is an understanding of who was supposed to be the beneficiary of the free speech guaranty—the individual. The Court assumed in cases like *Bellotti* and *Pacific Gas & Electric* that the scope of the First Amendment's protection could be extended to new entities without impairing its value to the original beneficiaries. In *Bellotti* it finessed its conclusion by characterizing the First Amendment interest protected as the individual's right to be informed,[111] but *Pacific Gas & Electric* was a bolder stroke. There the Court recognized a public utility's First Amendment right not to carry a consumer group's insert in its billing envelope. By conferring negative speech rights—the right not to speak—on the corporate entity, the Court blessed it with a status indistinguishable from that of the natural person. In doing so, the Court impeded rather than enhanced the information flow to the public. The Court, of course, did not initially see it that way. But, its vision was clouded by two fictions—that corporations and individuals have equal opportunities to acquire the resources needed to send their messages to market, and that the marketplace contains un-

[108] See generally Meiklejohn, Free Speech and Its Relation to Self-Government (1948); Blasi, The Checking Value in First Amendment Theory, 1977 ABF Res. J. 521.

[109] See Baker, Scope of the First Amendment Freedom of Speech, 25 UCLA L. Rev. 964 (1978).

[110] See generally Schneider, Free Speech and Corporate Freedom: A Comment on First National Bank of Boston v. Bellotti, 59 S. Cal. L. Rev. 1227 (1986); Baker, note 103 *supra*.

[111] 435 U.S. 765, 777 (1978).

limited shelf space. In *Austin*, the Court rejects both myths—the first explicitly,[112] the second more tacitly.[113] Conferring full speech rights on corporate entities inevitably diminishes the value of those rights to natural persons. The Court has not put either *Bellotti* or *Pacific Gas & Electric* to bed, but it is surely finished reciting the fairy tale.

Austin does not spell the end of speech protection for the corporate entity,[114] but the Court now seems prepared to recognize that when government seeks to promote speaker diversity there are First Amendment values on *both* sides of the equation.[115] No matter how we may balance the competing interests in other instances, *Austin* suggests that at least when corporations sit on one side of the scale and natural persons on the other, ordinarily the First Amendment may best be served by coming down on the side of the Amendment's intended beneficiaries.[116]

It is easier to cabin *Austin* than *Metro* on such a principle. After all, *Metro* is not a case about corporate speech rights. Indeed, it is not literally a speech case at all. But, on two levels, the result in *Metro* is consistent with an understanding that indiscriminately extending the full umbrella of a constitutional protection beyond its intended beneficiaries may seriously undermine the clause's original premise.

On the most obvious level, *Metro* signifies a triumph of the view that affording whites the identical degree of judicial scrutiny made available to blacks under the Equal Protection Clause may diminish legislative ability to protect the Clause's historical beneficiaries. The Equal Protection Clause was no more designed by its drafters to protect the white majority than the First Amendment was enacted to

---

[112]See text accompanying notes 35–36 *supra*.

[113]The Court's "distortion" and "domination" imagery, see 110 S.Ct. at 1397, is somewhat ambiguous but it is more difficult to conceptualize distortion and domination in an infinite market.

[114]No doubt Chief Justice Rehnquist joined *Austin* in the hope that it would be the first step in this direction. *See* First National Bank v. Bellotti, 435 U.S. 765, 822 (1978) (Rehnquist, J., dissenting); Pacific Gas & Electric Co. v. Public Utilities Comm'n, 475 U.S. 1, 26 (1986) (Rehnquist, J., dissenting).

[115]Justice White was well ahead of his colleagues here. See First Nat'l Bank of Boston v. Bellotti, 435 U.S. at 803–4 (1978) (White, J., dissenting) (Massachusetts' interest in limiting corporate speech is itself grounded in First Amendment and Court must decide whether State has correctly struck the balance between competing First Amendment interests). See also Schneider, note 110 *supra*, at 1269 (*Bellotti* presents situation where First Amendment interests are present on both sides).

[116]But see FEC v. Massachusetts Citizens for Life, Inc., 479 U.S. 238 (1986) (invalidating a prohibition against corporate political expenditures as applied to a nonprofit corporation formed solely for the promotion of political ideas).

shield the corporation from government regulation. I do not for one moment mean to suggest that courts should be constrained by some narrow conception of original intent in defining the scope of any constitutional provision, nor that classifications disadvantaging whites should be beyond the ambit of the Equal Protection Clause. Either proposition would be fundamentally unsound and extremely unwise. But when we expand the scope of a clause's coverage—and do so without sufficient sensitivity to the degree of coverage conferred—we must be aware, as several of the members of *Metro*'s majority seem to be, that you can't always give to Paul without taking away from Peter.[117] Conferring equal treatment to those with unequal resources will often deny the politically and economically weaker class its share of a finite pie.

But, as I have already argued, *Metro* was more than an equal protection case. The plaintiffs seeking relief from the Court were white-owned *corporations* and the domination of white views that the FCC was seeking to remedy was one principally proffered by business corporations.[118] Furthermore, the corporate domination of the airwaves is even more attributable to government largess than the electoral distortion noted in *Austin*. As Steven Shiffrin has pointed out, "the government appoints a corporation to manage a station reaching millions of people and grants the corporation virtually unfettered discretion to decide what issues will be discussed and who will discuss them."[119] The result in *Red Lion*, relied on so heavily by the *Metro* majority, admittedly did not rest on the corporate character of those whose speech rights were impaired, but it is surely one way to think about the case. As with *Austin*, there were First Amendment interests on both sides of the *Red Lion* equation and the decision weighed in on behalf of the individual's right to be informed by a diversity of views rather than with the speech interests of the corporate speaker.

---

[117]This view accurately characterizes the position of only three members of the *Metro* majority—Marshall, Brennan, and Blackmun—who consistently prefer a lower level scrutiny for benign racial preferences that have the effect of disadvantaging whites. See City of Richmond v. J.A. Croson Co,, 109 S.Ct. 706, 752 (Marshall, J., with whom Brennan, J., and Blackmun, J., join dissenting).

[118]Admittedly, the fact that one plaintiff—Shurberg Broadcasting, Inc.—was a one-man corporation, 110 S.Ct. at 3007 n.10, and the other plaintiff—Faith Center, Inc.—was a corporation with a religious mission, makes this case a somewhat unnatural one for the application of the principle I suggest. However, in contrast to the "as-applied" challenge of the Michigan Chamber of Commerce in *Austin*, see 110 S.Ct. at 1398, plaintiffs' challenge in *Metro* was strictly a facial one.

[119]Shiffrin, The First Amendment, Democracy and Romance 99 (1990).

The vast majority of the speakers disadvantaged by the regulations at issue in *Metro* might be said therefore to have historically benefited from a dual advantage—their corporate form and their white ownership.[120] Whether the challenge to the FCC's promotion of speaker diversity ultimately is styled as a bid for formal racial equality, which it clearly was in *Metro*, or as the speech infringement claim that Justice O'Connor hints might have been present,[121] the arguments rely on constitutional provisions not originally designed for the protection of this class of plaintiffs. That, as I have earlier noted, is hardly dispositive. What makes the claim perverse here, however, is that both constitutional provisions are invoked to the substantial detriment of their intended beneficiaries.

My suggestion that *Austin* and *Metro* might be susceptible of cabining along lines like these would be highly praised by being called half-baked. As previously noted, I have have no greater ambition in proposing these possibilities than to provide a starting point for discourse. On a practical level, wrestling with a cabining concept may be time poorly spent. With Justice Brennan's departure from the Court, only four of the current justices favor the FCC promotion of racially diverse voices. Although there remains a bare majority in support of Michigan's effort to constrain the use of treasury funds by corporate speakers, Justice Stevens is a soft vote.[122] Even if Justice Souter does not prompt a swift reversal of either precedent, it is unlikely that we shall witness their extension in the near future. For the time being, therefore, the answer to the question of where the Court's newfound willingness to tolerate the promotion of speaker diversity will ultimately lead may be as simple as "*Austin* and *Metro* and no further."

---

[120]True, Congress and the FCC did not justify the minority ownership policy "*strictly*" as a remedy for victims of racial discrimination. 110 S.Ct. at 3010 (emphasis supplied). But, as the Court noted, Congress believed that the "severe underrepresentation of minorities in the media of mass communications" was indeed attributable to "the effects of past inequities stemming from racial and ethnic discrimination." *Id.* at 3009–10. The FCC's role, if any, in this discriminatory history is less certain. *See* Spitzer, *supra* note 90, at 295 n.9.

[121]*See* 110 S.Ct. at 3036 (O'Connor, J., dissenting).

[122]See note 21 *supra*.

PAUL B. STEPHAN III

INTERNATIONAL LAW IN THE SUPREME COURT

Although the Constitution assigns to Congress the power "[t]o define and punish . . . Offenses against the Law of Nations,"[1] the Supreme Court long has played a major role in developing the body of international norms to which our government adheres. The Court does this by adducing principles of international obligation that it can assimilate into federal common law, by constructing doctrines derived from international law that can limit common law and statutory claims, and by using international law to guide its interpretation of statutes and the Constitution. Specialists might dispute whether such cases constitute "international law"—although inspired by international norms, the results bind only United States lawmakers—but no one can doubt that these decisions are the principal means by which international law becomes effective and consequential for most persons subject to United States jurisdiction.

The structural point—that the Supreme Court looks to international law in the course of performing its duties—seems uncontroversial, but the substantive outcomes are often disappointing. Three illustrative cases—two from the past Term, one from the Term before—are *Argentine Republic v. Amerada Hess Shipping Corporation*,[2] *W.S. Kirkpatrick & Co. v. Environmental Tectonics Corp.*,[3]

Paul B. Stephan III is Percy Brown, Jr. Professor of Law, University of Virginia.

AUTHOR'S NOTE: I am indebted to Glen O. Robinson, Robert E. Scott, Don Wallace, Jr., and David Westin for comments and criticisms. Any errors or misjudgments remain my own.

[1] U.S. Const. art. I, §8, cl. 10.

[2] 488 U.S. 428 (1989).

[3] 110 S.Ct. 701 (1990).

0-226-09573-8/91/1990-0007$02.00

and *United States v. Verdugo-Urquidez*.[4] *Hess* held that allegations that a foreign state violated international law cannot supersede the limitations on court jurisdiction established by the Foreign Sovereign Immunities Act (FSIA). *Verdugo-Urquidez* held that nonresident aliens (and their property) found outside the United States enjoy no protection under the Fourth Amendment; a contrary holding would have opened the door to the absorption of international human rights norms into constitutional doctrine. *Kirkpatrick*, the third case, rejected claims of international comity and due respect for the official acts of foreign governments and permitted our government to impose its own (perhaps parochial) judgments about business ethics on transactions involving foreign governments.

These cases contradict one approach to international law, long prevalent in the United States international law community and occasionally embraced by the Court. Historically, many have seen international law as a species of natural law—a morally unified body of precepts emanating from a basic conception of justice. The recent decisions, at best, manifest indifference toward this vision of a priori norms.

Instead, *Hess*, *Kirkpatrick*, and particularly *Verdugo-Urquidez* advance a conception of international law as a body of contingent principles derived from intergovernmental bargaining. This approach, supported by the insights of modern contracts scholarship, sees the Court as principally promoting international bargaining and cooperation, not coercing governments to reach particular outcomes. It expects the Supreme Court to reassure the other branches of government both that bargains struck will have legal consequences, and that the courts will not substitute new or different obligations for those accepted by the political branches.

I

A

The source and scope of immunity accorded foreign states has vexed the Supreme Court for the better part of two centuries. Before 1976 the issue was entirely a matter of federal common law. In *The Schooner Exchange v. McFaddon*,[5] Chief Justice Marshall recognized a

---

[4] 110 S.Ct. 1056 (1990).

[5] 7 Cranch 116 (1812).

French naval vessel's immunity from a libel. In this century, the Court first ruled that foreign states enjoyed absolute immunity from all claims in the United States courts, but in 1943, in *Ex Parte Peru*[6] the Court held that the executive branch has the authority to override this immunity. In 1952 the State Department announced that it would follow the "restrictive theory" of sovereign immunity, which permitted recognition of a "commercial exception" allowing litigants to sue foreign states for claims arising from business activity in which foreign states had engaged. Finally, Congress in 1976 enacted the FSIA to codify the exceptions to foreign state immunity and to eliminate the executive branch's role in resolving the cases. But because of the long tradition of common law development, members of the United States international law community tend to regard the FSIA more as a memorial of the doctrine's evolution than as a definitive legislative resolution of all issues concerning foreign sovereign immunity.[7]

Hess gave the Court its first opportunity to consider the scope of the FSIA's exceptions to sovereign immunity.[8] Hess owned an oil tanker that the Argentine military had attacked during the Falklands War, allegedly in violation of the rules of war and other international law norms. The ship contained oil destined for the United States but the bombing took place in international waters off the coast of Brazil. Hess sued the Argentine Republic under the Alien Tort Statute (ATS), a hoary and, until recently, moribund provision that gives federal courts "original jurisdiction of any civil action by an alien for a tort only, committed in violation of the law of nations or a treaty of the United States."[9] Hess claimed that the use of force outside the declared area of combat constituted an actionable breach of "the law

---

[6]318 U.S. 578 (1943).

[7]See generally Restatement (Third) of the Foreign Relations Law of the United States §§451–60 (1987); Born & Westin, International Civil Litigation in United States Courts—Commentary and Materials 335–402 (1989). The Restatement, while conceding that the "Foreign Sovereign Immunities Act is law of the United States," I Restatement, *supra*, at 395, does not exactly track the language of the Act and strongly hints that courts should remain free to follow customary international law in cases where the Act does not explicitly resolve an issue. For criticism of an earlier draft of the Foreign Sovereign Immunities Act on the ground that it did not give sufficient sway to the common law powers of courts, see Lillich, The Proper Role of Domestic Courts in the International Legal Order, 11 Va. J. Int'l L. 9, 27 (1970).

[8]In Verlinden B.V. v. Central Bank of Nigeria, 461 U.S. 480 (1983), the Court held that the FSIA permitted foreign plaintiffs to sue foreign sovereigns in United States courts, and that the exercise of such jurisdiction did not violate Article III of the Constitution. In First National City Bank v. Banco Para El Comercio Exterior de Cuba, 462 U.S. 611 (1983), the Court ruled that in applying the FSIA's commercial exception, courts could pierce the corporate veil.

[9]28 U.S.C. §1350.

of nations."[10] The Second Circuit previously had held that the ATS provided a substantive cause of action in federal courts for claims based on violations of international law.[11] In *Hess*, it extended that ruling by holding that the FSIA did not apply to suits grounded on the ATS.[12]

The Supreme Court unanimously rejected the Second Circuit's conclusion. Chief Justice Rehnquist's opinion reasoned that because the FSIA explicitly withdrew immunity for international law violations involving the taking of property, Congress must have meant to preserve immunity in all other cases not covered by the Act's exceptions. The Court also noted that no court of appeals had discovered a cause of action within the ATS until five years after Congress had enacted the FSIA. The Court concluded that Congress could not have intended to carve out an implicit exception to foreign sovereign immunity for suits under such a dormant statute.

After determining that no plaintiff could sue a foreign state without complying with the FSIA, the Court held that none of the Act's express exceptions applied to Hess's claim against Argentina. In particular, 28 U.S.C. §1605(a)(5), which allows suits for noncommercial torts occurring in the United States, did not cover Hess's claim. The Court viewed the tort as having occurred on the high seas, even though the bombing may have led to economic injury in the domestic oil market. The high seas, although subject to United States admiralty jurisdiction, did not constitute the "continental and insular" territory of the United States, and thus were not "in" the United States.[13]

Hess does not bar the door to all international tort claims in United States courts. First, the Court has not yet decided whether the ATS creates a general cause of action for persons injured by violations of international law. Were the Court to adopt that view, it might assimi-

---

[10]The alleged war crime was essential to Hess's case, because United States law does not recognize any duty to compensate for property destroyed in the course of legitimate military operations. See United States v. Caltex, 344 U.S. 149 (1952).

[11]The earlier case, Filartiga v. Peña-Irala, 630 F.2d 876 (2d Cir. 1980), involved allegations of torture by a Paraguayan police official. Although Peña-Irala had acted in his official capacity, the plaintiff had not included the Paraguayan government as a defendant. The District of Columbia Circuit and the Seventh Circuit, in alternate holdings of decisions grounded on the Foreign Sovereign Immunities Act, have rejected Filartiga's interpretation of the Alien Tort Statute. Tel-Oren v. Libyan Arab Republic, 726 F.2d 774 (D.C. Cir. 1984), cert. denied, 470 U.S. 1003 (1985); Frolova v. Union of Soviet Socialist Republics, 761 F.2d 370 (7th Cir. 1985).

[12]Amerada Hess Shipping Corp. v. Argentine Republic, 830 F.2d 421 (2d Cir. 1987).

[13]Justices Marshall and Blackmun did not join the Court's opinion as to the scope of the FSIA's exceptions.

late the doctrines used in the analogous area of Eleventh Amendment immunity. These cases permit most suits against government officials, even if the underlying claim stems only from the exercise of their official responsibilities.[14] Second, the FSIA does allow suits against foreign sovereigns for misconduct within United States territory, although plaintiffs may need to characterize the wrongful acts as violations of domestic criminal or tort rules rather than as breaches of the law of nations actionable under the ATS.[15]

Yet *Hess* must discourage those who hope to see the United States courts take an active role in creating international norms.[16] Not only does the substantive outcome make it harder to prosecute international- law-based claims, but the decision's structural underpinning implies a significant restraint on judicial power. At bottom, *Hess* held that the power of Congress "to define . . . Offenses against the Law of Nations" trumps judicial authority to assimilate international norms into domestic law. One might squint hard to find some limits on the judiciary's obligation to defer to Congress—the international law violation alleged in *Hess* did not involve genocide, torture, or comparable higher-order misconduct—but the Court did not suggest any such reservation.[17]

---

[14]See Home Telephone & Telegraph Co. v. City of Los Angeles, 227 U.S. 278 (1913); Ex parte Young, 209 U.S. 123 (1908); *cf.* Will v. Michigan Dept. of State Police, 109 S.Ct. 2304 (1989); Quern v. Jordan, 440 U.S. 332 (1979).

[15]*Cf.* Liu v. Republic of China, 892 F.2d 1419 (9th Cir. 1989).

[16]Before *Hess*, several scholars had argued that the FSIA should not obstruct claims arising under the Alien Tort Statute. See Bayzler, Litigating the International Law of Human Rights: A "How to" Approach, 7 Whittier L. Rev. 713, 732–34 (1985); Lillich, Invoking International Human Rights Law in Domestic Courts, 54 U. Cin. L. Rev. 367, 413 n.220 (1985); Paust, Federal Jurisdiction over Extraterritorial Acts of Terrorism and Nonimmunity for Foreign Violators of International Law under the FSIA and the Act of State Doctrine, 23 Va. J. Int'l L. 191 (1983); Document—Draft Brief Covering Claims to Foreign Sovereign Immunity and Human Rights: Nonimmunity for Violations of International Law Under the FSIA, 8 Houston J. Int'l L. 49 (1985); Randall, Federal Jurisdiction over International Law Claims: Inquiries into the Alien Tort Statute (II), 18 NYU J. Int'l L. & Pol'y 473, 509 (1985). For articulation of the view ultimately adopted by the Court, see Kirgis, Alien Tort Claims, Sovereign Immunity and International Law in U.S. Courts, 82 Am. J. Int'l L. 323 (1988).

[17]Some scholars have argued that international law consists of hierarchies, the highest level of which consists of norms that nations must observe regardless of a state's consent. See Hartman, Derogation from Human Rights Treaties in Public Emergencies, 22 Harv. J. Int'l L. 1, 15 (1981); Lobel, The Limits of Constitutional Power: Conflicts Between Foreign Policy and International Law, 71 Va. L. Rev. 1071, 1074–75 (1985); Parker & Neylon, Jus Cogens: Compelling the Law of Human Rights, 12 Hastings Int'l & Comp. L. Rev. 411 (1989); Randall, Federal Questions and the Human Rights Paradigm, 73 Minn. L. Rev. 349 (1988); *cf.* Committee of United States Citizens Living in Nicaragua v. Reagan, 859 F.2d 929, 935–36 (D.C. Cir. 1988). Although a prohibition of genocide and torture often tops the list, so does the ban on war crimes, which Argentina allegedly transgressed when without provocation it bombed Hess's ship outside the announced area of combat.

B

The act of state doctrine is a judge-made rule that compels a United States court to help implement an official act that a foreign state performed within its own territory. The leading modern case, *Banco Nacional de Cuba v. Sabbatino*,[18] required a United States buyer to pay to an instrumentality of the Cuban government, rather than to the original seller, money owed on the purchase of sugar. The buyer had bought the sugar from a private company owned by United States citizens, but before delivery Castro's revolutionary government had confiscated it. The Court acknowledged that the seizure may have violated international law, but it declared that the act of state doctrine required a United States court to give effect to a taking of property by a foreign government within its own territory "in the absence of a treaty or other unambiguous agreement regarding controlling legal principles."[19]

Both the foundation and purpose of the doctrine are somewhat obscure. The earlier cases suggested that it rested on notions of international comity: The United States agreed to respect the official acts of other states, taken within their jurisdiction, in the expectation that other nations would reciprocate. Justice Harlan's opinion for the Court in *Sabbatino*, however, stated that the doctrine had "'constitutional' underpinnings" although neither international law nor the Constitution compelled it.[20] Were the Court to pick and choose among foreign official acts that it would recognize, Justice Harlan reasoned, it would encroach upon the executive branch's constitutional responsibility to conduct foreign relations.

Sabbatino provoked immediate opposition in Congress, which enacted the Second Hickenlooper Amendment to eliminate use of the doctrine in expropriation cases.[21] In two subsequent decisions the Court refused to apply the out-of-state principles, but in neither instance could a majority agree why.[22] Lower courts have responded

---

[18] 376 U.S. 398 (1964).

[19] *Id.* at 428.

[20] *Id.* at 423.

[21] 22 U.S.C. §2370(e)(2); see Restatement (Third) of the Foreign Relations Law of the United States §444 (1987). The Amendment does permit the executive branch to override the command to adjudicate by determining that the foreign policy interests of the United States require application of the act of state doctrine. The First Hickenlooper Amendment, enacted in 1962, directed the President to withhold foreign aid from countries (primarily Cuba) that confiscated United States property in violation of international law. 22 U.S.C. §2370(e)(1).

[22] Alfred Dunhill of London, Inc. v. Republic of Cuba, 425 U.S. 682 (1976); First National City Bank v. Banco Nacional de Cuba, 406 U.S. 759 (1972).

with confusion, and commentators have attacked the doctrine, some calling for its outright repudiation.[23]

The act of state doctrine serves many functions: It can negate a challenge to property rights;[24] it can insulate a foreign government's human rights violations from judicial review;[25] and it can take a transaction out of the ambit of a United States statutory rule.[26] The first two functions can force a court to reject international law-based challenges to the acts of another nation, and thus may frustrate the development of international law norms by United States courts.[27] But deployed to temper the international scope of United States legislation, the doctrine furthers rather than hinders international cooperation and norm building. It gives courts a basis for modifying United States rules affecting international commerce, such as the securities laws and the Sherman Act, in light of the regulatory systems of other nations. Such modifications reduce the instances in which international businesses face the dilemma of complying with the prescriptions of another sovereign, acting within its own jurisdiction, only at the cost of violating United States law. Unable themselves to assert the foreign sovereign immunity defense, these businesses, without the act of state doctrine, could avoid the consequences of United States rules only by severing all contacts with our country and by keeping all their assets overseas.

In spite of the potential benefits, *Kirkpatrick*, the first act-of-state decision since *Sabbatino* to command a majority of the Court, may have ended the statute-limiting function of the act of state doctrine. Environmental Tectonics, a frustrated bidder, sued Kirkpatrick, a company that had bribed its way into a Nigerian government construction contract. Environmental Tectonics contended that the bribes violated the Foreign Corrupt Practices Act (FCPA),[28] a federal criminal statute, and that these violations constituted a "pattern of

[23]See Restatement (Third) of the Foreign Relations Law of the United States §443 (1987); Born & Westin, note 7 *supra*, at 489–560.

[24]*E.g.*, Banco Nacional de Cuba v. Sabbatino, 376 U.S. 398 (1964); Ricaud v. American Metal Co., 246 U.S. 304 (1918); Oetjen v. Central Leather Co., 246 U.S. 297 (1918).

[25]*Cf.* Underhill v. Hernandez, 168 U.S. 250 (1897).

[26]See O.N.E. Shipping v. Flota Mercante Grancolombiana, 830 F.2d 449 (2d Cir. 1987); Clayco Petroleum Corp. v. Occidental Petroleum Corp., 712 F.2d 404 (9th Cir. 1983), cert. denied, 464 U.S. 1040 (1984); IAM v. OPEC, 649 F.2d 1354 (9th Cir. 1981), cert. denied, 454 U.S. 1163 (1983); Industrial Inv. Dev. Corp. v. Mitsui & Co., 594 F.2d 48 (5th Cir. 1979), cert. denied, 445 U.S. 903 (1980); *cf.* Born & Westin, note 7 *supra*, at 516.

[27]*E.g.*, Lillich, note 7 *supra*, at 36–37.

[28]15 U.S.C. §§78dd-1, -2.

racketeering activity" within the ambit of the civil remedies portion of the Racketeering Influenced Organizations Act (RICO).[29] Kirkpatrick responded by invoking the act of state doctrine. It argued that a finding that the Nigerian contract rested on a bribe in effect would invalidate a public act of a foreign sovereign. The Third Circuit ruled that Environmental Tectonics could use RICO to enforce a FCPA claim and rejected Kirkpatrick's act of state defense.[30]

Justice Scalia, writing for a unanimous Court, agreed that the act of state doctrine did not bar Environmental Tectonics' RICO claim. The case, he concluded, involved facts predicate to a finding of invalidity rather than the actual invalidation of a governmental act. That is, although a determination that Kirkpatrick had paid a bribe might, if accepted by a Nigerian tribunal in a subsequent proceeding, lead to cancellation of the contract, Environmental Tectonic's suit by itself would not undo the contract award.[31] The Court rejected the position advanced by the Solicitor General: that the doctrine should apply to cases involving predicate findings of invalidity as well as to the direct invalidation of official acts, but that the executive branch should have the power to override the doctrine if it believed the suit did not implicate any foreign policy concern of the United States.[32]

Although the Court did not consider whether persons injured by a FCPA violation may seek damages under RICO, the outcome in *Kirkpatrick*, at least for now, has the effect of vitalizing the FCPA.[33] A firm seeking to do business with foreign governments will regard the possibility of RICO damages as a substantial deterrent, additional to the risk of criminal prosecution under the FCPA. Civil plaintiffs face a lower burden of proof than do criminal prosecutors; the exercise of the executive branch's prosecutorial discretion will not screen out

---

[29] 18 U.S.C. §§1962–68.

[30] 847 F.2d 1052 (3d Cir. 1988).

[31] 110 S.Ct. at 705.

[32] In First National City Bank v. Banco Nacional de Cuba, 406 U.S. 759 (1972), three members of the Court had embraced a rule, originally developed in the lower courts, that delegated to the executive branch the power to invoke the doctrine. See Bernstein v. N.V. Nederlandsche-Amerikaansche Stoomvaart-Maatschappij, 210 F.2d 375 (2d Cir. 1954). The Second Hickenlooper Amendment takes a parallel approach, allowing the executive branch to revive an act of state defense in cases where it believes foreign policy interests require such action. See note 21 *supra*. The executive branch exercised similar control over foreign sovereign immunity from 1943 until 1976. See note 21 *supra* and accompanying text.

[33] Lawsuits such as Environmental Tectonics's still might fail, if the Court ultimately were to hold either that a Foreign Corrupt Practices Act violation does not constitute the "pattern of racketeering activity" required to make out a RICO claim, or that persons who lose a bid do not have injuries of the sort for which RICO provides compensation.

embarrassing or problematic suits; and Congress designed RICO's damages rules to encourage bounty seekers.

This additional deterrent makes bidding on foreign government contracts more costly for firms covered by the FCPA. In many cases foreign states will end up absorbing some of these costs. Any fall off in competition for these contracts should raise the remaining contractors' bids, and those United States firms with a sufficient competitive advantage to continue to seek foreign government work probably have the capacity to pass through a portion of the risk premium.

It is by no means obvious that Congress intended to inflict such a burden on foreign governments. The FCPA itself, by not providing for private enforcement, limits most of these costs. The act of state doctrine, applied to cases such as *Kirkpatrick*, might preserve that result—prosecutions of United States firms and citizens could proceed, but foreign government buyers would not pay for what might be RICO's overdeterrence of wrongful behavior.[34]

By rejecting this application of the doctrine, the Court sacrificed respect for the legitimate interests of other nations—here controlling the cost of government procurement—in favor of reinforcing the unilateral conception of international business ethics embodied in the FCPA. Of course, the door remains open for the Court to deal with the problem directly by interpreting RICO and the FCPA restrictively. But by not using the act of state doctrine in a case where the ultimate issue rested on a predicate finding about the validity of a foreign official act, the Court lost an opportunity more generally to restrict the assertion of United States regulatory jurisdiction over foreign transactions.

C

The last case in the trilogy, *Verdugo-Urquidez*, involves the most fundamental questions concerning the relationship between international and domestic law. During the mid-1970s a few lower courts had held that aliens residing outside the territory of the United States could claim the benefit of United States constitutional protection of

[34]The Foreign Corrupt Practices Act does not criminalize the conduct of foreign citizens that accept bribes, and a conviction does not require proof that the bribe paid by a United States citizen or firm was accepted or, if accepted, affected an official act. See 15 U.S.C. §§78dd-1, -2.

individual liberties.[35] Several commentators celebrated these rulings, in part because they provided a doctrinal basis for assimilating international human rights norms into United States constitutional law.[36] Although its older decisions seemed inconsistent with this development, the Court had not considered the issue since the criminal procedure revolution of the 1950s and 1960s.[37] *Verdugo-Urquidez* finally provided that opportunity.

Mexican police apprehended Verdugo-Urquidez in response to a United States arrest warrant and handed him over to United States authorities. While he remained in a United States jail, Drug Enforcement Agency officers, acting with the Mexican police, carried out a warrantless search of his Mexican residences and seized various incriminating documents. The lower courts ordered suppression of this evidence on the ground that the warrantless searches in Mexico violated Verdugo-Urquidez's Fourth Amendment protection.

Five Justices held unequivocally that Verdugo-Urquidez, although detained against his will in the United States, did not qualify as a "resident" of this country and therefore enjoyed no Fourth Amendment protection as to the overseas acts of the government.[38] Chief Justice Rehnquist, writing for the majority, focused on the language of the Fourth Amendment, which refers to the right of the

[35]See United States v. Toscanino, 500 F.2d 267 (2d Cir. 1974); United States v. Tiede, 86 F.R.D. 227 (U.S. Ct. Berlin 1979); Stephan, Constitutional Limits on the Struggle Against International Terrorism: Revisiting the Rights of Overseas Aliens, 19 Conn. L. Rev. 831, 842–45 (1987).

[36]See Henkin, The Constitution as Compact and as Conscience: Individual Rights Abroad and at Our Gates, 27 Wm. & Mary L. Rev. 11 (1985); Lobel, The Constitution Abroad, 83 Am. J. Int'l. L. 871 (1989); Lowenfeld, U.S. Law Enforcement Abroad: The Constitution and International Law, Continued, 84 Am. J. Int'l. L. 444 (1990); Paust, An Introduction to and Commentary on Terrorism and Law, 19 Conn. L. Rev. 697, 722–24 (1987); Ragosta, Aliens Abroad: Principles for the Application of Constitutional Limitations to Federal Actions, 17 NYU J. Int'l L. & Pol'y 287 (1985); Saltzburg, The Reach of the Bill of Rights Beyond the Terra Firma of the United States, 20 Va. J. Int'l L. 741 (1980); Note, 72 Va. L. Rev. 649 (1986); *cf.* Christenson, The Uses of Human Rights Norms to Inform Constitutional Interpretation, 4 Hous. J. Int'l L. 39 (1981); Lillich, The United States Constitution and International Human Rights Law, 3 Harv. Hum. Rts. Y.B. 53 (1990); Lillich & Hannum, Linkages Between International Rights and U.S. Constitutional Law, 79 Am. J. Int'l L. 158 (1985).

[37]In Johnson v. Eisentrager, 339 U.S. 763 (1950), the Court held that German prisoners of war detained overseas by the United States military had no constitutional basis for challenging their confinement. However, a plurality of the Court declared in Reid v. Covert, 354 U.S. 1 (1957), that American citizens continued to enjoy constitutional protection when they travelled abroad. See Stephan, Constitutional Limits on International Rendition of Criminal Suspects, 20 Va. J. Int'l L. 777, 785–90 (1980). Dicta in Haig v. Agee, 453 U.S. 280, 308 (1981), in turn cast doubt on the broader aspects of the *Reid* plurality opinion.

[38]Justice Stevens argued that Verdugo-Urquidez enjoyed full constitutional protection because he resided lawfully, albeit involuntarily, in the United States. He joined the result, however, because he believed that the warrant clause did not apply to searches of noncitizens'

"people" to be secure in their person and possession. These "people," he argued, were only persons with some substantial connection to the United States, whether citizens or legal residents. Responding to the argument that the Equal Protection Clause forbade distinctions based on citizenship, and that an earlier decision had recognized the existence of constitutional protection for overseas citizens, the Chief Justice presented a parade of horribles that would follow from the active assertion of Fourth Amendment rights by overseas aliens. He ended with an instrumental argument about the relationship of constitutional protection to international affairs:[39]

> For better or for worse, we live in a world of nation-states in which our Government must be able to "functio[n] effectively in the company of sovereign nations." . . . Some who violate our laws may live outside our borders under a regime quite different from that which obtains in this country. Situations threatening to important American interests may arise half-way around the globe, situations which in the view of the political branches of our Government require an American response with armed force. If there are to be restrictions on searches and seizures which occur incident to such American action, they must be imposed by the political branches through diplomatic understanding, treaty, or legislation.

Verdugo-Urquidez does not close all possibilities of constitutional redress for wrongs inflicted on overseas aliens by the United States government. The Court expressly excluded from its ruling rights relating to the trial process, including the introduction of confessions obtained in violation of an accused's privilege against self-incrimination. Perhaps the Court still might rule that the Due Process Clause of the Fifth Amendment, which protects "persons" rather than "the people," imposes a universal and international check on governmental power.[40] But the Court's posture seems fairly clear: Injuries inflicted on overseas aliens by the United States govern-

---

homes in foreign jurisdictions, and that the searches otherwise were reasonable. 110 S.Ct. at 1068. Justice Blackmun agreed with Stevens that the Fourth Amendment applied but the Warrant Clause did not, but he wanted the lower court to determine whether the searches had been reasonable. *Id.* at 1078.

[39] *Id.* at 1066.

[40] The Chief Justice's opinion, in describing the Court's earlier decisions, stated that "we have rejected the claim that aliens are entitled to Fifth Amendment rights outside the sovereign territory of the United States." 110 S.Ct. at 1063. One might dismiss this remark as dicta about stale precedent. Taken at face value, however, it indicates that the *Verdugo-Urquidez* majority would reject the holding of United States v. Toscanino, 500 F.2d 267 (2d Cir. 1974), which extended Fifth Amendment protection to an overseas alien who alleged that Drug Enforcement Agency had tortured him before his rendition to the United States.

ment, presumably including torture and other violations of international norms, will not bring constitutional relief.[41]

* * *

Each of these decisions invites some consideration of the Court's role in fashioning international law. The Court has had at least two basic approaches to the resolution of international law litigation. Often it has treated international law as a set of norms determined primarily by reference to a priori principles, but on occasion it has viewed these norms as contingent on some positive act of consent by at least one of the political branches of government.

II

A

Under the first, a priori approach, the Court's job is to make international law, and it fulfills this function by embracing the "best"—the most moral, just, humane—rules. These are the norms that the other branches of government (and other nations) also would adopt if they were armed with sufficient detachment and moral intuition. A link to international declarations and practice is essential, but the Court can choose among a variety of sources: treaty declarations, actual state behavior, and the views of reputable commentators. Moreover, the rule for choosing among these sources is more or less openly normative: The discovery of international law involves, wherever possible, the rejection of declarations, practice, and comments that (in the view of the Court) do not lead to peace, security, or justice.

Of particular relevance to the a priori approach are the views of jurists: the authors of treatises and monographs, whether diplomats, judges, or academics. Their importance rests partly on historical accident—outside the common-law tradition, jurists traditionally have played a larger role in shaping legal norms and structures—and partly on the jurist's supposed comparative advantage at abstract moral reasoning.[42] Since international law is mostly gloss rather than positive enactment, the commentators can in effect become the law.

---

[41] One might frame an attack on torture and similar cruelties by invoking Eighth Amendment rights, but the Court so far has refused to extend the "cruel and unusual punishment" prohibition beyond criminal trials. See Ingraham v. Wright, 430 U.S. 651, 664–68 (1977).

[42] See Stephan, note 35 *supra*, at 852–53.

B

Many of the Court's leading international law decisions employ the a priori methodology, albeit not always self-consciously. Three examples should suffice. In *The Schooner Exchange v. McFaddon*, Chief Justice Marshall observed that, in the absence of precedential and legislative authority, the Court would have to reach its decision by relying "on general principles, and on a train of reasoning, founded on cases in some degree analogous to this."[43] He first expounded on the "mutual benefits" of contacts among sovereigns in terms of "those good offices which humanity dictates and its wants require."[44] He then reasoned that immunity from suit promoted benign contacts, and that the extension of immunity from the sovereign's person and ministers to naval vessels furthered those benefits. Having identified immunity for the Navy as a norm founded upon moral reasoning, Marshall looked for confirmation from the jurists. Although one commentator had rejected the principle of immunity he sought, Marshall distinguished away that authority.[45] Finally, after aligning the rule with such commentary as endorsed it, Marshall proclaimed it the law of the United States.

Nearly a century later the Court decided *The Paquete Habana*,[46] a case involving the right of the United States to seize a Spanish-flag fishing vessel incident to the Spanish-American War. Justice Gray, writing for the majority, asserted that, "[b]y an ancient usage among civilized nations, beginning centuries ago, and gradually ripening into a rule of international law, coast fishing vessels, pursuing their vocation of catching and bringing in fresh fish, have been recognized as exempt, with their cargoes and crews, from capture as a prize of war."[47] He noted that this rule was "founded on conditions of humanity to a poor and industrious order of men, and of the mutual convenience of belligerent states."[48]

Having deduced a reasonable rule, Gray sifted through both state practice and the treatises of commentators to find support for it. He disposed of contraindications essentially on moral grounds, dismissing as confused and irrational the instances where state practice and treatise commentary endorsed the seizure of fishing vessels. Finally, Gray incorporated his rule into the law of the United States. "International law is part of our law," he declared, "and must by ascer-

[43] 7 Cranch at 136.

[44] *Ibid.*

[45] *Id.* at 144–45.

[46] 175 U.S. 677 (1900).

[47] *Id* at 686.

[48] *Id.* at 708.

tained and administered by the courts of justice of appropriate jurisdiction, as often as questions of right depending upon it are duly presented for their determination."[49] The boats and their cargo thus were returned to the enemy alien owners, in spite of the absence of a treaty or statute mandating this result.

A final and particularly vivid example is Justice Brennan's dissent in *Verdugo-Urquidez*. Brennan did not pretend that the Court's precedents mandated the extension of Fourth Amendment protection to overseas aliens, and did not suggest that other nations observed comparable restraints in their extraterritorial activities. Rather he grounded his argument on moral reasoning:[50]

> Fundamental fairness and the ideals underlying our Bill of Rights compel the conclusion that when we impose "societal obligations," such as the obligation to comply with our criminal laws, on foreign nationals, we in turn are obliged to respect certain correlative rights, among them the Fourth Amendment.

To be sure, Brennan followed this appeal to first principles with what at first blush might seem to be instrumental arguments. Constitutional self-restraint, he claimed, would "encourage other nations to respect the rights of our citizens," and would send "a powerful message about the rule of law to individuals everywhere."[51] Conversely, allowing our government to disregard "the privacy and sanctity of the home" undermines these values and undercuts our national self-conception as "the world's foremost protector of liberties."[52] But Justice Brennan's reasoning cannot depend solely on how other nations react to what our courts do. The case involved the interpretation of the Constitution, which if not fixed at least does not change quickly in response to the conduct of other states. It seems incredible that Justice Brennan would alter his conception of what "fundamental fairness" requires if he faced overwhelming evidence

[49] *Id.* at 700. His remarks on the methodology of discovering international law, which immediately followed the statement in text, have brought joy to the hearts of generations of international law professors: "[W]here there is no treaty, and no controlling executive or legislative act or judicial decision, resort must be had to the customs and usages of civilized nations; and, as evidence of these, to the works of jurists and commentators, who by years of labor, research and experience, have made themselves peculiarly well acquainted with the subjects of which they treat." Unstated here, but demonstrated by the structure of his opinion, is the rule for choosing among these evidences of custom and usage: Courts should adhere only to those customs that are reasonable, *i.e.*, that would, in the view of the judge, lead to greater peace, security, and justice.

[50] 110 S.Ct. at 1071.

[51] *Ibid.*

[52] *Id.* at 1072.

proving the failure of the United States' human rights commitment to induce other nations to respect the interests of our citizens.

C

Verdugo-Urquidez majority, if it meant what it said, might tolerate gross abuses of overseas aliens, with torture and murder not expressly excluded. Why leave it to the executive and legislative branches to deter government lawlessness, if the Court by deploying conventional doctrinal tools can interpret the Constitution as forbidding such activity? One can find many declarations emanating from our government, the Congress, and distinguished academics that our country deplores human rights abuses. All the Court has to do is put deed to word by making available the usual techniques of constitutional adjudication to back up these statements of principle. Even if the typical remedy for constitutional violations—in the case of illegal searches, the suppression of the evidence obtained—differs from normal international practice, the Court at least can insist on some recognition of the alien's right not to suffer unjustified invasions of the privacy surrounding his home and possessions.

Although a procedural rather than a substantive case, *Hess* also prevents United States courts from redressing concededly blatant violations of international law. *Hess* may not block suits against foreign officials, as opposed to those against foreign states, but that does not help much. Unlike state and local officials, over whom plaintiffs easily can get jurisdiction when pressing civil rights claims, foreign officials normally can avoid subjecting themselves to United States judicial power.

In *Hess*, also, the Court had at its disposal doctrinal techniques for reaching the opposite result. The Court has considered itself free to override statutory language if a literal reading would lead to an absurd result.[53] The FSIA particularly lends itself to judicial reconstruction, given the long common law history behind it and the fact that foreign sovereign immunity rests on customary law throughout much of the world. Congress's express authorization of some international-law-based suits against foreign sovereigns does not compel an inference that it intended to exclude all other international law claims. It may have meant only to emphasize, in light of *Sabbatino*

[53]See, *e.g.*, United Steelworkers of America v. Weber, 443 U.S. 193 (1979); Textile Workers Union v. Lincoln Mills, 353 U.S. 448 (1957); Holy Trinity Church v. United States, 143 U.S. 457 (1892).

and the Cuban experience, the importance of vindicating property rights against illegal appropriations. In all likelihood, Congress did not consider the applicability of the FSIA to human rights lawsuits one way or the other. Nothing barred the Court from following customary international law in the face of this silence and permitting suits for claims such as Hess's.

Unlike the other cases, *Kirkpatrick* does not flout the a priori approach to international law. But it nonetheless may undermine the Court's ability to arbitrate among competing national regulatory systems, and thus impede the implementation of choices derived from a priori principles. What makes the decision problematic are the ambivalent role of the Foreign Corrupt Practices Act and the fundamental indeterminacy of the Court's opinion.

Some commentators view the FCPA as a United States contribution to international law, because they believe it checks the corrupting influence of United States–owned capital and allows developing countries a better chance of economic and political progress.[54] But one can just as easily attack the FCPA as an imperialist effort to impose a particular business culture on societies that have developed useful, if different, customs of commerce. Especially if the Act raises the costs developing countries must bear when procuring goods and services (a result that a marriage to RICO almost certainly achieves), the case for tempering its scope becomes strong. A court guided by the a priori principle of effecting a North-to-South redistribution of wealth could conclude that it should use every doctrinal and interpretive technique at its disposal to frustrate FCPA-based RICO claims.

Another problem that complicates the application of the a priori approach to the act of state doctrine is the possibility that behind the simple doctrinal formulation there may lurk not one but several disparate rules, each turning on the context. A dispute among private parties over title to property, for example, might invite a different rule of judicial abstention from a suit asserting either an international law or United States statutory claim, and different statutory schemes might require different degrees of abstention. The courts have not acknowledged this possibility, but a sub rosa sensitivity to context may underlie the otherwise inexplicable welter of decisions. An

[54]See, *e.g.*, Bayzler, Abolishing the Act of State Doctrine, 134 U. Pa. L. Rev. 325, 380–81 (1986); *cf.* Chu & McGraw, The Deductibilit y of Questionable Foreign Payments, 87 Yale L.J. 1091 (1978).

analogy to standing doctrine suggests itself: The Court talks as if a single formula can explain its standing decisions, but the outcomes make sense, if at all, only in light of each case's substantive background.[55]

What makes *Kirkpatrick* particularly difficult to analyze, however, is the irreducibly cryptic quality of the Court's opinion. Portions are barely plausible; others are completely opaque. In the first category falls the line drawn between direct invalidation of an official act, which the Court said would trigger the doctrine, and findings predicate to invalidation. To some extent this line may reflect the differences between property and contract: The failure to recognize a title derived from an act of state would directly invalidate that act, while imposing damages for the formation of a contract with a foreign government does not immediately undo the contract. But what does this distinction have to do with either international comity or separation of power concerns, the two policies that supposedly underlie the doctrine?[56]

The holding may be merely problematic, but the Court's justification for it is completely insupportable. Justice Scalia acknowledged that factual findings of an official act's invalidity implicate comity and the separation of powers, but argued that those policies affect only the narrowing of the doctrine, not its expansion.[57] The doctrine's entire history contradicts this contention: The United States courts have assumed for almost a century that only those two policies justify its existence. How can rationales that explain a doctrine's existence have no bearing on its extent?

Justice Scalia's difficulty in framing plausible arguments for his limitation of the act of state doctrine may reflect an ongoing division within the Court as to the doctrine's content and purpose. Perhaps he could obtain a majority, something the Court's prior two decisions had lacked, only by making the decision so confusing that no propo-

---

[55]See Currie, Misunderstanding Standing, 1981 Supreme Court Review 41; Stephan, Nontaxpayer Litigation of Income Tax Disputes, 3 Yale L. & Pol'y Rev. 73, 81–83 (1985).

[56]Lower courts have used this distinction to limit the applicability of the Second Hickenlooper Amendment. See Hunt v. Coastal States Gas Producing Co., 583 S.W.2d 322 (Tex. 1979); Born & Westin, note 7 *supra*, at 558. But note that the effect of those cases is to expand the applicability of the act of state doctrine, not shrink it, and that the language of that statute supports, if it does not compel, the distinction.

[57]But what is appropriate in order to avoid unquestioning judicial acceptance of the acts of foreign sovereigns is not similarly appropriate for the quite opposite purpose of expanding judicial incapacities where such acts are not directly (or even indirectly) involved. 110 S.Ct. at 706.

nent of any more coherent version of the doctrine would feel threatened. At the same time, the decision might serve to implement a hidden agenda (or, more likely, it might drive a majority toward an as yet unrealized consensus). The Court yet may conclude that comity and the separation of powers, as interpreted by judges, are never sufficient reasons for overriding a legislative decision to authorize a particular claim. *Kirkpatrick* might be the first step in a whipsaw: The Court first interprets the act of state doctrine in a manner that makes no sense, then announces that the doctrine no longer fulfills any rational purpose and declares it extinct.

But if this is the Court's intended destination, then followers of the a priori approach have much to deplore. It means in effect that courts may not limit the scope of United States statutes in light of the law and practices of other nations. But the reconciliation of conflicting national regulatory systems is one of the principal objectives of international law.

III

The other view of international law, implicit in a few Court opinions but not much favored by contemporary jurists, assigns primary importance to the international bargaining process as the source of international norms. Because judges usually do not participate in international negotiations, their role must be subordinate and adjunct. If the courts are to contribute, they must do so by enforcing the bargains struck by the other branches of government, not by fulfilling a priori principles.

A

Over the last decade and a half private law scholars have developed important insights into the bargaining dynamic:

1. Judicial enforcement enhances the value of promises. A naked promise—a statement of intent about some future course of action—creates value by supplying information, but conforming the promise to rules that ensure judicial enforcement enhances that value by upgrading that information's reliability.[58] Parties (including nations) ra-

[58]See Goetz & Scott, Enforcing Promises: An Examination of the Basis of Contract, 89 Yale L.J. 1261, 1286–88 (1980). Similarly, courts can enhance the value of legislative enactments by acting as agents of the legislature—*i.e.*, offering themselves as mechanisms for ensuring the

tionally will seek judicial enforcement of their commitments, so as to reassure other parties and thereby increase the return they can receive on their commitments. Conversely, parties have less reason to commit to judicial enforcement if they do not anticipate a return.

2. In the case of complex cooperative relationships where considerable residual uncertainty exists, bonding and other kinds of precommitment strategies can enhance a party's welfare. In a sense, the precommitment principle is a more general formulation of the insight that holding oneself to legal enforcement of one's promises enhances value. Precommitment—the decision to bind one's behavior to a preannounced standard, even though application of that standard in some situations may lead to outcomes that one regrets—is a useful technique for managing uncertainty.[59] Courts can reinforce the benefits of precommitment by holding actors to the initial choice, in the face of circumstances that cause regret.

Of course, courts must know when a precommitment has occurred before they can bind an actor, and actors must know what they have to do to satisfy a court that they have made a precommitment. The task involves both a retrospective inquiry into the parties' intent and, where appropriate, the announcement of "off-the-rack" formalities that parties can employ to signal a precommitment.[60] In formulating signalling rules, courts face a dilemma: Insisting on too stringent an adherence to formalities will result in nonenforcement of precommitments on which parties may have relied (and parties will lower their reliance because of doubts about enforcement), but making it too easy to "declare" a precommitment will force unintended obligations on parties and may deter actors from undertaking socially beneficial behavior that courts might misinterpret as the declaration of a precommitment.

3. Where direct bargaining between parties is costly but cooperative activity can generate gains (as in the prisoner's dilemma), parties

ongoing enforcement of bargains worked out within a particular legislature. See Landes & Posner, The Independent Judiciary in an Interest-Group Perspective, 18 J.L. & Econ. 875 (1975).

[59]See Schelling, Choice and Consequence 83–112 (1984); Williamson, Credible Commitments: Using Hostages to Support Exchange, 73 Am. Econ. Rev. 519 (1983).

[60]See Goetz & Scott, The Limits of Expanded Choice: An Analysis of the Interactions Between Express and Implied Contract Terms, 73 Calif. L. Rev. 261, 286–89, 311–16 (1985); Scott, Error and Rationality in Individual Decisionmaking: An Essay on the Relationship Between Cognitive Illusions and the Management of Choices, 59 S. Calif. L. Rev. 329, 353–61 (1986). For the related problem of developing signaling rules that enable a legislature to indicate its intent to courts, see Sunstein, Interpreting Statutes in the Regulatory State, 103 Harv. L. Rev. 405 (1989).

can optimize their welfare by pursuing a "tit-for-tat" strategy. The player makes his first choice in a way that signals cooperative intentions, even though it renders him vulnerable to the other party's opportunism. Thereafter he will match exactly the other player's behavior, responding to cooperation with cooperation and retaliating to each defection with a parallel act of opportunism.[61]

To encourage such "patterned cooperation," courts must allow each party the freedom to reciprocate, which means they must tolerate the imposition of tough sanctions on defectors. Moreover, they normally must recognize the parties' information advantage and allow them to determine whether a defection has occurred.[62] This need for deference where parties have reserved the power to retaliate increases the significance of judicial strategies for determining where precommitments exist. Because so much will ride on whether a court views a party as bound to a commitment, the courts must develop rules and procedures that allow easy and explicit signalling of intent. Where multiple jurisdictions might have the power to regulate a category of activity (as is the case in international transactions, whether private or intergovernmental), courts also must take care to choose rules that do not deviate too greatly from those used in other jurisdictions where the parties might seek to enforce an agreement.

4. The likelihood that parties will arrive at a cooperative outcome decreases as the number of parties representing different interests increases. One could restate this principle as the rule of small numbers—the amount and scope of legal rules of general application tend to increase as the number of participants in their formulation decrease.[63] Among the three branches of government, congressional action involves the most participants and therefore is the most costly. Whether the executive or the judiciary generally enjoys a comparative advantage in rule creation (in the sense that it can promulgate more rules at lower cost) depends on one's view of how each branch functions. The executive has a unified head, but most of its rulemaking takes place several levels below the President and includes many institutional actors. The Supreme Court, at the top of the judiciary,

[61]For a discussion of the prisoner's dilemma in the context of international law, see Abbott, Modern International Relations Theory: A Prospectus for International Lawyers, 14 Yale J. Int'l L. 335 (1989).

[62]See Scott, Conflict and Cooperation in Long-Term Contracts, 75 Calif. L. Rev. 2005, 2042–53 (1987).

[63]See Ehrlich & Posner, An Economic Analysis of Legal Rulemaking, 3 J. Leg. Stud. 257 (1974).

still comprises nine actors, each with his or her own values and preferences.[64] In the realm of international law, the Court's inability to bargain directly with foreign lawmakers complicates the problem. Although the Court, unimpeded by the need to obtain any other sovereign's assent, can more easily declare as "international law" rules that bind the United States, the executive branch through treaties and executive agreements can generate more rules to which at least one other nation has assented.

These insights of private law scholarship suggest how courts might apply a contingent-norm approach to international law. They reinforce the idea that courts should vigorously enforce international commitments, including those of the United States, to enhance the value of a nation's promises. But if a court-generated rule were to take away a nation's power to retaliate for the opportunism of other international actors, nations would choose to expose themselves less frequently to the risk of defection and generally would have less incentive to engage in patterned cooperation. Moreover, courts should not extend an international obligation past what the obligor intended. Courts can announce hermeneutical formulations that allow nations more easily to opt into international precommitments, but they must avoid imposing rules that lead to interpretations of commitments that vary widely among jurisdictions.

The contingent-norm approach does not bar the courts completely from the creation of international norms. Many cases arise, particularly in litigation among private parties, where an international norm could affect the outcome but the political branches have not announced any principles or policies. Nothing should prevent a court from positing an international norm in such a case, as long as it leaves room for a later reversal by the other branches.[65] Rules concerning the enforcement of foreign judgments, admiralty, and implementation of choices of law or forum are examples of areas where courts have developed a kind of international law without encroaching on the powers of the President or Congress.[66] The real legal challenge of

---

[64] *Cf.* Easterbrook, Ways of Criticizing the Court, 95 Harv. L. Rev. 802 (1982).

[65] See Garcia-Mir v. Meese, 788 F.2d 1446 (11th Cir.), cert. denied *sub nom.* Ferrer-Mazorra v. Meese, 479 U.S. 889 (1986); *cf.* Restatement (Third) of the Foreign Relations Law of the United States §155, n. 3 (1987).

[66] E.g., Hilton v. Guyot, 159 U.S. 11 (1989); The Bremen v. Zapata Off-Shore Co., 407 U.S. 1 (1972); Mitsubishi Motors Corp. v. Soler Chrysler-Plymouth, Inc., 473 U.S. 614 (1985). Other examples of "gap-filling" international rules include the law of foreign sovereign immunity before its codification by the FSIA and reliance on the act of state doctrine in instances not involving a federal statute or a generalized executive-branch statement of policy. Of

the contingent-norm approach is the determination of exactly when the political branches have addressed an issue; otherwise courts too easily can find "silences" to fill up with their own pronouncements on international norms.

B

A review of the Court's decisions suggests an occasional and inchoate appreciation of the contingent-norm approach. Of course, the notion of international law as essentially contractual has distinguished antecedents. In *The Schooner Exchange*, Chief Justice Marshall used a contract metaphor to organize his argument for creating sovereign immunity. But *The Schooner Exchange* implicitly assumed that the Court, through its law-making capacity, could participate in the bargaining. Marshall appeared to expect that whatever outcome the Court chose would influence courts and governments in other nations. He determined the rule for which our nation should bid and adopted the outcome that he thought the other parties—the civilized nations—would embrace. Only in this century has the Court explicitly defined its role as adjunct to the other branches, rather than as their mentor, in the bargaining for international law.

United States v. Curtiss-Wright Corp.[67] provides a good example of this posture. The case is notorious for its overblown rhetoric on the special capacity of the executive branch to implement foreign policy, and one might dismiss it as an atavism. Justice Sutherland's disquisition on executive branch power depends on a dubious predicate, namely, that the Court should take seriously constitutional limitations on the power of Congress to delegate authority.[68] Nonetheless, the opinion illustrates the Court's intuitions about bargaining dynamics.

The case tested the validity of a criminal conviction for violation of an embargo that President Roosevelt had imposed pursuant to an act of Congress that authorized him, upon the announcement of certain

course, some of the positions the Court has taken may conflict with the contingent-norm approach. In particular, the Court's past tendency in sovereign immunity and act-of-state cases to let the executive branch authorize suits on a case-by-case basis demonstrated an ignorance of the virtues of precommitments. See text at notes 58–60 *infra*.

[67]299 U.S. 304 (1937).

[68]Within a few years of *Curtiss-Wright*, the Court had effectively interred the nondelegation doctrine. See Yakus v. United States, 321 U.S. 414 (1944). The modern Court instead tends to focus on whether a delegation took place, rather than on its constitutionality. See, *e.g.*, FEA v. Algonquin SNG, Inc., 426 U.S. 548 (1976).

findings, to forbid the sale of arms to Bolivia and Paraguay, the countries involved in the Chaco conflict. The defendant argued that the grant of power to the President to turn the sanctions on and off violated the constitutional separation of powers. Justice Sutherland, writing for the majority, rejected that argument. He based his response on a distinction between international activity and domestic transactions.

Justice Sutherland asserted that the government's power to assert its legal sovereignty outside its territorial limits—unlike its power to regulate domestic affairs—derives only from international engagements : "[O]perations of the nation in such territory must be governed by treaties, international understandings and compacts, and the principles of international law."[69] The executive branch in particular needs a free hand to develop these understandings:[70]

> It is quite apparent that if, in the maintenance of our international relations, embarrassment—perhaps serious embarrassment—is to be avoided and success for our aims achieved, congressional legislation which is to be made effective through negotiation and inquiry within the international field must often accord to the President a degree of discretion and freedom from statutory restriction which would not be admissible were domestic affairs alone involved.

Bowing to this necessity (and revealing an unstated preference for greater projection of extraterritorial United States authority), the Court withheld a judicially crafted tool (the nondelegation doctrine) that would have blocked this particular exercise of executive power.

Beneath these arguments lies an intuitive appreciation of several of the private law insights associated with the contingent-norm approach. In arguing for the President's need to turn the arms embargo on and off, the Court appeared to have grasped the significance of the tit-for-tat strategy. By assuming that the President could act more effectively on his own, without waiting for case-by-case congressional approval, the Court followed the rule of small numbers. These intuitions impelled it not to impose a barrier (which, because of its constitutional foundation, only a later Supreme Court or a constitutional amendment could have lifted) to delegations of what otherwise would have constituted excessive discretionary authority.

Justice Harlan's opinion in *Sabbatino* offers a second illustration of

---

[69] 299 U.S. at 318.

[70] *Id.* at 320.

the contingent-norm approach. In exploring the dimensions of the act-of-state doctrine, he emphasized the principal role of the executive in developing international law, and the need of courts not to interfere with the executive's discretion:[71]

> The traditional view of international law is that it establishes substantive principles for determining whether one country has wronged another. Because of its peculiar nation-to-nation character the usual method for an individual to seek relief is to exhaust local remedies and then repair to the executive authorities of his own state to persuade them to champion his claim in diplomacy or before an international tribunal. . . . Although it is, of course, true that the United States courts apply international law as part of our own in appropriate circumstances, . . . the public law of nations can hardly dictate to a country which is in theory wronged how to treat that wrong within its domestic borders.

In particular, he argued, a United States court should not attempt to rectify international wrongs in a manner that "may hinder rather than further this country's pursuit of goals . . . in the international sphere."[72] But the courts should enforce those obligations that have been clearly signalled as binding commitments, the product of "codification or consensus concerning a particular area of international law," because under those circumstances courts would be acting less like lawgivers and more like agents of the parties: "[T]he courts can then focus on the application of an agreed principle to circumstances of fact rather than on the sensitive task of establishing a principle not inconsistent with the national interest or with international justice."[73]

Finally, consider the dissenting opinions in *Pfizer Inc. v. Government of India.*[74] A five-member majority held that foreign governments should have the same rights to sue under the Sherman Act that state governments enjoyed, including the possibility of obtaining treble damages. Chief Justice Burger and Justice Powell each attacked that result, essentially on the ground that the failure of Congress to exclude foreign states from the Sherman Act did not permit an inference in favor of extending coverage. Burger emphasized the power of foreign states to enact antitrust laws that would protect their own interests, and at the same time to engage in price fixing, boycotts, and other anticompetitive behavior that the Sherman Act

---

[71] 376 U.S. at 422–23.

[72] *Id.* at 423.

[73] *Id.* at 428.

[74] 434 U.S. 308, 320 (1978).

forbade nonsovereign actors to undertake.[75] Powell put the point succinctly:[76]

> The solicitude that we assume Congress has for the welfare of each of the United States, especially when the subject matter of legislation largely has been removed from the competence of the States and has been entrusted to the United States, cannot be assumed with respect to foreign nations.

At least implicit in Burger and Powell's argument are the assumptions that Congress might wish to encourage foreign states to eschew anticompetitive behavior, and that Sherman Act standing could serve as a carrot to induce good behavior. If these assumptions are correct, then the majority, by giving away this advantage without extracting any return benefit, impaired the ability of the political branches to develop common international norms of free competition . Seen in this light, Burger and Powell become the supporters of international cooperation, and the majority become unwitting promoters of economic nationalism .

The last point can be generalized. A critic could dismiss any or all of these cases as expressing a jingoist conception of national self-interest. But the contingent-norm approach suggests otherwise. A commitment to the development of extensive and meaningful international norms may lurk behind judicial deference and reluctance to create international law. In each of the above cases the Court (in *Pfizer*, the dissenters) distinguished subjects covered by binding international obligations, for which enforcement would increase the value of the United States's commitment, from areas where the political branches had retained the freedom to adjust their behavior reciprocally to the actions of other governments. If the political branches consider the Court's posture toward enforceability when they decide whether to assume international obligations, then the Court's unwillingness to substitute its norms for those already chosen might encourage the political branches to create more, and ultimately more meaningful, international commitments.

C

Of the new cases, *Verdugo-Urquidez* most clearly conforms to the contingent-norm model. Both Rehnquist and Brennan expose the

---

[75] *Id*. at 327–28.

[76] *Id*. at 331.

fundamental question—should the Court bind the United States to a standard of conduct in the treatment of overseas aliens that might inspire the international community to similar self-constraint? By making the answer dependent on the political branches, Rehnquist signals the Court's willingness to support a tit-for-tat strategy until such time as those branches make a contrary commitment. In contrast, Brennan's position, resting as it does on an interpretation of the Constitution, would bind the other branches without their consent.

What makes *Verdugo-Urquidez* interesting is the direct clash between a priori and contingent-norm principles. The moral issue seems especially poignant. Although the case involved only the search of an unoccupied dwelling, the ruling may tolerate a wide range of horrifying government behavior. Assuming that the Court does not wish to encourage our government's abuse of human rights, the outcome represents a significant judgment about means and ends. The Court, at least implicitly, must expect that our government's power to retaliate against the misbehavior of other nations will discourage barbarous conduct more effectively than would the imposition of unilateral and irreversible restraints on the United States.

The conflict is hardly less sharp in *Hess*. By holding that the international obligations of other nations are not enforceable in United States courts absent an explicit endorsement by Congress, the Court simultaneously reduced the impact of international norms and made it more likely that nations will embrace them. Governments will disavow emerging norms if the price of silence is significant risk of lawsuit in United States courts.[77] For example, tribunals such as the European Court of Human Rights and the Inter-American Court of

[77]Such concerns also might explain the failure of the United States to endorse many international human rights conventions, and the insistence of the Senate that those conventions it does ratify not be self-executing. Starting with the indisputable assumption that these conventions deal with propositions that any civilized society must embrace—e.g., that genocide and torture are bad and should be discouraged—an a priori approach would lead courts to declare that the norms codified in those conventions are now part of customary international law and as such have become part of United States law in the absence of an express declaration by Congress to the contrary. The justification for such action would stem from an assumed aberration in the ratification process that prevented Congress from understanding the manifest wisdom of the principles involved. See U.S. Ratification of the Human Rights Treaties: With or Without Reservations (Lillich, ed., 1981); Sohn, International Protection of Human Rights: Suggestions for the New Administration, 1989, 28 Va. J. Int'l L. 913, 914–15 (1988). The contingent norm approach, by contrast, would wait on Congress to implement those conventions and would accept any restrictions Congress might announce at the time of ratification. It would justify this deference by arguing that legitimate reasons for nonratification exist (principally asymmetries among nations in information about human rights violations and in enforcement mechanisms) and that too aggressive behavior by courts will discourage the political branches from engaging in any international activity to promote human rights norms.

Human Rights have the power to encourage members of a particular community to observe international norms, but for the most part they issue only declaratory judgments. Were these decisions, presumptively declarative of international law, to become the basis for tort suits in United States courts, the governments that have submitted to those tribunals might reconsider their commitments.

Hess does not stand for the proportion that international law claims should never be the basis of United States tort suits. Its premise is rather that the political branches enjoy a comparative advantage in formulating precise rules about sovereign immunity in a way that promotes reciprocity in the international environment. Consider the case of expropriation, for which the FSIA expressly abolishes sovereign immunity. Congress quite reasonably might have concluded that United States lawsuits seeking compensation form foreign sovereigns for wrongful expropriations give United States owners of overseas investment a level of protection roughly equivalent to what the Takings Clause provides to foreign investors in the United States.[78] The fact that Congress made this judgment does not suggest the wisdom of all international-law based suits, but rather indicates the capacity of the political branches to identify areas where litigation can flourish without harming national or international interests.

Finally, *Fitzpatrick* also follows the contingent-norm approach, in subtle as well as obvious ways. By shifting to Congress the responsibility for restraining the extraterritorial effect of statutes such as RICO, the Court relies on the implicit assumption that the political branches can do a better job of negotiating the appropriate limits of competing national regulatory schemes. In a sense the outcome mirrors the result sought by the *Pfizer* dissenters: the Court gives Congress the power to bestow an advantage (freedom from the effects of RICO in *Kirkpatrick*, antitrust standing in *Pfizer*) on foreign governments that conform their economic behavior to international standards.

But by rejecting the Solicitor General's position—that the Court should give the executive branch exclusive authority to decide whether a broad range of suits should proceed—the Court also revealed an intuitive understanding of the value of precommitments. Unless the executive branch is bound by some external standard, generated by either a legislative rule or a judicially created presump-

[78]*Cf.* Damrosch, Foreign States and the Constitution, 73 Va. L. Rev. 483 (1987).

tion, it would face intense if short-term pressures to permit or block particular suits. Lawsuits raising act-of-state issues depend on choices made by private parties, whose goals may not reflect broader foreign policy concerns and who have every incentive to lobby the executive for a favorable act-of-state ruling. The resulting unpredictability would create costly risks, and also might invite opportunism on the part of foreign governments acting either in their own interests or on behalf of their citizens. For all these reasons, some kind of precommitment, whether a rule allowing all cases falling into a particular category to proceed or one automatically barring such suits, seems preferable to unfettered executive branch discretion.

IV

The Court's new international law cases may reflect a plausible theory about the optimal strategy for developing international norms, but that does not prove that the Court is doing the right thing. Just as the a priori approach may exaggerate the Court's ability to influence the behavior of other nations, the contingent-norm construct may ignore the moral authority and persuasive power of the Court's decisions. Each is fundamentally problematic: The contingent-norm approach assumes that all rules, including those fundamental principles that make up the tissue and spirit of civilized society, remain subject to negotiation; the a priori approach regards induced responses as irrelevant. Each rests ultimately on behavioral assumptions that can be exposed but not easily verified.

The conflict between the two approaches also implicates opposing conceptions of judicial competence. Just as contemporary constitutional theory centers on debates over the Court's ability to act as the guardian and inspiration of our national moral discourse, the validity of the new cases turns on how one sees the Court shaping the logos of international norms. Can the Court speak with moral, if not political, authority to the international community? Does the international community listen, and does it matter if the Court fails to move other nations? In this, the cruelest of centuries, can the Court afford to ignore the brutality and horror that nations, unchecked by the threat of reciprocal force, can inflict on innocents? But can it overlook barbarisms rationalized by their prophylactic deterrence of even greater evils?

These are not questions that admit only one response. In part the answers turn on how one views judges in general as well as the Court in particular—whether one emphasizes the peculiar features of the judiciary (legal training and methodology, insulation from the rawer forms of politics) or the general characteristics its members share with all lawgivers (susceptibility to moral reasoning). The answers also depend on what, for want of a better term, could be called risk preferences toward judging. Should we celebrate a methodology that allows our most brilliant and intuitively wise judges to rise above the rest of us? Do we instead want a style of judging that frustrates the bumptious hacks who seeks to impose their foolish preferences on our lives?

My own sympathy for the contingent-norm approach reflects both risk aversion and a taste for the marshalling of legal skills, for which I believe judges to have a particular talent. By regarding international law as primarily contractual, and by limiting the Court's role to providing a hospitable environment for international bargaining, the contingent-norm methodology requires the Justices to be clever, but does not seduce them with the illusion of superior wisdom. Instead it expects them to be good at traditional legal skills, to parse out rights and duties, and to distinguish commitments from mere assumptions about the future, working against a background of received doctrine about the meaning of particular statements and actions. It does not ask them to comprehend the evolving norms of international behavior, either among states or between states and individuals. What it does require is a degree of intellectual humility that, over the long haul, may lend greater authority to the Court's pronouncements.

DAVID LUBAN

THE DISENGAGEMENT OF THE LEGAL PROFESSION: KELLER v. STATE BAR OF CALIFORNIA

For the legal profession these may be the best of times and the worst of times. In every material respect, the profession thrives as never before. Between 1960 and 1985 the bar grew 129%, and has become increasingly youthful (in 1985 over 30% of lawyers were under 34 years old) and better educated.[1] It has also become staggeringly rich, with over $35 billion expended on legal services in 1985.[2] After several years of slump, law school applications are swelling once again.

At the same time, the legal and general press reports a rather profound malaise in the profession.[3] Many lawyers discover that they simply do not like the practice of law or the environment of the contemporary law firm. According to a recent ABA survey of over 2,200 lawyers from all walks of practice, the number of lawyers saying they are "very satisfied" with their work has decreased from 41% in 1984 to 33%—and the number of lawyers reporting that they consume six or more drinks a day has risen from .5% in 1984 to 13%, including

David Luban is Professor of Law, University of Maryland, and Research Scholar, Institute for Philosophy and Public Policy, University of Maryland.

Author's Note: I wish to thank David Bogen, Michael Kelly, David Wasserman, Marley Weiss, and Robin West for their advice on an earlier draft of this paper.

[1]Galanter & Palay, The Tournament of Lawyers 66 (forthcoming).

[2]*Id.* at 68.

[3]See, *e.g.*, Marcus, Gloom at the Top: Why Young Lawyers Bail Out, Wash. Post, May 31, 1987, at C1. Margolick, More Lawyers Are Less Happy at Their Work, a Survey Finds, N.Y. Times, Aug. 17, 1990, at B5.

0-226-09573-8/91/1990-0001$02.00

20% of women lawyers.[4] Where in 1984 only 9% of male partners in private practice said they were dissatisfied with their work, the share is now 22%; among female partners, it has risen from 15% in 1984 to 42%.[5] Given that these are partners, whose professional self-assurance ought to be very high, these percentages are quite astonishing. And among sole practitioners, 43% of men and 55% of women said they are dissatisfied with their work.[6]

Burnout and dissatisfaction, however, is only part of the malaise. Paradoxically—or perhaps the paradox is only on the surface—at the very moment the profession enjoys unparalleled prosperity, it appears to be undergoing one of its periodic paroxysms of concern over its loss of what is called "professionalism." In 1984, the American Bar Association felt it necessary to establish a Commission on Professionalism, which began its 1986 report with the gloomy question "Has our profession abandoned principle for profit, professionalism for commercialism?" and continued with the not-very-reassuring response: "The answer cannot be a simple yes or no."[7] The ABA now publishes a regular newsletter on issues of professionalism; a recent issue lists 18 professionalism reports and 32 professionalism codes issued by state and local bar associations within the past four years alone.[8]

What sort of "professionalism" issues agitate the profession? A cover story in the newsletter describes bar association concern over a new District of Columbia ethics rule permitting law firms to take on non-lawyers as partners. Dennis Block, a member of the ABA's Special Coordinating Committee on Professionalism, comments on the rule—employing rhetoric that has become quite familiar in the professionalism debate—[9]

> It goes to the whole question of whether or not the profession of law is going to remain a unique and learned profession or just be like any other business, and if the latter is the case, whether we

---

[4]Margolick, note 3 *supra*.

[5]*Ibid*.

[6]*Ibid*.

[7]ABA Commission on Professionalism, ". . . . In the Spirit of Public Service:" A Blueprint for the Rekindling of Lawyer Professionalism 1 (1986).

[8]Growing Attention to Professionalism, 1 Prof. Lawyer 12 (Fall/Winter 1989/90).

[9]D.C. Rule Intensifies Debate Over Non-Lawyer Partners, 1 Prof. Lawyer 1 (Fall/Winter 1989/90).

> will be allowed to preserve our right to self-regulation, which is important not just to the profession, but to society as a whole. . . . Without the lawyer playing his traditional role as the buffer between the state and the citizen, something he can only do because of self-regulation, society will be the big loser in all of this.

Mr. Block's comment contains a noteworthy mix of arguments and perhaps of motives. We find both a concern for professional prerogatives—"our right to self-regulation"—and also a reference to the lawyer's "traditional role as the buffer between the state and the citizen." The argument promotes both lawyer interests and public interests, or rather promotes lawyer interests in the name of the public interest.

In this respect, it mirrors a long-standing debate in the sociology of the professions. On one side we find Max Weber and his followers, who understood the professional project as an anti-competitive effort at market control for largely self-interested reasons.[10] This plausible view is supported by Professor Abel's recent book *American Lawyers*, which argues strongly that the organization and self-regulation of the legal profession has been primarily an effort to control the market for legal services from the supply side.[11]

Durkheim, on the other hand, believed that social differentiation along lines of family and tribe would be replaced by a purely functional division of labor as economies modernize. This reorganization, he feared, could lead to the erosion of traditional moral norms and to the loss of social solidarity, resulting in a dangerously anomic society. The solution, according to Durkheim, lay in assigning to occupations—the functional units of society—the same moral role played in premodern societies by familial and tribal units. He envisioned professions and professional organizations that would serve as "intermediary bodies" (*corps intermédiaires*) between individuals and the state, associations that would remoralize the modern social world and help combat the *anomie* that characterizes it.[12] These intermediary bodies would develop collective moral codes and ideals, mitigat-

[10] Max Weber on Law in Economy and Society 202–03 (Rheinstein ed. 1954).

[11] Abel, American Lawyers (1989). Abel summarizes Weberian theories of the professions, including the legal profession, at 15, 18–30.

[12] Durkheim, Professional Ethics and Civic Morals (Brookfield trans. 1957); Durkheim, The Division of Labor in Society (Simpson trans. 1933).

ing the "amoral character of economic life" that "amounts to a public danger."[13]

Talcott Parsons held related views. He too believed that professions play a moral and not only an economic role in modern societies. In an address to The University of Chicago Law School, he argued that because lawyers represent private clients in a context of public right they are uniquely suited to reconcile individual self-interest and community needs; indeed, the concept of lawyers as "buffers" between state and citizen comes directly from Parsons.[14] It indirectly echoes Tocqueville's opinion that lawyers would mediate between people and government because they "belong to the people by birth and interest, and to the aristocracy by habit and taste; they may be looked upon as the connecting link between the two great classes in society."[15]

As Professor Abel observes, there is no reason to believe that either the Weberian or the functionalist analysis[16] of the legal profession is wholly correct or wholly false; the profession may well be partly self-interested and oligopolistic *and* partly altruistic and concerned with the public good. Associations of lawyers may likewise serve both functions. That bar associations aim to promote the interests of lawyers is hardly surprising; that they aim to promote public interests as well is a more noteworthy phenomenon.

That under some circumstances they should be constitutionally barred from using their members' dues for this latter aim is an ironic twist on the professionalism debate that merits some scrutiny. Yet so the Supreme Court held this year in *Keller v. State Bar of California*.[17] Far from offering a vision of the profession that might allay the current sense of crisis, *Keller* contracts the scope of public engagement by the bar and thereby makes the meaning of legal professionalism more enigmatic than ever.

---

[13]Durkehim, Professional Ethics and Civic Morals, note 12 *supra*, at 12.

[14]Parsons, A Sociologist Looks at the Legal Profession, in Essays in Sociological Theory, 370, 375, 384 (rev. ed. 1954).

[15]1 Tocqueville, Democracy in America 275–76 (Bradley ed. 1945). For discussion of the commonalities between Tocqueville, Durkheim, and Parsons, see Luban, The Noblesse Oblige Tradition in the Practice of Law, 41 Vand. L. Rev. 717, 718–25 (1988); Simon, Babbitt v. Brandeis: The Decline of the Professional Ideal, 37 Stan. L. Rev. 565 (1985).

[16]For a survey of contemporary functionalist views of the legal profession, see Halliday, Legal Professions and the State: Neocorporatist Variations on the Pluralist Theme of Liberal Democracies, in Lawyers in Society: Comparative Theories 375 (Abel & Lewis, eds., 1989).

[17]Keller v. State Bar of California, 110 S.Ct. 2228, 2237 (1990).

I. The Keller Case

Since 1927, California has maintained an "integrated" or "unified" bar, that is, a state bar fused with the state bar association. The term "state bar" refers collectively to all those licensed to practice law in a state. By contrast, the term "bar association" refers to an organization of lawyers. Unification fuses the bar with the bar association, and thus makes membership in the state's bar association mandatory for lawyers. In 19 states membership in the bar association remains voluntary. The business of all state bars, unified or not, is the regulation of the legal profession, including bar admissions, discipline, and such additional functions as maintaining a client security trust fund, fee arbitrations, enforcement of unauthorized practice regulations, and proposing ethical rules to the authoritative state court.

By contrast with state bars, bar associations, be they voluntary or mandatory, have generally undertaken business of both Weberian and Parsonian kinds. Bar associations aim to promote the interests of the legal profession, but also sponsor programs to educate and improve the competence of practitioners. In addition, they tender advice on law reform—primarily the reform of law concerning procedure and the administration of justice, but also more substantive and broad-ranging reform endeavors. Thus, the State Bar of California operates under the statutory mandate to "aid in all matters pertaining to the advancement of the science of jurisprudence or to the improvement of the administration of justice . . . ." as well as to aid in "all matters that may advance the professional interests of the members of the State Bar and such matters as concern the relations of the bar with the public."[18] In addition, bar associations—like other groups and professional organizations—often take stands on public issues, including controversial political issues. The California bar endorsed a nuclear freeze; the Colegio de Abogados de Puerto Rico—like California's, a mandatory bar association—has condemned the Soviet invasion of Afghanistan, declared itself in solidarity with the people of El Salvador, and sent official representatives to the United Nations to request that the U.N. declare Puerto Rico an American colony and take up the cause of Puerto Rican independence.[19]

---

[18]Cal. Bus. & Prof. Code §6031, subd. (a).

[19]*Keller*, 110 S.Ct. at 2237; Schneider v. Colegio de Abogados de Puerto Rico, 565 F. Supp. 963, 966–67 (D. Puerto Rico 1983).

Unifying a state bar fuses these various functions into an untidy amalgam, the purpose of which is often hard to hold in steady focus.[20] The various functions of a unified bar may be pictured as concentric circles radiating outward from the purely regulatory functions of non-integrated state bars, to the lawyer-improvement function (continuing education, informing the bar about new developments, etc.), to the narrow law reform function of advising the courts about procedural law and the administration of justice, to the wide law reform function of deliberating and commenting about substantive law ("all matters pertaining to the advancement of the science of jurisprudence," in the words of the California statute), to the political function of attempting to influence public debate on controversial issues of the day. It is unclear where the advancement of lawyers' self-interest belongs in this schema, or indeed whether it belongs in the schema at all.

No aspect of bar activity has been immune from controversy, including the narrowly regulatory functions. Over the years the most significant Supreme Court decisions regarding the legal profession have arisen from lawyers' challenges to bar regulations and bar discipline. In *Lathrop v. Donahue*[21] the Court turned back a First Amendment challenge to bar unification. Yet, the wider circles of bar activity, and especially the political function of mandatory bar associations, have continued to excite controversy, anger, and litigation.

In *Keller*, the Court decided a First Amendment challenge brought by dissident members of the California bar to the bar's expenditure of their dues for law reform and political activities. The California bar "for many years has lobbied the Legislature and other governmental agencies, filed amicus curiae briefs in pending cases, held an annual conference of delegates at which issues of current interest are debated and resolutions approved, and engaged in a variety of education programs."[22] Among the activities that the dissident members protested, the Court singles out[23]

> (1) Lobbying for or against state legislation prohibiting state and local agency employers from requiring employees to take polygraph tests; prohibiting possession of armor piercing handgun

---

[20]For a particularly trenchant critique of the unified bar concept, see Schneyer, The Incoherence of the Unified Bar Concept: Generalizing from the Wisconsin Case, 1983 ABF Res. J. 1 (1983).

[21]367 U.S. 820 (1960).

[22]47 Cal. 3d 1152, 1156 (1989), quoted in *Keller*, 110 S.Ct. at 2231.

[23]*Keller*, *id.* at 2231n–32n.

> ammunition; creating an unlimited right of action to sue anybody causing air pollution; creating criminal sanctions for violation of laws pertaining to the display for sale of drug paraphernalia to minors; limiting the right to individualized education programs for students in need of special education; creating an unlimited exclusion from gift tax for gifts to pay for education tuition and medical care; providing that laws providing for the punishment of life imprisonment without parole shall apply to minors tried as adults and convicted of murder with a special circumstance; deleting the requirement that local government secure approval of the voters prior to constructing low-rent housing projects; requesting Congress to refrain from enacting a guest worker program or from permitting the importation of workers from other countries. (2) Filing *amicus curiae* briefs in cases involving the constitutionality of a victim's bill of rights; the power of a workers' compensation board to discipline attorneys; a requirement that attorney-public officials disclose names of clients; the disqualification of a law firm. (3) The adoption of resolutions by the Conference of Delegates endorsing a gun control initiative; disapproving the statements of a U.S. senatorial candidate regarding court review of a victim's bill of rights; endorsing a nuclear weapons freeze initiative; opposing federal legislation limiting federal court jurisdiction over abortions, public school prayer, and busing.

In addition, the state bar had intervened in a controversial 1982 judicial retention election over several state supreme court justices who opposed capital punishment. In the words of appellant Eddie Keller, a former prosecutor who believes strongly in capital punishment, "It was the straw that broke the camel's back. It was the bar's involvement in that retention election that brought on the suit."[24]

Relying principally on *Abood v. Detroit Board of Education*,[25] which confronted a similar issue in the context of agency shops, a unanimous Court prohibited the California bar from expending the dues of protesting members for any activities not "necessarily or reasonably incurred for the purpose of regulating the legal profession or 'improving the quality of the legal service available to the people of the State.'"[26] Thus, *Keller* forbids the bar from expending dissenters' dues for political or wide law reform purposes—indeed, on its face *Keller*'s holding forbids the expenditure of dissenters' dues even for purposes of narrow law reform.

---

[24]Evans, Partial Victory in Bar Dues Suit Is Sweet, Keller Says, S.F. Banner Daily Journal (June 5, 1990), p. 11.

[25]Abood v. Detroit Board of Education, 431 U.S. 209 (1976).

[26]*Keller*, 110 S.Ct. at 2236 (quoting *Lathrop*, 367 U.S. at 843).

As we shall see, both *Keller* and *Abood* (upon which *Keller* rests) expound First Amendment doctrine that is highly problematic. More importantly, *Keller*'s drastic paring-back of the integrated bar's expenditure of dissenters' dues for anything beyond the regulatory and lawyer-improvement functions implies an impoverished view of the bar's role that I believe to be substantially mistaken. Active involvement in law reform, I shall argue, forms an essential part of the social role of lawyers—essential in that without active involvement in law reform, legal ethics as it has traditionally been understood cannot be justified. Bar associations are the most plausible institutional setting for this centrally-important activity. Thus the *Keller* Court's judgment that law reform is a more problematic activity of mandatory bar associations than self-regulation or lawyer improvement betrays a misunderstanding of the nature of legal professionalism. Its implicit distinction between an essential apolitical "core" of bar activities and a dispensable periphery of engagement in political issues leaches the publicly-significant content out of legal professionalism, which has always, and correctly, signified an active engagement in public affairs. Detached from that engagement, "professionalism" means little more than white-collar self-congratulation.

II. A Genealogy of Keller

On the surface, nothing could be less problematic than *Keller*, a short opinion written by Chief Justice Rehnquist for a unanimous Court. The argument is a straightforward application of *Abood*, which held that although the legalization of union- and agency-shop contracts does not violate the First Amendment, unions with such contracts may not expend the dues or assessments of protesting workers for political or ideological activities with which they disagree. Dues and assessments may be spent by a union only for its nonpolitical core activity of collective bargaining and other activities germane to collective bargaining. The *Keller* Court likens a unified bar to a union shop. Like a union shop contract, bar unification conditions one's job on (eventual) membership. Like a labor union, bar associations have a nonpolitical core activity, namely professional self-regulation and self-improvement. And thus, like a labor union, mandatory bar associations may spend protesting members' dues only for the nonpolitical core activity.

This does not mean that labor unions or bar associations must abandon their political activities. *Abood* and its successor cases[27] established a different remedy. Unions must set up procedures for identifying workers who protest union political activities and reduce protesting workers' assessments in proportion to the amount of the union's budget dedicated to protested political expenditures; in addition, protesting workers must receive a proportional rebate for political expenditures that have already taken place. *Keller* adopts this "*Abood/Hudson* remedy."

Moreover, the analogy *Keller* draws between bar unification and union shop contracts is an old one, going back 35 years to the first case in which the Court reviewed the constitutionality of union security agreements. In *Railway Employees' Department v. Hanson*,[28] the Court rejected a challenge, based on the First and Fifth amendments, to Congress' authorization of union shop contracts in section 2, Eleventh of the Railway Labor Act. There the Court wrote, "On the present record, there is no more an infringement or impairment of First Amendment rights than there would be in the case of a lawyer who by state law is required to be a member of an integrated bar."[29] Five years later, the Court upheld the constitutionality of bar unification in a case decided the same day as the next major constitutional challenge to union security agreements; Justice Brennan authored both opinions, and the Court stressed the relatedness of the cases.[30]

I am persuaded that the reasoning in both lines of cases, union-shop and unified-bar, is deeply flawed. In particular, the effort to impart constitutional significance to a distinction between nonpolitical core activities and peripheral political activities fails. To see this will require some delving into the most important cases in this line.

A. HANSON

Hanson unanimously upheld the constitutionality of federal legislation permitting railway unions to bargain for union shop contracts.

---

[27]Ellis v. Railway Clerks, 466 U.S. 435 (1983); Chicago Teachers Union v. Hudson, 475 U.S. 292 (1985).

[28]351 U.S. 225 (1955).

[29]*Hanson*, 351 U.S. at 238. Justice Douglas, the author of *Hanson*, subsequently disowned this question-begging dictum in his dissenting opinion in *Lathrop*, 367 U.S. at 820 (Douglas, J., dissenting).

[30]Lathrop v. Donahue, 367 U.S. 820 (1960); International Assoc. of Machinists v. Street, 367 U.S. 740 (1960).

However, the *Hanson* Court expressly insisted that "if the exaction of dues, initiation fees, or assessments is used as a cover for forcing ideological conformity or other action in contravention of the First Amendment, this judgment will not prejudice the decision in that case."[31]

But what "other action" did the Court have in mind? Trade unions have always been in the business of organizing new locals, backing pro-labor electoral candidates, and actively promoting advantageous legislation: pursuing these activities is among the fundamental purposes of unions. Obviously, when it upheld union shop contracts the *Hanson* Court knew what a trade union is. Did the Court therefore mean to exclude traditional union political activities from the domain of "action in contravention of the First Amendment," or did it on the contrary view union withdrawal from the wider political arena as a *quid pro quo* for the permission to bargain for union security agreements? The second position seems less plausible, since the opinion contains no hint that the Court proposes such a significant shift in public policy regarding trade unions. Nevertheless, neither reading seems obviously wrong, and thus the *Hanson* Court seemed to duck the First Amendment issue raised by union political activities. It thereby obscured the question of exactly what the institutions were whose authorization to negotiate union shop contracts it was sustaining.

Admittedly, the Court held "that the requirement for financial support of *the collective-bargaining agency* by all who receive the benefits of its work . . . does not violate either the First or the Fifth Amendments,"[32] and this way of referring to the unions suggests that the Court identified the essence of unionism with collective bargaining. But the holding in fact carries no such implication, and indeed contains a significant ambiguity. The quoted language might mean only that the requirement for financial support of *collective bargaining* does not violate the First or the Fifth Amendments. However, with no strain it also sustains a wider reading, namely, that the requirement for financial support of the collective-bargaining *agency* in the full range of its legitimate activities, including activities other than collective bargaining, does not violate the First or the Fifth Amendments. Presumably, union members cannot be compelled to contribute to activities far removed from legitimate trade-unionism; they cannot, for example, be compelled to subsidize a professional hockey team that the union leadership had decided to launch. But

[31]*Hanson*, 351 U.S. at 238.

[32]*Ibid.* (emphasis added).

since political activity has always been the heart and purpose of the labor movement, *Hanson*'s holding is open to an interpretation that upholds the constitutionality of such traditional activity of collective bargaining agencies.

One additional feature of the *Hanson* opinion supports the plausibility of reading its holding widely. Justice Douglas wrote for a unanimous Court: "Industrial peace along the arteries of commerce is a legitimate objective; and Congress has great latitude in choosing the methods by which it is to be obtained. The choice by the Congress of the union shop as a stabilizing force seems to us to be an allowable one."[33] At the core of the constitutional argument, then, lies the understanding that the underlying policy is the pursuit of "industrial peace." The Railway Labor Act was, in fact, a kind of treaty with the unions, and the unions had been pressing for union security agreements for decades. It is scarcely credible that the unions would energetically demand a clause in the treaty that significantly pared back the range of activities through which they had traditionally pursued the interests of their members.

From the unions' point of view collective bargaining is not the essence of union activity. Pursuit of their members' workplace interests is the essence of their activity, and collective bargaining—along with political action—is simply a principal means for that pursuit. It may be that Congress did not share the unions' holistic point of view, and perhaps the *Hanson* Court did not either. But the language in *Hanson*'s holding entitles us to no inference one way or the other.

It might be objected that *Hanson* can sustain only the narrow reading. The Court, after all, expressly left open the First Amendment issue raised by "the exaction of dues . . . used as a cover for forcing ideological conformity," suggesting that union ideological activities lay outside the scope of its First Amendment holding. However, the opinion makes clear that "forcing ideological conformity" refers to prevalent union policies much more repressive than expending dues for political ends. The opinion cites several union rules that expressly barred individuals who held specific ideological commitments (e.g., to communism or to fascism) from union membership, or forbade union members from publicly supporting legislation disapproved by the union. Since a union-shop contract conditions the right to work on eventual union membership, such restrictions clearly *are* a literal case of "forcing ideological conformity," whereas

[33] *Id.* at 233.

the expenditure of dissident members' dues on political activity counts as forcing ideological conformity only figuratively.[34] To guard against ideological litmus tests for union membership, the Railway Labor Act explicitly barred union-shop contracts that conditioned union membership on anything other than payment of dues. It was solely on the basis of this provision that the Court concluded that the record in *Hanson* did not raise the First Amendment issue.

B. STREET

The next decision in the series proved to be the most significant. In *International Association of Machinists v. Street*,[35] machinists subject to a union shop agreement protested on First Amendment grounds the use of their dues by the union to finance the election campaigns of federal and state candidates they opposed and to promote "political and economic doctrines"[36] with which they disagreed. Justice Brennan, writing for the Court, sought to avoid the constitutional question. He argued that the purpose of the Railway Labor Act as a whole was to preserve industrial peace by creating a framework for collective bargaining. And the sole purpose of permitting union shop contracts was to avoid the unfairness of permitting free riders on union collective bargaining efforts.

By itself, the first proposition proves nothing beyond the uncontroversial point that Congress regarded collective bargaining as necessary for the preservation of industrial peace. Justice Brennan nevertheless concluded from these two propositions that the only union activity Congress meant to encourage by permitting union shop contracts to avoid free riders was collective bargaining, and thus that Congress regarded collective bargaining as sufficient (not merely necessary) for the preservation of industrial peace. He based this conclusion on a strained and unpersuasive reading of the Railway Labor Act's legislative history, which in fact said virtually nothing on the subject. On this reading, which a subsequent Court gently characterized as "an interpretation of the Railway Labor Act not without its difficulties,"[37] section 2, Eleventh granted unions with security agreements

---

[34] *Id.* at 236n–237n.

[35] 367 U.S. 740 (1960).

[36] *Id.* at 744.

[37] *Abood*, 431 U.S. at 232. In his concurring opinion, Justice Powell describes *Street*'s reading of section 2, Eleventh as a "strained construction." *Id.* at 248.

authority to collect dues in support of collective bargaining, but no authority to collect dues to support other union activities, in particular protested political activities. The case thereby fell against the union on statutory rather than constitutional grounds.

Street quotes language from *Crowell v. Benson:* "When the validity of an act of the Congress is drawn in question, . . . this Court will first ascertain whether a construction of the statute is *fairly possible* by which the question may be avoided."[38] Justice Brennan adds that the Court's reading of section 2, Eleventh is "not only 'fairly possible' but entirely reasonable."[39] But, whether fairly possible or entirely reasonable, what is not asserted is that the reading is correct, or superior to alternative readings. The desire to avoid constitutional questions may thus lead the Court to a statutory interpretation that it would reject if the question it faced concerned only the meaning of the statute. "Fairly possible" and even "entirely reasonable" sets a lower threshold for acceptable statutory interpretation than "most plausible." An interpretation of a statute may be fairly possible or entirely reasonable even though a different interpretation is clearly superior.

Indeed, Justices Black, Frankfurter, and Harlan were convinced that the effort to avoid the constitutional question had led the majority to a gross misreading of section 2, Eleventh. They argued that Congress fully intended section 2, Eleventh to permit union shop agreements under which unions would be able to use members' dues to pursue the full range of their traditional activities, including political and ideological activities. Frankfurter and Harlan would have con fronted the constitutional question and upheld section 2, Eleventh, while Justice Black would have held it a violation of free speech.

On the issue of interpreting section 2, Eleventh, Frankfurter's dissent, joined by Justice Harlan, is devastating:[40]

> To write the history of the Brotherhoods, the United Mine Workers, the Steel Workers, the Amalgamated Clothing Workers, the International Ladies Garment Workers, the United Auto Workers, and leave out their so-called political activities and expenditures for them, would be sheer mutilation. . . . Viewed in this light, there is a total absence in the text, the context, the history and the purpose of the legislation under review of any indication that Congress, in authorizing union-shop agreements,

---

[38]285 U.S. 22, 62 (emphasis added), quoted at 367 U.S. 749–50.

[39]*Street*, 367 U.S. at 750.

[40]*Id.* at 800–01 (Frankfurter, J., dissenting).

> attributed to unions and restricted them to an artificial, non-prevalent scope of activities in the expenditure of their funds. An inference that Congress legislated regarding expenditure control in contradiction to prevailing practices ought to be better founded than on complete silence.

Frankfurter is right. The force of the plurality's reading of section 2, Eleventh lies principally in the thought that if Congress had meant to grant unions operating under security agreements authority to collect dues from dissident members for political expenditures the legislative history should have reflected this fact: an affirmative grant of power requires an affirmative demonstration of congressional intent.[41] This argument evaporates, however, once we understand that forbidding unions from expending dissidents' dues for political purposes would mark a departure from prevailing and well-known practice. As Frankfurter says in the final sentence of the passage quoted above, it simply makes no sense to infer congressional intent to depart from prevailing practice from a largely silent record. As between two interpretations of a silent record—that Congress intended to preserve the *status quo ante* and that Congress intended to grant unions a narrower power of the purse than they currently possessed—the former seems clearly better than the latter, even if the latter is "fairly possible" or even "entirely reasonable." Silence implies the status quo.

Like *Hanson*, *Street* thus ducked the constitutional issue raised by union expenditures of dues for political purposes, answering the question on purely statutory grounds. But it also, albeit tacitly, resolved the ambiguity we have noted between the narrow and wide readings of *Hanson*. If section 2, Eleventh never authorized the expenditure (under union security agreements) of dissidents' dues for political activities in the first place, then *Hanson*'s holding "that the requirement for financial support of the collective-bargaining agency by all who receive the benefits of its work . . . does not violate either the First or the Fifth Amendments" cannot be read to sustain political activities undertaken by the collective bargaining agency. This proves to be a decisive point in the subsequent cases, and it is a perfect object lesson—if another is needed—in how the passive virtues may influence constitutional decisions under the guise of ducking them.

[41] "One looks in vain for any suggestion that Congress also meant in §2, Eleventh to provide the unions with a means for forcing employees, over their objection, to support political causes which they oppose." *Street*, 367 U.S. at 764.

C. ABOOD

The Court finally confronted the constitutional issue in *Abood v. Detroit Board of Education*,[42] when the Michigan court of appeals authoritatively construed the state's agency shop statute to "sanction[] the use of nonunion members' fees for purposes other than collective bargaining"[43] and upheld its facial constitutionality on the authority of *Hanson*. The Court disagreed. Though it reaffirmed the constitutionality of union security agreements upheld in *Hanson*, it vacated the state court's judgment, holding that a statute permitting protested political expenditures violates the First Amendment.

Abood characterized the protesting employees' First Amendment interests in the strongest of terms, declaring that "at the heart of the First Amendment is the notion that an individual should be free to believe as he will, and that in a free society one's beliefs should be shaped by his mind and his conscience rather than coerced by the State."[44] In the Court's view, the rather slight and indirect impingement on freedom of belief created by protested political expenditures does not lessen the applicability of this principle. In support of its view the Court invokes Madison ("Who does not see . . . that the same authority which can force a citizen to contribute three pence only of his property for the support of any one establishment, may force him to conform to any other establishment in all cases whatsoever?"[45]) as well as Jefferson ("[T]o compel a man to furnish contributions of money for the propagation of opinions which he disbelieves, is sinful and tyrannical."[46]).

Yet these ringing categorical declarations highlight a puzzling feature in *Abood*'s argument, namely, its ready acceptance of *Hanson*. If the First Amendment truly prohibits *any* assessment, even of three pence, in support of abhorrent political or ideological views, how can it permit assessments in support of collective bargaining? One pos-

---

[42] 431 U.S. 209 (1976).

[43] *Id.* at 232, quoting 230 N.W. 2d, at 326. An agency shop, as distinct from a union shop, requires financial support for the union from all workers—so-called "fair share" contributions—but does not require any worker to join the union. For simplicity, I will use the word "dues" to refer both to dues paid by union members and fair share contributions paid by non-members under an agency shop agreement.

[44] *Abood*, 431 U.S. at 234–35.

[45] Madison, Memorial and Remonstrance Against Religious Assessments, in The Complete Madison: His Basic Writings 299 (Padover ed. 1953).

[46] Jefferson, A Bill for Establishing Religious Freedom, in Thomas Jefferson: Writings 346 (Peterson ed. 1984).

sible answer is that collective bargaining does not partake of politics or ideology—but *Abood* explicitly (and correctly) rejects this answer:[47]

> To compel employees financially to support their collective-bargaining representative has an impact upon their First Amendment interests. An employee may very well have ideological objections to a wide variety of activities undertaken by the union in its role as exclusive representative. His moral or religious views about the desirability of abortion may not square with the union's policy in negotiating a medical benefits plan. . . . The examples could be multiplied. To be required to help finance the union as a collective-bargaining agent might well be thought, therefore, to interfere in some way with an employee's freedom to associate for the advancement of ideas, or to refrain from doing so, as he sees fit. But the judgment clearly made in *Hanson* and *Street* is that such interference as exists is constitutionally justified by the legislative assessment of the important contribution of the union shop to the system of labor relations established by Congress.

The final sentence of this passage provides the key to *Abood*. Notwithstanding its categorical libertarian rhetoric, *Abood* actually rests on a balancing test: although all assessments under union security agreements have "an impact upon . . . First Amendment interests," this impact may be "constitutionally justified" by a sufficiently weighty social goal.[48]

As I shall now argue, however, both *Abood*'s reading of *Hanson* and the terms of the constitutional balancing upon which *Abood* rests derive from *Street*'s construction of section 2, Eleventh. This fact drastically undermines *Abood*'s argument, for two related reasons. First, it seems questionable to derive a general constitutional test, applicable to state statutes such as Michigan's, from a federal statute that does not preempt the state statute. Second, even if *Street*'s faulty reading of the statute must be taken as authoritative in other contexts, it cannot be employed in answering *Abood*'s question. As we have seen, the Court construed section 2, Eleventh as it did only in order to avoid the constitutional question raised in *Abood*, and thus on logical grounds section 2, Eleventh, thus construed, cannot form the premise for resolving that very constitutional question. If the con-

[47] *Abood*, 431 U.S. at 222.

[48] The bar's argument in *Lathrop v. Donahue* also employed a balancing argument on behalf of integrated bars, as did the Wisconsin Supreme Court opinion. This led Justice Black to deliver a forceful polemic against First Amendment balancing in his dissenting opinion. 367 U.S. at 871–74 (Black, J., dissenting).

stitutional question was to be reached, the construction of section 2, Eleventh should have faced (and failed) a higher standard of acceptable interpretation. *Abood*, and thus *Keller*, rests on a mistake.

As we have seen, by construing section 2, Eleventh narrowly, *Street* backhandedly eliminated the wide reading of *Hanson*,[49] limiting the latter's validation of union interests so that it encompasses only interests unrelated to politics. In addition, *Street* identified the important-sounding aim of preserving industrial peace—the policy underlying *Hanson*—with the significantly narrower aim of promoting collective bargaining. *Street* thereby set the terms for *Abood*'s constitutional balancing test. The passage quoted above from *Abood* identifies the state interest to be balanced against complaining workers' First Amendment interests as "the important contribution of the union shop to the system of labor relations established by Congress," a "system" that *Abood* follows *Street* in equating with collective bargaining, rather than with the full gamut of traditional union activities. On the basis of this balancing, *Abood* found that collective bargaining, but no other union activity, serves state interests sufficient to outweigh the First Amendment interests that the Court characterized in the remarkably strong terms we have seen. It consequently rejected the more plausible argument that *any* union activities, including political activities, that promote industrial peace suffice to outweigh the First Amendment interest in not contributing to causes of which one disapproves.

Abood thus marches to the beat of *Street*'s drum. Therein lies the problem. *Street* purported to settle no constitutional question; indeed, it imposed a problematic construction upon section 2, Eleventh for the sole and express purpose of avoiding constitutional questions. Yet by construing section 2, Eleventh narrowly, *Street* cast a shadow that retroactively transformed the meaning of *Hanson*, and decisively influenced *Abood* and the cases (including *Keller*) that followed upon it. In this way, the *Street* Court's strained interpretation of section 2, Eleventh—an interpretation that *Abood* concedes was "not without its problems"—determines the constitutional contours of an agency shop agreement authorized by a state statute having nothing to do with section 2, Eleventh.

As we have seen, the key maneuver in this argument consists of attributing to Congress the view that collective bargaining is not

[49]As Justice Powell noted in his concurrence in *Abood*, 431 U.S. at 248–49.

merely a necessary condition for industrial peace, but a necessary *and sufficient* condition for industrial peace. In this way the Court manages to have its cake and eat it too: it finds a union activity, collective bargaining, that suffices to secure an important national aim and yet lies outside the sphere of ideology and political controversy. It seems like wishful thinking to suppose that any national end can be attained that is at once vitally important and untainted by political controversy.

D. ELLIS

Abood's successor case amply illustrates the artificiality of distinguishing between the collective bargaining core and the political periphery of union activities—a distinction that makes no sense from the standpoint of the unions, as I have earlier argued. *Ellis v. Railway Clerks*[50] involved a challenge by workers to union expenditure (under a security agreement) of dues for activities that were neither directly associated with collective bargaining nor obviously political. These included expenditures for holding a national convention, purchasing refreshments for meetings, putting out a union publication, organizing new locals, litigation, and the payment of death benefits. As it happens, the appellee Brotherhood of Railway Clerks was subject to the Railway Labor Act, and thus the Court based its argument directly on section 2, Eleventh (which it elected to construe along the lines of *Street*[51]) as well as on the First Amendment analysis of *Abood*.[52]

The Court now reaped the fruits of its own artificial distinction between the collective bargaining core and political periphery of union activities: it was forced to determine which of the challenged union expenditures were "necessarily or reasonably incurred for the purpose of performing the duties of an exclusive representative of the employees in dealing with the employer on labor-management issues"[53] and which were not. Given the interconnectedness of various union activities, it should come as no surprise that the Court's arguments seem rather casuistical. Thus, though it acknowledges that

[50] 466 U.S. 435 (1983).

[51] *Ellis*, 466 U.S. at 447–48.

[52] *Id.* at 455–56.

[53] *Id.* at 448.

expanding the union through organizing can enhance a union's bargaining power, the Court finds that organizing bears only an "attenuated connection with collective bargaining."[54] Serving refreshments at Grand Lodge meetings, however, is "sufficiently related to [collective bargaining] to be charged to all employees."[55] So is holding a national convention, and so is putting out a monthly magazine, though only the portion of the magazine that reports on bargaining-related activities may be charged to the assessments of objecting workers. This is because "[i]f the union cannot spend dissenters' funds for a particular activity, it has no justification for spending their funds for writing about that activity" (even, apparently, if that is the only way dissenters can find out what political activities the union is undertaking).[56] Thus, the union publication must be subjected to a content-tent-based analysis to separate the apolitical wheat from the political chaff.

Justice Powell's concurrence goes a step further. He advocates applying a similar content-based analysis to the union's national convention. Powell would grant rebates to protesting workers of that portion of their dues used to finance segments of the convention in which politicians make speeches. This argument, like the Court's approach to the monthly magazine, seems hard to limit—why not further subdivide the convention based on what was discussed in each 20-minute segment?—and so invites ever-finer-grained content-based distinctions within union activities. Such are the perils of the armchair inquiry into the workings of labor unions upon which *Ellis* embarks. It is an inquiry, let us not forget, that results directly from the Court's bifurcation of union activities into a supposedly apolitical core—the "apolitical good" that outweighs dissident members' First Amendment interests—and a political periphery.

---

[54] *Id.* at 451.

[55] *Id.* at 449.

[56] *Id.* at 451. Two terms later, in *Hudson*, 475 U.S. 292 (1985), the Court held that an adequate *Abood* remedy would require unions to provide sufficient information to employees about the nature of various union expenditures; perhaps this requirement would obviate the need to discuss political expenditures in the monthly publication. But the Court's argument is still puzzling. Suppose that a union officer was convicted for embezzling union funds. It seems to follow from the Court's argument that the union publication could not use dissenters' assessments to defray the costs of reporting on the scandal in the union magazine. As a general proposition, "if *X* cannot spend dissenters' funds for a particular activity, it has no justification for spending their funds for writing about that activity" seems quite fallacious.

E. LATHROP

Precisely the assumption of such an apolitical good lies at the heart of the unified bar cases as well. *Lathrop v. Donahue* involved a challenge by a Wisconsin lawyer to the integration of the state bar by order of the Wisconsin Supreme Court. Like *Hanson*, *Lathrop* sustained the constitutionality of compelled membership against a First Amendment challenge. Like the workers in *Hanson*, the protesting bar members claimed that the organization they were compelled to join was objectionably ideological and political in character.[57] Like *Hanson*, the Court ducked the issue of protested political expenditures because it believed that the record of the case did not present that issue.[58] And thus, like *Hanson*, *Lathrop* obscured the question of exactly what sort of institution the mandatory bar was whose constitutionality the Court was sustaining.

Moreover, *Lathrop*, like *Hanson*, offered a holding that shifts ambiguously between narrow and wide readings. At one point in its argument, *Lathrop* characterizes the policy underlying bar unification as "elevating the educational and ethical standards of the Bar to the end of improving the quality of the legal service available to the people of the State, without any reference to the political process."[59] The *Lathrop* Court adds: "It cannot be denied that this is a legitimate end of state policy."[60] On one reading, then, *Lathrop* sustains bar unification only for the pursuit of this rather narrow end of state policy—an end that on its face excludes not only the political and wide law reform functions of bar associations, but the narrow law reform function (that is, tendering advice about procedural law and the administration of justice) as well. "Elevating the educational and ethical standards of the Bar" includes only self-regulation, ethical advice (tendered through ethics opinions or ethics hotlines), continuing education, and such related activities as gathering and disseminating information about legal and professional matters through newsletters, bar-maintained law libraries, or annual meetings. State bar associations typically engage in all these activities, and *Lathrop* may have intended to limit them to this menu.

---

[57] "'A major portion of the activities of the State Bar as prescribed by the Supreme Court of Wisconsin are of a political and propaganda nature.'" *Lathrop*, 367 U.S. at 822, quoting a letter by the complaining lawyer.

[58] *Id.* at 845–48.

[59] *Id.* at 843.

[60] *Ibid.*

However, Justice Brennan's opinion explicitly quotes the stated purpose of the Wisconsin State Bar: "'to aid the courts in carrying on and improving the administration of justice; . . . to provide a forum for the discussion of subjects pertaining to the practice of law, the science of jurisprudence and law reform, and the relations of the bar to the public, and to publish information relating thereto. . . .'"[61] These clauses allude specifically to law reform functions. Oddly enough, although the Court insists that "legislative activity is not the major activity of the State Bar,"[62] it does so at the conclusion of a detailed four-page summary of bar political activities, in which it notes that "[t]he standing committees . . . and the sections have devoted considerable time to the study of legislation, the formulation of recommendations, and the support of various proposals."[63] In addition, the Court quotes from the State Bar committee assignments that the public services committee is to be involved in "'disseminating information of interest to the public in relation to the functions of the departments of government . . . ; and to that end the committee may operate a speakers' bureau and employ the facilities of the public press and other channels of public communication.'"[64] This seemingly-innocuous activity generated one of the controversies underlying *Keller*, when the California State Bar's president used his office to lay out the organization's view of the sizzling political debate over reconfirming controversial state supreme court justices.

Thus, it is by no means a simple matter to determine just what activities the *Lathrop* plurality thought it was sustaining. On the one hand, it formulates its holding by reference to a narrow policy involving only the educational and ethical edification of the bar. On the other hand, the decision sustains compulsory membership in a state bar admittedly engaged in a range of unquestionably political activities without holding that the bar must desist from any of these activities. As we shall see, a similar ambiguity clouds the holding of *Keller*.

[61] *Id.* at 828–29, quoting the Rules of the Wisconsin State Bar. An additional state purpose of the unified bar was "'to safeguard the proper professional interests of the members of the bar,'" quoted in *id.* at 829—the self-regarding interest that Weberians believe constitutes the real motive for professional organization.

[62] *Id.* at 839.

[63] *Id.* at 835–39. The quoted passage at 837.

[64] Quoted in *id.* at 830n.

F. KELLER

We are now in a position to understand *Keller*'s argument and holding, which are compounded of elements drawn from *Abood*, *Ellis*, and *Lathrop*.

From *Abood* the Court draws its fundamental constitutional argument that protested political expenditures by mandatory bar associations violate the First Amendment, though nonpolitical expenditures consistent with the policy underlying bar integration do not. Drawing an analogy between *Abood*'s treatment of unions and the parallel question regarding bar associations, Justice Rehnquist writes: "Here the compelled association and integrated bar is justified by the State's interest in regulating the legal profession and improving the quality of legal services."[65] Clearly, this passage employs an *Abood*-like balancing test: regulating the legal profession and improving the quality of legal services represents an apolitical good that outweighs the First Amendment interests of lawyers who do not wish to join a mandatory bar association, whereas other state interests served by the bar association—notably, state interests in obtaining the bar's advice on matters of law reform or politics—do not.

From *Ellis* the *Keller* Court derives a standard for distinguishing political from nonpolitical expenditures. *Ellis* distinguished union activities for which the dues collected from objecting members may nevertheless be spent from those for which such dues cannot be spent: "the test must be whether the challenged expenditures are necessarily or reasonably incurred for the purpose of performing the duties of an exclusive representative of the employees in dealing with the employer on labor-management issues."[66] Quoting this language, the *Keller* Court explicitly models its test for permissible expenditures on it:[67]

> the guiding standard must be whether the challenged expenditures are necessarily or reasonably incurred for the purpose of regulating the legal profession or "improving the quality of the legal service available to the people of the State." *Lathrop*, 367 U.S., at 843 (plurality opinion).

And, as the final citation makes clear, the Court takes the policy underlying bar integration from the narrow reading of *Lathrop*.

---

[65] 110 S.Ct. at 2236.

[66] *Ellis*, 466 U.S. at 448.

[67] *Keller*, 110 S.Ct. at 2236.

This is an extraordinarily narrow range of permissible expenditures—significantly narrower, in fact, than the Court itself intimated earlier in the opinion. Quoting language describing the State Bar of California' s narrow law reform function,[68] the Court had stated that the State Bar "also engages in a number of other activities which are the subject of the dispute in this case."[69] The word "also" implies that narrow law reform is not the subject of the dispute in the case, and thus that it *is* an activity for which protesting members' dues may be expended. But narrow law reform goes well beyond the standard of "regulating the legal profession or 'improving the quality of the legal service available to the people of the State.'" *Keller*, no less than *Lathrop*, admits of both a narrow and a wide reading. In the end, then, *Keller*'s explicit standard constricts the range of permissible expenditures more than its opinion suggests, and this ambiguity leaves unanswered the question of how much of the bar's narrow law reform mission the Court has pared away. Even though the Court may believe it is finally through with the issue, the issue is probably not through with the Court.

Unions and bar associations typically spend only a relatively small proportion of their budgets on political activities, and the actual amounts of money levied are rather small.[70] The demand to be excused from small contributions obviously serves only a symbolic function: withholding money is a tangible surrogate for political disaffiliation. But one's expressive interest in symbolic disaffiliation can be satisfied in many ways, not just noncontribution, and so the First Amendment interest in noncontribution must be regarded as inconsequential. *Abood* to the contrary, exacting a nominal contribution that will be spent furthering an organization's political agenda is simply not an infringement of liberty that can with a straight face be likened to forced loyalty oaths, compulsory political party memberships,

[68]The Court quotes the Bar's statutory mandate to promote "the improvement of the administration of justice" as well as the California Supreme Court's explication of the Bar's mission as "engaging in study and recommendation of changes in procedural law and improvement of the administration of justice." *Keller*, 110 S.Ct. at 2231.

[69]*Ibid*.

[70]As of September 1990, the California bar has not computed the dues rebates required by *Keller*. According to Susan Scott, media relations officer of the State Bar of California, the Bar spent only 6.1% of its budget last year on "administration of justice" matters, and this rubric includes other activities besides protested political expenditures. Maximum current bar dues are $440 annually, and thus the rebates should not exceed $26.44 (assuming that previous years involve comparable numbers).

coerced speech, or even unwilling message-bearing as in *Wooley v. Maynard*.[71]

Clearly the *Abood* Court was sensitive to this argument. As we have seen, it shored up its exposition of the First Amendment interest in freedom from enforced contributions with the authority of Madison's statement, "Who does not see . . . that the same authority which can force a citizen to contribute three pence only of his property for the support of any one establishment, may force him to conform to any other establishment in all cases whatsoever?"[72] and Jefferson's "that to compel a man to furnish contributions of money for the propagation of opinions which he disbelieves is sinful and tyrannical."[73] Indeed, many other cases on these issues quote the same two sentences, which impart ancestral *gravitas* to what might otherwise be regarded as litigation over trivia.[74]

Yet the invocation of the Framers in the present context is perhaps the most perfect example of the absurdly overstated rhetoric surrounding the debate. Of the many judges who cite their words, only Justice Douglas has the courtesy to remind us that Madison's sentence is lifted from his "Memorial and Remonstrance Against Religious Assessments" while Jefferson's comes from his 1779 Bill for Religious Liberty.[75] Madison and Jefferson were speaking against compulsory financial exactions by government in support of religion, a context that has almost nothing to do with the issues presented by *Abood* and *Keller*. Many religious adherents believe that support of false religions, no matter how indirect or minor, can consign their souls to eternal perdition. ("For I am a jealous God.") Given such sentiments, it is indeed sinful and tyrannical to confront the believer with a choice between secular punishment and eternal torment. But outside the context of Judgment Day, Jefferson's and Madison's statements seem like absurd exaggerations, and we may

---

[71]430 U.S. 705 (1977). See Gaebler, First Amendment Protection Against Government Compelled Expression and Association, 23 B.C. L. Rev. 995, 1019–23 (1982).

[72]The Complete Madison, note 45 *supra*, at 299.

[73]Thomas Jefferson: Writings, note 46 *supra*, at 346.

[74]Madison's statement is cited in *Street*, 367 U.S. at 778 (Douglas, J., concurring); *Street*, 367 U.S. at 790 (Black, J., concurring); *Abood*, 431 U.S. at 234–35n.; *Hudson*, 475 U.S., at 305n.; and *Keller*, 767 P. 2d at 1034. Jefferson's is cited in *Street*, 367 U.S. at 778 (Douglas, J., concurring); *Street*, 367 U.S. at 790 (Black, J., concurring); *Abood*, 431 U.S. at 234–35n.; *Hudson*, 475 U.S., at 305n.; *Keller*, 110 S.Ct. at 2234; *Keller*, 767 P. 2d at 1034; and *Schneider*, 565 F. Supp. at 974.

[75]*Street*, 367 U.S. at 778 (Douglas, J., concurring).

well expect that Jefferson and Madison—who were not habitually given to hyperbole—would agree.

Once we have come to appreciate the lightness of the First Amendment interest in being freed from minuscule exactions, we must turn to the societal interests advanced by union security and bar unification. There is little reason to doubt that union security agreements play a key role in maintaining unionism, which has been one of the mainstays of American society for over a century. *Hanson*, *Street*, and *Abood* rightly judge that the societal interests advanced by union security agreements outweigh dissidents' First Amendment interest in avoiding compulsory contribution to collective bargaining. Dissidents' additional First Amendment interest in avoiding tiny contributions to union political activities is too slight to tip the balance in the other direction. Thus, the right outcome for the union security cases would have been to uphold the rights of unions to bargain for security agreements under which dues could be expended for any legitimate union purposes, including politics.

The integrated bar cases present a different picture. The day after *Keller* was issued the president of the California state bar expressed relief that the Court did not hold mandatory bars unconstitutional.[76] This suggests that the real aim of the plaintiffs may have been the disintegration of the bar.

Yet this may be a non-issue. Professor Schneyer has argued plausibly that bar integration has outlived whatever usefulness it had.[77] During the heyday of the bar integration movement in the early-to-mid-twentieth century, bar association memberships were quite low, and an argument could be made that, supposing bar associations to be socially beneficent, their activities should be enhanced by making them mandatory. Now, however, voluntary bar associations have learned to attract the membership of (typically) 75% of the lawyers in their states by the time-honored expedient of offering attractive side-benefits such as "many types of insurance, car rental and travel discounts, lawyer placement and referral services, meeting facilities, and a journal, newletter, and legislative bulletin."[78] Thus, the societal interest in bar unification may no longer be sufficient to sustain the *Lathrop* balance. If bar unification remains constitutionally accept-

[76]State Bar Loses Dues Fight, The Recorder, June 5, 1990, p. 10.

[77]Schneyer, note 20 *supra*.

[78]*Id.* at 11. By 1970, of the 15 largest voluntary bar associations, only New York had membership below 70%. *Id.* at 10.

able, however, our argument indicates that the unified bar should be able to expend dues on law reform activities. *Keller* was wrongly decided.

Keller's practical importance does not reside in the direct effects of its holding: the noncontribution of dissident lawyers will probably make only a slight dent in bar associations' public affairs budgets. The mischief in the case lies in the Court's endorsement of the dubious distinction between the supposedly apolitical core of bar activity and a suspect politicized periphery. This distinction suggests a rather drastic misunderstanding of what the mission of bar associations is.

III. Law Reform and Visions of the Legal Profession

It is possible to view the legal profession as a commercial enterprise and nothing more. Lawyers offer a valuable service for which they extract rents; any view of legal professionalism that characterizes the provision of legal services in more exalted terms is mystification. This view, however, has difficulty explaining the fact that lawyers typically believe that professionalism means something more than an economic transaction between lawyer and client.

But lawyers are apt to disagree over what professionalism means. In a fascinating study of lawyers in a small New England town, Austin Sarat found a rather sharp split between two competing versions of professionalism.[79] One is the familiar idea that professionalism consists in the zealous pursuit of client interests. The second—equally familiar in its own way—regards lawyers as "bearers of an autonomous, public-regarding civic culture" who would "harmonize the pursuit of private interest with the universal interest of the whole [community]."[80]

A. THE BRANDEISIAN VISION

It is not difficult to see why activity in law reform would occupy a prominent position in this second image of professionalism, which

[79] Sarat, Ideologies of Professionalism: Conflict and Change Among Small Town Lawyers, in Lawyers' Ideals and Lawyers' Practices: Professionalism and the Transformation of the American Legal Profession (Nelson, Trubek, Solomon, eds., forthcoming 1991).

[80] *Id.* at 15, quoting Gordon, Lawyers as the American Aristocracy 2–3, 9 (unpublished lectures 1986).

Sarat assimilates to the tradition of civic republicanism.[81] Louis Brandeis, the paradigm of the republican vision of legal professionalism, argued that a lawyer's training "fits him especially to grapple with the questions which are presented in a democracy."[82] He described reform activity as "the opportunity in the law," and wrote: "Such questions as the regulation of trusts, the fixing of railway rates, the municipalization of public utilities, the relation between capital and labor, call for the exercise of legal ability of the highest order."[83] The research of Robert Gordon has disclosed an almost unbroken tradition of such public activity on the part of lawyers throughout the nineteenth and twentieth centuries,[84] and Terrance Halliday's recent in-depth study of the Chicago Bar Association has confirmed the civic involvement of lawyers along the lines of what I shall call "the Brandeis vision."[85]

In the Brandeis vision, the centrality of law reform activity to legal professionalism is virtually definitional. However, as I shall now argue, activity in law reform forms a crucial component in the first, more familiar, vision of professionalism as well.

B. NEUTRAL PARTISANSHIP

That vision centers around what William Simon has called "the ideology of advocacy," but which I shall call "neutral partisanship," since it appears prominently in legal contexts other than advocacy as well as in advocacy itself.[86] Neutral partisanship may be defined as

---

[81]Sarat, note 79 *supra*, at 15. I am not confident in assigning a civic-republican pedigree to this "republican vision," which seems rather to find its roots in the progressive movement and in functionalist social theory (Gordon's description of lawyers who work to "harmonize the pursuit of private interest with the universal interest of the whole [community]" sounds very much like Parsons). See Simon, note 15 *supra*, Luban, note 15 *supra*.

[82]Brandeis, The Opportunity in the Law, in Business: A Profession 322 (1914).

[83]*Id.* at 322. I have discussed Brandeis's vision in Luban, Lawyers and Justice: An Ethical Study 169–74 (1988) [cited below as Lawyers and Justice] and Luban, note 15 *supra*, at 717, 720–23. See also Shaffer, American Legal Ethics: Text, Readings, and Discussion Topics 241–315 (1985). See generally Strum, Louis D. Brandeis: Justice for the People (1984).

[84]Gordon, note 80 *supra*.

[85]Halliday, Beyond Monopoly: Lawyers, State Crises, and Professional Empowerment (1987).

[86]Simon, The Ideology of Advocacy: Procedural Justice and Professional Ethics, 1978 Wisc. L. Rev. 29 (1978). Elsewhere I have described this view as "the standard conception of the lawyer's role." Lawyers and Justice, note 83 *supra* at 23. However, critics have denied that this conception is in any sense "standard." Schneyer, Moral Philosophy's Standard Misconception of the Lawyer's Role, 1984 Wisc. L. Rev. 1529 (1984); Ellmann, Lawyering for Justice in a Flawed Democracy, 90 Colum. L. Rev. 116, 120–29 (1990). Though I remain convinced

the conjunction of a "principle of partisanship," which demands that in representing clients lawyers do everything within the bounds of the law to advance their clients' interests, with a "principle of nonaccountability," which insists that lawyers are morally nonaccountable for the means used or ends pursued in a representation. Neutral partisanship may take as its credo Lord Brougham's well-known adage for the courtroom advocate:[87]

> An advocate, in the discharge of his duty, knows but one person in all the world, and that person is his client. To save that client by all means and expedients, and at all hazards and costs to other persons, and, amongst them, to himself, is his first and only duty; and in performing this duty he must not regard the alarm, the torments, the destruction which he may bring upon others.

The lawyer is to act as though a client's interests, whatever they may be, outweigh the interests of anyone else, and indeed outweigh the interests of everyone else combined. Such a view seems highly problematic as a moral proposition. To defend it, one must show that neutral partisanship is a requirement imposed by the adversary system, and then justify the adversary system.[88] Even then, however, it is not at all obvious that a morally decent person could undertake a career in a profession so ruthlessly indifferent to "the alarms, the torments, the destruction" of others. It is here that law reform plays a crucial role: though the advocate exploits the law on behalf of clients, the lawyer may later attempt to rectify the law. Let us examine some examples of the role law reform plays in the ideology of advocacy.

1. Discussing one of the classic "hard cases" in legal ethics, Monroe Freedman asks whether a criminal defense lawyer should cross-examine a rape victim about her sex life in order to suggest that she is promiscuous and that she invited sexual intercourse with the defendant she later accused. The defendant, Freedman stipulates, has credibly confessed to his lawyer that he has in fact forcibly raped the prosecutrix, but insists on arguing consent because he has gotten away with rape before (in another state) by so doing.[89]

Freedman argues on the basis of the requirements of the adversary system that "the attorney is bound to provide [the defense] on the

---

that the conception is indeed standard, I shall use the less conclusory term "neutral partisanship." See Luban, Partisanship, Betrayal and Autonomy in the Lawyer-Client Relationship: A Reply to Stephen Ellmann, 90 Colum. L. Rev. 1004 (1990).

[87] 2 The Trial of Queen Caroline 8 (Nightingale ed. 1820–21).

[88] I have argued that this justification fails. Lawyers and Justice, note 83 *supra*, chs. 5–7.

[89] Freedman, Lawyers' Ethics in an Adversary System 43–44 (1975).

client's behalf."[90] Some may reject his argument; my concern here is not with its merits, however, but with one of Freedman's subsequent remarks:[91]

> For the lawyer who finds the presentation of that defense, and perhaps others in rape cases, to go beyond what he or she can in good conscience do, there are two courses that should be followed. The first is to be active in efforts to reform the law in that regard; the second is to decline to accept the defense of rape cases. . . .

Of course, some lawyer will eventually have to represent the defendant, so declining to accept the defense of rape cases merely displaces the problem onto someone else. Thus, the preponderant weight of Freedman's suggestion falls on law reform: working to enact shield laws is an indispensable safety valve to release the pressure of the dilemma.

2. A similar argument appears in Fuller and Randall's *Professional Responsibility: Report of the Joint Conference of the ABA-AALS*,[92] the closest thing we have to an official ABA vindication of the adversary system. The purpose of this document is straightforward:[93]

> Confronted by the layman's charge that he is nothing but a hired brain and voice, the lawyer often finds it difficult to convey an insight into the value of the adversary system or an understanding of the tacit restraints with which it is infused. Accordingly, it was decided that the first need was for a reasoned statement of the lawyer's responsibilities, set in the context of the adversary system. The document printed below is intended to meet that need.

The report offers a series of arguments to demonstrate the efficacy of the adversary system as a truth-finder.[94] Shortly after these arguments, Fuller and Randall relate an incident in the life of Thomas Talfourd. As a barrister Talfourd had successfully represented a father in a suit over the custody of a child. Judgment for Talfourd's client was based on his superior legal right, though the court recognized in the case at bar that the mother had a stronger moral claim to custody than the father. Having thus encountered in the course of his practice an injustice in the law as then applied by the courts, Tal-

[90] *Id.* at 48–49.

[91] *Id.* at 49.

[92] 44 A.B.A.J. 1159 (1958) (cited below as Joint Conference Report).

[93] *Id.* at 1159.

[94] I have criticized these arguments in Lawyers and Justice, note 83 *supra*, at 71–74, 79–81.

fourd later as a member of Parliament secured the enactment of a statute that would make impossible a repetition of the result his own advocacy had helped to bring about.[95] As in Freedman's discussion of the rape cross-examination, Talfourd's law reform activity seems like a necessary counterweight to mitigate the moral anomalies of the advocate's role. Indeed, this point lies close to the heart of Fuller's and Randall's theory, which consists largely of an argument that the excesses of any given lawyerly role are counterbalanced by other roles.

3. The ABA Code of Professional Responsibility cites the Fuller/Randall report in its analysis of the adversary system[96] as well as in several of its pronouncements on the law reform function.[97] Citing Fuller and Randall, the Code states in Canon 8 that lawyers "should participate in proposing and supporting legislation and programs to improve the system, without regard to the general interests or desires of clients or former clients" (EC 8–1). The same point appears in EC 7–17 as part of an argument that activity in law reform contrary to the interests of clients does not violate the duty of loyalty to clients:

> The obligation of loyalty to his client applies only to a lawyer in the discharge of his professional duties and implies no obligation to adopt a personal viewpoint favorable to the interests or desires of his client. . . . [H]e may take positions on public issues and espouse legal reforms he favors without regard to the individual views of any client.

In a footnote to this passage, the Code's drafters quote one of the Fuller/Randall report's most fulsomely self-congratulatory sentences: "It is one of the glories of the profession that it admits of this freedom." The same footnote quotes language from an article on the lawyer as tax adviser:[98]

> No doubt some tax lawyers feel constrained to abstain from activities on behalf of a better tax system because they think that their clients may object. Clients have no right to object if the tax adviser handles their affairs competently and faithfully and independently of his private views as to tax policy. They buy his expert services, not his . . . silence on issues that gravely affect the public interest.

These references to the profession's "freedom" and "independence" highlight a crucial feature in the world view of neutral partisanship.

---

[95]Joint Conference Report, note 92 *supra*, at 1162.

[96]EC 7–19, note 32.

[97]EC 7–17, n. 29, EC 8–1, n. 2, EC 8–2, n. 4.

[98]ABA Code, EC 7–17, n. 29, quoting Paul, The Lawyer as a Tax Adviser, 25 Rocky Mt. L. Rev. 412, 434 (1953).

On that world view, lawyers need not believe or endorse any of the arguments they offer on behalf of clients; indeed, lawyers in a courtroom setting are actually forbidden from asserting their personal opinion as to the justness of a cause.[99] It is this distance between the lawyer's personal convictions and the arguments she vicariously offers as the client's "legal voice" that justifies her claim of moral nonaccountability;[100] but the same distance between personal beliefs and professional arguments implies the lawyer's independence from the client.

The importance of law reform activity follows from this linkage between the principle of nonaccountability and the lawyer's independence from her client. If the lawyer wishes to disclaim accountability for furthering morally dubious client projects, she must demonstrate, not merely assert, that her conscience really is distinct from that of her clients. Otherwise, her claim of distance between personal convictions and professional arguments is empty and self-serving. In this sense, activity in law reform forms the linchpin of the system of neutral partisanship.

Notice that Freedman, Fuller and Randall, and the Code of Professional Responsibility are not talking merely about what I have called narrow law reform, that is, advising the courts about procedural law and the administration of justice. The idea, rather, is that in the ordinary course of their practice lawyers will have their noses rubbed repeatedly in the infirmities and irrationalities of the substantive law they deal with. Neutral partisanship insists that they exploit those infirmities and irrationalities on behalf of their clients, but the antiphonal strain I have been emphasizing insists in addition that they then go to work to correct the law. This is the wide law reform function of deliberating and commenting about substantive law, what the California statute refers to quaintly as "all matters pertaining to the advancement of the science of jurisprudence."

C. THE ROLE OF BAR ASSOCIATIONS

Where might bar associations fit into this picture? Let me sketch a utopian picture of a bar association in its full Durkheimian glory, supposing for the moment that it actually dedicated part of its activities to "the advancement of the science of jurisprudence." Such

---

[99] ABA Code DR 7–106(C)(4); Model Rules of Professional Conduct, rule 3.4(e).

[100] On the justification of zealous advocacy as an attempt to allow legally mute clients to speak, see Lawyers and Justice, note 83 *supra*, at 85–87, 193.

an association would advance the law reform efforts of lawyers in two ways. First, it would provide moral and practical support to lawyers' efforts at independence from their clients—assuming, of course, that lawyers actually desire that independence. Many lawyers, we will assume, share that desire.

Others, however, do not. Obviously, many lawyers would much prefer that law benefiting their clients stay exactly as it is, regardless of its effects on others. Such lawyers will involve themselves in law reform activities only when they benefit clients. Given this fact of life, a bar association can advance law reform by providing a forum in which other lawyers—lawyers who do not have a client interest to serve or who have adverse client interests to serve—can participate in formulating proposals.

Bar associations can thus simultaneously reinforce civic-minded lawyers in their efforts to exercise independence from their clients, and counteract the efforts of lawyers who view law reform as nothing more than zealous advocacy of their clients in an alternative forum. For the altruists the association provides moral support; for the advocates, it provides a Madisonian arena in which interest may counteract interest. Let me briefly elaborate these two functions.

1. *Encouraging the altruists.* Fuller and Randall assert that "It is one of the glories of the profession that it admits of . . . freedom" from the interests and world-views of clients. But winning independence from client interests is easier said than done; independence from clients is a precarious and hard-to-attain goal, not a given of the lawyer's moral world.

Professor Mark Osiel points out that the lawyer's "independence" is built on paradoxical foundations. Independence requires more than a good will. It requires power and money, and the American legal profession has acquired its extraordinary levels of power and money by assiduously advancing the interests of the same wealthy clients from whom lawyers are supposed to be independent.[101] An attempt by lawyers to reform the law contrary to client interests inevitably amounts to biting the hand that feeds them, and in this respect the project of wide law reform may well be a machine that turns itself off: lawyers who engage in wide law reform may antagonize and lose clients, thereby forfeiting the material basis of their independence. Conversely, lawyers obtain power and wealth, the raw materials of independence, by orbiting around powerful and wealthy clients. In

[101]Osiel, Lawyers as Monopolists, Aristocrats, and Entrepreneurs (review of Abel & Lewis, Lawyers in Society), 103 Harv. L. Rev. 2009, 2016–21, 2046 (1990).

Professor Osiel's words, "American lawyers were . . . denied the possibility of leadership *within* the corporate world without becoming *of* it."[102] Thus, the Tocquevillean, Brandeisian, and Parsonian agenda for lawyers—to mediate between conflicting social interests, remaining independent of all—"was riddled with irresoluble tensions."[103]

Yet matters are not as bad as this way of posing the problem suggests. It is as easy to exaggerate the constraints on lawyers as it is to exaggerate their freedom, and we should not entertain too seriously the idea of a successful and lucrative law practice as in actuality nothing more than a gilded cage.[104] Much as they may wish to deny it, lawyers enjoy significant degrees of power and freedom, and the more powerful they are the more degrees of freedom they enjoy. The key to professional involvement in law reform lies in creating institutional structures that amplify that freedom and enhance lawyers' resolve to employ it.

Bar associations buttress lawyers' freedom to engage in wide law reform in at least two related ways. First, a lawyer who works at law reform through the regularized channels of professional-association activity simply presents a less prominent target for client anger than a lawyer operating entirely as a free agent. Not only is the lawyer less conspicuous, but activity in a professional association is more obviously the lawyer's own and proper business. Second, a collegial association can provide a kind of support—moral support in the most literal sense of the term—that solitary lawyers lack. Professor Osiel writes, "When social theorists of the past sought reinforcement for professional independence from the antisocial demands of clients, they turned to the professional community of peers as a buttress. . . ."[105] If bar associations insist on the propriety, and indeed the necessity, of wide law reform undertaken independently of the advancement of client interests they enhance the independence of lawyers. Conversely, a decision like *Keller*, which implies that the wide law reform function of bar associations is somehow improper, diminishes professional independence and undermines the justification of the entire professional role.

2. *Tempering the Fixers*. In a study of Chicago large-firm lawyers, Robert Nelson discovered that a large number held political views

---

[102] *Id*. at 2046.

[103] *Ibid*.

[104] See Gordon, The Independence of Lawyers, 68 B.U.L. Rev. 1 (1988) for imaginative suggestions about how lawyers may exercise their independence from clients.

[105] Osiel, note 101 *supra*, at 2017.

quite skeptical of the corporations who comprise virtually their entire clientele. Forty percent of these lawyers believed that "there is too much power concentrated in the hands of a few large companies for the good of the country";[106] 43% denied that consumer interests are better protected by competition among sellers than by federal intervention;[107] 46% disagreed that "economic profits are by and large justly distributed in the United States today" as compared with only 30% agreement.[108]

However, when Nelson queried his subjects about particular law reforms they would support, he discovered[109]

> a consistent pro-client cast to the suggestions. Specific recommendations came out against government regulation, for management, for the defense in litigation, for wealthy taxpayers, and for banks and creditors. . . . If there is a distance between large-firm lawyers and their corporate clientele over general social and political questions, there is not much disparity between client concerns and the lawyers' agenda for change in the legal fields in which they actually practice.

This should come as no great surprise. Closing loopholes that benefit your clients seems manifestly irrational, for a variety of obvious reasons, not the least of which is that it makes your job more difficult on a day-to-day basis. Nor is the crusading tax lawyer likely to mollify an aggrieved client by reading aloud the Code's admonition that "[c]lients have no right to object if the tax adviser handles their affairs competently and faithfully and independently of his private views as to tax policy."[110] These are uncomfortable facts that functionalists ignore at their peril; as Niklas Luhmann wryly observes, "Most astonishing . . . —especially because of a theory proposed by Karl Marx—is Durkheim's neglect of the ability of *money* to neutralize morality in face-to-face interaction."[111]

Thus, while many lawyers desire the independence necessary to engage in law reform, many others will have no desire to close the loopholes they make a living exploiting. On the contrary, they will

---

[106] Nelson, Ideology, Practice, and Professional Autonomy: Social Values and Client Relationships in the Large Law Firm, 37 Stan. L. Rev. 503, 514 (1985).

[107] *Id.* at 515.

[108] *Id.* at 517.

[109] *Id.* at 524–25.

[110] ABA Code, EC 7–17, n. 29, quoting Paul, The Lawyer as a Tax Adviser, 25 Rocky Mt. L. Rev. at 434.

[111] Luhmann, The Differentiation of Society 15 (Holmes & Larmore trans. 1982).

become active in law reform activities only to press reforms that benefit their clients, or to quash reforms that might remove such benefits. From this perspective, Fuller's and Randall's edifying anecdote about Thomas Talfourd should be regarded as an unrepresentative fable. Lawyers who lobby for "law reforms" may well be fixers aiming solely at promoting client interests in the legislative arena.

Yet here too bar associations may have a salutary effect, by pitting special-interest subsections of the bar against each other. If, for example, the insurance bar attempts to throw the bar association's prestige behind a tort-reform package, plaintiffs' attorneys will labor to counteract the effort. Of course, before accepting this argument one would wish to know whether the politics of a bar association and its relevant policy-making committees are open and democratic, and bar associations may differ greatly along these dimensions.[112] But assuming the best—and we should remember that in a unified bar all subsections are of necessity represented—bar associations offer rather unique possibilities for Madisonian checks on lawyers whose sole aim is to advance client interests.

I have described the picture I have just drawn as "a utopian picture of a bar association as it might be," and a final question that might be asked is whether the picture has anything to do with bar associations as they are. Professor Abel has argued that bar associations should be understood much more cynically, as attempts to control legal markets through the supply side.[113] Other sociologists of the profession have likewise argued that professional associations play a largely self-interested and probably discreditable role.[114] Still others argue that a professional organization diverse enough to be truly representative will be prevented by its very diversity from "taking action on any but the least controversial, most innocuous questions."[115] Common sense lends some support to these arguments. The one in-depth study we possess of the actual workings of a bar association nevertheless points to a different conclusion. Terrance Halliday, aided by stenographic transcripts of all meetings of the Chicago Bar Association's governing

[112] See Halliday & Cappell, Indicators of Democracy in Professional Associations: Elite Recruitment, Turnover, and Decision Making in a Metropolitan Bar Association, 1979 ABF Res. J. 697 (1979).

[113] Abel, note 11 *supra*.

[114] See, *e.g.*, Larson, The Rise of Professionalism: A Sociological Analysis (1977); Auerbach, Unequal Justice: Lawyers and Social Change in Modern America (1976).

[115] Heinz *et al.*, Diversity, Representation, and Leadership in an Urban Bar, 1976 ABF Res. J. 717, 771 (1976).

board between 1950 and 1970, found an organization substantially involved in civic affairs in a variety of ways that seemed largely independent of professional self-interest.[116] Whether this result can be generalized is, of course, a matter of speculation; but there is no reason to suspect that the Chicago Bar Association is atypical.

Let me summarize the argument. First: wide law reform is an essential, not an accidental, part of legal ethics—not only on the Brandeis vision that I support, but also on the powerfully important view of neutral partisanship. Second: because of the paradoxical and self-undercutting nature of professional independence, collegial associations play an essential, not an accidental, role in the enterprise of wide law reform. As Professor Osiel rightly observes, "If the primary problem, then, lies in the social underpinnings of legal ethics rather than in their logical incoherence, effective reform might best be directed at these underpinnings."[117] Bar associations form an important part of the underpinnings of professional independence. Third: although bar associations may often busy themselves in self-regarding projects, they do not always. It is unwarranted empirical speculation to suppose that they do not also play the role that Durkheim, Brandeis, and Parsons regard as "the opportunity in the law": the opportunity to reform law in the public interest.

What should one say, however, about the political function of bar associations, over and above the wide law reform function? The California bar, remember, took a position on the nuclear freeze, while the Puerto Rican Colegio de Abogados appears to have conducted an entire foreign policy. Obviously, neither of these political stances is tied to law reform, no matter how wide, in more than fanciful and nominal ways. More importantly, neither issue is tied to any special competence that lawyers' training or experience may be expected to confer on them. In adopting these and similar stances, bar associations are not acting as a deliberative forum or advisory body; rather, they are acting as pressure groups. Now as a general proposition there is nothing wrong with lawyers organizing as a pressure group, and thus there is no particular reason for a voluntary bar association to refrain from taking political positions—no reason, that is, beyond respect for its membership, and a sense that its credibility may be squandered if it issues a flurry of manifestos. A unified bar, however, goes beyond its own justification if it takes political posi-

[116]Halliday, note 85 *supra*.

[117]Osiel, note 101 *supra*, at 2049.

tions to which the special competences of lawyers have no obvious relevance. In this respect, the analogy between mandatory bar associations and labor unions operating under security agreements breaks down. A labor union is, and is meant to be, a pressure group advancing the interests of workers (including their ideological interests). The aim of labor legislation such as the National Labor Relations Act has been to normalize the operations of such pressure groups by at once legitimizing and channeling the pressure they exert. This is entirely different from the aim of statutes and court orders unifying the bar. The goal of the latter, we have seen, is primarily to turn bar associations to other-regarding purposes tied to the work and competences of lawyers.

This is not to suggest that the distinction between wide law reform and political activity to which the special competences of lawyers bear no obvious relevance is an easy one to draw. Particularly in light of the powerful arguments of critical legal scholars that law is through-and-through political, to say nothing of Tocqueville's observation that Americans habitually turn every political question into a legal question, we may be skeptical of the law/politics distinction. Yet unless we wish to deny that lawyers know anything distinctive at all, we must admit that legal knowledge is about something. The watershed test is then whether a given political issue has aspects that legal knowledge is about.

What is striking in *Keller* is how many of the bar activities that the appellants and Chief Justice Rehnquist catalogue—evidently with the expectation that to read of them is to disapprove of them—have obviously legal aspects, and therefore pass this test with no difficulty. Chief Justice Rehnquist offers a list of bar positions on criminal procedure and other constitutional issues, issues of legal ethics, the creation of causes of action and the limitation of federal court jurisdiction, possible tax law reforms, and similar matters that obviously have a great deal to do with the special competences of lawyers. These are matters of law reform, not politics in its purely extralegal sense. Even the bar's gun control positions implicate constitutional judgments as well as the expertise of the numerous lawyers (such as prosecutors) who work closely with police. Obviously, lawyers will differ about these issues, and thus the bar's position will anger many of its members. This, however, is an inevitable and perhaps not even regrettable consequence of majority rule in an organization. Those who lose out have a complaint only if the vote was unfair or if the matter was not appropriate for the organization to put to a vote.

In Chief Justice Rehnquist's list, only "creating criminal sanctions for violation of laws pertaining to the display for sale of drug paraphernalia to minors," "requesting Congress to refrain from enacting a guest worker program or from permitting the importation of workers from other countries," and the endorsement of a nuclear freeze, are proposals about which we would not expect lawyers to have any special knowledge or insight to contribute (and even these assessments could be disputed). Only these did not belong on the agenda of a mandatory bar. In the end, the *Keller* opinion reveals a rather shocking underestimate of the capacities of the bar and the relevance of law to public policy.

IV. Conclusion

The issues and arguments in *Keller* and the labor cases it rests upon possess a curiously metaphysical character, in which the passions and rhetoric far outstrip the phenomena that excite them. Consider first the appellants' side. The appellants—opponents of mandatory bar membership—press a freedom of association argument even though they lie under no compulsion whatever actually to associate with their fellow members. They press a free speech argument even though bar membership does not restrict their freedom of speech. And they protest the use of their compulsory dues for political purposes even though the actual amount of money at stake is little more than the price of a case of beer.

Yet bar unification has provoked a nonstop stream of apocalyptic negative rhetoric, of which Justice Douglas's fear in *Lathrop* that "we practically give *carte blanche* to any legislature to put at least professional people into goose-stepping brigades"[118] is unfortunately typical. Nor is the rhetoric on the other side, which typically employs fulsomely overstated terms to characterize the state's interest in obtaining the bar association's advice, much of an improvement.

All in all, the arguments in *Keller* provide no reason to revise the assessment offered by Professor Schneyer of *Lathrop:*[119]

> [T]he court had good reason not to overestimate the constitutional gravity of compelled association in the unified bar. In particular,

[118]*Lathrop*, 367 U.S. at 884 (Douglas, J., dissenting).

[119]Schneyer, note 20 *supra*, at 52. See also Gaebler, note 71 *supra*, at 1019–23.

> there is only a negligible risk that forced membership would cause people mistakenly to associate a lawyer with a state bar position she opposed. Insofar as bar membership and dues are understood to be prerequisites for law practice and not simply matters of choice, they presumably are also taken as very flimsy evidence that a lawyer supports bar positions. This point aside, if lawyers *are* sometimes misidentified as supporting bar positions, it may well be because they are lawyers, not bar members. . . . [A]n unaffiliated lawyer in a voluntary bar state faces a comparable problem. To illustrate: the Minnesota State Bar Association now claims about 80% of Minnesota's practicing lawyers as members; . . . consequently, association positions cannot be much less often misattributed to lawyer nonmembers than a unified bar's positions would be misattributed to captive members.

On the other side of the issue, and precisely because the amounts of money actually at stake are so slight, it should cause no diminution of law reform activity on the part of a unified bar association to refund the proportional dues of objecting members, and mere respect for the membership may often recommend this course. It seems in the end that no tangible interest would be threatened by *Keller* no matter how the case came out. As seems to be true of so many issues, this one seems to be all spin control with no object actually spun—a Cheshire cat's smile.

What is the real issue in this through-the-looking-glass debate? It is reasonably clear that the purpose of the litigation in the various *Abood*-based challenges to bar political activities has not been to obtain an *Abood/Hudson* dues reduction but rather to stop the bar from taking public positions, perhaps as a step toward abolishing the unified bar altogether. The *Keller* appellants asked for an injunction "prohibiting the State Bar from using its name to advance political and ideological causes or beliefs," arguing "that they cannot be compelled to associate with an organization that engages in political or ideological activities beyond those for which mandatory financial support is justified under the principles of *Lathrop* and *Abood.*"[120] Though the Court declined to address this argument "in the first instance," it invited state courts to consider it, and thus left open the possibility that it might in the future smile upon the total disengagement of integrated bars from law reform.

This year, at any rate, this may not be necessary. Though *Keller*

[120] *Keller,* 110 S.Ct. at 2238.

specifically declined to order the California bar to abjure the wide law reform and political functions, the bar responded by deleting 45 items from the agenda of its annual meeting.[121] Other states' integrated bars, apprehensive about litigation initiated by well-financed adversaries such as the Pacific Legal Foundation (which represented the *Keller* plaintiffs), are quite likely to engage in similar self-censorship. Such voluntary self-censorship would be the worst of all possible outcomes—worse, in fact, than overturning *Lathrop* and holding integrated bars unconstitutional. As Professor Schneyer argues, the existence of a mandatory bar inevitably discourages the formation of voluntary organizations to take up the slack.[122] Thus, driving the integrated bar out of law reform activities will have the effect of eradicating the only effective collegial forum available for lawyers to debate these matters. This, in turn, may shrivel the state bar as a forum even for the issues left to it; as one California lawyer worried, "If people can't talk about anything other than the dull stuff [at the bar's Conference of Delegates], will people pay the money to go?"[123]

It is perhaps no coincidence that shortly after *Keller* was decided, the ABA House of Delegates voted to rescind a previously-passed resolution supporting the claim that women enjoy a constitutional right to abortion. The politicking around the issue was predictably fierce,[124] and in the end the ABA adopted a *Keller*-like position that it is inappropriate for the organization to adopt resolutions concerning volatile public issues. This is noteworthy because the ABA is a voluntary, not a mandatory, bar association, and therefore remains totally unaffected by *Keller*. The Court's resounding 9–0 endorsement of a depoliticized conception of the bar may well have influenced the House of Dele-

---

[121]Peters & Checchio, State Bar Berated for Response to Keller, The Recorder (July 12, 1990). The action was taken at the advice of the bar's general counsel for several reasons. First and foremost, it was too late in the year to permit protesting members to opt out of expenditures, and the bar wished to comply in good faith with *Keller*. Telephone conversation with Diane Yu, General Counsel of the State Bar, September 22, 1990. According to Ms. Yu, the deletion of items from the House of Delegates' agenda is a one-time remedy that will not be repeated in future years. Second, the State Bar was dismayed by the 9–0 defeat in *Keller;* since the matter has been remanded to the California courts the bar wishes to proceed cautiously. Third, after eight years of litigation the bar simply wants to close the issue. Telephone conversation with Starr Babcock, State Bar's general counsel office, September 11, 1990.

[122]Schneyer, note 20 *supra*, at 34.

[123]Peters & Checchio, note 121 *supra*.

[124]It also transcended the bar itself: The New York Times discovered that the ad hoc group attempting to overturn the resolution was being run secretly from the national headquarters of a long-established anti-abortion group. Lewis, Abortion Issue a Magnet for A.B.A. Annual Event, N.Y. Times (July 27, 1990) at B5.

gates' sense of the boundary between proper and improper bar association activity. Together, *Keller* and the ABA's anti-controversy vote project a curiously stunted sense of the public responsibilities of lawyers.[125]

So do other decisions of the Court. The term before *Keller*, the Court held 5–4 that federal courts lack statutory authority to compel attorneys to represent the poor in civil cases;[126] it expressly reserved the question whether federal courts possess inherent authority to compel attorneys to take such cases, thereby inviting a challenge to that authority.[127] Though the Court insisted that it believes firmly in a *pro bono publico* obligation of attorneys, *Mallard* together with *Keller* lead one to wonder what the content of that obligation might be. The same day as *Keller* the Court decided its latest lawyer-advertising case, holding in *Peel v. Attorney Registration and Disciplinary Commission of Illinois*[128] that lawyers have a constitutional right to advertise certification as a trial specialist by the National Board of Trial Advocacy; two terms earlier the Court had recognized a constitutional right of lawyers to engage in targeted mass-mail advertising.[129] The Court thereby expands the rights of lawyers while simultaneously contracting their responsibilities.

The majority opinions in these and other lawyer advertising cases straightforwardly embrace a notion of legal professionalism as a means to the end of efficient delivery of legal services to legal consumers.[130] The economic arguments for the efficiency of advertising scarcely need discussion, and the only real question posed by the Court's position is where it will end. There are powerful economic arguments that such forbidden practices as selling shares in large-scale lawsuits will lead to more efficient delivery of legal services; yet

---

[125]This is not to say that it would be proper for a mandatory bar association to take a position on the abortion issue. Although the issue clearly contains significant constitutional and legal aspects about which the opinion of the bar is germane, these are hardly the most important issues in the abortion debate. Thus, the abortion issue straddles the divide between the wide law reform and political functions of the bar.

[126]Mallard v. The United States District Court for the Southern District of Iowa, 109 S.Ct. 1814 (1989).

[127]*Id.* at 1822–23.

[128]110 S.Ct. 2281 (1990).

[129]Shapero v. Kentucky State Bar, 108 S.Ct. 1916 (1988).

[130]I have taken the notion of professionalism as a means to the end of client service from an interesting paper of Murray Schwartz, Lawyers and the Supreme Court: Of Means and Ends, 3 Ga. State L. Rev. 179 (1987).

one wonders what legal professionalism would mean if tort futures were traded on Wall Street.[131] The point is more general: the concept of professionalism incipient in the advertising cases cannot sustain the usual contrast with commercialism, for the concept simply *is* commercialism.

This obviously troubles Justice O'Connor, who describes *Bates* and its successors as a "line of cases built on defective premises and flawed reasoning."[132] She explains: "The roots of the error in our attorney advertising cases are a defective analogy between professional services and standardized consumer products."[133] Justice O'Connor believes that whatever their economic significance, advertising restrictions play "a delicate role . . . in preserving the norms of the legal profession," a profession whose "goal is public service."[134] This sounds quite promising. On inspection, however, this "delicate role" proves to consist in pure symbolism: "Such restrictions act as a concrete, day-to-day reminder to the practising attorney of why it is improper for any member of this profession to regard it as a trade or occupation like any other."[135] Professionalism will be instilled by hanging the pre-*Bates* albatross of detailed restrictions on the size and shape of business cards and letterheads around the collective neck of the bar. Lacking a more robust conception of legal professionalism, Justice O'Connor is compelled to fall back on the legal ethics of yesteryear, which imposed obligations largely in order to maintain professional status by maintaining professional decorum.

Thus, in the end the disengagement of the legal profession evidenced in *Keller* distorts both the Court's majority and minority jurisprudence of the legal profession. In addition, I have argued, the Court's view that the legal profession's core is apolitical and disengaged from public affairs can only reinforce the sense of *anomie*

---

[131]See Shukaitis, A Market in Personal Injury Tort Claims, 16 J. Leg. Stud. 329 (1987). The argument for claim selling is offered in powerful form by Peter Schuck: "The legal system cannot have it both ways. If it desires the end, then it must desire (or at least accept) the only practical means to that end. If it wishes to encourage so-called public interest tort litigation on behalf of diffuse, poorly financed interests over extremely complex issues of scientific or technical uncertainty, then it must either transform the government into a tort litigator on behalf of these interests (a solution with enormous problems of its own), or it must countenance, indeed welcome, private arrangements for securing the resources necessary for effectively prosecuting such cases." Schuck, Agent Orange on Trial 204 (1986).

[132]*Shapero*, 108 S.Ct. at 1925 (O'Connor, J., dissenting).

[133]*Id.* at 1928.

[134]*Id.* at 1929, 1930.

[135]*Id.* at 1930.

within the profession. *Keller* plays directly to the forces that Justice O'Connor decries—forces that have thrown the contemporary profession into deep turmoil. It may be well to end with an admonition offered in 1959 by Hannah Arendt:[136]

> More and more people in the countries of the Western world, which since the decline of the ancient world has regarded freedom from politics as one of the basic freedoms, make use of this freedom and have retreated from the world and their obligations within it. This withdrawal from the world need not harm an individual; he may even cultivate great talents to the point of genius and so by a detour be useful to the world again. But with each such retreat an almost demonstrable loss to the world takes place; what is lost is the specific and usually irreplaceable in-between which should have formed between this individual and his fellow men.

The "in-between which should have formed between this individual and his fellow men" may be taken as a formula defining legal professionalism at its best.

---

[136]Arendt, Men in Dark Times 4–5 (1968).

JOHN H. LANGBEIN

THE SUPREME COURT FLUNKS TRUSTS

When the administrator of a pension or employee benefit plan denies a participant's claim for a benefit under the plan, and the dissatisfied participant sues to recover the benefit, what standard of review should the court apply in evaluating the reasonableness of the administrator's decision? Should the court adopt a deferential standard of review, presuming the correctness of the administrator's decision and requiring the participant to bear the burden of showing that the decision was unreasonable? Or should the court apply a de novo standard of review, considering the merits of the benefit denial without any presumption in favor of the plan's internal decisionmaking?

Because ERISA, the 1974 regulatory scheme,[1] federalizes the field of pension and employee benefit plans, the question of the appropriate standard of review of benefit denials is one of federal law. Because, however, the statutory text fails to speak to the standard of review, the federal courts have had to deal with the question as a matter of decisional law. By the late 1980s, deferential review under the so-called arbitrary-and-capricious standard was the norm among the courts of

John H. Langbein is Chancellor Kent Professor of Law and Legal History, Yale University.

AUTHOR'S NOTE: I acknowledge with gratitude helpful suggestions from Richard A. Posner, Alan Schwartz, Lawrence Waggoner, and Charles B. Wolf; and from law school workshop participants at Chicago, Connecticut, Harvard, Syracuse, and Yale.

[1]Employee Retirement Income Security Act of 1974, P.L. No. 93–406, 88 Stat. 829 (1974), codified as amended primarily in 29 USCS §1001 *et seq* (1982 & Supp 1990). Citation hereafter is to ERISA § numbers rather than to USCS numbers.

0-226-09573-8/91/1990-0002$02.00

appeal,[2] although some significant exceptions were being carved from that standard, especially in the Third Circuit. In *Firestone Tire & Rubber Co. v. Bruch*,[3] the Supreme Court astonished the ERISA bar by overturning the arbitrary-and-capricious standard and instituting de novo review.

The issue in *Bruch* is one of considerable practical importance, on account of the extent of ERISA's turf. Although ERISA is often called the "pension reform law," the statute governs employee benefit plans of all sorts. Among the nonpension plans (called "welfare benefit plans") that ERISA regulates are those that provide most of the nation's health care, as well as plans that provide for severance pay, childcare services, accident and life insurance, tuition and educational assistance, and a variety of other fringe benefits. Health plans alone make millions of benefit determinations every month. Fortunately, most of these decisions flow automatically from unambiguous plan terms, but doubts inevitably arise at the margin. For example: How much vision impairment must a worker suffer in order to qualify as blind under a disability plan?[4] Or, does a novel medical procedure fall within the definition of covered benefits under a health plan?[5] Because the number of plans and of benefit determinations is so enormous, benefit denial cases have come to constitute the largest category of ERISA litigation.

There are solid justifications for insisting on more searching review of plan decisionmaking than was occurring in pre-*Bruch* practice. However, the Supreme Court in *Bruch* dealt with the problem so awkwardly that plan drafters have been able to evade the Court's decision. There is reason to think that the very dissatisfaction that brought the issue in *Bruch* to the Supreme Court in the first place will recur, and that the Court will have to face the question anew. Understanding why the *Bruch* decision miscarried is, therefore, a matter of consequence for the future of pension law. Furthermore, because the Supreme Court's opinion in *Bruch* rests on an elementary error in applying long-settled principles of trust law, it is important from the standpoint of trust law to make clear why the Court's position is

---

[2]Firestone's Brief in the Supreme Court collects authority from the circuits, at 8, note 5. See also Flint, ERISA: The Arbitrary and Capricious Rule under Siege, 39 Cath. U. L. Rev. 133, 139–43 (1989).

[3]109 S.Ct. 948 (1989).

[4]Pokratz v. Jones Dairy Farm, 771 F.2d 206 (7th Cir. 1985).

[5]*E.g.*, Egbert v. Connecticut General Life Ins. Co., 900 F.2d 1032 (7th Cir. 1990) (in vitro fertilization procedure held covered).

insupportable. The Supreme Court is the final arbiter of federal statutory law under ERISA, but not of the common law of trusts that the Court purported to apply in *Bruch*. Trust law is predominantly a state-law field. The Court can impose a nonsense reading of ERISA by fiat, but it cannot force state courts to repeat the error in ordinary trust law settings.

I. Pension and Employee Benefit Trusts

A. Why Plans Are Trusts

ERISA requires that pension and employee benefit plans take the trust form.[6] The idea of mandating that plan assets be trusteed was not novel to ERISA. The Taft-Hartley Act of 1947 requires that a union-sponsored multiemployer plan take the form of a trust with equal numbers of employer-designated and union-designated trustees.[7] Since 1921 the Internal Revenue Code has insisted upon the use of the trust for pension plans as a precondition for what we now call "qualifying" the plan for tax benefits.[8] Back into the last century, at the dawn of the private pension system, employers set up pension plans in the trust form.[9]

1. *Segregation of assets*. There are two main reasons why our legal system has found it convenient to structure plans in the trust form. The trust is a characteristic device for situations in which there is some reason to have a separate entity or conduit. Pension plans have such a need: achieving the deferral of wages. Instead of paying wages directly to the employee, the employer contributes to a segregated fund in which assets accumulate for future payment of benefits. This segregation of the fund is the attribute that made the pension trust attractive for the purposes of the Internal Revenue Code.[10]

---

[6]Unless plan assets take the form of insurance contracts, ERISA §403 requires that "all assets of an employee benefit plan shall be held in trust . . . ." ERISA §403(a).

[7]Labor Management Relations (Taft-Hartley) Act §302(c)(5), 29 USC §186(c)(5).

[8]See discussion in Fischel & Langbein, ERISA's Fundamental Contradiction: The Exclusive Benefit Rule, 55 U. Chi. L. Rev. 1105, 1108, and text at note 14.

[9]*E.g.*, McNevin v. Solvay Process Co, 32 App. Div. 610, 53 N.Y. Supp. 98 (1898), aff'd per curiam 167 N.Y. 530, 60 N.E. 1115 (1901).

[10]Ordinarily, the employer would not receive a deduction for wages paid until the employee receives the payment and is subject to taxes on it. Pension plans are exceptions. The employer gets the deduction currently although the employee receives the benefit in later years. As a general matter (depreciation apart), the Internal Revenue Code is reluctant to allow deductions for mere bookkeeping entries. By requiring that the employer make pension payments into a separate trust, the Code assures that the employer does not get a deduction until the pension

2. *Trust fiduciary law.* The other great advantage of trust law is that it imports a set of well-developed fiduciary standards and ancillary remedial rules. The great rubrics of substantive trust law are the duty of prudent management and the duty of loyalty.[11] The trustee is required to invest trust assets and to conduct trust functions in accordance with objectively reasonable standards (prudence). And the trustee is required to deal with trust property for the sole interest of the trust beneficiaries, thus not for the trustee's own gain (loyalty).

The Taft-Hartley Act imposed the trust form on multiemployer plans in 1947 in order to prevent John L. Lewis and other labor leaders from using plan assets for union organizing or for self-enrichment.[12] ERISA was enacted in 1974 in the wake of more than a decade of Congressional investigation into looting and other abuses of plans by some union leaders, and ERISA fiduciary law was meant to be the cure. The drafters of ERISA determined to "apply rules and remedies similar to those under traditional trust law to govern the conduct of fiduciaries."[13] ERISA insists that persons exercising discretion over plan assets[14] be subject to fiduciary standards that are derived from trust law and that are spelled out in the statute. Lest plan drafters be tempted to use the plan documents to squelch the safeguards of ERISA fiduciary law, the statute contains an anti-opt-out measure, section 404(a)(1)(D), requiring that plan documents be "consistent with the provisions of [ERISA]."[15]

3. *The exclusive benefit rule.* The centerpiece of ERISA fiduciary law, commonly called the exclusive benefit rule, is ERISA's version of the trust-law duty of loyalty. An ERISA fiduciary "shall discharge his duties with respect to the plan solely in the interest of the beneficiaries and for the exclusive purpose of . . . providing benefits to participants and their beneficiaries."[16]

---

contribution is segregated from the corporate accounts. Segregation into a trust account also has the effect of putting the pension fund beyond the reach of a troubled employer's general creditors.

[11]Restatement of Trusts (2d) §§170 (loyalty), 174 (prudent administration) (1959); Restatement of Trusts (3d) §227 (prudent investing) (1990).

[12]See Comment, 23 Duquesne L. Rev. 1033 (1985).

[13]Conference Report on HR 2, Pension Reform, HR Rep. No. 93–1280, 93d Cong., 2d Sess. 295, reprinted in 3 Legislative History of the Employee Retirement Income Security Act of 1974, 94th Cong., 2d Sess. 4277, 4562 (1976).

[14]On the definition of "fiduciary" in ERISA §3(21), see Langbein & Wolk, Pension and Employee Benefit Law 495–97 (1990).

[15]ERISA §404(a)(l)(D).

[16]ERISA §404(a)(1)(A)(i).

The drafters of ERISA adapted the exclusive benefit rule from the trust-law duty of loyalty in order to prevent knaves from looting plan funds. The protective purpose that led Congress to impose a federal fiduciary regime to prevent and to remedy abuse of pension plan assets applies equally to nonpension plans. A dollar is a dollar. It does not much matter whether Jimmy Hoffa wants to steal from your pension plan or your health plan. Thus, ERISA fiduciary law applies both to pension plans and to nonpension (welfare benefit) plans, even though ERISA exempts welfare benefit plans from various pension-specific parts of ERISA.[17]

B. THE MISMATCH OF PRIVATE TRUST AND ERISA TRUST[18]

Alas, there are important differences between the private trust and the pension trust, and ERISA is sometimes insensitive to these differences. That is the problem that underlies the litigation in *Bruch*. The conventional private trust—created, for example, in my will for the support of my widow and children—is a donative transfer. The distinctive logic of a donative transfer is that the benefits are not reciprocal. Unlike a business deal, a gratuitous transfer benefits only the donees. Pension and employee benefit plans, by contrast, arise from contract rather than gratuity. Although the pension and employee benefit system is said to be voluntary, in the sense that regulatory law does not require employers to offer such plans, when an employer does offer a plan, the plan is not a gratuity. Fringe benefits substitute for cash wages. Employers are not donors. Employers offer plans for reasons of economic advantage, in the competition to attract and retain employees. Thus, the employer has continuing economic interests in the plans that it sponsors.[19]

The most important of the employer's continuing interests is the employer's liability for plan expenses. A welfare benefit plan pays its

[17]In particular, from the vesting and funding rules and the pension plan termination insurance system.

[18]This section follows Langbein, The Conundrum of Fiduciary Investing under ERISA, in Proxy Voting of Pension Plan Equity Securities 128 (Pension Research Council, Wharton School) (McGill ed. 1989); and Fischel & Langbein, note 8 *supra*.

[19]Employers incur administrative and regulatory costs in delivering wages in the form of fringe benefits. Employees have various reasons for preferring some fringes over the equivalent in cash wages. Many fringes are tax advantaged, and some (such as group insurance) embody cost reductions that result from economies of scale. A further attraction of pension and employee benefit plans for employers is that such plans facilitate the departure of superannuated employees; they constitute a part of the employer's program of personnel management. For a

expenses on a current basis. In the typical case—for example, my employer's health care plan—my employer is directly responsible for the portion of my health care costs that the plan covers. If I am healthy this year, the savings flow through to the employer. If I am sick, the plan's costs for my health care are expensed to my employer (subject to whatever steps the employer has taken to lay off some of that risk in the insurance markets). Those expenses pass through directly to my employer's income statements as diminutions of net income. As regards pension plans, under the most characteristic type of pension plan, the defined benefit plan, the employer usually bears a similar exposure to plan costs.[20]

Because the settlor of a private trust does not have a continuing economic interest in the trust fund that he has already given away,[21] trust fiduciary law quite sensibly imposes a duty of loyalty that directs all the economic benefits of the trust to the trust beneficiaries. By contrast, the defined benefit pension plan or a welfare benefit plan such as a health care or severance pay plan manifests a complex contract in which both employer and employee have important interests. In subjecting these plans to a comparable duty of loyalty—that is, to the exclusive benefit rule—ERISA transposes from the realm of the unilateral donative transfer a regime that in some respects does not fit the characteristics of pension and benefit law. The employer has important economic interests in the operation of its plans, unlike the settlor of a private trust. In truth, ERISA plans are not for the exclusive benefit of the employees; they are for the joint benefit of employer and employees.[22] The exclusive benefit rule works well in preventing thugs from looting plans, but in other settings it misdescribes the economic reality of ERISA plans.

---

more detailed discussion, see Why Are Pension Plans Employment-Based? in Langbein & Wolk, note 14 *supra*, at 27–31.

[20]Under a defined benefit plan, the employer promises to pay a future benefit, commonly expressed in a formula as a fraction of final average salary. Even though the employer has been funding the plan by means of regular contributions, if the fund turns out to be inadequate to pay the accrued benefits, the employer is liable to make up the shortfall. Thus, the employer who sponsors a defined benefit plan bears the plan's investment risk. The healthier the investment returns that the plan experiences, the less that the employer will have to contribute to honor the plan's pension promises.

[21]Restatement of Trusts (2d) §200 provides: "No one except a beneficiary . . . can maintain a suit against the trustee to enforce the trust . . . ." Comment *b* declares that this principle precludes the settlor from enforcing the trust, unless the settlor acts in another capacity under the trust, such as the beneficiary of a retained interest.

[22]A main theme of Fischel & Langbein, note 8 *supra*, at 1118–19.

C. THE NONNEUTRAL FIDUCIARY

Perhaps the feature of ERISA architecture that most clearly manifests the tension within ERISA's transposed norms of private trust law is ERISA's authorization of the nonneutral fiduciary. This is the creature who holds center stage in *Bruch*. ERISA section 408(c)(3) authorizes the employer or other plan sponsor to have its own "officer, employee, agent, or other representative" serve as the trustee or in other fiduciary capacities for the plan. Employers routinely exercise this authority, using management personnel to conduct both investment activities (for funded plans) and benefit determinations. ERISA's authorization of nonneutral fiduciaries is difficult to reconcile with ERISA's exclusive benefit rule. As the lower court observed in *Donovan v. Bierwirth*, the most celebrated ERISA fiduciary case, "section 408(c)(3) expressly contemplates fiduciaries with dual loyalties," and this arrangement is "an unorthodox departure from the common law rule against dual loyalties . . . ."[23]

ERISA's authorization of nonneutral fiduciaries represents an unmistakable concession to the employer's interest in pension and benefit plans. Congress could have adopted the opposite rule, requiring outside persons to serve as plan fiduciaries, but the price would almost certainly have been lower benefit levels and lower levels of plan formation. We have seen that welfare benefit plan expenses come more or less directly off the employer's bottom line, and that the investment experience of defined benefit plans has a comparable bearing on the employer's profit account. Employers view the investment of plan assets and the control of plan expenses as important centers of cost containment , hence as an integral management function. ERISA Section 408(c)(3) necessarily embodies the acceptance of that view, but ERISA neglects to reconcile the resulting conflict between the nonneutral fiduciary and the exclusive benefit rule.[24]

II. Bruch in the Third Circuit

The *Bruch* case arose out of one of those corporate "downsizings" or "deconglomeritizations" that so typified the 1980s.

[23]538 F. Supp. 463, 468 (E.D.N.Y. 1981) (citation omitted), aff'd as modified, 680 F.2d 263 (2d Cir. 1982).

[24]See the discussion in Fischel & Langbein, note 8 *supra*.

Firestone, the tire company, sold off its plastics division, comprising five plants, to Occidental Petroleum. Occidental took over most of the Firestone employees, who, as Firestone employees, had been covered under Firestone's severance pay plan. It provided: "If your service is discontinued, . . . you will be given termination pay [calculated on a length-of-service formula, if you are] released because of a reduction in work force . . . ."[25]

Some of the employees whose employment with Firestone terminated when they were transferred to Occidental contended that they were within the terms of the plan and entitled to receive severance pay, even though they had employment continuity with Occidental. The plan fiduciaries, who were Firestone managers, denied the claimed benefits "on the ground that the sale of the Plastics Division to Occidental did not constitute a 'reduction in work force' within the meaning of the termination pay plan."[26] The employees sued in respect of the benefit denial. The district court held for Firestone, unremarkably applying the deferential arbitrary-and-capricious standard of review.

The Third Circuit reversed. In a learned and thoughtful opinion, Judge Becker held that de novo as opposed to deferential review should pertain. He reasoned that "under ERISA courts must be cognizant of the features that distinguish the ERISA arrangements from the paradigmatic common law situation."[27] Under Firestone's severance pay plan, "every dollar saved by the administrator on behalf of his employer is a dollar in Firestone's pocket."[28] Judge Becker pointed out that trust law has long applied a standard of searching review in situations in which the trustee "is thought to have acted in his own interest and contrary to the interest of the beneficiaries . . . ."[29] In this case Firestone "is clearly not disinterested in the amount of severance pay awarded; its impartiality therefore cannot be relied upon to produce a fair result."[30]

The Third Circuit's departure from deferential arbitrary-and-capricious review had been anticipated in a few earlier cases, in which

---

[25] 109 S.Ct. at 951.

[26] *Ibid.*

[27] 828 F.2d at 143.

[28] *Id.* at 144.

[29] *Id.* at 145.

[30] 828 F.2d at 145.

intense conflicts of interest on the part of the plan fiduciaries had led the reviewing courts to scrutinize the benefit denials more carefully.[31] On the eve of the *Bruch* case, Judge Posner attempted to sum up the authorities by remarking that "the arbitrary-and-capricious standard may be a range, not a point. There may be in effect a sliding scale of judicial review of trustees' decisions—more penetrating the greater is the suspicion of partiality . . . ."[32]

In pre-*Bruch* case law some courts had undertaken to justify deferential review on the ground that the court should respect the special expertise of the plan fiduciaries. The arbitrary-and-capricious standard "exists to ensure that administrative responsibility rests with those whose experience is daily and continuous, not with judges whose exposure is episodic and occasional," Judge Wilkinson wrote in a prominent Fourth Circuit case.[33]

Judge Becker in *Bruch* considered and rejected Judge Wilkinson's view. A benefit denial case does not ordinarily "turn on information or experience which expertise as a claims administrator is likely to produce." Rather, Judge Becker reasoned, the case "is likely to turn on a question of law or of contract interpretation. Courts have no reason to defer to private parties to obtain answers to these kinds of questions."[34] Judge Becker contrasted fiduciary investment functions; the court should defer to a plan fiduciary's "decision about how to invest plan funds," absent evidence of abuse.[35]

Embodied in this line of reasoning are two rather different arguments, a law/fact distinction and a challenge to the notion that plan administrators possess expertise. Pure construction of the words of an instrument may be likened to the "law" side of the law/fact line, hence for the court, but it is an old truism that issues of law fade into issues of fact. Judge Becker thought that the issue in *Bruch* did not require him to "deal with a determination of fact by a plan administrator," and he was prepared "to leave for another day the definition of the context, if any, in which courts should defer to such determinations."[36]

---

[31]The case law is reviewed in Fischel & Langbein, note 8 *supra*, at 1133–35.

[32]Van Boxel v. Journal Co. Employees Pension Trust, 836 F.2d 1048, 1052 (7th Cir. 1987).

[33]Berry v. Ciba-Geigy Corp., 761 F.2d 1003, 1006 (4th Cir. 1985).

[34]828 F.2d at 144.

[35]*Id.* at n. 9.

[36]*Ibid.*

The situation in *Bruch* may not have involved the plan in making close determinations of fact, but in most benefit denial settings, construction entails application. The further suggestion that plan administrators do not bring real expertise to their work is problematic. Employee benefits professionals commonly argue, for example, that (especially in small and medium size firms) because they know their workforce, they have a better feel than would a reviewing court for a question such as whether a worker was malingering or hurting.

Actually, Judge Becker did not wholly deny that the administrator may possess expertise. Rather, his main emphasis was on the proposition that the imbedded conflict of interest that inclines a servient administrator to decide in favor of his employer outweighs whatever expertise the administrator may bring to the table. The "significant danger that the plan administrator will not be impartial . . . offsets any remaining benefit which the administrator's expertise might be thought to produce."[37]

Despite the intuitive appeal of Judge Becker's conflict-sensitive position, there is, at least in some cases, a respectable counterargument. Most plan decisionmaking occurs in the setting of long term or repeat player relations. Employer-dominated fiduciaries have strong incentives not to acquire a reputation for sharp practice in handling benefit claims, a reputation that would harm employee morale and cause employees to devalue plan benefits. Employer-dominated fiduciaries are common in plan administration, even in single-employer plans that have been collectively bargained. This seems to bespeak the sense that—ordinarily—employees do not have much to fear from putting their heads in this particular lion's mouth. Employees (even when unionized) may have recognized that they are better off leaving substantial discretion over benefit denials to the employer, because the employer is more likely to offer plans, and to enrich the benefits, if the employer is left in control of the cost containment decisions at the plan margins.

On the other hand, there are many circumstances in which the employer's incentives for fairness grow attenuated, and the facts in *Bruch* exemplify such a case. The employer's reputational interest is not likely to be effective when the long term relationship between the firm and the workers is dissolving, as in a plant closing or in a corporate restructuring such as Firestone's transfer of the workers in *Bruch*.

[37] 828 F.2d at 144.

III. The Supreme Court Opinion

Justice O'Connor's opinion for the Supreme Court in *Bruch* sustained the Third Circuit's result, but substituted quite a different rationale. Recall that the issue in *Bruch* is whether the reviewing court should presume the correctness of the plan's internal decision-making when an employer-dominated fiduciary renders a decision that benefits the employer.

Judge Becker was self-consciously following trust-law tradition in scrutinizing fiduciary conduct more closely when conflict of interest is suspected.[38] The Supreme Court, however, expressly declined to "rest our decision on the concern for impartiality that guided the Court of Appeals," hence refused to pay attention to "whether the administrator or fiduciary is acting under a possible or actual conflict of interest."[39] Thus, the Supreme Court decided to require de novo review not on account of the factors that persuaded the Third Circuit to impose de novo review, but even in circumstances in which those factors were absent.

A. Does Trust Law Defer to Trustee Decisionmaking?

Despite its refusal to follow the Third Circuit in basing the requirement of searching review on the conventional trust-law standard of heightened scrutiny for fiduciary conflicts of interest, the Supreme Court purported to derive its requirement of de novo review from trust law. "In determining the appropriate standard of review for actions under [the ERISA section allowing plan participants to sue in respect of benefit denials], we are guided by principles of trust law."[40] The Court compacted its discussion of what it deemed to be the relevant trust law into the passage reproduced here:[41]

---

[38]Judge Becker's opinion, 828 F.2d at 141, reproduces Comment *g* to Restatement of Trusts §187: "The court will control the trustee in the exercise of a power where he acts from an improper even though not dishonest motive . . . . In the determination of the question of whether the trustee in the exercise of power is acting from an improper motive the fact that the trustee has an interest conflicting with that of the beneficiary is to be considered." See also 828 F.2d at 145 ("The principles of trust law instruct that when a trustee is thought to have acted in his own interest and contrary to the interest of the beneficiaries, his decisions are to be scrutinized with the greatest possible care").

[39]109 S.Ct. at 956.

[40]*Id.* at 954.

[41]*Ibid.* The "omitted citations" are references to the standard treatises on trust law, Bogert and Scott.

> Trust principles make a deferential standard of review appropriate when a trustee exercises discretionary powers. See Restatement (Second) of Trusts § 187 (1959) ('[w]here discretion is conferred upon the trustee with respect to the exercise of a power, its exercise is not subject to control by the court except to prevent an abuse by the trustee of his discretion'). [Citation omitted.] A trustee may be given power to construe disputed or doubtful terms, and in such circumstances the trustee's interpretation will not be disturbed if reasonable. [Citation omitted.] Whether 'the exercise of a power is permissive or mandatory depends upon the terms of the trust.' [Citation omitted.] Hence, over a century ago we remarked that '[w]hen trustees are in existence, and capable of acting, a court of equity will not interfere to control them in the exercise of a *discretion vested in them by the instrument under which they act*.' *Nichols v. Eaton*, 91 U.S. 716 (1875) (emphasis added)." . . . Firestone can seek no shelter in these principles of trust law, however, for there is no evidence that under Firestone's termination pay plan the administrator has the power to construe uncertain terms or that eligibility determinations are to be given deference.

It takes very little probing to see why this passage abuses the principles of trust law that it purports to apply. The Court begins by invoking the authority of section 187 of the Restatement of Trusts, which calls for the very deference to trustee decisionmaking that the Court is about to deny in *Bruch*. The trustee's discretion, the Restatement says, is "not subject to control by the court, except to prevent an abuse by the trustee of his discretion." This abuse-of-discretion standard is simply the arbitrary-and-capricious standard by another name. And indeed, the Court says in introducing section 187 that "[t]rust principles make a deferential standard of review appropriate when a trustee exercises discretionary powers."

How, then, did the Court manage both to invoke section 187 and to refuse that deference to fiduciary decisionmaking that section 187 requires? The leap occurs toward the end of the quoted passage. The Court recalls its century-old trust-law precedent, *Nichols v. Eaton*, and underscores a phrase from that opinion—a phrase endorsing judicial deference to trustees' "exercise of a *discretion vested in them by the instrument under which they act*." The Court then draws a negative inference from the underscored words. "Firestone can seek no shelter in these principles of trust law, however, for there is no evidence that under Firestone's termination pay plan the administrator has the power to construe uncertain terms or that eligibility determinations are to be given deference." Thus, the Supreme Court reasons that, as a matter of trust law, deference to the trustee's decisionmaking is appropriate only when the trust power in question is particularly granted by the trust instrument.

This distinction between trust powers that derive from the background law of trusts, and those that derive from the trust instrument, is fundamentally mistaken. It is refuted in the very source that the Court treats as authoritative, section 187 of the Restatement of Trusts. Official Comment *a* to section 187 says: "When powers are discretionary. The exercise of a power is discretionary except to the extent to which its exercise is required by the terms of the trust or by the principles of law applicable to the duties of trustees." In other words, discretion does not depend upon an explicit grant in the instrument. The trustee has discretion unless the instrument or some particular doctrine of trust law denies discretion. Discretion is the norm.[42] What the Supreme Court in *Bruch* calls "the trust law *de novo* standard of review"[43] is simply nonexistent in trust law.

B. EXALTING FORTUITY

The Supreme Court's distinction between the law of the instrument and the background law of trusts would frequently lead to bizarre results. For example, legislation such as the Uniform Trustees' Powers Act[44] or a local equivalent is in force in most American jurisdictions. These acts grant to trustees of private trusts extensive powers to manage and to invest trust assets. Under the reasoning in *Bruch*, if a trust instrument happens to incorporate these powers by terms, the reviewing court should defer to the trustee's decisionmaking. When, however, the trust instrument is silent on the matter because the drafter has chosen to rely upon the statutebook that authorizes the same powers rather than copy them into the instrument, the rule in *Bruch* would deny judicial deference to the decisionmaking of the trustees of that trust. Accordingly, the distinction

[42]So fundamental is this point that the Seventh Circuit has lately reiterated it even while obeying the Supreme Court's commands in *Bruch:* "Under the common law courts will not review the discretionary decisions of trustees and other fiduciaries *de novo*, but will look only for the trustee's abuse of its discretionary authority." Exbom v. Central States Welfare Fund, 900 F.2d 1138 (7th Cir. 1990) (Eschbach J., citing Restatement (2d) of Trusts §187).

[43]109 S.Ct. at 948.

[44]7B Uniform Laws Annotated 741 (1985)

between the background law of trusts and the law of the trust instrument exalts a pure fortuity.

If I had to hazard a guess about why the Court took this distinction, my answer would be that a peculiarity of the facts in *Bruch* made the distinction useful for deciding the particular case, and that not much thought was given to the shortsightedness of letting freak facts resolve the ERISA standard-of-review issue. The peculiarity in *Bruch* is that "[a]t the time of the sale of its Plastics Division, Firestone was not aware that the termination pay plan was governed by ERISA, and therefore had not set up a claims procedure . . . with respect to that plan."[45] The plan in litigation in *Bruch* was dramatically exceptional in having no written terms regarding claims matters. By insisting that deference to plan trustees had to rest on the language of the trust instrument, the Court seized on a criterion that the plan in *Bruch* could not satisfy. Other plans, however, can indeed satisfy that criterion, especially after the *Bruch* case alerts plan drafters to the need.

C. INVITING EVASION

The Court in *Bruch* may have thought it was being prudential in resting its decision on a narrow ground, but in conditioning its requirement of de novo review on the language of the plan document, the Court may have found a ground so narrow as to be self-defeating. The Court's emphasis in *Bruch* on the trust instrument as the basis for deferential review raises the prospect that an ERISA plan may opt out of *Bruch*'s de novo review and back into the pre-*Bruch* world of judicial deference merely by inserting some boilerplate to that effect in the plan instrument. Indeed, in a remarkable passage toward the end of the *Bruch* opinion, the Court seems to invite plan drafters to trump the decision by instrument. *Bruch*'s de novo standard of review pertains, says the Court, "unless the benefit plan gives the administrator or fiduciary discretionary authority to determine eligibility for benefits or to construe the terms of the plan."[46]

Consider, for example, *Lowry v. Bankers Life & Casualty Retirement Plan*,[47] first decided in the Fifth Circuit four days before the Supreme Court released its opinion in *Bruch*. The question was

[45] 109 S.Ct. at 948.

[46] 109 S.Ct. at 956.

[47] 865 F.2d 692 (5th Cir 1989).

whether the plan fiduciaries had correctly calculated the employee's compensation base, on which the plan based its retirement benefits. The court emphasized the Fifth Circuit's arbitrary-and-capricious standard and routinely deferred to the plan fiduciaries' calculation. "Discretion is a touchstone of trusteeship, and we invade the province of the trustee only when he violates the proper exercise of his discretion."[48] The claimant obtained a rehearing in the light of *Bruch* but lost anyhow. "The instruments in this case sharply contrast with the termination pay plan in *Bruch*. [The plan in this case] grants permissive authority to the Plan Committee to 'interpret and construe' the [plan] and the power 'to determine all questions of eligibility and status under the [plan].'" Similar language appeared in a related plan instrument. "Unlike in *Bruch*, there is 'evidence that under' the trust instruments 'the administrator has the power to construe uncertain terms [and] that eligibility determinations are to be given deference.'"[49]

The post-*Bruch* law is now replete with such cases, in which the court decides that a provision in the instrument begets the pre-*Bruch* standard. "In actions challenging the denial of benefits under an ERISA plan which gives the administrator discretion in administering the plan, review is deferential and is limited to determining whether the administrator's action is arbitrary and capricious . . . ."[50]

1. *Construing opt-out terms.* The immediate post-*Bruch* case law has been troubled by the question of whether particular language in various pre-*Bruch* plans is adequate to invoke the opt-out deferential review that *Bruch* invites.[51] This is, however, a transitional phenomenon. As drafters amend[52] pre-*Bruch* plans to make deferential review unambiguous, and as pre-*Bruch* disputes are resolved, this issue will pass out of contention. The players will learn their lines. Boilerplate effective to claim deferential review will be all but universally inserted in plan instruments.

2. *Opt-out policy.* The puzzle about the Supreme Court's handling of the *Bruch* case is now easy to state but impossible to solve. If the

---

48 *Id.* at 694.

49 871 F.2d at 525 (5th Cir. 1989) (quoting *Bruch*).

50 McConnell v. Texaco, Inc., 727 F. Supp. 751 (D. Mass. 1990). See also, *e.g.*, Davis v. Kentucky Finance Cos. Retirement Plan, 887 F.2d 689, 694 (6th Cir. 1989); Jader v. Principal Mutual Life Ins. Co., 723 F. Supp. 1338 (D. Minn. 1989); O'Dom v. GCIU Supplemental Retirement & Disability Funds, 722 F. Supp. 365 (S.D. Ohio 1989).

51 De Nobel v. Vitro Corp., 885 F.2d 1180 (4th Cir. 1989).

52 ERISA §402(b)(3) requires that plans be amendable.

Court was right to think that the arbitrary-and-capricious standard worsened the situation of plan participants and beneficiaries unacceptably, why did the Court permit plan drafters to reinstitute the arbitrary-and-capricious standard by means of boilerplate grants of discretion? Indeed, quite a plausible argument can be made that ERISA's effort to prevent plan drafters from escaping ERISA's fiduciary norms should prevail in such cases. The statute should be treated as preventing plan drafters from ousting the ordinarily applicable standard of review. Recall that ERISA section 404(a)(1)(D) contains an anti-opt-out clause, requiring plan instruments to be "consistent with the provisions of" ERISA.[53] If the purpose of ERISA fiduciary law is to protect plan participants from abusive management by the plan fiduciary, it seems transparently counterproductive to allow the employer to bootstrap around the safeguards of the statute by inserting boilerplate in the plans ordering the courts not to pay much attention to the misbehavior of an employer-dominated fiduciary.

3. *Full circle?* Once plan drafters respond to *Bruch* by modifying plan instruments to insist on deference to plan fiduciaries, the question that Judge Becker confronted in *Bruch* will recur. Should courts defer to plan fiduciaries regardless of the circumstances, or should the courts adjust the scope of deference to take account of factors such as the degree of disinterestedness of the particular fiduciary? Remarkably, the Supreme Court in *Bruch* appears to have anticipated that issue. Toward the end of its opinion, after priding itself on not following the Third Circuit in devising a standard of review that is sensitive to "whether the administrator or fiduciary is operating under a possible or actual conflict of interest," the Court announces: "Of course, if a benefit plan gives discretion to an administrator or fiduciary who is operating under a conflict of interest, that conflict must be weighed as a 'factor[] in determining whether there is an abuse of discretion.'"[54]

Thus, the Supreme Court appears to invite the use of a conflict-sensitive standard of the sort that the Third Circuit tried to devise, once plan drafters have inserted the necessary boilerplate to claim deferential review. The Eleventh Circuit accepted this invitation

---

[53]See text at note 15 *supra*. See also ERISA §410(a), declaring "any provision in [an] instrument which purports to relieve a fiduciary from responsibility or liability for any responsibility, obligation, or duty [to] be void as against public policy."

[54]109 S.Ct. at 956.

with alacrity, holding in *Brown v. Blue Cross & Blue Shield of Alabama* "that when a plan beneficiary demonstrates a substantial conflict of interest on the part of the fiduciary responsible for benefits determinations, the burden shifts to the fiduciary to prove that its interpretation of plan provisions committed to its discretion was not tainted by self-interest."[55]

To conclude: The Supreme Court made such a tangle of the trust law it purported to apply in *Bruch* that the informed observer will have difficulty understanding what the Court's purposes really were. Judge Becker trod a perfectly conventional trust-law[56] path to the Third Circuit's result in *Bruch*, imposing stricter scrutiny in cases of fiduciary conflict of interest, impliedly preserving deferential review for neutral fiduciaries. The Supreme Court's decision to impose de novo review in all cases extends the requirement of a searching standard of review to cases in which it hardly seems needed, that is, to cases in which the fiduciaries are genuinely neutral. But if the Court wanted to institute such a dramatically protective standard of review, then the Court's willingness to allow plan drafters to reinstitute the less searching arbitrary-and-capricious standard by means of a few pen strokes seems inexplicable.

IV. Contract

Since the Supreme Court was determined to institute de novo review (with whatever tolerance for evasion) as the notional standard, the question arises of why the Court did not follow a more conventional doctrinal path to de novo review—contract law. Pension and employee benefit plans originate in the employment contract.[57] ERISA requires as a matter of regulatory law that plan assets be placed in trust, but ERISA does not delimit the boundaries of trust and contract.

A. DE NOVO REVIEW

De novo review is the norm in contract law for two main reasons. First, contracting parties are expected to be self-interested. The

[55] 898 F.2d 1556, 1566 (11th Cir. 1990); accord, Newell v. Prudential Insurance Co., 904 F.2d 644 (11th Cir. 1990).

[56] See text at note 38 *supra*.

[57] See discussion in text at notes 18–19 *supra*.

premise that underlies deferential review in trust law—namely, that fiduciaries are disinterested—is absent in contract.[58] Second, contracts seldom institute a decisionmaker analogous to a trustee. Thus, in ordinary contract settings, there is neither reason to defer nor anyone to whom to defer.

In the period before ERISA, standard-of-review questions arising from pension and employee benefit plans were understood to be contract questions, and the Supreme Court in *Bruch* refers to that tradition in attempting to justify its reasoning in *Bruch*. The arbitrary-and-capricious standard that Firestone urged in *Bruch* "would require us to impose a standard of review that would afford less protection to employees and their beneficiaries than they enjoyed before ERISA was enacted."[59] Elsewhere in its opinion, the Supreme Court draws upon contract notions,[60] even while asserting that "[i]n determining the standard of review for actions under [ERISA], we are guided by principles of trust law."[61] Such passages invite the suggestion that the Court may have thought contract while it talked trust.

Indeed, the Supreme Court's strongest argument for de novo review is drawn directly from contract law. It occurs in a paragraph immediately following that awkward passage in which the Court tries to rest its rationale for a trust-law-based de novo standard of review on the insupportable distinction between discretion granted under the trust instrument and discretion granted under the background law of trusts. The Court says: "As they do with contractual provisions, courts construe terms in trust agreements without deferring to either party's interpretation."[62] This argument echoes Judge Becker's suggestion, mentioned above, that benefit denial cases are "likely to turn on a question of law or of contract interpretation.

[58]By contrast, we have seen that, as applied to the pension or employee benefit trust, the premise that fiduciaries are disinterested is faulty. Such a trust is not a true donative transfer. See text at notes 18–22 *supra*.

[59]109 S.Ct. at 956.

[60]"The trust law de novo standard of review is consistent with the judicial interpretation of employee benefit plans prior to the enactment of ERISA. Actions challenging an employer's denial of benefits before enactment of ERISA were governed by principles of contract law. If the plan did not give the employer or administrator discretion or final authority to construe uncertain terms, the court reviewed the employee's claim as it would have any other contract claim—by looking to the terms of the plan and other manifestations of the parties' intent." *Id.* at 954.

[61]*Ibid.*

[62]*Id.* at 955.

Courts have no reason to defer to private parties to obtain answers to these kinds of questions."[63] We have questioned whether Judge Becker's argument overstates the extent to which benefit denial cases fall on the "law" or "construction" side of the law/fact or construction/administration line, but the distinction is surely sound at the margin. When a benefit denial case entails the construction of an instrument in circumstances in which there is no application to particular facts, there would not be much ground for deferring to the internal decisionmaker either in contract or in trust.

The view that the issue in *Bruch* would be better resolved as a matter of contract law than as trust law is not an academic afterthought. The Solicitor General's *amicus* brief, which the Court in *Bruch* cites,[64] urged the Court to view the issue as one of contract. The Solicitor General argued that ERISA's objectives "are best served by resolving questions of plan interpretation under established principles of contract interpretation."[65] The brief observed that "ERISA's own reliance on trust principles is selective, and in no way suggests that Congress intended that a highly deferential standard be applied here."[66] The Supreme Court opinion took over from the Solicitor General's brief (without attribution) the passage arguing that deferential review under the arbitrary-and-capricious standard leaves employees "worse off than they were before ERISA was enacted."[67] However, the Supreme Court opinion suppresses the Solicitor General's underlying argument—that the comparison to pre-ERISA conditions should incline the Court to a contract-based standard of review.[68]

If there is an advantage to treating the issue in *Bruch* as one of contract law, it is candor. The de novo standard of review that the Supreme Court thought appropriate to benefit denial cases follows automatically as a normal incident of contract law. The Court would not have had to distort trust law to obtain de novo review. De novo review was there for the asking in contract. The puzzle about *Bruch* is

---

[63]Text at note 34 *supra*.

[64]109 S.Ct. at 954 (column 2, end).

[65]Brief for the United States as Amicus Curiae Supporting Respondents, at 6.

[66]*Ibid.*

[67]*Id.* at 7. Compare 109 S.Ct. at 956, quoted in text at note 59 *supra*.

[68]Judge Becker also recommended attention to contract law on the remand that the Third Circuit ordered in *Bruch*. "We suggest several principles of contractual construction" for ascertaining what the parties intended in the particular circumstances. 828 F.2d at 147.

not only that the Court insisted on de novo review, but also that the Court insisted on deriving it from trust law (where it is not the rule) rather than contract law (where it is).

B. THE PROTECTIVE POLICY

Was there any reason for the Court to have preferred a distorted version of trust law to a candid version of contract law as the basis for a de novo standard of review? One possibility is that the Court feared that the regime of contract law would allow plan drafters too much latitude for overreaching at the employee's expense. The employer is economically dominant in many employment relationships. Most pension and employee benefit plans are unilateral contracts, offered on a take-it-or-leave-it basis. It's a rare employee who has had the chance to bargain about a pension or health plan, although there is reason to think that employees sort themselves (in choosing among employers and in deciding whether to remain with an employer) in part on the basis of the comparative merits of competing employers' fringe benefits.

In a prominent pre-*Bruch* opinion, *Van Boxel v. Journal Co. Employees Pension Trust*,[69] Judge Posner voiced the concern that contract standards of review might not adequately vindicate the protective purposes of ERISA. "A Congress committed to the principles of freedom of contract would not have enacted a statute that interferes with pension arrangements voluntarily agreed on by employers and employees. ERISA is paternalistic; and it seems incongruous therefore to deny disappointed pension claimants a meaningful degree of judicial review on the theory that they might be said to have implicitly waived it."[70]

Because, however, the de novo standard of review in contract law is more protective than the deferential standard of trust law as commonly understood before *Bruch*, contract should have been better suited than trust to vindicate this concern to protect employees from overreaching. Actually, the serious problem under either contract or trust is not the implicit waiver to which Judge Posner refers, but explicit waiver, that is, the use of the plan documents to oust the more favorable default rule by imposing deferential review. An employer bent on overreaching may as easily arrange to have the plan docu-

---

[69] 836 F.2d 1048 (7th Cir. 1987).

[70] *Id.* at 1052.

ments oust the default regime of de novo review whether that regime is thought to rest on trust or on contract. Since the Supreme Court in *Bruch* invites plan drafters to reinstitute deferential review (albeit subject to the possibility of stricter scrutiny in conflict of interest cases), it seems unlikely that the Court was much concerned with that aspect of the contract standard of review.

If the Court had been worried that a contract-based standard of de novo review might be too easy for plan drafters to evade, ERISA offered an easy statutory basis for preventing such maneuvers. Section 404(a)(1)(D)—the measure that requires that plan documents be "consistent with the provisions of" ERISA—could easily have been read to restrict or to prohibit attempts to oust de novo review, at least in situations of conflict of interest. Moreover, quite apart from statute, contract law is not defenseless to such moves when protective values are offended. Just as trust law exhibits that tradition of strict scrutiny of a fiduciary's conflict-tainted transactions upon which Judge Becker relied, so in contract law there are familiar doctrines—unconscionability, contra proferentum—for responding to overreaching.[71]

Thus, the deep issue that lurks in the standard-of-review dispute when analyzed from the standpoint of contract law is not whether the particular plan actually claims discretion for the employer, but rather whether the protective policy of ERISA should allow such a plan to enforce its claim. ERISA is silent on the precise question. The Supreme Court in *Bruch*, we have seen, waffled on the question, inviting plan drafters to try it, while holding out the possibility that the resulting conflict of interest might be offensive enough to qualify "as a 'factor[] [to be weighed] in determining whether there is an abuse of discretion.'"[72]

ERISA abridges freedom of contract in some respects, but not others. For example, ERISA's vesting rules[73] greatly restrict the parties' freedom to agree upon forfeiture of accrued pension benefits, yet ERISA's vesting rules do not apply to nonpension benefits such as health care. The courts have repulsed efforts to extend the protective policy of the vesting rules to such benefits.[74] ERISA contains doc-

---

[71]See, *e.g.*, Farnsworth, Contracts §§4.28, at 495–517 (unconscionability), 7.11, at 265–68 (contra proferentum) (1990 ed.).

[72]Text at note 54 *supra*.

[73]ERISA §203(a).

[74]Most prominently, in Hansen v. White Farm Equipment Co., 788 F.2d 1186 (6th Cir. 1986). See generally Langbein & Wolk, note 14 *supra*, at 421–23.

trinal pegs, such as the anti-opt-out provision[75] and the exclusive benefit rule[76] that could be used to defeat contractual provisions enhancing the discretion of employer-dominated administrators. The question is whether and in what circumstances the protective policy of ERISA may be said to justify the use of these doctrines to interfere with plan terms. How protective, in other words, is ERISA meant to be? Likewise, the contra proferentum rule, construing the benefit plan contract strictly against the drafter, could be adopted.[77] But the price of any of these measures will be lowered levels of plan formation and less generous funding. From the standpoint of the protected persons, it seems unlikely that that is the optimal outcome. Here, as elsewhere in the law, it is all too easy to overprotect. That is why Judge Becker's focus on actual conflict of interest as the criterion for strict scrutiny seems to strike such a sensible balance.

V. Conclusion

The Supreme Court's opinion in *Bruch* garbles long-settled principles of trust law, confuses trust and contract rubrics, and invites plan drafters to defeat the stated objectives of the decision. *Bruch* is such a crude piece of work that one may well question whether it had the full attention of the Court. I do not believe that either Justice O'Connor or her colleagues who joined this unanimous opinion[78] would have uttered such doctrinal hash if they had been seriously engaged in the enterprise.

Unfortunately, *Bruch* is not the first instance in which the Supreme Court has discharged ERISA business shoddily.[79] I understand why a Court wrestling with the grandest issues of public law may feel that its mission is distant from ERISA. The Court may increasingly view itself as having become a supreme constitutional

---

[75]ERISA §404(a)(1)(D), discussed in text at notes 15, 71 *supra*.

[76]ERISA §404(a)(1)(A), discussed in text at notes 16–17 *supra;* of comparable import is the anti-inurement rule of ERISA §403(c)(1).

[77]A Ninth Circuit panel has started down this path, holding in a recent case against an ERISA-covered health insurer "that the rule of *contra proferentum* applies [either] . . . as a matter of uniform federal law or because federal law incorporates state law on this point." Kunin v. Benefit Trust Life Ins. Co., 910 F.2d 534, 540 (9th Cir. 1990).

[78]Justice Scalia expressed a reservation about the Court's reasoning in an unrelated question decided in the same case, see 109 S.Ct. at 958–59.

[79]*E.g.*, Connolly v. PBGC, 106 S.Ct. 1018 (1986); Metropolitan Life Ins. Co. v. Massachusetts, 471 U.S. 724 (1985); PBGC v. Gray, 467 U.S. 717 (1984); International Brotherhood of Teamsters v. Daniel, 439 U.S. 551 (1979).

court, resembling the specialized constitutional courts on the Continent. If so, the time may have come to recognize a corollary. If the Court is bored with the detail of supervising complex bodies of statutory law, thought should be given to having that job done by a court that would take it seriously.

The solution long familiar on the Continent is to have separate courts of last resort superintend such fields. A supreme court specializing in ERISA matters, and probably in Social Security and tax law as well, would treat these subjects with respect, which is more than can be said for the U.S. Supreme Court in *Bruch*. Within legal policy circles in the United States, the caseload problem of the federal courts has given rise to renewed interest in specialized courts.[80] ERISA is an ideal field for experimenting with specialized courts: It is complex, it is important, and it is relatively well delimited from other fields. The evidence from *Bruch* is that this is a sphere of subject matter jurisdiction that the Supreme Court would scarcely miss.

[80]See the symposium on specialized adjudication in 1990 BYU L. Rev. 377–575.

FREDERICK SCHAUER

STATUTORY CONSTRUCTION AND THE COORDINATING FUNCTION OF PLAIN MEANING

The Justices have not been reading their Derrida. Indeed, despite the lengthy importunings of legions of law professors, the Justices have been neglecting to read not only Derrida, but Foucault, Gadamer, Rorty, and Heidegger as well. Instead, as the statutory construction cases of the 1989 Term demonstrate, they have been spending their time reading (Noah) Webster, relying, both in fact and in articulated justification, on notions of plain meaning routinely derided in contemporary legal scholarship.

A number of explanations for the move to plain meaning are possible, and there is no reason to suppose that one is true and the others false. Any of these explanations, however, would have to start with the premise that plain meaning is to the Justices a usable tool. Why plain meaning is usable is debatable, but that debate is more about the explanation of a phenomenon than of its existence. Occurrence precedes explanation, and just as the inability to explain the source or composition of the rings of Saturn does not show that they do not exist, so too does the inability of philosophers or linguists or literary theorists yet to explain satisfactorily the deepest nature of the workings of language say little about the ability of language to serve some number of important and obvious social functions. The Justices may not read Foucault or talk to Derrida, but they read the newspapers

Frederick Schauer is Frank Stanton Professor of the First Amendment, John F. Kennedy School of Government, Harvard University.

0-226-09573-8/91/1990-0003$02.00

and talk to each other, giving them an understanding of the idea of plain meaning that they can then apply to the construction of statutes. For whatever they seem not to know, the Justices do know that when they ask a law clerk for a tuna fish sandwich and the briefs in *Roe v. Wade*, what they get is a tuna fish sandwich and the briefs in *Roe v. Wade*. Unsophisticated as it is, this insight provides the underpinnings for a view of language that in turn supports an explanation of recent statutory construction cases in terms of the use of plain language as a second-best coordinating device for multiple decisionmakers attempting to reach some methodological consensus in the face of substantive disagreements among them.

To provide a descriptive explanation is not to provide a normative justification. Still, there turns out to be a plausible normative argument supporting the Court's approach. This is not to say that there could not be equally plausible normative arguments supporting other approaches. But the one the Court has chosen, one that takes plain meaning as presumptively but not conclusively controlling, can be justified by recognizing the simultaneous virtues and vices of plain meaning. I do not wish to dispute the extent to which plain meaning builds on and in all of the political and other contingent normative and categorial choices of the linguistic community within which it exists. But for the Court to lessen its reliance on plain meaning would serve only to substitute for the community's contingent normative choices the equally contingent and equally normative choices of individual interpreters. The reliance on plain meaning, therefore, as one form of a solution to a coordination problem, substitutes a second-best coordinating solution for a theoretically optimizing but likely self-defeating search for first-best solutions by multiple decisionmakers with different goals and different perspectives. In achieving some semblance of coordination, the reliance on plain meaning serves a stabilizing function as well, bringing together to some suboptimal equilibrium a process that might otherwise be much better, but also might otherwise be much worse. As with all stabilizing solutions, therefore, the evaluation of this one turns partially on an estimate of the likelihood and consequences of solutions generated by different decision procedures, and partially on the inevitably value-laden determination of the desirability of a status quo that any stabilizing solution will necessarily entrench.

Although I will say at least a small bit about all of those cases from the 1989 Term in which questions of plain meaning were relevant, I will focus on *Pavelic & LeFlore v. Marvel Entertainment Group*,[1] in which the Court held that sanctions under Rule 11 of the Federal Rules of Civil Procedure were available not against law firms but only against individual attorneys. I choose this case not because there is anything exceptional about it. It is entirely exemplary, but as such it provides an accessible entry into a perspective illustrating not only this case, but many others whose greater complexity makes them less appropriate vehicles for my primary attention.

I. The Case

Pavelic & LeFlore involved a sanction in the amount of $100,000 imposed on a two-member law firm for signing a pleading raising a claim (forgery of a copyright permission) that "had no basis in fact and had not been investigated sufficiently by counsel."[2] The relevant pleadings had been signed in the name of the law firm, with the form of:

"Pavelic & LeFlore
By /s/ Ray L. LeFlore
(A Member of the Firm)
Attorneys for Plaintiff"

Upon finding no basis for the forgery claim raised above the foregoing signature line, the District Court awarded sanctions against Pavelic & LeFlore for violation of the requirement in Rule 11 that:

> The signature of an attorney or party constitutes a certificate by the signer that the signer has read the pleading, motion, or other paper; that to the best of the signer's knowledge, information, and belief formed after reasonable inquiry it is well grounded in fact and is warranted by existing law or a good faith argument for the extension, modification, or reversal of existing law, and that it is not interposed for any improper purpose, such as to harass or to cause unnecessary delay or needless in the cost of litigation.

The sanction itself was authorized by further language in the Rule providing that:

> If a pleading, motion, or other paper is signed in violation of this rule, the court, upon motion or upon its own initiative, shall impose upon the person who signed it, a represented party, or both,

---

[1] 110 S.Ct. 456 (1989).

[2] 110 S.Ct. at 457.

> an appropriate sanction, which may include an order to pay to the other party or parties the amount of the reasonable expenses incurred because of the filing of the pleading, motion, or other paper, including a reasonable attorney's fee.

Central to this case was the "upon the person who signed it" language of Rule 11. The District Court had rejected Pavelic & LeFlore's contention that this language authorized the Court to impose sanctions only upon the individual attorney who signed the pleading and not upon that attorney's law firm,[3] and the Court of Appeals for the Second Circuit affirmed,[4] thus creating a conflict with the rule in the Fifth Circuit, pursuant to which sanctions were available only against the individuals lawyers who signed the court papers.[5] With the opinion written by Justice Scalia, the Supreme Court sided with the Fifth Circuit and against the Second, reversing the latter and holding that the "plain meaning" of Rule 11 did not permit the imposition of sanctions against any person or entity other than an individual attorney.

Justice Scalia acknowledged that the phrase "person who signed," when taken in isolation, was ambiguous on the point at issue, for "[i]n other contexts the phrase 'the person who signed it' might bear the somewhat technical legal meaning of the natural or juridical person in whose name or on whose behalf the paper was signed; . . ."[6] But reading the entire paragraph, Justice Scalia argued, particularly its requirement of an "individual " signature and its discussion of the implications of that individual signature, made it clear that "references to the signer in the later portions must reasonably be thought to connote the individual signer mentioned at the outset."[7] "Just as the requirement of signature is imposed upon the individual, we

---

[3]Calloway v. Marvel Entertainment Group, 650 F. Supp. 684, 687 (S.D.N.Y. 1986).

[4]Calloway v. Marvel Entertainment Group, 854 F.2d 1452, 1479 (2d Cir. 1988).

[5]Robinson v. National Cash Register Co., 808 F.2d 1119, 1128–30 (5th Cir. 1987).

[6]110 S.Ct. at 458. Imbedded in this conclusion is the important point that plain meaning is not equivalent to ordinary meaning. Although much of legal language is parasitic on ordinary language, see Morrison, Excursions into the Nature of Legal Language, 37 Cleve. St. L. Rev. 271 (1989), much of it is technical, such that the lawyer's use of "party" or "contract" or "adhesion" is not identical to the use of those terms by the person on the Clapham omnibus. Thus, that which is "plain" within some moderately discrete professional linguistic community need not be plain within the larger linguistic community, and no one who takes as comprehensible the idea of plain or literal meaning makes (or should make) the implausible claim that this must necessarily be the same as ordinary non-technical meaning.

[7]110 S.Ct. at 458.

think the recited import and consequences of signature run *as to him*."[8]

Although the Court offered the possibility that this reading was consistent with an underlying purpose of increasing the psychological and economic deterrent effect of the sanctions,[9] its construction of a purpose consistent with the plain reading of the text seems to have been added almost as an afterthought. Moreover, the constructed purpose seems particularly strained, as Justice Marshall's lone dissent makes clear. Relying heavily on the Advisory Committee's Notes, Justice Marshall concluded that[10]

> The policies underlying Rule 11 decisively indicate that "person" should be interpreted broadly so that a court can effectively exercise discretion in formulating appropriate sanctions. . . . Admittedly, in some case, sanctions imposed solely on the individual signer may halt abusive practices most effectively. In other cases, however, deterrence might best be served by imposing sanctions on the signer's law firm in an attempt to encourage internal monitoring. The trial judge is in the best position to assess the dynamics of each situation and to act accordingly.

The greater plausibility of Justice Marshall's view of the result best indicated by Rule 11's underlying purpose, however, merely underscores the majority's main point: that the purpose—whatever it was—was irrelevant, for the language was sufficiently clear to make recourse to underlying purpose not merely unnecessary but impermissible. "We give the Federal Rules of Civil Procedure their plain meaning, . . . and generally with them as with a statute, '[w]hen we find the terms . . . unambiguous, judicial inquiry is complete.'"[11] "Even if it were entirely certain that liability on the part of the firm would more effectively achieve the purposes of the Rule, we would not feel free to pursue that objective at the expense of a textual interpreta-

---

[8] *Id.* at 459.

[9] *Id.* at 462.

[10] *Id.* at 461–62 (Marshall, J., dissenting). Moreover, the last sentence of the relevant paragraph of Rule 11 makes clear that the Rule has a compensatory as well as a deterrence goal, and serving the goal of compensation appears compatible not with limiting the number of pockets out of which compensation might be drawn, but instead with keeping open the option of imposing sanctions on a law firm as well as on an individual attorney. For general background on the purposes of Rule 11, see Carter, The History and Purposes of Rule 11, 54 Fordham L. Rev. 4 (1985); Schwarzer, Rule 11 Revisited, 101 Harv. L. Rev. 1013 (1988); Note, 88 Mich. L. Rev. 344 (1989).

[11] 110 S.Ct. at 458, quoting Rubin v. United States, 449 U.S. 424, 430 (1981).

tion as unnatural as we have described. Our task is to apply the text, not to improve upon it."[12]

II. Pavelic & LeFlore as Exemplar

Pavelic & LeFlore thus comes down squarely on one side of a divide that is embedded within all decisionmaking environments other than those whose decisionmakers are simply instructed to make the best all-things-considered decision in each case. Where decisionmakers are instructed in accordance with more specific directives, these directives are necessarily actually or potentially both under- and over-inclusive vis-à-vis their background justifications. As a result, cases will arise in which the meaning of the terms of the directive (which I will call a "rule-formulation") points in one direction and the direct application of background purposes points in another. Given this actual or potential divergence, decisionmaking environments must choose between reflecting the purpose or reflecting the meaning of the rule-formulation when the two are in conflict. A long and distinguished tradition, represented by *McBoyle v. United States*,[13] H. L. A. Hart's side of his debate with Lon Fuller,[14] and traditional rule-utilitarianism,[15] embodies in one way or another the latter view, and an equally long and equally distinguished tradition, represented by *Church of the Holy Trinity v. United States*,[16] Fuller's response to Hart,[17] and traditional act-utilitarianism,[18] prefers the former.

It is important to understand that this divide is not about what to do when the words in a statute or rule are vague or ambiguous. On

[12]110 S.Ct. at 459–60.

[13]283 U.S. 25 (1931) (Holmes, J.).

[14]Hart, Positivism and the Separation of Law and Morals, 71 Harv. L. Rev. 593 (1958).

[15]See Brandt, Fairness to Indirect Optimific Theories of Ethics, 98 Ethics 341 (1988); Rawls, Two Concepts of Rules, 64 Phil. Rev. 3 (1955); Urmson, The Interpretation of the Moral Philosophy of J.S. Mill, 3 Phil. Q. 3 (1953). See also Hare, Moral Thinking: Its Levels, Method, and Point (1981).

[16]143 U.S. 457 (1892).

[17]Fuller, Positivism and Fidelity to Law—a Reply to Professor Hart, 71 Harv. L. Rev. 630 (1958). See also Fuller, The Case of the Speluncean Explorers, 62 Harv. L. Rev. 20, 27–30 (1949) (Foster, J.).

[18]See Lyons, Forms and Limits of Utilitarianism (1965); Regan, Law's Halo, in Philosophy and Law 15 (J. Coleman & E. Paul eds. 1987); Regan, Reasons, Authority, and the Meaning of 'Obey': Further Thoughts on Raz and Obedience to Law, 3 Can. J. L. & Jurisp. 3 (1990); Smart, Extreme and Restricted Utilitarianism, 6 Phil. Q. 344 (1956).

this there is (or should be) much less controversy, for choosing plain meaning over purpose is impossible when the meaning simply is not plain.[19] But when there is a plain meaning, as there seems to have been to eight Justices in *Pavelic & LeFlore*, then there is a real difference between whether the plain meaning of a rule-formulation will be treated on the one hand as opaque or on the other as transparent to its underlying purpose. Moreover, my reference to purpose is a simplification. The contrast between language and purpose parallels the contrasts between language and original intent, language and equity (or justice), and language and policy. Although purpose, intent, justice, and policy are all different, they each represent a version of an approach pursuant to which statutory language is defeasible in the service of, or transparent to, a range of factors likely to be truncated by the literal meaning of some specific rule-formulation.

Pavelic & LeFlore's preference for opacity and the primacy of the meaning of the rule-formulation might be attributed simply to Justice Scalia's own views,[20] but seven other Justices, operating in an environment in which having one's own different reasons for reaching the same result is increasingly a sufficient condition for setting forth those reasons in the form of a concurring opinion, joined the opinion with nary a qualifying syllable.[21] Moreover, the one dissenting Justice, Justice Marshall, was the author of one of the more noto-

[19]Conversely, my disagreements with some contemporary commentators on statutory construction are less with respect to those commentators whose prescriptions seem at times to be restricted to the domain of linguistic indeterminacy. See, *e.g.*, Eskridge, Dynamic Statutory Interpretation, 135 U. Pa. L. Rev. 1479, 1483–84 (1987); Sunstein, Interpreting Statutes in the Regulatory State, 103 Harv. L. Rev. 405, 415–24 (1989). A fair reading of the entirety of the foregoing, however, would still support the conclusion that Eskridge and Sunstein, along with others, see note 81 *infra*, would quarrel with the Court's increasing tendency to take meaning as dispositive when plain, and would thus take issue with my attempt here to provide some justification for that approach.

[20]See, *e.g.*, Blanchard v. Bergeron, 109 S.Ct. 939, 946–47 (1989) (Scalia, J., concurring in part); Green v. Bock Laundry Machine Co., 109 S.Ct. 1981, 1994–95 (1989) (Scalia, J., concurring in the judgment); Immigration and Naturalization Serv. v. Cardoza-Fonseca, 480 U.S. 421, 452–53 (1987) (Scalia, J., concurring in the judgment); Scalia, The Rule of Law as a Law of Rules, 56 U. Chi. L. Rev. 1175 (1989); Scalia, Judicial Deference to Administrative Interpretations of Law, 1989 Duke L.J. 511.

[21]Let me make clear that the statement in the text is not only descriptive, but also normative and prescriptive. I recognize full well the various political and resource-allocation constraints on the decisionmaking process that would lead a Justice simply to sign on to a decision the reasoning of which he or she might question. But just as we commonly in conversation and many other contexts hold people responsible for their overt actions or words regardless of their divergent deepest beliefs, so too do I believe it important that judges and other public decisionmakers be held responsible for those actions they explicitly support and those opinions they explicitly sign.

rious recent opinions treating opaquely a quite plainly mistakenly drafted procedural requirement.[22]

The ease with which the Court in *Pavelic & LeFlore* chose plain meaning over inconsistent purpose or preferable policy is neither aberrational nor a function of the special role of procedural rules, a conclusion demonstrated by the Court's other statutory construction cases decided in the 1989 Term. Recognizing that it is far too easy to generalize from a few carefully selected cases to the thesis the support of which guided the selection of the cases in the first place, I have attempted to analyze all of the Court's 1989 Term statutory construction cases. Some of these cases involve undeniably indeterminate language as to which the divide between determinate language and purpose (or between determinate language and justice, or between determinate language and legislative intent) does not arise.[23] But the bulk of the remaining cases demonstrate a consistent theme of taking the plain meaning of statutory terms as dispositive if clear, and primary even if not.[24]

---

[22]United States v. Locke, 471 U.S. 84 (1985), scorned in Posner, Legal Formalism, Legal Realism, and the Interpretation of Statutes and the Constitution, 37 Case West. Res. L. Rev. 179 (1986).

[23]See, *e.g.*, Chesapeake and Ohio Ry. Co. v. Schwalb, 110 S.Ct. 381 (1989) (whether employees were "engaged in maritime employment" for purposes of Longshore and Harbor Workers' Compensation Act); Commissioner of Internal Revenue v. Indianapolis Power & Light Co., 110 S.Ct. 589 (1990) (definition of "income"); Dole v. United Steelworkers of America, 110 S.Ct. 929 (1990) (definition of "collection of information" under Paperwork Reduction Act); Ngiraingas v. Sanchez, 110 S.Ct. 1737 (1990) (whether Guam is a "person" for purposes of 42 U.S.C. §1983); Reves v. Ernst & Young, 110 S.Ct. 945 (1990) (definition of "security"); United States v. Goodyear Tire and Rubber Co., 110 S.Ct. 462 (1989) (determination of whether "accumulated profits" for a multinational corporation were to be measured according to United States or foreign tax principles); United States v. Ojeda Rios, 110 S.Ct. 1845 (1990) (definition of "satisfactory explanation" in federal wiretapping statute).

Note that the well-known sample bias in favor of hard cases in appellate courts, see Llewellyn, The Common Law Tradition: Deciding Appeals 6, 64–68 (1960); Posner, The Jurisprudence of Skepticism, 86 Mich. L. Rev. 827, 828, 840 (1988); Schauer, Judging in a Corner of the Law, 61 S. Cal. L. Rev. 1717 (1988); *cf.* Priest & Klein, The Selection of Disputes for Litigation, 13 J. Legal Stud. 1 (1984), tolerates any number of divergent determinants of easiness and hardness. Thus, the presence in significant numbers of linguistically easy cases before the Supreme Court provides some evidence that the existing legal environment is such that linguistic easiness is hardly coextensive with legal easiness. As long as this is so, then it will be fruitful for lawyers and litigants to pursue cases in which the plain meaning of a statute is against them, so long as they have some legally respectable argument (purpose, or intent, or current desirable policy, or equity between the parties, for example) that can non-laughably counter the appeal to plain meaning. Conversely, insofar as the Court's reliance on plain meaning increases, it is less likely that the Court will see many plain meaning cases, for those will be the cases whose newly established legal easiness will provide impediments to rising up the appellate ladder.

[24]Moreover, the 1989 Term saw a unanimous opinion, written by Justice Stevens, relying on the plain meaning of the Militia Clauses of the Constitution in holding that gubernatorial con-

Guidry v. Sheet Metal Workers National Pension Fund[25] provides a good starting point, largely because of its intriguing contrast with *Riggs v. Palmer*.[26] In *Guidry*, a unanimous Court, with Justice Blackmun writing the opinion, held that a union official's union pension was immune from an attempt by that union to impose a constructive trust on it as a way of recouping part of what the official had embezzled from the union. Interpreting the prohibition on assignment and alienation contained in §1056(d)(1) of the Employee Retirement Income Security Act of 1974 (ERISA), Justice Blackmun operated on the assumption that "It is an elementary tenet of statutory construction that '[w]here there is no clear intention otherwise, a specific statute will not be controlled or nullified by a general one . . . .' We do not believe that congressional intent would be effectuated by reading the LMRDA's general reference to 'other appropriate relief' as overriding an express, specific congressional directive that pension benefits not be subject to assignment or alienation."[27] And then, "Understandably, there may be a natural distaste for the result we reach here. The statute, however, is clear."[28]

In *Sullivan v. Zebley*,[29] the issue was the definition of "disability" in the context of eligibility for benefits under the Supplemental Security Income Program, and Justice Blackmun's majority opinion again relied on the "plain words"[30] of the authorizing statute to strike down regulations of the Secretary of Health and Human Services defining disability for children in terms of an exhaustive list rather than in the functional terms employed for adults. This disparity, the Court held, was plainly inconsistent with the statutory requirement

sent is unnecessary for Congress to authorize the President to order members of the National Guard to active training duty outside the United States during peacetime. Perpich v. Department of Defense, 110 S.Ct. 2418 (1990). Note also the reliance on the plain meaning of constitutional text in Justice Scalia's dissent, joined by Justices Brennan, Marshall, and Stevens, in Maryland v. Craig, 110 S. Ct. 3157 (1990).

[25]110 S.Ct. 680 (1990).

[26]115 N.Y. 506, 22 N.E. 188 (1889), made famous by Ronald Dworkin in Dworkin, Taking Rights Seriously 23 (1977); Dworkin, Law's Empire 15–20 (1986).

[27]110 S.Ct. at 687.

[28]*Id.* at 688. Note also in this regard Carden v. Arkoma Associates, 110 S.Ct. 1015 (1990), in which Justice Scalia's majority opinion, joined by Justices Rehnquist, White, Stevens, and Kennedy, acknowledged that its result in concluding that the citizenship of all partners of a limited partnership must be considered in determining diversity of citizenship "can validly be characterized as technical, precedent-bound, and unresponsive to policy considerations raised by the changing realities of business organization." *Id.* at 1021.

[29]110 S.Ct. 885 (1990).

[30]*Id.* at 890.

that a child be considered disabled "'if he suffers from any . . . impairment of comparable severity' to one that would render an adult 'unable to engage in any substantial gainful activity.'"[31]

In *United States v. Dalm*,[32] there was no dispute that a taxpayer's claim for a refund did not fall under any of a number of different provisions providing exceptions to the otherwise applicable limitations period. In light of that, Justice Kennedy's majority opinion refused to apply to doctrine of equitable recoupment to provide an exception other than those explicitly designated in the Internal Revenue Code.

In *Adams Fruit Co., Inc. v. Barrett*,[33] Justice Marshall wrote for a unanimous Court. In concluding that exclusivity provisions in state workers' compensation laws did not preclude those who had availed themselves of benefits under those laws from bringing an action under the Migrant and Seasonal Agricultural Protection Act, Justice Marshall relied almost entirely on a close reading of the relevant law, a reading that followed his early assertion that "As a general rule of statutory construction, where the terms of a statute are unambiguous, judicial inquiry is complete."[34] Justice Marshall used similar language in *Hughey v. United States*,[35] where for a unanimous Court restricting restitution to the offense for which a defendant was convicted he relied both "on the language of the statute itself" and on Webster's Third New International Dictionary and Black's Law Dictionary in interpreting that language.[36] And in *Northbrook National Ins. Co. v. Brewer*,[37] Justice Marshall was joined by seven other Justices in basing on "pellucid" statutory language "that could not be more clear"[38] the conclusion that diversity jurisdictional limitations with respect to actions brought "against" insurers were inapplicable to direct action litigation brought "by" insurers.

---

[31] *Ibid.*

[32] 110 S.Ct. 1361 (1990).

[33] 110 S.Ct. 1384 (1990).

[34] *Id.* at 1387.

[35] 110 S.Ct. 1979 (1990).

[36] *Id.* at 1983. Justice Marshall used similar language in Pennsylvania Department of Public Welfare v. Davenport, 110 S.Ct. 2126 (1990), but there his close analysis of the language seemed more based on policy and less on language *simpliciter* than in most of the other cases in which plain meaning was the announced guideline.

[37] 110 S.Ct. 297 (1989).

[38] *Id.* at 299.

In *Kaiser Aluminum and Chemical Corp. v. Bonjorno*,[39] it was Justice O'Connor who carried the banner of plain meaning. In holding that postjudgment interest runs from the date of judgment and not the date of verdict, she relied on the specific "date of judgment" language in 28 U.S.C. §1961:[40]

> The starting point for interpretation of a statute "is the language of the statute itself. Absent a clearly expressed legislative intention to the contrary, that language must ordinarily be regarded as conclusive." Both the original and the amended versions of sec. 1961 refer specifically to the "date of judgment," which indicates a date certain. . . . Even though denial of interest from verdict to judgment may result in the plaintiff bearing the burden of the loss of the use of the money from verdict to judgment, the allocations of the costs accruing from litigation is a matter for the legislature, not the courts.

And Justice O'Connor used similar language, saying that the relevant statute "could not be clearer," in concluding for the Court in *Hallstrom v. Tillamook County*[41] that a "flexible or pragmatic construction"[42] was impermissible where in an action involving a statutory precondition of notice prior to litigation the flexible or pragmatic construction "flatly contradict[ed] the language of the statute."[43]

Plain meaning can include not only what is plainly in a statute, but also what is plainly not in it. Thus in *Yellow Freight System, Inc. v. Donnelly*,[44] Justice Stevens wrote for a unanimous Court in holding that the federal courts do not have exclusive jurisdiction over suits brought under Title VII of the Civil Rights Act of 1964. "Title VII contains no language that expressly confines jurisdiction to federal courts or ousts state courts of their presumptive jurisdiction. The omission of any such provision is strong, and arguably sufficient, evidence that Congress had no such intent."[45] To the same effect is *Venegas v. Mitchell*,[46] where Justice White for a unanimous Court

---

[39] 110 S.Ct. 1570 (1990).

[40] *Id.* at 1575–76. Justice White's dissent, joined by Justices Brennan, Marshall, and Blackmun, did not disagree on the point in the text, but only on the question of retroactive application of an amendment to §1961.

[41] 110 S.Ct. 304, 308 (1989).

[42] *Id.* at 309.

[43] *Ibid.*

[44] 110 S.Ct. 1566 (1990).

[45] *Id.* at 1569. Justice Stevens also referred later to the statute's "plain text." *Ibid.*

[46] 110 S.Ct. 1679 (1990).

determined that nothing in the federal civil rights laws prohibited a contingent-fee arrangement that exceeded in amount the statutory "reasonable fee" awarded against a losing defendant. "But there is nothing in the section to regulate what plaintiffs may or may not promise to pay their attorneys if they lose or if they win. Certainly § 1988 does not on its face prevent the plaintiff from promising an attorney a percentage of any money judgment that may be recovered."[47]

Just as at times the Court relies on the exclusionary import of plain language, so too does it at times rely on the fact that some language may be literally inclusive, thus defeating arguments for exclusion. In *California v. American Stores, Inc.*,[48] Justice Stevens's unanimous opinion relied on the "literal text" of §16 of the Clayton Act to hold that mandating divestiture was a permissible remedy because the section did not limit the authority to grant "injunctive relief . . . against threatened loss or damage."[49] Because the divestiture had been ordered in the form of injunctive relief, and because there was no question as to the presence of threatened loss or damage, Justice Stevens found no basis for creating an exclusion not literally authorized. Similarly, Justice White's opinion for an 8–1 Court in *United States v. Energy Resources Co.*[50] relied in the literal absence of a limitation on the power of the Bankruptcy Court as a virtually conclusive argument for not creating such a limitation.

As in *Pavelic & LeFlore* itself, plain meaning is rarely a function of just a few words taken in isolation. In *Maislin Industries, U.S., Inc. v. Primary Steel, Inc.*,[51] Justice Brennan's opinion for the Court found a statute's "clear meaning,"[52] but found it not on the basis of a few words, but from the "basic structure"[53] of the Interstate Commerce Act that the language revealed. Even more interestingly, where the plain meaning is subject to dispute, there still seems to be agreement that it remains the appropriate focus of legal argument. In *John Doe Agency v. John Doe Corp.*,[54] for example, much of the dispute turned

[47] *Id.* at 1682.

[48] 110 S.Ct. 1853 (1990).

[49] *Id.* at 1860.

[50] 110 S.Ct. 2139 (1990).

[51] 110 S.Ct. 2759 (1990).

[52] *Id.* at 2768.

[53] *Id.* at 2769.

[54] 110 S.Ct. 471 (1989).

on the meaning of the word "compiled" in the context of the exemption from the Freedom of Information Act for "records or information compiled for law enforcement purposes."[55] Writing for the majority, Justice Blackmun left little doubt about the contours of the inquiry:[56]

> As is customary, we look initially at the language of the statute itself. The wording of the phrase under scrutiny is simple and direct: "compiled for law enforcement purposes." The plain words contain no requirement that compilation be affected at a specific time. . . . A compilation, in its ordinary meaning, is something composed of materials collected and assembled from various sources or other documents. See Webster's Third New International Dictionary 464 (1961); Webster's Ninth New Collegiate Dictionary 268 (1963). . . . We thus do not accept the distinction the Court of Appeals drew between documents that originally were assembled for law-enforcement purposes and those that were not so originally assembled but were gathered later for such purposes. The plain language does not permit such a distinction.

And although Justice Scalia's dissent disputed the majority's view that compilation could not include "more creative activity," as "[W]hen we say that a statesman has 'compiled an enviable record of achievement,' or that a baseball pitcher has 'compiled a 1.87 earned run average,'" he relied not only on his own linguistic intuitions, but also on *Roget's Thesaurus of Synonyms and Antonyms*, making quite clear that the grounds for the debate, even when there was a debate, were not whether plain meaning would dominate, but just what the plain meaning was.[57]

Similarly, *Sullivan v. Everhart*[58] was a 5–4 opinion, with Justice Scalia writing for the majority and Justice Stevens for the dissent. The majority and the dissent divided on the question whether the Secretary of Health and Human Service's regulations for error correction ("netting") were within the scope of his authorization pursuant to the Old Age, Survivors, and Disability Insurance program,

---

[55] 5 U.S.C. §552(b)(7).

[56] 110 S.Ct. at 476–77. The Court went on to note that "If, despite what we regard as the plain meaning of the statutory language, it were necessary or advisable to examine the legislative history of Exemption 7, . . . we would reach the same conclusion." *Id.* at 477.

[57] *Id.* at 480 (Scalia, J., dissenting). A similar debate about the "explicit statutory direction" was at the center of Hoffman-La Roche v. Sperling, 110 S.Ct. 482, 487 (1989), with Justice Kennedy writing for the majority and Justice Scalia in dissent.

[58] 110 S.Ct. 960 (1990).

but the dispute was at least on the surface about meaning, with even Justice Stevens's dissent relying initially and primarily on his interpretation of the "plain terms of the statute."[59]

So too in *Department of Treasury v. Federal Labor Relations Authority*,[60] where Justice Scalia's majority opinion on an issue of federal employee labor relations relied on the "plain text" in determining that a Federal Labor Relations Authority interpretation was "flatly contradicted " by the relevant statutory language.[61] Although Justice Stevens dissented, his disagreement was not with the majority's plain meaning construction of the basic statutory structure, but only about whether the "plain language," a phrase he used twice in a one-paragraph opinion, required outright reversal rather than mere remand.[62]

Thus the ability to argue about plain meaning should not be taken to rebut its relevance. A dispute over plain meaning looks different from one about justice, or equity, or purpose, or policy, or intent,[63] drawing on different sources and employing a different argumentative style and structure. This is perhaps most apparent in *Sullivan v. Stroop*,[64] where the issue was whether Title II Social Security payments were to count as "child support payments" for purposes of a statute exempting the first fifty dollars of child support payments (per month) from the calculation of eligibility for AFDC purposes. Both in the briefs and argument, and in the opinions themselves, the case turned on the meaning of the phrase "any child support payments," and more particularly on whether "child support payments" was to be defined in accordance with its technical legal meaning, which arguably is restricted to court-awarded payments from a parent or guardian, or its ordinary language meaning, which arguably includes government benefits for the purpose of child support as well. In choosing the former, Chief Justice Rehnquist relied in part

---

[59]110 S.Ct. at 968 (1990) (Stevens, J., dissenting). Similarly, Justice O'Connor relied on Webster's New International Dictionary to reach the conclusion that "for the use of" in the Internal Revenue Code "could support any number of different meanings." Davis v. United States, 110 S.Ct. 2014, 2019 (1990).

[60]110 S.Ct. 1623 (1990).

[61]*Id.* at 1627.

[62]*Id.* at 1632 (Stevens, J., dissenting).

[63]See Texaco Inc. v. Hasbrouck, 110 S.Ct. 2535, 2542 n.12 (1990), in which Justice Stevens's majority opinion in a Robinson-Patman case refused to follow the direction indicated by the legislative history where it conflicted with the "blunt direction of the statutory text."

[64]110 S.Ct. 2499 (1990).

on Black's Law Dictionary to support the technical meaning, and in part on the Random House Dictionary of English Usage to show that even the ordinary language meaning urged by those objecting to the failure to exclude, and even the very dictionary on which they relied, lent some support to the Secretary's interpretation. Justice Blackmun's dissent reached a different conclusion, but was an inquiry quite similar in style, concluding "that the plain language of the statute does not unequivocally support the Secretary's interpretation."[65] And Justice Stevens's separate dissent, acknowledging the closeness of the case, reached its conclusion by "put[ting] aside legal terminology and consider[ing] ordinary English usage."[66]

Sullivan v. Stroop involved conflicting claims of plain meaning, but was a decision in which questions of plain meaning dominated. But even when neither side is able to claim that the meaning is "plain," an opinion that is focused almost entirely on wrestling with the meaning and interrelationship of various technical statutory provisions, as with Justice Marshall's opinion for himself and seven others in the bankruptcy/tax case of *Begier v. Internal Revenue Service*,[67] or Justice White's opinion for himself and seven others in *Sullivan v. Finkelstein*,[68] dealing with the circumstances under which an order invalidating certain administrative regulations may be appealed as a "final decision," is quite different from an opinion that wrestles with the deepest purposes of the Bankruptcy Code or with the current policies served by the diversity jurisdiction or with the conflicting equities of the particular parties in a securities case. Similarly, Justice Blackmun's opinion for a unanimous Court in *General Motors Corp. v. United States*[69] is devoted mainly to the kind of extraordinarily close textual analysis of the Clean Air Act that would seem superfluous if purpose or intent or justice rather than linguistic meaning were to be the primary determinant of statutory import.[70]

---

[65]*Id.* at 2505 (Blackmun, J., dissenting).

[66]*Id.* at 2510 (Stevens, J., dissenting).

[67]110 S.Ct. 2258 (1990).

[68]110 S.Ct. 2658 (1990).

[69]110 S.Ct. 2528 (1990).

[70]I use the word "import" here to avoid the begging the central question by talking of statutory "meaning." Whether a statute means what its words mean is just what the dispute is all about, and that is why I earlier referred to the meaning of a rule-formulation rather than the meaning of the rule, since whether the meaning of the rule is the meaning of its formulation is just the matter at issue.

III. The Tilt Toward Plain Meaning

I suspect that most readers will have found the foregoing litany of cases only slightly less tedious to read than it was for me to write.[71] And I do not claim to have described each with the same care, subtlety, or accuracy as might have been the case were I a specialist in the relevant areas, were I more interested in the substantive disputes involved in the cases, or had I more time or space to devote to each case. As shall become apparent, that is a big part of the point I wish to make. Still, a number of themes emerge from this survey. First among these is that plain language discourse dominates the Court's statutory interpretation cases. Almost every case mentions plain language in just those words, many opinions rely on specific definitions in specific dictionaries, and many disputes are couched as disputes over the meaning of language rather than as disputes about policy or purpose or intent or justice.[72] Moreover, the use of "plain meaning" discourse is hardly limited to its most prominent proponent, but is employed by every member of the Court, not only in the opinions they join but also in the opinions they write, and not only in the opinions they write when Justice Scalia is joining them, but also in the opinions they write when Justice Scalia is on the other side.

Now it could be that this language in the opinions is all fluff, disguising analyses and conclusions based on policy, or purpose, or justice between the parties, or something else. Am I making too much of what might very well be merely boilerplate? I think not, for such a Realist conclusion is unsupported by the evidence. First of all, the use of plain meaning boilerplate, in the current academic/ professional climate, seems hardly necessary to serve the legitimizing purpose that the Realist thesis would posit. If the purpose of writing an opinion that does not accurately replicate the actual decisional processes of the Court is to attempt to appeal to some constituency outside the Court, it is not clear to me just who the constituency for this kind of plain meaning rhetoric would be. And even if it is true that neither the Justices nor their clerks care very much whether their discourse looks academically respectable, the actual results in the cases

[71]No research assistants were used in the preparation of this article.

[72]Because it is as hard to cite to what the Court did not say as it is to listen to a dog that does not bark, let me simply assert my impression that almost all of the opinions I describe demonstrated far less attention to purpose or justice or equity between the parties than would have been expected were these factors the actual focus of the decisionmaking process.

do not support the conclusion that the articulated justifications are simply disingenuous. There are just too many cases in which the alignment of Justices is not explicable in terms of expected sympathy with one side or the other, or one policy position or another. Now one could complicate the Realist-based policy analysis, attempting to explain the alignment of Justices in terms of their views not only on some reductionist and misleading liberal/conservative dichotomy, but also in terms of their views about the role of courts, the role of administrative agencies, the functioning of legislatures, the virtues of particular statutory schemes, the importance of certain social policies, and so on and on and on. But once we add all of these factors to an allegedly Realist analysis, it seems quite unrealistic to suppose that the one factor that the Justices disregard among so many factors that they consider is what the statutes actually say, the one factor they describe as being so important. It might be plausible to hypothesize that the Justices' views in statutory construction cases are all political, and that they choose the side most appealing to them as a matter of policy and then craft a textual argument to fit the predecided conclusion. This hypothesis, however, is not supported by the evidence. Given that, there seems little basis for even the conjecture that the one factor that so pervades the Justices' articulated justifications is the one factor out of so many that played no role in how the Justices reached the conclusions they did.

That plain meaning seemed in the aggregate to dominate political inclination for this sample of cases should come as little surprise. For there was one factor that (to me) was present in every one of these cases: None of them was interesting. Not one. Compared to flag burning or affirmative action or separation of powers or political patronage, these cases struck me as real dogs. That is not to say they were socially unimportant. Far more of the public welfare of the United States turns on questions of qualification for AFDC benefits than on the question of flag desecration. But the moral, political, and social insensitivity of my own judgments is hardly unique (consider which among the foregoing cases taken in isolation are likely candidates for articles in *The Supreme Court Review* or the Supreme Court issue of the *Harvard Law Review*). And the relevance of all of this is that my morally and socially erroneous judgments about the interestingness or political consequences of these cases seem reflective of similarly morally and socially erroneous judgments reached by the Court itself. This array of cases is disproportionately dominated by cases decided early in the Term, by 7–2, 8–1, or 9–0 opinions, and with comparatively brief opinions, the latter being especially surprising given the enormous complexity of the issues. It only takes two or three sentences to get to the point with respect to flag desecration, but three or four pages are necessary just to figure out what is going on in some of the AFDC or ERISA or tax cases.

The 1989 Term statutory interpretation cases were perhaps unusual in that few if any of them involved issues as to which the Justices seemed to hold strong political or moral or economic (as opposed to jurisprudential) views.[73] As long as it is professionally respectable to rely both on plain meaning and on underlying purpose,[74] it is not at all surprising that the use of one or the other will be decision-rationalizing rather than decision-generating where the issue is as morally and politically charged as discrimination on the basis of race[75] or gender.[76] Conversely, however, where the substance of the dispute seems to the Justices (or to me) less politically or morally or economically charged, as with some of this Term's cases involving, for example, diversity jurisdiction for direct action litigation, the coverage of the Longshore and Harbor Workers' Compensation Act, and the non-alienation provisions of the Employee Retirement Income Security Act of 1974, it is more likely that jurisprudential views about methods of legal decisionmaking, views that are themselves political or substantive at the wholesale rather than retail level, are more likely to dominate.

---

[73]This is not to make the claim that jurisprudential positions are politically or morally or economically sterile. It is to say, however, that there is a difference between a jurisprudential view, itself chosen on wholesale political grounds, and a view about which side, for political reasons, ought to win this case. The distinction I draw is no more than, and no less than, the distinction that enables opinions or judges to be labeled as "result-oriented." Insofar as that distinction suggests that the opposite of result-orientation is political neutrality, I disavow it. The opposite of result-orientation is holding process-oriented views, themselves political, that *may* dominate the political desirability of one result rather than another in a particular case.

[74]The standard citation here is Llewellyn, Remarks on the Theory of Appellate Decisions and the Rules or Canons about How Statutes Are to Be Construed, 3 Vand. L. Rev. 395 (1950), no less true today than in 1950.

[75]*E.g.*, Firefighters Local Union No. 1784 v. Stotts, 467 U.S. 561 (1984); Steelworkers v. Weber, 443 U.S. 193 (1979). My claim about these cases is only that as a descriptive matter the Justices' jurisprudential views about the role of plain meaning or purpose were dominated by their views about the merits of the particular controversy before them.

[76]California Federal Savings & Loan Ass'n v. Guerra, 479 U.S. 272 (1987). My conjecture about cases like *Weber* and *CalFed* is simply that if in both cases the plain meaning of the statutes had supported the race- or gender-conscious program and the underlying purpose of those statutes could plausibly be interpreted as prohibiting it, the alignment of Justices would likely have been no different. This conjecture receives some oblique support from the frequency as this article is being written of reliance on the plain meaning of the "declaration of war" clause in Article I, §8 by those who otherwise have little good to say about plain meaning.

Thus, my interpretive claim about this array of cases is not that inquiry into plain meaning is the only inquiry that takes place, nor that for any Justice the outcome-independent consultation of what is indicated by the plain meaning of the statutory terms is always dispositive. Rather, the statutory interpretation cases of the 1989 Term do indicate that arguably for all of the Justices their outcome-independent reading of the plain meaning of the statutory terms is at the very least a factor in their decisionmaking. I might be willing to go further and suggest that for most it appears to be a presumptive factor, being by itself presumptively controlling in the same sense that distinctions based on gender are, by themselves, presumptively violative of the equal protection clause,[77] or that content-based restrictions are, by themselves, presumptively inconsistent with the first amendment.[78] But whether I am correct in this conjecture about presumptiveness or not, I am willing to conclude with more confidence that plain meaning appears now for all of the Justices to be a strong factor in their decisionmaking, the consequence of which is that plain meaning is increasingly likely to be dispositive as other factors, most prominently a strong political or moral or social or economic tilt towards one side or the other, are diminished. With an array of cases like that presented in the 1989 Term, therefore, in which many appear to the decisionmakers to present issues of great complexity and relative political and moral equipoise, and in which many involve quite clear language, it should come as less of a surprise to discover that plain meaning would dominate both the Court's actual decisionmaking process and its articulated justifications for its decisions. But to reemphasize what should be obvious, this is not to make a uniform claim. My conclusions about the import of plain meaning are conclusions much like the claims that Swiss cheese has holes or that German wine is sweet. These are probabilistic generalizations, true in many or most cases, but not in all. So too with my claim that plain meaning is very important—not a claim that it is the only thing that is important, and not inconsistent with the claim that in some cases it is not important at all.

---

[77]Mississippi University for Women v. Hogan, 458 U.S. 718 (1982).

[78]Boos v. Barry, 485 U.S. 312 (1988). Obviously the term "presumptive" is compatible with presumptions of varying strength, and even if I am correct in concluding that the plain meaning of a statute is treated as presumptively controlling by the Court, there is as yet too little evidence from which one could extract a characterization of the strength of the presumption that would be analogous to a level of scrutiny in the constitutional domain.

IV. Plain Meaning as Common Ground

My claim so far is entirely descriptive. Moreover, the descriptive claim is a modest one. In light of the comparative frequency of purpose-oriented or policy-oriented or intent-oriented decisions in recent years,[79] even in cases in which the plain language of the statute involved pointed in the other direction, I want to claim only that this Term's results and justifications appear to represent something of a departure, and perhaps the beginning of a new direction,[80] one whose sights are set more on *McBoyle* than on *Church of the Holy Trinity*, more on text than on policy, and more on meaning than on value. It is far too early to determine if this trend will hold, or whether instead 1989 is aberrational. But it is not too early to try to offer some explanation of why this might (even if unintentionally) be happening, and some explanation of why it might be more justifiable than one would think merely by reading much of the contemporary statutory interpretation literature.[81]

I start with the usability of plain meaning, and the claim that plain meaning is what makes it possible for me to converse with an English speaker with whom I have nothing in common but our shared language, to read a newspaper or book written in English by people from different backgrounds writing at very different times (I learn much more from reading Shakespeare in the original than I do from reading Plato in the original, and that is because I read English but I

[79]*E.g.*, United States v. Fausto, 484 U.S. 439 (1988); Rose v. Rose, 481 U.S. 619 (1988); Midlantic Nat'l Bank v. New Jersey Dept. of Environmental Protection, 474 U.S. 494 (1986); Dickman v. Comm'r, 465 U.S. 330 (1984); Rose v. Lundy, 455 U.S. 509, 516–18 (1982).

[80]Or perhaps the somewhat firmer entrenchment of a trend that had begun earlier. See Sunstein, Interpreting Statutes in the Regulatory State, 103 Harv. L. Rev. 405, 415 (1990) ("Textualism appears to be enjoying a renaissance in a number of recent cases").

[81]I refer here to a literature that has usefully helped to open up an unfortunately recently neglected area for academic inquiry, but has at the same time done so with a striking unity of voice and approach. See, *e.g.*, Calabresi, A Common Law for the Age of Statutes (1982); Aleinikoff, Updating Statutory Construction, 87 Mich. L. Rev. 20 (1988); Eskridge, Dynamic Statutory Interpretation, 135 U. Pa. L. Rev. 1479 (1987); Eskridge & Frickey, Statutory Interpretation as Practical Reasoning, 42 Stan. L. Rev. 321 (1990); Eskridge & Frickey, Legislation Scholarship and Pedagogy in the Post-Legal Process Era, 48 U. Pitt. L. Rev. 691 (1987); Farber, Statutory Interpretation and Legislative Supremacy, 78 Geo. L.J. 281 (1989); Farina, Statutory Interpretation and the Balance of Power in the Administrative State, 89 Colum. L. Rev. 452 (1989); Langevoort, Statutory Obsolescence and the Judicial Process: The Revisionist Role of the Courts in Federal Banking Regulation, 85 Mich. L. Rev. 672 (1987); LaRue, Statutory Interpretation: Lord Coke Revisited, 48 U. Pitt. L. Rev. 733 (1987); Sunstein, Interpreting Statutes in the Regulatory State, 103 Harv. L. Rev. 405 (1989); Note, 95 Harv. L. Rev. 892 (1982).

do not read Greek), and to do far better with traffic signs in Nigeria than in Szechuan.

Thus members of a linguistic community, a community stretching across both time and space, are members of that community precisely because they are able to make minimal sense out of some number of signs standing alone. Whether we call this literal meaning, or plain meaning, or sentence meaning,[82] or something else, it is a phenomenon that undergirds much of our existence, including my writing of this article and your reading of it. Moreover, members of linguistic subcommunities do the same things with the linguistic understandings of those subcommunities, and that is why in this article I am not explaining the meaning of "Supreme Court" or "statutory interpretation," or telling the reader that H. L. A. Hart and Henry Hart were different people. Within the linguistic subcommunity whose membership includes me and many readers of this text, certain things are plain that would not be plain outside of this subcommunity.

I make no claim that plain meaning or Basic English or lawyer's English or whatever is value-free. Plain meaning incorporates numerous categorial choices, all of which are contingent and value-laden. Nor, more relevantly here, do I claim that plain meaning is an

---

[82]The expression "sentence meaning," as distinguished from "utterer's meaning," is commonly used within the speech act tradition in the philosophy of language to distinguish what a sentence means from what a speaker intends or attempts to do by use of that sentence. See Grice, Utterer's Meaning, Sentence-Meaning, and Word-Meaning, in The Philosophy of Language 54 (Searle, ed., 1971). Although there are real debates about the relationship between literal meaning and other more speaker- or hearer-oriented phenomena, see generally Philosophical Grounds of Rationality: Intentions, Categories, Ends (Grandy & Warner, eds., 1986), the notion of a rule- or convention-based literal meaning, undeniably incorporating certain contextual presuppositions of the linguistic community but still independent of the particular context of utterance, is widely held. See, *e.g.*, Alston, Philosophy of Language 103–3 (1964); Chomsky, Reflections on Language (1975); Davidson, Inquiries into Truth & Interpretation 243–80 (1984); Dummett, The Interpretation of Frege's Philosophy 108–47 (1981); Holdcroft, Words & Deeds: Problems in the Theory of Speech Acts (1978); Lewis, Convention: A Philosophical Study (1969); McGinn, Wittgenstein on Meaning: An Interpretation and Evaluation 88–92 (1984); Quine, Use and Its Place in Meaning, in Theories and Things 42, 50 (1981) ("our core language, Basic English so to say, which all English speakers command"); Searle, Literal Meaning, in Expression and Meaning: Studies in the Theory of Speech Acts 117 (1979); Strawson, Intention and Convention in Speech Acts, 73 Phil. Rev. 439 (1964). I use the phrase "widely held" before the previous string cite advisedly, and I use it in order to deny any originality or idiosyncrasy in my views about language, while at the same time (*a*) denying that the pages of a law journal are the appropriate forum for debating or resolving the deepest questions of the philosophy of language; (*b*) denying that the kinds of people, including me, who write in law journals are qualified to debate or resolve the deepest questions of the philosophy of language; (*c*) disclaiming any reliance on the authoritativeness of non-specialist interpretations of what well-known philosophers have said; and (*d*) refusing to brand as philistine, backwards, or ignorant those who disagree with me.

infallible reflector of the intentions of the user of the language, or a universally reliable guide to the background purposes of a statute written in language, or a particularly adaptable vehicle for keeping up with various social or political changes, or a particularly sensitive tool for applying the necessarily general notion of meaning to the necessarily particular components of individual cases.[83] Plain meaning, quite simply, is a blunt, frequently crude, and certainly narrowing device, cutting off access to many features of some particular conversational or communicative or interpretive context that would otherwise be available to the interpreter or conversational participant.

The comparative crudeness of plain meaning explains why interpreting a statute according to its plain meaning will at times generate an absurd result, or at least a result at odds with the best direct application of the purposes underlying that statute, or at odds with best current policy in light of changed circumstances, or at odds with what the drafters would have desired were they faced with the current situation in light of current circumstances. But such suboptimal outcomes are little different from those that would emerge when we attempt to conduct conversations solely on the basis of plain meaning, because in doing so we ignore a wide range of contextual and conversational cues that make sentence meaning different from utterance meaning, that make what a speaker's words mean different from

[83]And that is why so many attacks on plain meaning as being unable to reproduce "faithfully" or "accurately" or "precisely" what the first user of the language intended, or what the purpose of the statute indicates for the case at hand, or what is best in light of changes in society, miss the point. Of course plain language cannot meet these goals, and no one except the straws commonly attacked claims it can. Plain language is sparse rather than rich, a blunt cleaver and not a sharp scalpel. As such reliance only on plain meaning will frequently misperceive some speaker's intention, or misapply some background purpose or goal, or be incapable of responding without lag to a world that changes faster than its language. As to this there is no debate, however much those of us with some attraction to text or plain meaning are commonly taken to have made various preposterous claims for the perfection of text or plain meaning. The real question, the one that it is the aim of this article to open for discussion, is whether in some contexts the reliance on text or plain meaning, for all its imperfections and consequent suboptimal results in individual cases, might still be preferable to the use of theoretically richer and more sensitive tools by multiple and decidedly suboptimal decisionmakers. Here the relevant analogy to me is the MacKinnonesque perspective on rape offered by Susan Estrich in Real Rape (1987). Recognizing that relying on the plain meaning of "No!" will for the universe of reliers produce some cases in which the relier will act on "no" when the speaker wanted the relier to understand "yes," and when it might be best "in context" to interpret "no" as meaning something else, Estrich quite properly focuses on the identity and predilections of the actual array of actual reliers, concluding that the number of legal and moral mistakes made by reliance on plain meaning will be lower than the number of legal and moral mistakes that are now made by actual reliers and actual judges and actual juries in trying to determine when "no" might mean "yes." My claim is only that those who find this perspective appealing ought to consider whether its appeal might be generalizable.

what a speaker means to say, and that lead us into confusions that would not be present were we at all times maximally sensitive to the context of utterance.

So it is therefore common ground (at least among those of us who accept that there is such a thing as plain meaning) that plain meaning is far from perfect, if the measure of perfection is what some maximally sensitive interpreter would glean from consideration of every aspect of the context of utterance. So why then would we find a Court of nine quite intelligent people and thirty-odd quite intelligent assistants making use of such a crude tool?

I put the question in this way in order to indicate that there is a question here. Unfortunately much of the contemporary literature refuses to acknowledge that there is an issue, making a few debaters' points about the confusions and absurdities that can be produced by plain meaning, obligatorily quoting Wittgenstein's example of games and dice, and (as if Wittgenstein had or offered a theory of statutory construction or judicial power) making the remarkable leap from the imperfections of plain language to the conclusion that it is the job of the judiciary to correct those imperfections whenever and wherever they occur. To put the question in this way, however, is to beg the entire question, and thus we must ask a different question: Given that plain meaning is far from perfect, what (if anything) might suggest the desirability of employing a consequently imperfect decision procedure that relies on it?

In trying to offer one possible answer to this question, I want to return to some characteristics of the array of statutory interpretation cases that dominated the 1989 Term. First, as I noted above, I did not find these cases very substantively interesting. I offer this not as an absolute claim about anything, but only as some evidence that it is possible that neither the Justices nor their clerks did either, a conclusion buttressed by the brevity of the opinions, their unanimity, and the almost complete absence, even when there were differences, of the kind of extraodinarily fragmented (and acrimonious) opinions that mark much of the Court's recent work.[84]

In addition, these did not look like the kinds of cases as to which either the Justices or their clerks had much context-sensitive expertise. Context is not for dabblers, and it is almost definitional of a

[84] *E.g.*, City of Richmond v. J.A. Croson Co., 488 U.S. 469 (1989); County of Allegheny v. American Civil Liberties Union, 109 S.Ct. 3086 (1989); DeShaney v. Winnebago Dept. of Social Services, 489 U.S. 189 (1989); Webster v. Reproductive Health Services, 109 S.Ct. 3040 (1989).

context-based inquiry that the inquirer have the expertise and internal-participant knowledge that enables the inquirer to know what is really going on beneath and around and next to the raw external clues, including among those raw external cues ordinary meanings of the words used by the participants in the enterprise.[85]

If these perceptions are correct, then the Justices are faced with a coordination problem.[86] Given their lack of expertise about the areas involved, and given what seems to be some lack of interest in the areas involved, and given some presumed time and related constraints, how are the Justices to achieve some degree of agreement? Here the virtues of plain meaning seem more compelling. If we take as a given the relative unwillingness of the Justices to get totally involved in the detailed ramifications of the cases involved, or take as an alternative given the likelihood that were they to do so a great deal of disagreement would result, then the reliance on plain meaning may be a hardly novel suboptimizing second-best solution, a way in which people with potentially divergent views and potentially different understandings of what the context would require may still be able to agree about what the language they all share requires. Plain language may provide some minimal mutual understanding that

[85]See, *e.g.*, Kahn, The Supreme Court's Misconstruction of a Procedural Statute—a Critique of the Court's Decision in Badaracco, 82 Mich. L. Rev. 461 (1983), a good example of the way in which a specialist might read a statute, even the literal language of a statute, differently from the way the Court read it. But even assuming Kahn is right about this case, he does not address the question whether this decision procedure, when employed by these nine people with the amount of time spent on the cases as fixed, would produce better results over a run of cases by employing a different procedure. My instinct is that these Justices with these clerks with this amount of time will make less of a hash of tax law in the long run by trying to rely on plain meaning than by trying to divine and apply the deepest purposes and equities of the Internal Revenue Code. And even if I am wrong about this, it would not surprise me if the Justices themselves thought this.

[86]I draw my inspiration from a reading (and misreading) of a rich literature including Gauthier, Morals By Agreement (1986); Hardin, Collective Action (1982); Lewis, Convention: A Philosophical Study (1969); Regan, Utilitarianism and Co-operation (1980); Olson, The Logic of Collective Action (1965); Schelling, The Strategy of Conflict (1960); Slote, Beyond Optimizing: A Study of Rational Choice (1989); Ullman-Margalit, The Emergence of Norms (1977); Axelrod, The Emergence of Cooperation among Egoists, 75 Am. Pol. Sci. Rev. 306 (1981); Axelrod & Hamilton, The Evolution of Cooperation, 211 Science 1390 (1981); Lindblom, The Science of Muddling Through, 19 Pub. Admin. Rev. 79 (1959); Tversky & Kahnemann, The Framing of Decisions and the Psychology of Choice, 211 Science 453 (1981). For applications of these perspectives to law, see Finnis, The Authority of Law in the Predicament of Contemporary Social Theory, 1 Notre Dame J. .of Law, Ethics and Pub. Pol. 115 (1984); Green, Law, Co-ordination and the Common Good, 3 Ox. J. Legal Stud. 299 (1983); Heiner, Imperfect Choice and Self-Stabilizing Rules, 5 Econ. & Phil. 19 (1989); Heiner, Imperfect Decisions and the Law: On the Evolution of Legal Precedent and Rules, 15 J. Legal Stud. 227 (1986); Postema, Coordination and Convention at the Foundations of Law, 11 J. Legal Stud. 165 (1982); Reynolds, Law as Convention, 2 Ratio Juris 105 (1989).

guards something that is shared in the face of widely disparate political views and social experiences.

All of this presupposes that the Justices have some reason for seeking agreement, if not as to results then at least as to the permissible sources for the inquiry. Here there are a number of different stories that might be told, but at least one would see the Justices as people who both want to agree in fact and want to be seen as people who agree with some frequency. Justice Marshall and Justice Scalia are likely never to agree about affirmative action, but they can agree that December 30 is not the same day as December 31, just as they can agree that an action brought by an insurance company is not the same as one brought against one. But if there is shared agreement among all of the Justices that something shared is worth preserving (and here the increase in reliance on plain meaning from the 1988 Term to the 1989 Term may bear some relationship to the decrease in acrimony from the 1988 Term to the 1989 Term), then the search for some common ground is understandable, and the finding of plain meaning as that common ground, despite all its failings, is understandable as well.

The normative contingency of this approach ought to be obvious. That is, the desirability of reliance on plain meaning is a function of the desirability of (*a*) the Court's marshalling its human resources in such a way that it is undesirable for the Justices and their clerks to become truly internally expert in every subject that comes to their attention; (*b*) the Court's agreeing on the results in some significant number of cases; (*c*) the Court's agreeing on the methods of inquiry in some significant number of cases; (*d*) the institutional stability brought by (*b*) and (*c*). The desirability of these goals is far from obvious. But it is equally obvious that their desirability is far from implausible. In this respect almost all of the contemporary statutory interpretation literature has failed to address at least one quite important question. We have numerous answers to the question, "How should the individual Justices reach their decisions if their goal is to make the best possible decision in each case?" Unfortunately, we have many fewer answers to the question, "What decision procedure should a nine-member body employ to reach the best decisions *they* can over an array of cases highlighting experiential and political differences among the nine decisionmakers?"

The premise of this essay is that these are not the same questions, and that an attempt to answer the second will lead to consideration of a menu of second-best or satisficing solutions that are not even thought about if only the first of these questions are asked. And if attention is then turned to the contingent and contextual desirability of acontextual inquiry, to the contingent optimality of sub-optimizing decision procedures, and to the circumstances in which the second-best is the best we can do, then some number of second-best approaches are before us for consideration. Reliance on plain meaning is only one of these among many, but if this is the focus of the inquiry, then the admitted limitations of plain meaning need no longer be considered dispositive. From this perspective, the lesson of the 1989 statutory interpretation cases is not that it is unilluminating to read Derrida or Gadamer, but that it can also be illuminating and useful to read Webster's dictionary in a society that for generations has thought it useful to produce it.

JEFFREY D. HOCKETT

JUSTICE ROBERT H. JACKSON, THE SUPREME COURT, AND THE NUREMBERG TRIAL

Justice Robert H. Jackson regarded his service as United States Chief of Counsel at the Nuremberg War Crimes Trial as "the most satisfying and gratifying experience" of his life and "infinitely more important" than his work on the Supreme Court. While there is "only a very temporary distinction in the work of a judge," Jackson said, the Nuremberg Trial marked an event "rather unique in the annals of law."[1] It was at Nuremberg that individuals were first held responsible for waging a war of aggression and for committing crimes against humanity, or genocide. Jackson stood to be identified closely with the Trial: He negotiated the Charter on which the Trial was based, marshaled the evidence supporting the charge that the Nazis planned and waged a war of aggression, wrote and made the opening and closing statements for the prosecution, expounded the theory and purpose of indicting Nazi organizations, and assumed primary responsibility for cross-examining Goering, Schacht, and Speer.[2]

Many lauded Jackson's efforts and agreed that Nuremberg repre-

Jeffrey D. Hockett is Assistant Professor of Political Science, the University of Tulsa.

AUTHOR'S NOTE: I would like to thank the University of Tulsa for grant support used in the research of this paper.

[1]Jackson, Oral History, 1475–76, The Papers of Robert H. Jackson, Box 191, Library of Congress, Manuscript Division (cited below as RHJP; subsequent references to the Oral History contain only page numbers for the reader's convenience). See also Jackson, Justice Jackson's Final Report to the President Concerning the Nurnberg War Crimes Trial, 20 Temple L. Q. 342–44 (1946); Jackson, Introduction to Harris, Tyranny on Trial: The Evidence at Nuremberg xxxvii (1954).

[2]Jackson, Oral History at 1205, 1246–48; Jackson, The Nurnberg Case (1947).

0-226-09573-8/91/1990-0004$02.00

sented a landmark in international law.[3] Others denied the legitimacy of the Trial and excoriated Jackson for participating. The Trial, some argued, was a negation of principles that lie at the heart of any system of justice under law.[4] Put another way: "Nurnberg was at best a political 'court' aimed at administering punishment spectacularly for political reasons and by virtue of victory, i.e., power."[5] Even Chief Justice Harlan Stone privately characterized the Trial as a "high-grade lynching party."[6] When asked to administer the oath to the American members of the International Tribunal, the Chief Justice said that he "did not wish to appear, even in that remote way, to give my blessing or that of the Court on the proposed Nurnberg trials."[7]

At the very least, Jackson's decision to participate in this off-the-bench activity posed several risks. Extra-judicial involvement is potentially hazardous since it might (1) impair the Court's institutional integrity if the event deserves condemnation; (2) impede the work of the Court by diverting time and energy from primary judicial obligations; or (3) affect the participating Justice's jurisprudence, usually by leading to actual bias or the appearance of bias in cases related to the activity.[8] These dangers, however, suggest certain potential benefits. If sufficient public and elite opinion regard the activity in question as honorable or an event of some moment, the Court benefits from the notoriety received by the participating Justice. Furthermore, a Justice can enhance his or her judicial performance if an extra-judicial experience reinforces or cultivates important legal or constitutional values.

In view of the range of opinion regarding Nuremberg's merit, and considering that the War Crimes Trial is perhaps the most famous extra-judicial mission in the Court's history, it is odd that there is no sustained assessment of Jackson's decision to participate in the event.

---

[3]Harris, note 1 *supra*; Gerhart, America's Advocate: Robert H. Jackson (1958); Taylor, The Nuremberg Trials, 55 Colum. L. Rev. 488–525 (1955); Stimson, The Nuremberg Trial: Landmark in Law, 25 Foreign Affairs 179–89 (1947).

[4]Woetzel, The Nuremberg Trials in International Law 94 (1960); Wyzanski, Nuremberg—A Fair Trial? Atl. Monthly 66 (April 1946).

[5]Solow, The Integrity of the Supreme Court, Fortune 101 (1954).

[6]Quoted *ibid.*

[7]Harlan F. Stone to Luther Ely Smith, Jan. 2, 1946, The Papers of Harlan Fiske Stone, Box 27, Library of Congress, Manuscript Division (cited below as HFSP).

[8]McKay, The Judiciary and Nonjudicial Activities, 35 Law & Contemp. Probs. 12, 19–26 (1970). See also Bell, Extrajudicial Activity of Supreme Court Justices, 22 Stan. Law Rev. 587–617 (1970); Note, 47 Iowa L. Rev. 1026–48 (1962).

Conclusions drawn from an analysis of the Nuremberg assignment, it should be noted, are not necessarily applicable to other examples of extra-judicial involvement. The variety and number of these activities make generalizations inappropriate.[9] But an examination of Jackson's Nuremberg experience is of more than historical interest, since requests for judicial participation in international trials seem possible in an increasingly interdependent world.

I. The Nuremberg Trial: Landmark in Law or Instance of Victor's Justice?

The most important question to consider in assessing Jackson's decision to participate in the Nuremberg Trial is whether the charges of his harshest critics were valid. If the Trial was a manifest instance of "victor's justice," it would be impossible to justify Jackson's involvement in view of the damage it would have caused to legal values and to the integrity of the judiciary in general and the Supreme Court in particular. Political trials, in which a cooperative judiciary sanitizes the prosecuting party's efforts to eliminate its political enemies, violate fundamental notions of justice and law.[10] As Jackson himself noted: "The world yields no respect to courts that are merely organized to convict."[11]

A. Why a Trial?

The standard by which to judge the fairness of a trial is found in the fundamental legal principle, *nullem crimen sine lege, nulla poena sine lege praevia*—no crime and no punishment without pre-existing law.[12] Critics of the Nuremberg Trial argued that the nascent state of international law rendered claims against the enemy non-justiciable. This, however, did not preclude resort to forms of retribution not connected to judicial procedures, such as direct political action or summary justice. Indeed, the argument ran, the virtue of this alternative is "its naked and unassumed character;" "[i]t confesses itself to be not legal justice but political." In this instance, political action

---

[9]See McKay, note 8 *supra*, at 27–36 *passim*.

[10]Shklar, Legalism 149 (1986).

[11]Jackson, The Rule of Law among Nations, 19 Temp. L. Q. 141 (1945).

[12]Woetzel, note 4 *supra*, at 111; Shklar, note 10 *supra*, at 152.

would render a deserved punishment without compromising legal values and judicial prestige.[13]

Jackson conceded that political action would not imperil the integrity of the judiciary, but he was concerned about the consequences of violating another juridical principle, that there must be no punishment without demonstrated proof of a criminal act. "[U]ndiscriminating executions or punishment without definite findings of guilt, fairly arrived at," he argued, "would not set easily on the American conscience or be remembered by our children with pride."[14] As one British member of the Nuremberg Tribunal said: "[T]he view that men could be shot without trial, whatever their alleged crimes might have been, would . . . savour far too much of the Nazi doctrine itself to have any wide commendation to reasonable people."[15] Furthermore, if the Allies were to have any hope of promoting the resurgence of a legalistic ethos in post-war Germany, the Nazis could not be made into martyrs. Punishment without public proof of individual wrongdoing and an opportunity for the accused to defend themselves risked creating a myth of martyrdom.[16]

Of course, a trial that was high politics masquerading as law also would have had this effect.[17] But if, contrary to the critics, the Nuremberg Trial did not offend legal principles, the superiority of this method for dealing with the Nazis could not be questioned. Jackson identified numerous accomplishments stemming from the Trial that would not have attended political executions. Foremost among these attainments, the Trial "made explicit and unambiguous what was theretofore . . . implicit in International Law," namely, that

[13]Wyzanski, note 4 *supra*, at 70. See also April, An Inquiry into the Juridical Basis for the Nuernberg War Crimes Trial, 30 Minn. L. Rev. 327–29 (1946). The British initially favored executions without trial (Taylor, note 3 *supra*, at 493; Jackson, Oral History at 1027, 1033).

[14]Jackson, Justice Jackson's Report to President Truman on the Legal Basis for Trial of War Criminals, 19 Temp. L. Q. 148 (1945); see also Jackson, Oral History at 1027, 1033.

[15]Birkett, International Legal Theories Evolved at Nuremberg, 23 Int'l Affairs 319 (1947). See also Stimson, note 3 *supra*, at 179; Wright, The Nuremberg Trial, 246 Annals of the American Academy of Political and Social Sciences 74 (1946); Biddle, The Nurnberg Trial, 33 Va. L. Rev. 681 (1947); Glueck, The Nuernberg Trial and Aggressive War, 59 Harv. L. Rev. 400 (1946). The fact that several of the defendants were found innocent of all charges (see note 35 *infra* and accompanying text) revealed as unfounded the belief that any trial would appear farcical because of the obvious culpability of the Nazis. Birkett, note 15 *supra*, at 319; Taylor, note 3 *supra*, at 511; Jackson, Oral History at 1069.

[16]Jackson, Introduction to Tyranny on Trial, note 1 *supra*, at xxxiv; Shklar, note 10 *supra*, at 159–60. Jackson realized that care had to be taken to prevent the Nazis from using the Trial as a means for spreading propaganda. Jackson, Oral History at 1049–51, 1270, 1277, 1288.

[17]Finch, The Nuremberg Trial and International Law, 51 Am. J. Int. L. 24–25 (1947); April, note 13 *supra*, at 330; Wyzanski, note 4 *supra*, at 69.

acts of international aggression and the systematic extermination or enslavement of political, racial, or religious groups are international crimes for which individuals may be held responsible. Second, the Trial demonstrated that it is possible to reconcile diverse legal systems in order to try the perpetrators of international crimes. Third, it replaced uncontrolled vengeance with a measured process of determining guilt. And finally, Nuremberg documented Nazi aggressions, persecutions, and atrocities, and illuminated the methods by which the Nazis obtained and held power; it provided "the world's first post-mortem examination of a totalitarian regime." The exposure of the violence and meanness of the accused not only thwarted their becoming patriotic martyrs, according to Jackson, but also provided a valuable lesson to nations concerned with maintaining the conditions necessary for freedom.[18]

B. FORMAL JUSTICE

It is ironic that Jackson's assessment of Nuremberg appears vulnerable when the Trial is measured against the principle that he believed made judicial procedures preferable to political executions. While the production of proof of a criminal act is critical, it is also important that the evidence be presented to an *impartial* judge.[19] The Nuremberg Tribunal was composed only of representatives of Allied countries, and the Soviet participants, because of their nation's involvement in aggressions against Poland, were particularly interested in having the Nazis assume the blame for crimes against peace. To rectify this situation, some called for the participation of neutrals and representatives of the vanquished states.[20]

The explanations for the failure to follow this suggestion are singularly unconvincing. Jackson contended that "[t]he scope of the war . . . left few neutrals and formal neutrality did not mean disinterestedness on the part of all its citizens."[21] A more representative

---

[18]Jackson, Final Report, note 1 *supra*, at 342–44. See also Jackson, Oral History at 1469–71.

[19]Goodhart, Reprint of the Legality of the Nuremberg Trials, at 1, RHJP, Box 105.

[20]Kelsen, Will the Judgment in the Nuremberg Trial Constitute a Precedent in International Law?, 1 Int. L. Q. 170–71 (1947); Kelsen, Collective and Individual Responsibility in International Law with Particular Regard to the Punishment of War Criminals, 31 Cal. L. Rev. 562 (1943); Wyzanski, note 4 *supra*, at 68; Lauterpacht, The Law of Nations and the Punishment of War Crimes, 21 Brit. Y. B. Int. L. 82–83 (1944). The makeup of the Tribunal disturbed at least some German nationals (see memo headed German Public Reaction to the Nuremberg Trial, at 4, and memo headed Reactions to the Nuremberg Verdicts, at 1, 5–6, RHJP, Box 107).

[21]Jackson, Nuremberg in Retrospect: Legal Answer to International Lawlessness, 35 ABA J. 881 (1949).

Tribunal, however, would have appeared and been more impartial than one made up of the victims of Nazi aggression and the most powerful of the victorious nations. The claim that the inclusion of neutrals would have been impracticable because of the complexities of translation appears unfounded, in view of the fact that the Tokyo Tribunal was composed of representatives of eleven nations.[22] It was also argued that Nuremberg was no different from a prosecution in a conventional criminal trial where the injured party—the state—provides the court as well as the prosecution.[23] This analogy is unpersuasive, because a state has a lesser stake in punishing individuals accused of violating criminal statutes than the Allies did in persecuting their enemies from a devastating world war. One is also unconvinced by the argument that the Leipzig Trials of 1921 revealed the ill-advisedness of German participation at Nuremberg.[24] The presence of Allies and neutrals on the Tribunal would have prevented the exoneration of culpable defendants if sympathetic German judges voted to acquit.[25]

The Soviet influence at Nuremberg was neutralized in a similar manner, as a conviction required the affirmative votes of at least three of the four Tribunal members (two in addition to the Soviet vote). Jackson was at pains to emphasize that "[n]o defendant . . . was found guilty or punished because of Soviet participation."[26] Russian involvement, however, still threatened to undermine Jackson's assertion in his opening remarks that the laws applied at Nuremberg were "of general application to any nation and were not merely rules gotten up for the occasion."[27] Jackson believed the stability of post-war Europe necessitated Russian participation and that America could only hope its insistence, against Russian opposition, on a general statement of principles (as opposed to charges mentioning only Nazi crimes) would be viewed as a condemnation of Soviet aggression.[28] Others offered the apology that "it is never open to a murderer to object to his trial on

---

[22]Birkett, note 15 *supra*, at 320; Woetzel, note 4 *supra*, at 227–30.

[23]Wright, note 15 *supra*, at 79.

[24]Birkett, note 15 *supra*, at 321.

[25]Lauterpacht, note 20 *supra*, at 84–86; Woetzel, note 4 *supra*, at xi–xii, 27–36.

[26]Jackson, note 21 *supra*, at 882. See also Jackson, Oral History at 1473.

[27]*Id.* at 1139. See Jackson, The Nurnberg Case, note 2 *supra*, at 81.

[28]Jackson, Some Problems in Developing an International Legal System, 22 Temp. L. Q. 151–55 (1948); Jackson, note 21 *supra*, at 882; Taylor, note 3 *supra*, at 518–19.

the grounds that there are other untraced murderers at large."[29] This observation, however, does not apply when it is known that one of the judges trying the case was closely connected to the murder. In this situation, the impartiality of all judges and the fairness of the proceedings are suspect. For this reason, Jackson prophesied that "judgment by Russians . . . will always injure the repute of the trial [especially] with the German people."[30]

Jackson's fears did not come to pass. In spite of its organizational flaws, the Nuremberg Trial was regarded, even by its critics and German citizens, as "a model of forensic fairness."[31] This perception was owing in part to the extraordinary efforts that were made to ensure due process and to present unimpeachable evidence and render verdicts based upon this proof. The prosecution's case was based upon documents culled from Nazi files instead of rhetorical testimony that would have had greater public interest and made for a more dramatic case. It was thought that "witnesses, many of them persecuted and hostile to the Nazis, would always be chargeable with bias, faulty recollection, and even perjury."[32] Prosecution documents were given to defense counsel in advance of presentation in court. These lawyers were chosen by the defendants and were paid, fed, and housed by the military government. A transcript of court proceedings was furnished daily (in German) to each counsel, access was provided to documents not used by the prosecution, and the defendants were granted the deposition or presence of any witness that had information relevant to their defense. Finally, the Germans were afforded both the common law right to testify in their own behalf and the continental right to make an unsworn statement not subject to cross-examination at the conclusion of all proceedings.[33] In view of

---

[29]Woetzel, note 4 *supra*, at 46. See also Wright, The Law of the Nuremberg Trial, 51 Am. J. Int. L. 46–47 (1947).

[30]Jackson, note 21 *supra*, at 882.

[31]Wyzanski, Nuremberg in Retrospect, Atlantic Monthly 59 (December 1946). See also Schwarzenberger, The Judgment of Nuremberg, 21 Tul. L. Rev. 336, 337, 358 (1947); Finch, note 17 *supra*, at 23; Glueck, note 15 *supra*, at 453; Carter, The Nurnberg Trials: A Turning Point in the Enforcement of International Law, 28 Neb. L. Rev. 385 (1949); Wright, note 15 *supra*, at 75–76; Wright, note 29 *supra*, at 48, 52; Birkett, note 15 *supra*, at 321; Biddle, note 15 *supra*, at 680–83. 74% of German nationals believed that the Trial "was carried out in a just manner" (see memo headed Reactions to the Nuremberg Verdicts, at 4, RHJP, Box 107).

[32]Jackson, Introduction to Tyranny on Trial, note 1 *supra*, at xxxv. See also Jackson, note 14 *supra*, at 149–50; Jackson, Oral History at 1239–40, 1254, 1476.

[33]Jackson, note 28 *supra*, at 150–51; Jackson, note 21 *supra*, at 881; Jackson, Oral History at 1136–37; Birkett, note 15 *supra*, at 680; Stimson, note 3 *supra*, at 186–87; Wright, note 29 *supra*,

the fact that the defendants offered evidence for nearly five months, compared to the prosecution's three months, and the closing speeches of each side took twenty days and three days, respectively, Jackson was justified in saying that the "future will never have to ask, with misgiving: 'What could the Nazis have said in their favor?' History will know that whatever could be said, they were allowed to say."[34]

The most convincing demonstration of impartiality came with the acquittal of three individual defendants—Schacht, Von Papen, and Fritsche. This result belied the early suspicion that "[t]he basic approach [at Nuremberg] is that these men should not have a chance to go free." Alternatively, it realized Jackson's hope that the Trial would be faithful to "[t]he ultimate principle . . . that you must put no man on Trial under the forms of judicial proceedings if you are not willing to see him freed if not proven guilty."[35]

C. SUBSTANTIVE JUSTICE

Yet, the presence of formal or procedural justice did not ensure the success of the Trial. It was also necessary that it not offend the fundamental principle of legality, that crimes must not be invented after the fact. Critics contended that the law applied at Nuremberg was patently retroactive, since it violated existing tenets of international law. Since the nineteenth century, it has generally been accepted that the courts of a state are not competent to judge the acts of individuals of another state because of inevitable bias. The consequence of this tenet is that international law acknowledges only collective responsibility. This is illustrated by the fact that the usual sanctions of international law—reprisals and war—are directed, not against the individual whose conduct was illegal, but against the home state of

---

at 52; Schwarzenberger, note 31 *supra*, at 337 n.27; Biddle, note 15 *supra*, at 680; Shklar, note 10 *supra*, at 168; Woetzel, note 4 *supra*, at 250.

[34]Jackson, The Nurnberg Case, note 2 *supra*, at 122. See also Jackson, note 21 *supra*, at 881. Jackson believed the Nazis were allowed to say too much, as the Tribunal ruled that the defendants could take as much time as needed to answer the prosecution's questions. Jackson's belief that this ruling risked turning the proceedings into a propaganda event for the Nazis caused him to lose his temper. His outburst in court hurt his reputation at the Trial. See Jackson, Oral History at 1281–82, 1285; Hutchinson, The Black-Jackson Feud, 1988 Supreme Court Review 212–213.

[35]Wyzanski, note 4 *supra*, at 69; Jackson, note 11 *supra*, at 140–41. See also Jackson, Oral History at 1132; Woetzel, note 4 *supra*, at 14–15; Wyzanski, note 31 *supra*, at 59. This is not to say that Jackson was not disappointed that these individuals were acquitted (Jackson, Oral History at 1447–53).

the offender.[36] Admittedly, there are exceptions to this rule. For instance, it is generally acknowledged that nations possess the right to punish foreign nationals engaged in the trade of illicit items (e.g., narcotics or pornography), the destruction of submarine cables, and piracy.[37] But individualized punishment has been viewed as particularly inappropriate for acts performed in an official capacity. The "act of state" doctrine specifically exempts an individual from prosecution by another nation for violations of international law committed in the exercise of official duties. The only way, consistent with international law, to punish an individual for an act performed as the instrument of his government is to receive the consent of the offender's home state—to conclude a treaty that grants jurisdiction over transgressors to a national or international court.[38]

Defenders of the Nuremberg Trial (Jackson, in particular) were troubled by "the paradox that legal responsibility should be the least where power is the greatest."[39] The immunity from individual responsibility granted to acts of state, it was argued, frustrates the maintenance of world peace, since experience has revealed the ineffectiveness of collective sanctions in reducing international criminalism.[40] For this reason, some scholars put forth the unorthodox view that the act of state doctrine does not extend to violations of international law.[41] As one proponent of this view explained, drawing upon the German situation:[42]

> Surely it is more reasonable to assume that by invading neighboring countries in flagrant violation of treaty obligations and for purposes of aggression, conquest and the mass-extermination of

[36]Kelsen, Collective and Individual Responsibility, note 20 *supra*, at 533–34, 540; Woetzel, note 4 *supra*, at 58–64.

[37]*Id.* at 61–64.

[38]Kelsen, Collective and Individual Responsibility, note 20 *supra*, at 537–40; Woetzel, note 4 *supra*, at 67–69; Wright, Legal Positivism and the Nuremberg Judgment, 42 Am. J. Int. L. 409–10 (1948). There are exceptions to the acts of state doctrine (*e.g.*, espionage and war treason), but none that would allow for the prosecution of the Nazis (Kelsen, Collective and Individual Responsibility, note 20 *supra*, at 552). The prosecution of the Nazi defendants could not have been justified on the basis of the rights of occupying powers, either (Woetzel, note 4 *supra*, at 76–84). The defense counsel at Nuremberg focused more on the violation of the act of state doctrine than the controversial aggressive war charges (Jackson, note 28 *supra*, at 152–53; see notes 45–66 *infra* and accompanying text).

[39]Jackson, note 14 *supra*, at 148.

[40]Jackson, Oral History at 1052; Glueck, note 15 *supra*, at 406, 419, 428–29, 451; Wright, note 29 *supra*, at 63–64 (quoting Jackson).

[41]Woetzel, note 4 *supra*, at 71–74; Wright, note 38 *supra*, at 410–11; Jackson, note 28 *supra*, at 152.

[42]Glueck, note 15 *supra*, at 424–25.

> the subjects of neighboring States, an offending sovereign destroys any implied consent that he be exempt from the jurisdiction of others, and strips himself and his agents of any mantle of immunity he may have claimed by virtue of international comity. . . . An examination of the act-of-state doctrine from such a point of view shows it to be so unreasonable and dangerous to law-abiding peoples as to cast grave doubt on the question whether it ever was sound law.

Similar reasoning is found in the Nuremberg judgment, with the added observation that "individuals have international duties which transcend the national obligations of obedience imposed by the individual state."[43]

Critics of the Trial regarded this argument as problematic, since it was unmindful of the value of the act of state doctrine and effectively rendered the concept meaningless.[44] Furthermore, considerations of retroactivity were again relevant, as it was questionable whether the Nuremberg defendants committed any illegal (as opposed to immoral) acts. The most controversial charge in the indictment, ironically, was the one Jackson regarded as Nuremberg's greatest legacy: crimes against peace or waging a war of aggression.[45] It was largely through Jackson's efforts that this charge was incorporated into the Nuremberg Charter, as he insisted on its inclusion over strong Allied opposition.[46] Jackson's case for the illegality of aggressive war stressed the significance of the Pact of Paris, better known as the Kellogg-Briand Pact of 1928. It was through this treaty, he argued, that[47]

---

[43]As quoted in Biddle, note 15 *supra*, at 688–89. See also Wright, note 38 *supra*, at 409; Wright, International Law and Guilt by Association, 43 Am. J. Int. L. 753–54 (1949).

[44]Kelsen, Collective and Individual Responsibility, note 20 *supra*, at 551–52. See the all too brief treatment of this argument in Woetzel, note 4 *supra*, at 72.

[45]As defined in the Nuremberg Charter, crimes against peace involve "planning, preparation, initiation or waging of a war of aggression, or a war in violation of international treaties, agreements or assurances, or participation in a common plan or conspiracy for the accomplishment of any of the foregoing" (as quoted in Woetzel, note 4 *supra*, at 246).

[46]Jackson, note 28 *supra*, at 153–55; Jackson, Oral History at 1049, 1245; Shklar, note 10 *supra*, at 239 n.78 and accompanying text; Glueck, note 15 *supra*, at 397; Woetzel, note 4 *supra*, at 155–57.

[47]Jackson, note 14 *supra*, at 153. See also Jackson, note 21 *supra*, at 886. The Preamble to the Pact states: "All changes in their relations with one another should be sought by pacific means and be the result of a peaceful and orderly process, and that any signatory Power which shall hereafter seek to promote its national interests by resort to war should be denied the benefits furnished by this Treaty." Article I reads: "The High Contracting Parties solemnly declare, in the names of their respective peoples, that they condemn recourse to war for the solution of international controversies and renounce it as an instrument of national policy in their relations with one another." Article II provides: "The High Contracting Parties agree that the settlement or solution of all disputes or conflicts, of whatever origin they may be, which may arise among them, shall never be sought except by pacific means" (as quoted in Woetzel, note 4 *supra*, at 143–44).

> Germany, Italy, and Japan, in common with ourselves and practically all the nations of the world, renounced war as an instrument of national policy, bound themselves to seek the settlement of disputes only by pacific means, and condemned recourse to war for the solution of international controversies.

Jackson emphasized that the sentiment in Kellogg-Briand was not novel; the treaty was preceded by several (albeit not universal) international agreements declaring the illegality of aggressive war. In short, this series of agreements evidenced the evolution of an international custom outlawing aggression.[48]

Jackson conceded that Kellogg-Briand failed to satisfy the conventional requirement for individual prosecutions, since it did not declare individual responsibility for the violation of its provisions.[49] But he contended, in an alternative argument for the limitation of the act of state doctrine, that punishment of the accused was permissible, since international law "grows, as did the Common-Law, through decisions reached from time to time in adapting settled principles to new situations." And "it is clear that by 1939 the world had come to regard aggressive war as so morally wrong and illegal that it should be treated as criminal if the occasion arose."[50] Instead of destroying the act of state doctrine, this approach would only prevent its extension to egregious violations of international law. Jackson added that construing a treaty to include individualized punishment was not unprecedented. Individual liability for violations of the laws and customs of war is now recognized under international law, even though the Hague Conventions , which forbid such conduct, do not identify this behavior as criminal, establish courts to try offenses, or fix any penalties.[51]

Jackson's argument for the illegality of aggressive war was severely criticized. Some pointed out that aggressive war is apparently undefinable: no practical definition was provided in the Kellogg-Briand Pact, the Nuremberg Charter, or the judgment of the Tribunal. When an illegal act is not defined, it was argued, only retroactive punishment can be meted out.[52] This criticism, however, was not

[48]Jackson, note 14 *supra*, at 154; Jackson, note 21 *supra*, at 886. See also Glueck, note 15 *supra*, at 408–12; Woetzel, note 4 *supra*, at 141–45.

[49]Jackson, The Challenge of International Lawlessness, 27 ABA J. 691 (1941).

[50]Jackson, note 14 *supra*, at 153; Jackson, note 21 *supra*, at 885.

[51]*Id.* at 886. See also Biddle, note 15 *supra*, at 686–87; Woetzel, note 4 *supra*, at 26–27, 116, 157–58, 166. This argument was borrowed from the Nuremberg Tribunal (Kelsen, Will Nuremberg Constitute a Precedent?, note 20 *supra*, at 159–60; Wright, note 29 *supra*, at 62–64).

[52]Finch, note 17 *supra*, at 36; Woetzel, note 4 *supra*, at 152–53, 159, 164. For listings of the

particularly damaging to the Trial. As Jackson noted, Hitler's actions against other nations were arguably "aggressive by any test."[53] Several factors—the rigid hierarchy of the Third Reich, the Nazi ideology of conquest, Hitler's stated willingness to violate international law, and the reluctance of other European states to enter the war—supported the contention that Nazi assaults clearly constituted aggression, even in the absence of a definition of the concept.[54] Of course, the inability to define aggressive war doomed Jackson's hope that the Trial would contribute to "the great effort to make peace more secure," since the cause of subsequent wars was unlikely to be as apparent, and the nebulous concept of aggression could not influence the future conduct of statesmen.[55] But this omission was not primarily responsible for compromising the legality of the aggressive war charge.

Rather, the practice of states between the signing of Kellogg-Briand and the end of the Second World War did the most damage to Jackson's argument. Critics of Jackson's position (most notably, Germans) drew attention to such acts of international warfare as the Soviet and Japanese invasions of Manchuria; Italian aggression against Abyssinia, followed by British and French recognition of the King of Italy as Emperor of Italian East Africa; and the intervention of Italy, Germany, France, and the Soviet Union in the Spanish War. Furthermore, the initial responses of the Trial's prosecuting nations to Nazi aggressions did not suggest recognition of an international crime. Indispensable raw materials were still traded to the aggressors, German aggression upon Czechoslovakia was followed by the Munich agreement, and the United States responded to the war upon Poland with a formal proclamation of neutrality. The argument that customary international law outlawed aggression was thus unfounded, since custom implies usage or near continuous conformity of behavior. Flagrant violations of anti-war agreements and acquiescence in acts of aggression revealed that Kellogg-Briand had no legal force.[56]

---

numerous articles supporting and criticizing the charge of crimes against peace, see Wright, note 29 *supra*, at 42–43 n.14; Woetzel, note 4 *supra*, at 167–68 nn.46–48.

[53]Jackson, Oral History at 1139–40.

[54]Jackson, note 28 *supra*, at 155–57; Jackson, note 21 *supra*, at 882–83; Shklar, note 10 *supra*, at 172, 178, 199; Woetzel, note 4 *supra*, at 165; Kelsen, Collective and Individual Responsibility, note 20 *supra*, at 546–47; Wyzanski, note 31 *supra*, at 57–58.

[55]As quoted in Schwarzenberger, note 31 *supra*, at 360. Shklar, note 10 *supra*, at 171–73, 177, 180.

[56]Schwarzenberger, note 31 *supra*, at 347–48; Finch, note 17 *supra*, at 26–33; Harlan F.

This behavior should be contrasted with the international response to the Hague Conventions. Many nations went so far as to incorporate these limitations upon the conduct of war into their own criminal law. The willingness of nations to punish their own citizens as well as foreign nationals for violating the rules of warfare, and the consistent enforcement of these provisions, denoted the existence of an international custom.[57] Jackson's attempt to equate the Kellogg-Briand Pact with the Hague Conventions was thus ill-fated.

The controversy surrounding the charge of aggressive war was exacerbated by a separate, but related, count—conspiracy to wage aggressive war. Like the aggressive war count, the inclusion of this charge in the Charter was the result of Jackson's insistence against Allied opposition. Jackson found the doctrine of conspiracy attractive, since it made possible the prosecution of individuals who may not have actually participated in specific acts of international aggression but whose cooperation was vital to Nazi wars of conquest. He also expected the doctrine to prove very useful in the long-term effort to dismantle the numerous organizations that had as their purpose the abetment of Nazi crimes, and the continued existence of which, he believed, threatened a resurgence of fascism. The Tribunal was thus empowered to declare organizations criminal for proceedings subsequent to the main Trial. Members of these organizations would essentially be guilty of conspiring to violate international laws.[58]

Use of the doctrine of conspiracy was criticized for two reasons. First, it had no basis in international law. International courts had never before declared organizations criminal, and most continental European countries abandoned the doctrine of conspiracy in the nineteenth century. Second, the potential for abuse was great, since a prosecutor was not required to prove individual criminal intent of action beyond the act of association.[59] Even Jackson noted that con-

---

Stone to Louis Lusky, Nov. 13, 1945, HFSP, Box 19; memo headed The Prosecution of War Criminals in the German-American Press, at 3, RHJP, Box 107; Wright, note 29 *supra*, at 62 n.101; Shklar, note 10 *supra*, at 166; Woetzel, note 4 *supra*, at 150–51, 165. The American decision to aid Britain through the "destroyer-for-bases" exchange and the Lend-Lease Act was made eighteen months after the German "crime" was committed. Finch, note 17 *supra*, at 31; see note 88 *infra* and accompanying text.

[57]Kelsen, Will Nuremberg Constitute a Precedent? note 20 *supra*, at 159–61; Wright, note 29 *supra*, at 59–60.

[58]Shklar, note 10 *supra*, at 174, 239 n.78 and accompanying text; Jackson, The Law Under Which Nazi Organizations are Accused of Being Criminal, 19 Temple L. Q. 373, 385 (1946); Jackson, Oral History at 1033; Woetzel, note 4 *supra*, at 190–91.

[59]*Id.* at 214–16; Carter, note 31 *supra*, at 373–74; Shklar, note 10 *supra*, at 171–72; Kelsen, Will Nuremberg Constitute a Precedent? note 20 *supra*, at 165–66; April, note 13 *supra*, at 320–21; memo headed German Public Reaction to the Nuremberg Trial, at 3, RHJP, Box 107.

spiracy "is the great dragnet of the law, rightly watched by courts lest it be abused."[60]

The Tribunal was very wary of these most controversial aspects of the indictment and acted to limit their impact. Taking advantage of ambiguous language in the Charter, the Court had restricted the charge of conspiracy to the crime of waging aggressive war, though the prosecution intended its application to all crimes named.[61] The Tribunal also rejected the prosecution's theory that "any significant participation in the affairs of the Nazi Party or government is evidence of a participation in a conspiracy that is itself criminal."[62] Instead, conspiratorial behavior had to "be clearly outlined in its criminal purposes" and "not be too far removed from the time of [actual] decision and action." Furthermore, the Tribunal insisted that an individual be part of a "concrete plan to wage war" and hold a sufficiently high position to exert influence upon this plan.[63] It was held that a group could only be declared criminal if it was so large that its members could not be tried separately, if its structure and purpose were sufficiently defined that it could be considered an "organization" as the word is commonly understood, and if it was apparent that it had been used for criminal purposes.[64]

The result of these rulings was the acquittal of fourteen of twenty-two defendants on the conspiracy charge and the exoneration of three of seven organizations accused of being criminal. Among the major war criminals, only Hess (sentenced to life imprisonment) was found guilty solely on the aggressive war counts. All but one of those sentenced to death had also been convicted of both remaining charges—war crimes and crimes against humanity.[65] In Henry Stimson's words, "the charge of aggressive war has not been established in international law at the expense of any innocent lives."[66]

The integrity of the Trial, however, could not be ensured by efforts to mute its most controversial aspects and by the mere fact that most defendants were found guilty of other crimes as well. It was

---

[60]Jackson, note 58 *supra*, at 378.

[61]Woetzel, note 4 *supra*, at 173–74; Wright, note 29 *supra*, at 67–68.

[62]As quoted in *id.* at 68.

[63]As quoted in Woetzel, note 4 *supra*, at 160–62. See also Biddle, note 15 *supra*, at 690–91.

[64]Woetzel, note 4 *supra*, at 196–99; Biddle, note 15 *supra*, at 692; Wright, note 29 *supra*, at 69.

[65]Woetzel, note 4 *supra*, at 163, 198–200; Birkett, note 15 *supra*, at 322, 325; Taylor, note 3 *supra*, at 518; Jackson, Oral History at 1142, 1447.

[66]Stimson, note 3 *supra*, at 187–88.

essential that these remaining charges not offend legal values and that they be of such moment as to vindicate the Nuremberg effort or compensate for its shortcomings. As noted, prosecutions and individualized punishment for violations of the laws of war were generally accepted as part of customary international law. Even vociferous critics of the Trial accepted the legality of the war crimes charge.[67] German war crimes were undeniable and numerous. They included the murder of commandos, captured Allied airmen, and prisoners who had escaped and been recaptured; the plunder of occupied territories; the ill-treatment of civilian populations; the exploitation of inhabitants of occupied countries for slave labor; the taking and shooting of hostages; and the destruction of towns without justification of military necessity. The Tribunal strengthened the moral and legal basis for conviction on this count by refusing to consider in the sentences of any defendant two charges pressed by the prosecution, namely, aerial and submarine warfare. Allied actions in these areas did not differ substantially from German practices, and only the vanquished were being tried for these offenses.[68]

But the count that served to vindicate the Nuremberg effort was the one that had not even a pseudo-legal basis: crimes against humanity.[69] This count was included in the indictment in order to punish the Nazis for persecuting German citizens on political, racial, or religious grounds—cruelties that preceded and continued during the war.[70] The legality of this charge was vulnerable: international law does not permit punishment by military occupants for crimes committed before the commencement of hostilities. Moreover, occupying nations are precluded from prosecuting acts perpetrated by

[67]See note 57 *supra* and accompanying text; Wyzanski, note 4 *supra*, at 66; Schwarzenberger, note 31 *supra*, at 343; Finch, note 17 *supra*, at 20–21; Stimson, note 3 *supra*, at 181; Lauterpacht, note 20 *supra*, at 61, 64–67. According to the Nuremberg Charter, war crimes are "violations of the law or customs of war. Such violations shall include, but not be limited to, murder, ill-treatment or deportation to slave labour or for any other purpose of civilian population of or in occupied territory, murder or ill-treatment of prisoners of war or persons on the seas, killing of hostages, plunder of public property, wanton destruction of cities, towns or villages, or devastation not justified by military necessity" (as quoted in Woetzel, note 4 *supra*, at 246–47).

[68]*Id.* at 174, 176, 188; Shklar, note 10 *supra*, at 161–62; Jackson, Oral History at 1450.

[69]Shklar, note 10 *supra*, at 158. As defined in the Nuremberg Charter, crimes against humanity include "murder, extermination, enslavement, deportation, and other inhumane acts committed against any civilian population, before or during the war, or persecutions on political, racial or religious grounds in execution of or in connection with any crime within the jurisdiction of the Tribunal, whether or not in violation of the domestic law of the country where perpetrated" (as quoted in Woetzel, note 4 *supra*, at 247).

[70]Finch, note 17 *supra*, at 23; Schwarzenberger, note 31 *supra*, at 353; Biddle, note 15 supra, at 694; Wright, note 29 supra, at 60.

nationals of the vanquished state against their own citizens. Determination of culpability for these acts is "generally considered the exclusive sovereign concern of the authorities of that state."[71] Neither the prosecution nor the Tribunal was able to invoke an international law or convention that carved out any exceptions to these principles.[72] The Tribunal, in order to make this count less controversial and in clear disregard of the Charter, limited itself to crimes committed after 1939 and would acknowledge the commission of crimes against humanity "only where proof also fully established the commission of war crimes."[73] Yet, these efforts could not completely disguise the fact that the defendants were being prosecuted on a novel charge.

The lack of a legal justification, however, did not compromise the legitimacy of this aspect of the Trial. There was no significant scholarly criticism of this charge. Punishment, it was believed, was warranted because of the enormity of Nazi offenses against German citizens, the record of which "reads like a fantastic fairy-tale unparalleled in its heinous proportions by even the wildest outrages of conquerors of the past." As Jackson argued, "[h]istory does not record a crime ever perpetrated against so many victims or one ever carried out with such calculated cruelty."[74] The Nazis' cold, systematic, and brutal extermination of non-Aryan Germans, especially Jews, and domestic opponents was so extraordinary that no moral or legal argument could excuse the defendants. Punishment in the absence of law, although it did not conform to legal values, did not offend these principles because the prohibition of retroactive legislation "is based on the ground that the actor might, at the time when he performed the act, have believed that he was entitled to perform it."[75] The only reason no international law made criminal the mass extermination of peoples was because such a practice was unthinkable before the Second World War.[76] Since the Nazis could not have fairly thought that genocide against a segment of their own population was undeserving of the most severe form of individualized punishment, a retroactive

[71]Finch, note 17 *supra*, at 23; Woetzel, note 4 *supra*, at 177–78.

[72]Shklar, note 10 *supra*, at 164; April, note 13 *supra*, at 324; Wyzanski, note 4 *supra*, at 67.

[73]Biddle, note 15 *supra*, at 694–95. See also Shklar, note 10 *supra*, at 165; Wright, note 29 *supra*, at 61–62; Finch, note 17 *supra*, at 23; Woetzel, note 4 *supra*, at 172–73; Schwarzenberger, note 31 *supra*, at 353–54; Stimson, note 3 *supra*, at 187.

[74]Woetzel, note 4 *supra*, at 175; Jackson, The Nurnberg Case, note 2 *supra*, at 54.

[75]Goodhart, note 19 *supra*, at 9.

[76]Shklar, note 10 *supra*, at 164.

law setting aside the act of state doctrine and making this practice criminal was acceptable; it was "not contrary to the moral idea which is at the basis of the principle in question."[77] Indeed, failure to execute the Nazis would have been a denial of justice—the perpetrators of the holocaust had to be punished.[78]

Due process had to precede the meting out of punishment, however, as the proceedings "fulfilled an immediate function which is both the most ancient and the most compelling purpose of all criminal justice," namely, substituting a reliable process of determining guilt for what was the most likely alternative—private, uncontrolled vengeance by those directly injured.[79] Those who would have testified to the wisdom of this argument included Hess, whose life was spared by his being found innocent of crimes against humanity and war crimes, and Fritsche, who was freed because he was cleared of these same charges as well as conspiracy to wage aggressive war.[80] Jackson, it will be recalled, made this argument in defense of the Nuremberg Trial.

The remainder of Jackson's assessment of the Trial was, for the most part, also borne out.[81] Numerous scholars and many German citizens rightly pointed out that Nuremberg did not justify the charge of waging aggressive war. But the Trial reaffirmed an international commitment to punish war crimes and made explicit the righteous sentiment that those guilty of genocide should be deprived of the traditional defenses afforded by international law. The Trial also demonstrated the practicability of reconciling diverse legal traditions to respond to these crimes in the future. And finally, Nuremberg prevented the creation of Nazi martyr figures by exposing fully the atrocities of the Third Reich; only a trial, with its emphasis upon disclosure and explanation, could document these crimes and reveal the sterility of the reasons and defenses advanced for such murderous behavior.[82]

---

[77]Kelsen, Collective and Individual Responsibility, note 20 *supra*, at 544. See also Woetzel, note 4 *supra*, at 112; Kelsen, Will Nuremberg Constitute a Precedent? note 20 *supra*, at 165. The enormity of Nazi offenses also deprived the defendants of the doctrine of "superior orders" (Woetzel, note 4 *supra*, at 68 n.31, 118–19; Lauterpacht, note 20 *supra*, at 69–74).

[78]Shklar, note 10 *supra*, at 160, 168.

[79]*Id.* at 158; Jackson, Oral History at 1038.

[80]Woetzel, note 4 *supra*, at 7, 14.

[81]See note 18 *supra* and accompanying text.

[82]Shklar, note 10 *supra*, at 160. Of the 65% of German nationals who said they had learned something from the proceedings that they had not known before, 29% indicated they had

The international response to the Trial was even more approving than one would anticipate from a critical analysis of the proceedings. All of the Nuremberg principles were accepted by the United Nations, and a sizable majority of German nationals assented to the results of the Trial.[83] It is thus fair to say that Jackson was involved in an internationally renowned event of considerable historical importance. Had it not led to other occurrences that proved damaging to judicial integrity, the Trial would have enhanced the prestige of the institution with which Jackson was most closely associated.

II. Nuremberg and the Supreme Court: The Impact of Jackson's Absence

It would be understandable if the accomplishments of the Nuremberg Trial were not as perceptible to the members of the Supreme Court as were the inconveniences caused by Jackson's extended absence. The Nuremberg assignment occupied Jackson from June of 1945 until October the following year. He missed all of the 1945–46 term. As a result, some twenty cases accumulated in which the vote stood at four to four, many requiring reargument upon Jackson's return. The Justices also were forced to shoulder added opinion writing duties.[84] These inconveniences obviously had the potential to produce severe conflict between Jackson and his brethren.

A. Why Jackson?

An attempt to explore this possibility and measure the Trial's costs against its achievements would not even be warranted if someone other than a Supreme Court Justice could have fulfilled Jackson's Nuremberg responsibilities; Jackson's involvement would have been indefensible. But the apparent ease with which he could have been replaced is deceiving. The participant nations were compelled to assign high-ranking, respected legal figures to the Trial because of the

"learned details about the concentration camps" (memo headed German Public Reaction to the Nuremberg Trial, at 3, RHJP, Box 107).

[83]Woetzel, note 4 *supra*, at 6, 15; Biddle, note 15 *supra*, at 684; 74% of German citizens believed the Trial "was carried out in a just manner," and 73% thought the verdicts in general were either "too mild" or "just right" (memo headed Reactions to the Nuremberg Verdicts, at 4, RHJP, Box 107).

[84]Gerhart, note 3 *supra*, at 257; Mason, Extra-judicial Work for Judges: The Views of Chief Justice Stone, 67 Harv. L. Rev. 212 (1953): Harlan F. Stone to Charles C. Burlingham, Nov. 30, 1945, HFSP, Box 7.

presence of a member of the United States Supreme Court—a position respected world wide, Jackson noted, by virtue of its life tenure. The expertise and reputation of these individuals were significant factors in the ultimate success of the proceedings.[85] Jackson's matchless drive and leadership, however, were even more important to the Trial.[86] There were several reasons for his zest. First, the Trial afforded him relief "from the sense of frustration at being in a back eddy with important things going on in the world. . . . "After the attack at Pearl Harbor," he said, "it was impossible for anyone who had recently been active to serve on the court without feeling a sense of frustration and dissatisfaction," and second, Jackson had "always loved advocacy and trial work, and this was about the most important trial that could be imagined. To represent the government in an international trial, the first of its kind in history, was a challenge that no man who loved advocacy would pass up willingly."[87]

Jackson's commitment was unrivaled, however, because Nuremberg afforded him an opportunity to vindicate a controversial wartime policy he championed as Attorney General under President Roosevelt. As the nation's chief legal officer, Jackson was charged with the responsibility of justifying to the international community the 1940 "destroyer-for-bases" exchange with Britain and the Lend-Lease Act of 1941. Concern was voiced that America had violated the international obligation of non-belligerent states to treat warring nations with impartiality. In a speech directed to South American countries, Jackson explained that the United States' policy of extending to Britain all aid "short of war" while avoiding entry into the conflict as a belligerent was justified, since recent changes in international law "swept away the nineteenth century basis for contending that all wars are alike and all warriors entitled to like treatment." The League of Nations Covenant, the Argentine Anti-War Treaty, and, especially, the Kellogg-Briand Pact "altered the dependent concept of neutral obligations" by implicitly conferring upon non-belligerents the right to discriminate against an aggressor. Since aggressive wars are now viewed as "civil wars against the international community," and "[i]ntelligent public opinion of the world . . . and the action of the American states has made a determination that the Axis powers are the aggressors" in the present conflict, the United States was warranted in

[85]Jackson, Oral History at 1043, 1048, 1125–28.

[86]Taylor, note 3 *supra*, at 522–23.

[87]Jackson, Oral History at 1009, 1015–16, 1040.

treating the "victims of aggression in the same way we treat legitimate governments when there is civil strife and a state of insurgency—that is to say, we are permitted to give to defending governments all the aid we choose," Jackson conceded that the lack of a reliable means for identifying aggression presented problems for his argument, but he answered that "[r]ough justice is done by communities long before they are able to set up formal governments"—a response that only could have struck his audience as inadequate.[88]

Nuremberg assumed great importance for Jackson in light of the insufficiency of this argument, since the assignment of individual responsibility for the war by an international tribunal would help to vindicate his earlier contentions and advance his efforts to impede war. As Jackson noted, the trial of the Nazis for illegal precipitation of war was "entirely in keeping with the philosophy of lend-lease which I had espoused, [and] with the destroyer exchange. . . ."[89] Deducing personal criminal liability from the aforementioned antiwar agreements, however, was even more controversial than employing the treaties to justify America's shift from formal neutrality.[90] Consequently, Jackson was compelled to work to ensure the overall integrity of the proceedings. Nuremberg's greatest contributions were rendered certain by Jackson's pursuit of his controversial aims.

Jackson made numerous strategic decisions that were critical to the success of the Trial. With respect to the quality of the evidence presented, he was responsible for the prosecution's policy, mentioned earlier, of relying on unimpeachable documents, as opposed to the more dramatic but vulnerable witnesses favored by his staff. Jackson also resisted counsel that the prosecution exploit the willingness of certain defendants to testify against others in return for leniency in sentencing. Acceptance of testimony from those attempting to save their lives, he believed, would discredit convictions.[91] Jackson's judgment on these matters proved sound, as "[f]ew, if any, of the critics . . . questioned that if the law is accepted, the evidence justified the convictions."[92]

---

[88]Jackson, International Order, 27 ABA J. 275–79 (1941). See also Jackson, Oral History at 785–814. The speech was actually delivered by the American Ambassador to Cuba, George Messersmith, as severe weather prevented Jackson from traveling to Havana (*id.* at 808–09).

[89]*Id.* at 1028.

[90]Finch, note 17 *supra*, at 33.

[91]See note 32 *supra* and accompanying text; Robert H. Jackson to Henry L. Stimson, June 5, 1946, RHJP, Box 110; Jackson, Introduction to Tyranny on Trial, note 1 *supra*, at xxxvi; Jackson, Oral History at 1476.

[92]Wright, note 29 *supra*, at 48. See also Schwarzenberger, note 31 *supra*, at 337 n.27.

With regard to the perceived fairness of the proceedings, Jackson opposed a United States Reparations Committee plan to turn over before trial as many as a half-million Nazis to the Soviet Union for "labor reparations." Despite being accused in this country of excessive lenience toward the enemy, he threatened to quit the Trial if the United States went ahead with this plan. He believed it would render the Nuremberg proceedings meaningless by punishing the defendants before a determination of guilt, and that it would compromise the moral position of the nation by tolerating labor camps.[93] Jackson also managed to persuade Francis Biddle, an American member of the Nuremberg Tribunal, to relinquish chairmanship of the Court to the British, lest the proceedings seem "a purely American enterprise," and he convinced Jewish leaders that a strong Jewish presence on the prosecution team might foster Nazi martyrs by making Nuremberg appear as a "vengeance trial."[94]

Nor was Jackson above acknowledging the weaknesses in the charges he regarded as most important to the Trial. He thought it best that the aggressive war counts, the "novel features" of the event, "not . . . bear the weight of the sentences alone." "[F]or this reason," he noted, "we were rather careful to get defendants who were [also] implicated in war crimes and crimes against humanity. . . ."[95] And when the Nuremberg Charter was drawn up, Jackson threatened to withdraw from the London Conference unless the aggressive war charges were stated generally and were not directed solely at the Nazis, as the Soviets desired.[96] As noted, Russian participation weakened the moral force of a general statement of principles.[97] But Jackson was right to assume that charges aimed only at the Nazis would have done more to align the proceedings with the conception of a political trial.

Finally, Jackson's opening statement contributed to the success of the proceedings. He was very much aware that his remarks would set a tone for the trial; he sought to convince his listeners that a dispassionate, careful inquiry into the facts would follow, and that justice would be done according to principles of international jurispru-

[93]Jackson, Introduction to Tyranny on Trial, note 1 *supra*, at xxxii-xxxiii; Jackson, Oral History at 1057–72.

[94]Jackson, Oral History at 1075–77, 1205–09.

[95]Robert H. Jackson to McGeorge Bundy, Nov. 8, 1946, RHJP, Box 110.

[96]Jackson, note 28 *supra*, at 155.

[97]See notes 27–30 *supra* and accompanying text.

dence. It is not an exaggeration to say that, perhaps with the exception of Cardozo's skilled pen, the brilliance and force of Jackson's prose was unmatched in the history of the Supreme Court. This talent, when combined with the belief that the task before him was "probably the most important . . . of my life," produced an address that was universally hailed as a brilliant introduction to an unprecedented international event.[98]

In fact, Jackson's felicity of expression and his demonstrated commitment to a fair trial of the Nazis led to his involvement at Nuremberg in the first place. President Truman grasped the importance of Jackson's participation in light of a speech on the proposed Trial that the Justice gave before the American Society of International Law. It was here that Jackson first voiced the principle that would later guide him: "any trials to which lawyers worthy of their calling lend themselves [should] be trials in fact, not merely trials in name, to ratify a predetermined result."[99]

B. A CATALYST FOR CONFLICT

Jackson's unrivaled interest, ability, and efforts may have been largely responsible for Nuremberg's success. But an evaluation of his involvement still requires an examination of his preparations for the event. Though Nuremberg was important, Jackson's primary obligation was the effective functioning of the Supreme Court. Therefore, the foremost consideration in his decision whether or not to accept the assignment should have been the impact of his absence on that institution. At the very least, Jackson needed to discuss with his brethren, especially Chief Justice Stone, whether his participation was prudent and how the institutional difficulties that would be caused by his involvement could be minimized.[100]

Jackson, however, sought no consultations with his associates. He "had some discussion [with President Truman] as to whether it was consistent with my duties as a member of the court."[101] But the Chief Justice "was not advised of Justice Jackson's participation until his

[98] Jackson, Oral History at 1243–51. See also Jackson, The Nurnberg Case, note 2 *supra*, at 30–94; memo headed German Public Reaction to the Nuremberg Trial, at 2, 4, and memo headed Memorandum for Mr. Justice Jackson, December 5, 1945, at 2–5, RHJP, Box 107.

[99] Jackson, note 11 *supra*, at 141; Taylor, note 3 *supra*, at 495.

[100] The possibility that Justices should not even consider participating in international trials is considered *infra* at pages xx–xx.

[101] Jackson, Oral History at 1036.

appointment by the Executive was announced in the newspapers."[102] Jackson's explanation for this blunder hardly redeems him: "I did not discuss the request with Chief Justice Stone . . . [because] I knew that he would disapprove of my doing it. I didn't have to ask him to know that."[103] Surely, Jackson could not have believed that the expectation that Stone would disapprove of his involvement obviated the need for consultations, even—especially—if he intended to ignore the Chief Justice's protestations. Since Stone's opposition-in-principle to extra-judicial activities was well known, Jackson's failure to explain his involvement and, more importantly, to express concern over problems that would stem from his absence was an invitation to conflict.[104]

Stone barely disguised his irritation and resentment in his correspondence with Jackson during the Trial. The Chief Justice's letters made reference to the increased opinion writing burden and, more frequently, to the equally divided cases caused by Jackson's absence. In a letter written approximately seven months after Jackson's departure, Stone responded as follows to his colleague's expressed disappointment over the delay caused by the long Christmas recess granted by the Tribunal:[105]

> We have not been troubled by too much recess over the holidays, and I found myself doing some work on both Christmas and New Year's day in order to keep up. At the moment all of my opinions are written, but I think there is no one else in the Court in that fortunate situation, although Douglas, as usual, is not very much behind and he has had one [*sic*] the whole rather heavier assignments than I have given to myself. We are continuing to develop four-to-four votes in cases which will, for that reason, have to be reargued. I am announcing three such today. As a result of this and the rearguments of cases which we heard last term, we are piling up quite a backlog which I think can be disposed of only by prolonging the term into late June or perhaps July. The extent will, of course, depend on when you are able to get back. I am not promising myself that you will be here much before June, if you are at that time.

This letter inspired a sense of guilt that was manifested in Jackson's offer to return temporarily to the Court in order to help clear the

---

[102]As quoted in Mason, note 84 *supra*, at 209–10.

[103]Jackson, Oral History at 1041–42.

[104]Mason, note 84 *supra*.

[105]Harlan F. Stone to Robert H. Jackson, Jan. 2, 1946, HFSP, Box 75, partially quoted in Mason, note 84 *supra*, at 212–13.

backlog.[106] Stone's refusal of this suggestion was not calculated to assuage Jackson's uneasiness:[107]

> I am very strongly of the personal opinion, both in the interests of the Court and of your own interest that it would be desirable for you not to attend a brief session of the Court and then return to Nurnberg for further proceedings there. It would, I think, be preferable not to return to the work of the Court until you are ready to take it up in the regular way without further interruptions, even at the cost of putting over cases which might otherwise be disposed of this term. I am only suggesting this for your consideration and decision, in light of what is best for the Court and for you as a Justice of the Court.

This response was attributable in part to Stone's contempt for the Nuremberg Trail and his embarrassment at the involvement of a member of the Supreme Court, sentiments he expressed more forthrightly in numerous letters to confidants. Since Stone believed Jackson was involved in a "Carthaginian vengeance" and was attempting to dress up a retroactive aggressive war charge "with a false facade of legality," he thought that judicial prestige would suffer if his colleague were to address Court matters before finishing at Nuremberg.[108] Stone's reply was also a not-so-subtle reminder to Jackson that proper attention to cases required his presence during the entire decision-making process, including the writing of opinions and announcement of decisions. Or, as Jackson said: "Between the lines, it was clear to me that he was saying, 'When you get here, you [had] better stay on the job.'"[109]

It might be argued that Jackson was not entirely to blame for the inconveniences caused by his absence, since he was assured before accepting the assignment "that the War Department had long been working on the matter and had assembled an extraordinary amount of detailed, accurate information, backed with exhibits, photographs, and other evidence, which would make a convincing case" against the Nazis. Thinking considerable legwork had been done,

---

[106] Robert H. Jackson to Harlan F. Stone, Jan. 11, 1946, HFSP, Box 75.

[107] Harlan F. Stone to Robert H. Jackson, March 1, 1946, HFSP, Box 75, partially quoted in Mason, note 84 *supra*, at 213.

[108] Harlan F. Stone to Sir Arthur and Lady Salter, June 23, 1945, HFSP, Box 25; Harlan F. Stone to Charles E. Wyzanski, Jr., Jan. 22, 1946, HFSP, Box 30. See also the following letters from the Chief Justice in HFSP: Louis Lusky, Nov. 13, 1945, Box 19; Charles Fairman, March 13, 1946, Box 12; Charles C. Burlingham, Nov. 30, 1945, Box 7; Luther Ely Smith, Jan. 2, 1946, Box 27.

[109] Jackson, Oral History at 1424.

Jackson was optimistic that the Trial would not interfere with his Court duties; his Nuremberg responsibilities were to begin at the end of the Court's 1944–45 term and could be completed, he hoped, before the beginning of the next term in October. This estimate, he later learned, was "foolishly optimistic," as preliminary work on the Trial was actually minimal.[110] Even after Jackson realized that he would have to assume responsibility for the endeavor, the magnitude of the task before him was not apparent. Five months into the assignment, he still thought he might finish in January, though the proceedings continued for ten months after that.[111]

These observations, however, do no more than mitigate Jackson's culpability for failing to consult his brethren. Consultations were necessary if there was any possibility that his off-the-bench activity would affect the Court. In fact, Jackson demonstrated an awareness of the need to obtain consensus on matters that were likely to be *less* disruptive to the Court than the War Crimes Trial. While at Nuremberg, he was contacted by counsel for the joint congressional committee investigating Pearl Harbor about the possibility of using his Court office as a base for research. Jackson replied that "it would seem presumptuous . . . for me to authorize this without consent of my associates."[112]

A slightly more convincing explanation for Jackson's negligence prior to Nuremberg is that he may have thought it unnecessary to trouble the Justices with the matter, since he believed he might resign from the Court before the beginning of the next term. His relationship with Justice Hugo Black had deteriorated to the point that Jackson thought Nuremberg might prove to be a good exit from an increasingly unpleasant situation. The animosity between the Justices had been building since Jackson joined the Court. Jackson was appalled by what he viewed as Black's partisan, non-judicial approach to cases.[113] His contempt for Black crystallized after an incident that occurred shortly before Jackson accepted the Nuremberg assignment. Jackson became convinced that Black was attempting to force the early release of a decision interpreting the Fair Labor Standards Act in order to influence a labor dispute that began during the Court's deliberations on the case. Although the effort to announce

---

[110]Jackson, Oral History at 1034–36, 1086–89, 1170–72.

[111]Robert H. Jackson to Harlan F. Stone, Oct. 11, 1945, HFSP, Box 75.

[112]*Ibid.*

[113]Jackson, Oral History at 1041, 1417.

the decision prematurely was unsuccessful, Jackson thought that Black's "sinister manipulation" of the timing of the decision was "indefensible and could not be condoned"; this incident "created [such] uneasiness" in Jackson's mind that he said he considered resigning from the bench.[114]

Even Jackson's belief that he might leave the Court before the beginning of its next term, however, could not explain and excuse his failure to consult his brethren about Nuremberg. In view of his awareness of the need to obtain consensus on matters that might affect the Court, Jackson must have realized that consultations were necessary if there was only a slight chance when he decided to accept the assignment that he would return to the bench. Apparently, there was such a chance, since Jackson said he was only "considering going back to private practice and getting off the Court," and, as noted, he accepted the assignment only after being assured that it would not interfere with his Court duties.[115] Even if Jackson had been certain he would resign, discussions still would have been warranted to consider and address any reservations his brethren may have had about his involvement and the mission's implications for the Court.

In view of the untenability of these explanations for Jackson's behavior, it must be considered whether he had cause not to consult his brethren. There is reason to believe that, when weighing the Nuremberg assignment, he had no real intention of resigning and possessed sufficient motive not to involve the Court in his decision. More specifically, Jackson may have agreed to participate in the Trial in part to improve his chances with Truman for appointment to the Chief Justiceship when Stone ultimately stepped down (this is not to say there was an explicit quid pro quo), and he may have assumed that his associates would assign this motive to his actions.[116] At one time, Jackson at least anticipated that he would be asked to succeed Stone. Roosevelt all but promised him the position, and Stone only could have heightened Jackson's expectation by mentioning that he would retire after a couple of years as Chief Justice, with the hope Jackson would succeed him. Upon his appointment to Chief Justice, Stone had also expressed surprise that Jackson had not been nomi-

---

[114]Memo headed The Black Controversy, at 35–37, and memo headed To President Truman Only From Justice Jackson, June 7, 1946, at 4, RHJP, Box 26. See also Hutchinson, note 34 *supra*, at 208–9, 229–38.

[115]Jackson, Oral History at 1412.

[116]Of course, as the previous subsection shows, Jackson was also motivated by a desire to promote the peaceful resolution of international disputes.

nated for the position. Roosevelt's death, however, rendered uncertain the choice of Stone's replacement. And Jackson was convinced that Black and perhaps William Douglas coveted the post for themselves. Jackson contended that they "couldn't help but regard me as one who stood in the way," since "[t]he story got around that I had been promised the chief justiceship."[117] The impression that several of his brethren, including Stone, regarded him as a contender for the Court's leading post, and the circumstance that his supposed benefactor was gone, most likely convinced Jackson that discussions with his associates about the War Crimes Trial would be counterproductive. He denied, however, that he had designs on the office and that his decision to go to Nuremberg was prompted by such a desire. "I suppose I could say that I had a sense of duty to respond to the President's request," Jackson remarked, "but I must say that was entirely secondary in my thinking. If it hadn't appealed to me, I wouldn't have hesitated at all to say I just didn't want to do it."[118]

Jackson's conduct after Stone's death in April of 1945, however, belied his contention that he had not hoped and planned to assume leadership of the Court. Stone's passing revived the stories that Roosevelt had promised to appoint Jackson Chief Justice, and Truman intimated that he would follow through on his predecessor's plan. A story then surfaced that two members of the Court would resign if Jackson were promoted, and another report suggested that the threatened resignations were the result of a "blood feud" between Black and Jackson. The detailed nature of the articles suggested to Jackson that certain of his colleagues were cooperating with the press.[119] Still at Nuremberg, he was concerned enough about the events unfolding back home to draft a memo explaining to Truman that his differences with Black were "not petty personal ones," as the reports suggested.[120] The memo was not sent, however, because Jackson believed he "could not volunteer information on this subject . . . without giving the impression of being a petitioner for the appointment."[121] Indeed, the memo would have convinced Truman of this. Jackson's recounting of Black's partisan treatment of cases,

[117]Jackson, Oral History at 969–72, 975–76, 1010, 1414–15.

[118]*Id.* at 1040–41, 1428.

[119]*Id.* at 1424–26.

[120]Memo headed "not used," RHJP, Box 26.

[121]Memo headed To President Truman Only From Justice Jackson, June 7, 1946, at 2, RHJP, Box 26.

and his apology that "I owe it to you to submit these facts before you make a new appointment lest you act without information which coming out afterwards would prove embarrassing," would have seemed less the product of one who cared only for the President's and the Court's integrity than one who sought to sabotage his rival's chances for the position.[122]

Jackson not only thought better of sending this memo, but, probably for similar reasons, had decided not to interrupt the Nuremberg proceedings to attend Stone's funeral. Jackson could have used the occasion to organize support for his appointment, but he most likely assumed his return would be so interpreted. By doing nothing, however, he was outmaneuvered by his opponents (primarily Justice Douglas and, former Chairman of the Democratic National Committee, Robert Hannegan, as Jackson later discovered), and he grew increasingly frustrated as friends informed him of these developments.[123]

Jackson's frustration boiled over when Fred Vinson was selected to lead the Court, and his outrage became public with a cable to the House and to the Senate Judiciary Committees, which followed a private dispatch to the President. Ostensibly, these communications were intended to respond to news reports about his conflict with Black, since the stories, in Jackson's view, trivialized the dispute and were partial to his colleague. Jackson contended that "the attacks upon me during my absence cannot in fairness to my future work on the court be left unanswered. . . ."[124] Yet, his bitterness over losing the nomination and his resentment towards the person he believed responsible for derailing the appointment set the tone of the cables. He wrote to Truman:[125]

> The impression has been created that appointment of me was considered but that opposition by Justice Black prevented it. As you know, I have never approached you directly or indirectly in reference to this office and have no knowledge of whether you ever had the slightest thought of naming me. Ordinarily it would have done me no harm to have been passed unnoticed. But the reports reaching me come to this: That Mr. Justice Black threat-

---

[122] Memo headed "not used," RHJP, Box 26. See also Hutchinson, note 34 *supra*, at 217–19.

[123] *Id.* at 214–17, 226–27.

[124] Memo headed Office U.S. Chief of Counsel for Morgan From Justice Jackson, June 10, 1946, at 10, RHJP, Box 26.

[125] Memo headed To President Truman Only From Justice Jackson, June 7, 1946, at 1, RHJP, Box 26. See also Hutchinson, note 34 *supra*, at 219–21.

> ened to resign should you promote me to Chief Justice and thereupon you agreed not to do so. These events were at once given wide publicity either by the White House or by Mr. Justice Black. I would be loathe to believe that you would concede to any man a veto over court appointments. Every Justice, every aspirant, every judge on the lower courts, and every litigant before the Court, is now given the impression that a judge may be denied promotion if he incurs the displeasure of Mr. Justice Black on grounds however trivial.

Jackson's cable to the congressional committees detailed Black's partisan behavior in past cases and concluded with the demand that his associate's conduct cease.[126] Jackson conceded that the timing of this communication, "however suitable to other reasons, lent itself perfectly to the answer that [my] statement was due only to personal disappointment."[127]

Jackson's outburst was costly to the Court. Columnists attacked both Justices (with Jackson bearing the brunt of the criticism), and calls were made for a congressional investigation (that never occurred).[128] Jackson acknowledged that the cable "badly missed its mark," since the public perceived the dispute as "petty and personal."[129] But he did not regret sending the memo, believing it was partly responsible for a modification of Black's behavior. "[S]ince that occasion," Jackson said, "Justice Black has never . . . given a cause for any resentment on my part. . . . Of course," he added, inadvertently acknowledging his desire for the Chief Justiceship, "another thing that contributed, perhaps, to the relative calm that settled upon the Court was the fact that the chief justiceship was apparently settled. There was no longer that rivalry which had been evident."[130]

This motive for accepting the Nuremberg assignment, then, ensured not only that the Trial would be a catalyst for conflict between the Justices, but that it would prompt an incident harmful to judicial integrity. Jackson's assumption that his participation would be regarded as politically motivated led him to forgo consultations with his brethren, which, in turn, caused resentment on their part for the

---

[126]Memo headed Office U.S. Chief of Counsel for Morgan From Justice Jackson, June 10, 1946, *passim*, RHJP, Box 26; Hutchinson, note 34 *supra*, at 221.

[127]Memo headed The Black Controversy, at 30, RHJP, Box 26.

[128]Hutchinson, note 34 *supra*, at 221.

[129]Untitled, undated memo, RHJP, Box 26.

[130]Jackson, Oral History at 1433–34.

inconveniences caused by his absence.[131] And Jackson's expressed resentment against those working to prevent his appointment was more damaging to the Court's prestige than the Nuremberg Trial possibly could have been. Had Jackson not participated in the Trial, it is likely that his enemies on the Court would have been less inclined to scheme against him. And Jackson also would have been less likely to lash out, as he could have monitored and had some impact upon events through intermediaries, thus preventing his frustration from overwhelming him. A weighing of these drawbacks against the accomplishments stemming from Jackson's participation at Nuremberg would be warranted, except that scholars point to further problems involving Jackson himself.

III. Nuremberg and Jackson: A Changed Constitutional Jurisprudence?

Concern over Nuremberg's impact on Jackson has not focused on what one would expect, namely, the extent to which his involvement biased him in cases linked to the continuing war crimes trials. This is because no cases related to Jackson's off-the-bench activity reached the Court after his return.[132] Moreover, a more disturbing possibility has been raised. It has been suggested that the Trial had a profound effect on how Jackson addressed issues of individual rights generally. More specifically, it is argued that the once-liberal or moderate Justice lost an appreciation for the protections afforded by the Bill of Rights because of his understanding of the events that led to the destruction of the Weimar Republic and the rise of fascism.[133] If Jackson was moved to support a supererogatory narrowing of the am-

[131]The Chief Justice was not the only member of the Court irritated by Jackson's absence (see *id.* at 1423).

[132]In Re Yamashita, 327 U.S. 1 (1946), was decided before Jackson returned. The continuing war crimes trials at Nuremberg led to several petitions to the Supreme Court; all were denied (Jackson, Oral History at 1423).

[133]See Abraham, Justices and Presidents: A Political History of Appointments to the Supreme Court 232–33 (New 2d ed. 1985). Abraham suggests that Jackson's opinions in West Virginia State Board of Education v. Barnette, 319 U.S. 624 (1943); Korematsu v. United States, 323 U.S. 214 (1944); and Thomas v. Collins, 323 U.S. 516 (1945), should be contrasted with his opinions in Terminiello v. Chicago 337 U.S. 1 (1949); Kunz v. New York, 340 U.S. 290 (1951); Dennis v. United States, 341 U.S. 494 (1951); and Adler v. Board of Education, 342 U.S. 485 (1952) (*id.* at 361–62 nn.72, 73, 74 and accompanying text). See also Freund, Individual and Commonwealth in the Thought of Mr. Justice Jackson, 8 Stan. L. Rev. 16–19 (1955); Gerhart, A Decade of Mr. Justice Jackson, 28 NYU L. Rev. 952–54 (1953); Jaffe, Mr. Justice Jackson, 68 Harv. L. Rev. 967–70 (1955).

bit of constitutional liberties, this would give further reason to question his acceptance of the Nuremberg assignment.

A. AN APPARENT SHIFT

An examination of Jackson's writings on Nuremberg and certain of his later free speech opinions suggests that he believed the event had important implications for liberty in this country. As noted, Jackson listed as an accomplishment of the Trial the lesson it provided to nations concerned with maintaining the conditions essential to freedom.[134] More specifically, Nuremberg illuminated the methods the Nazis used to obtain power. Jackson believed the Trial demonstrated that the Nazi party should not be thought of in terms of the unstructured organizations referred to in this country as political parties, since control of the German state was not acquired through conventional or republican means. Instead, the Nazis employed various forms of fraud, intimidation, and sabotage to seize power. For example, the SA (or *Die Sturmabteilungen*), a voluntary organization of young, fanatical Nazis, practiced violent interference with elections, the breaking up of opposition meetings, and the terrorization of adversaries. The members of the SA "boasted that their task was to make the Nazi Party 'master of the streets.'" The SD (or *Der Sicherheitsdienst*), a component of the SA, violated the secrecy of elections in order to identify those opposed to the Nazis. Finally, the burning of the Reichstag building in February of 1933, less than a month after Hitler was appointed Chancellor, helped solidify Nazi power. Hitler claimed that this act of arson was the beginning of a communist revolution, and he exploited the resulting hysteria to subdue his political enemies and lobby for dictatorial power to meet the crisis.[135]

The regrettable destruction of German freedom and the tragedy that followed in the wake of international aggression by the Nazis might have been averted, Jackson believed, had it not been for the "complacency and tolerance as well as the impotence of the Weimar Republic towards the growing organization of Nazi power." Nazi control over German society "was accomplished through an elaborate network of closely knit and exclusive organizations of selected volunteers, oath-bound to execute without delay and without question the commands of the Nazi leaders." "The party power resulting

---

[134]See note 18 *supra* and accompanying text.

[135]Jackson, The Nurnberg Case, note 2 *supra*, at 38–46.

from this system of organizations first rivaled, and then dominated the power of the state itself."[136] The German experience, Jackson argued, revealed the importance of controlling such aggregations of power in their incipient stages.[137]

These observations were starkly manifest in Jackson's dissent in *Terminiello v. Chicago*, where he excoriated the Court for reversing Arthur Terminiello's conviction for breach of the peace.[138] Terminiello, who had come to Chicago to address the Christian Veterans of America, preached an anti-communist, anti-Semitic message that attracted a large group of protestors and prompted several disturbances both inside and outside the building. But the Court held that an ordinance prohibiting speech that merely "stirs the public to anger, invites dispute, [or] brings about a condition of unrest"[139] seriously invades the province of speech protected by the First Amendment. In his scathing dissent, Jackson reproached the Court for deciding the case "by reiterating generalized approbations of freedom of speech with which, in the abstract, no one will disagree," and he accused the majority failing to realize that[140]

> [t]his was not an isolated, spontaneous and unintended collision of political, racial or ideological adversaries. It was a local manifestation of a world-wide and standing conflict between two organized groups of revolutionary fanatics, each of which has imported to this country the strong-arm techniques developed in the struggle by which their kind has devastated Europe. Increasingly, American cities have to cope with it. One faction organizes a mass meeting, the other organizes pickets to harass it; each organizes squads to counteract the other's pickets; parade is met with counterparade. Each of these mass demonstrations has the potentiality, and more than a few the purpose, of disorder and violence. This technique appeals not to reason but to fears and mob spirit; each is a show of force designed to bully adversaries and to overawe the indifferent. We need not resort to speculation as to the purposes for which these tactics are calculated nor as to their consequences. Recent European history demonstrates both.

In Jackson's view, "[t]he present obstacle to mastery of the streets by either radical or reactionary mob movements is not the opposing

---

[136] *Id.* at 95–96.

[137] Jackson, Final Report, note 1 *supra*, at 344.

[138] 337 U.S. 1, 13 (1949).

[139] *Id.* at 4–5.

[140] *Id.* at 23.

party." Rather, it is the authority of local governments—governments that "represent the free choice of democratic and law-abiding elements of all shades of opinion."[141] Jackson argued that free speech will be difficult to maintain in the long term if local officials are prevented from providing protection against abuses of that right. "There is danger," he warned, "that if the Court does not temper its doctrinaire logic with a little practical wisdom, it will convert the constitutional Bill of Rights into a suicide pact."[142]

Many were struck by the contrast this language presented to Jackson's celebrated majority opinion in *West Virginia State Board of Education v. Barnette*,[143] where the Court held that a compulsory flag salute ceremony violated the First Amendment rights of Jehovah's Witness school children. In his opinion, Jackson said:[144]

> The very purpose of a Bill of Rights was to withdraw certain subjects from the vicissitudes of political controversy, to place them beyond the reach of majorities and officials and to establish them as legal principles to be applied by the courts. One's right to life, liberty, and property, to free speech, a free press, freedom of worship and assembly, and other fundamental rights may not be submitted to vote; they depend on the outcome of no elections.

Jackson's efforts in *Terminiello* to convince the Court that an expansive interpretation of the right of speech constitutes an abuse of the First Amendment rather than its fulfillment appeared to be an implicit rejection of the preferred freedoms doctrine, which his *Barnette* opinion seemed to support.

B. THE CONSISTENCY OF JACKSON'S THOUGHT

There is no doubt that Jackson at one time accepted the idea that First Amendment rights have a preferred position in our constitutional system, and that he ultimately rejected this notion. Before his appointment to the bench, Jackson contended that "[t]he presumption of validity which attaches in general to legislative acts is frankly reversed in the case of interferences with free speech and free assembly. . . ."[145] And he explicitly repudiated this position in the post-

---

[141]*Id.* at 24.

[142]*Id.* at 36–37.

[143]319 U.S. 624 (1943).

[144]*Id.* at 638.

[145]Jackson, The Struggle for Judicial Supremacy 285 (1949).

Nuremberg, Fourth Amendment case, *Brinegar v. United States*,[146] where he said that "[w]e cannot give some constitutional rights a preferred position without relegating others to a deferred position."[147]

This shift in Jackson's jurisprudence, however, was caused by his exposure to the complexities of actual constitutional controversies rather than by his involvement at Nuremberg. In his *Brinegar* dissent, Jackson held that he had long disclaimed the preferred position theory, and he cited as evidence his pre-Nuremberg opinion in *Murdock v. Pennsylvania*.[148] In *Murdock*, the Court invalidated a license tax ordinance that was construed to apply to religious colporteurs (in this case Jehovah's Witnesses), holding that such a restriction on itinerant evangelism is a violation of the freedoms of press, speech, and religion, which "are in a preferred position."[149] In dissent, Jackson accused the Court of ignoring "the broad plan of campaign employed by Jehovah's Witnesses and its full impact on a living community."[150] This case, he believed, did not merely raise questions of religious freedom; it involved "the right to proselyte [which] comes into contact with what many people have an idea is their right to be let alone."[151] Employing a mere balancing formula, he concluded that local officials were justified in their attempts to restrain the aggressive door-to-door proselytizing of the Witnesses and their verbal attacks upon other faiths, which prompted many citizens to complain about the nuisance. While the Constitution protects all in their peaceful and orderly practice of the religion of their choice, "[c]ivil government can not let any group ride rough-shod over others simply because their 'consciences' tell them to do so."[152] As he said in another pre-Nuremberg case: "[T]he limits [on religious practices] begin to operate whenever [these] activities begin to affect or collide with the liberties of others or of the public."[153]

Jackson had even employed a traditional balancing test in *Barnette* (which stands to reason, since it was decided after *Murdock*). Though his opinion contained the earlier mentioned paean to First Amend-

[146] 338 U.S. 160 (1949).

[147] *Id.* at 180.

[148] 319 U.S. 105, 166 (1943), cited in 338 U.S. at 180.

[149] 319 U.S. at 115.

[150] *Id.* at 166.

[151] *Ibid.*

[152] *Id.* at 179.

[153] Prince v. Massachusetts, 321 U.S. 158, 177 (1943).

ment guarantees, this passage was preceded by a weighing of the conflicting claims, with no presumption of unconstitutionality. "The freedom asserted by these appellees," he said, "does not bring them into collision with rights asserted by any other individual."[154] The Jehovah's Witnesses' refusal "to participate in the ceremony does not interfere with or deny rights of others to do so."[155] Had there been such a conflict, or had the Witnesses not been "peaceable and orderly," Jackson indicated that the state would have been allowed "to determine when the rights of one end and those of another begin."[156]

Jackson later defended the consistency of his free speech decisions (with explicit references to *Barnette*, *Murdock*, and *Terminiello*) by maintaining he had always held that "our Constitution excludes both general and local governments from the realm of opinions, ideas, beliefs and doubts, heresy and orthodoxy, political, religious, or scientific."[157] But he also consistently "protested the degradation of these constitutional liberties to minimize and approve mob movements, whether those mobs be religious or political, radical or conservative, liberal or illiberal."[158] *Terminiello*, then, did not mark a shift in Jackson's First Amendment jurisprudence, since it fit comfortably within a free speech philosophy, developed early in his judicial tenure, that balanced liberty claims against societal interests in public order and tranquility.

Another possibility is that *Terminiello* signaled a modification in Jackson's approach to the doctrine of incorporation, what with his emphasis upon the need for deference to the decisions of local officials. He may have thought not only that the Illinois officials did not violate the First Amendment, but that they should not even be held to that standard. In fact, Jackson expressed doubt concerning the legitimacy of incorporation, as he requested that the Court "recall that our application of the First Amendment to Illinois rests entirely on authority which the Court has voted to itself."[159] The terms of the Fourteenth Amendment, he suggested, "gave no notice to the people that its adoption would strip their local governments of power to deal

---

[154]319 U.S. at 630.

[155]*Ibid.*

[156]*Ibid.*

[157]American Communications Assn. v. Douds, 339 U.S. 382, 443 (1950).

[158]*Id.* at 444.

[159]337 U.S. 1, 28 (1949).

with such problems of local peace and order as we have here."[160] And for years, the Court denied that the Fourteenth Amendment incorporates the First. Jackson, however, ultimately rested his opinion on his interpretation of the free speech guarantee, as he concluded, surprisingly, that he had "no quarrel"[161] with the Court's later application of the First Amendment against the states. Apparently, he felt compelled to remain consistent with his *Barnette* opinion (which he cited), where he held that "[t]he test of legislation which collides with the Fourteenth Amendment, because it also collides with the principles of the First, is much more definite than the test when only the Fourteenth is involved."[162]

Jackson's desire for consistency was absent, however, when the Court sustained an attempt by Illinois authorities to punish Joseph Beauharnais for violating a group libel law (the accused had distributed racist leaflets on Chicago streets).[163] Jackson dissented from the decision because he believed that the application of the statute violated due process (i.e., the state required no proof of injury to any person or group). But he agreed that group libel statutes are permissible; they "represent a commendable desire to reduce sinister abuses of our freedoms of expression—abuses which I have had occasion to learn can tear apart a society, brutalize its dominant elements, and persecute, even to extermination, its minorities."[164] In contrast to the majority, however, Jackson argued that the reason this sort of legislation does not violate the Constitution is that the First Amendment does not apply against the states. He explicitly rejected the argument that the Fourteenth Amendment incorporates the provisions of the First, because, in his view, the history of criminal libel demonstrates otherwise. More than forty state constitutions, which extend protection to speech and press, he noted, "reserve a responsibility for their abuse and implicitly or explicitly recognize validity of criminal libel laws."[165] It can be assumed "that the men who sponsored the Fourteenth Amendment in Congress, and those who ratified it in the State Legislatures, knew of such provisions then in many of their State Constitutions,"[166] and it would be unreasonable

[160] *Id.* at 28–29.

[161] *Id.* at 29.

[162] *Ibid.*, citing 319 U.S. at 639.

[163] Beauharnais v. Illinois, 343 U.S. 250 (1952).

[164] *Id.* at 304.

[165] *Id.* at 292.

[166] *Id.* at 293.

to believe that they were consciously canceling them, as the incorporation of the First Amendment would require. The "wise and historically correct view of the Fourteenth amendment,"[167] Jackson believed, was articulated by Justices Holmes and Brandeis in *Gitlow v. New York*.[168] There, the Justices stated that while "[t]he general principle of free speech" inheres in the Fourteenth Amendment, "a somewhat larger latitude of interpretation than is allowed to Congress" should be accorded to the states.[169]

Jackson acknowledged this change in his Fourteenth Amendment jurisprudence with an apology:[170]

> Whence we are to derive metes and bounds out of the state power is a subject to the confusion of which, I regret to say, I have contributed—comforted in the acknowledgement, however, by recalling that this Amendment is so enigmatic and abstruse that judges more experienced than I have had to reverse themselves as to its effect on state power.

He also conceded that his increased deference to local officials was attributable, in some measure, to his Nuremberg experience.[171]

Yet, this shift in his thought must not be overdrawn. Jackson's preference for the local resolution of problems can be traced to his pre-Nuremberg dissent in *Ashcraft v. Tennessee*,[172] an involuntary confession case, where he reproved the Court for setting aside a murder conviction. He argued that[173]

> [t]he burden of protecting society from most crimes against persons and property falls upon the State. Different States have different crime problems and some freedom to vary procedures according to their own ideas. Here, a State was forced by an unwitnessed and baffling murder to vindicate its law and protect its society. To nullify its conviction in this particular case upon a consideration of all the facts would be a delicate exercise of federal judicial power. . . . The use of the due process clause to disable the States in protection of society from crime is quite as dangerous and delicate a use of federal judicial power as to use it to disable them from social or economic experimentation.

The only actual jurisprudential change suggested by Jackson's *Terminiello* dissent, then, was the reinforcement of a conservative tendency

---

[167] *Id.* at 291.

[168] 268 U.S. 652 (1925).

[169] *Id.* at 672.

[170] 343 U.S. at 288.

[171] Jackson, Oral History at 573.

[172] 322 U.S. 143 (1944).

[173] *Id.* at 158, 174. See also Jackson, note 145 *supra*, at 19.

that preceded Nuremberg. And while liberal jurists might consider this sufficient reason to question Jackson's participation at Nuremberg, it could not be said that a retrenchment from the doctrine of incorporation (or, for that matter, from the preferred freedoms concept) would constitute a radical and indefensible innovation in constitutional law.[174]

C. AT ONCE A LIBERALIZING AND NOISOME INFLUENCE

The attention paid to Jackson's increased conservatism has led scholars to overlook the fact that his study of Nazi techniques for maintaining power had a liberalizing influence on his judicial philosophy. Jackson noted that the Nazis employed several means to perfect control over German society, including formation of the Gestapo, or secret police, whose role was to detect opposition. Secret arrest and indefinite detention were used against individuals objecting to the Nazi program and those belonging to opposition parties. Charges were not leveled against those whom the Nazis suspected or disliked, nor was evidence presented against them, as hearings with counsel were not allowed. In short, "[t]he German people were in the hands of the police, the police were in the hands of the Nazi Party and the Party was in the hands of a ring of evil men."[175] This highly centralized system of coercion existed "outside of and [was] immune to any law, with party-controlled concentration camps and firing squads [administering] privately decreed sanctions."[176] The Nazis seized property, deprived individuals of liberty, and even took away life itself "[w]ithout responsibility to any law and without warrant from any court."[177]

These insights occasioned a heightened appreciation on Jackson's part for the Constitution's procedural guarantees. Many of these provisions, he noted, are discredited "as 'technicalities' which irritate by causing delays and permitting escapes from what [public opinion] regards as justice. But by and large, sober second thought sustains most of them as essential safeguards of fair law enforcement and worth whatever delays or escapes they cost."[178]

---

[174]See Berger, Government by Judiciary 134–56, 249–82 (1977).

[175]Jackson, The Nurnberg Case, note 2 *supra*, at 42, 46.

[176]*Id.* at 96.

[177]*Ibid.*

[178]Jackson, Wartime Security and Liberty Under Law, 1 Buff. L. Rev. 105–6 (1951).

This principle guided him in *Shaughnessy v. Mezei*,[179] where the Court sustained the Attorney General's order, based ostensibly on national security grounds, to exclude an alien without a hearing. In his dissent, Jackson noted that the conspiratorial techniques of infiltration used by the communists tempts government to confine suspects on secret information secretly judged, and he conceded that he was not one to discount the communist threat. "But my apprehensiveness about the security of our form of government," he said, "are about equally aroused by those who will not see danger in anything else."[180] Here, the government's detention of Mezei had "unmistakable overtones of the [system of] 'protective custody' of the Nazis"[181] by which the arrested could claim no judicial or other hearing. Just as the Nazi "concentration camps were populated with victims of summary executive detention for secret reasons,"[182] this practice, "once established with the best of intentions, will drift into oppression of the disadvantaged in this country as surely as it has elsewhere."[183] In Jackson's view, "[p]rocedural fairness and regularity are of the indispensable essence of liberty."[184] And "the most scrupulous observance of due process, including the right to know a charge, to be confronted with the accuser, to cross-examine informers and to produce evidence in one's behalf, is especially necessary where the occasion of detention is fear of future misconduct, rather than crimes committed."[185]

Jackson's Fourth Amendment decisions also revealed the impact of Nuremberg. They disclosed his belief that the prohibition against unreasonable searches and seizures and the attendant requirement of particularity in search warrants is one of the most important procedural safeguards against arbitrary government. Or, as Jackson said:[186]

> Among deprivation of rights, none is so effective in cowing a population, crushing the spirit of the individual and putting terror in every heart [as is deprivation of Fourth Amendment free-

---

[179] 345 U.S. 206 (1952).

[180] *Id.* at 227.

[181] *Id.* at 226.

[182] *Id.* at 225–26.

[183] *Id.* at 226.

[184] *Id.* at 224.

[185] *Id.* at 225.

[186] *Brinegar*, 338 U.S. at 183.

> doms]. Uncontrolled search and seizure is one of the first and most effective weapons in the arsenal of every arbitrary government.

Requiring officers to have some valid basis in law for intrusions is "one of the most fundamental distinctions between our form of government, where officers are under the law, and the police state where they are the law."[187]

Nuremberg's liberalizing effect was more than offset, however, by a troubling development in Jackson's jurisprudence that was not evident in his *Terminiello* dissent. This aspect of the Trial's impact was seen in *Dennis v. United States*,[188] which involved an appeal from a conviction of eleven Communist party leaders for violating the Smith Act by conspiring to form a political party to teach violent overthrow of the government. Speaking for the majority, Chief Justice Vinson accepted Judge Learned Hand's revision of the "clear and present danger" test (the Appeals Court judge subordinated the requirement of a "present" danger to a "probable" one) and upheld the convictions.[189] Jackson concurred in the decision but refused to apply the clear and present danger test as redefined by Hand.[190] Jackson's refusal probably was based on the principle that guided him at Nuremberg, namely, that courts should not participate in the perversion of law. The Court's evisceration of the clear and present danger test essentially politicized the proceedings, and only Jackson seemed aware of the damage that a domestic political trial would cause to legal values and judicial prestige.[191]

But Jackson's concern for legal principles did not ensure that his approach was any less harmful to judicial integrity and constitutional values. He did not call for a proper application of the clear and present danger test, since he was disturbed by the implications of requiring the existence of an imminent danger before the state would be permitted to suppress radical speech. The problem with this test, he argued, is that it was fashioned when the primary forces viewed "as antagonists in the struggle between liberty and authority were

---

[187]Johnson v. United States, 333 U.S. 10, 17 (1948). See also his dissent in Harris v. United States, 331 U.S. 145, 195 (1947).

[188]341 U.S. 494 (1951).

[189]*Id.* at 510.

[190]*Id.* at 568.

[191]Shklar, note 10 *supra*, at 217–19.

the Government on the one hand and the individual citizen on the other."[192] The political situation has been complicated in recent times "by the intervention between the state and the citizen of permanently organized, well-financed, semisecret highly disciplined political organizations."[193] Employing the clear and present danger test would mean "that the Communist plotting is protected during its period of incubation; its preliminary stages of organization and preparation are immune from the law; the Government can move only after imminent action is manifest, when it would, of course, be too late."[194]

Drawing upon his belief, acquired at Nuremberg, that radical organizations must be curbed in their early stages, Jackson argued that resort should be had to a controversial doctrine he championed at the War Crimes Trial—the doctrine of conspiracy. Jackson again acknowledged that criminal conspiracy is "a dragnet device capable of perversion into an instrument of injustice in the hands of a partisan or compliant judiciary."[195] But he contended that this doctrine "has an established place in our system of law."[196] Since it has been used to frustrate concerted action that disturbs interstate commerce, it would be unreasonable to withhold its application to those attempting to undermine our government.[197]

So, while Nuremberg impressed upon Jackson the dangers presented to legal values and judicial prestige by involving courts in the distortion of law for political purposes, his analysis of the destruction of German liberty inured him to the perils associated with a legal doctrine that permits government to punish individuals for having done nothing more than agree to assemble and discuss radical politics. Only Jackson was willing to accept at face value the conspiracy provisions of the Smith Act and not insist on the demonstration of a danger. The conviction of the communists through use of the conspiracy doctrine would not have compensated for the harm done to liberal or constitutional values and to judicial integrity. The elimination of the Communist party would not have lessened the Soviet

[192] 341 U.S. at 577.

[193] *Ibid.*

[194] *Id.* at 570. See also *Douds*, 339 U.S. at 424–30.

[195] 341 U.S. at 572.

[196] *Ibid.*

[197] *Id.* at 575, 577.

threat appreciably, if at all; by contrast, the "history of the law of conspiracy . . . is such as to inspire only misgivings."[198] One might argue that the results of Jackson's approach were more desirable than the majority's transmogrification of the clear and present danger test, since the latter approach harmed legal values as well as constitutional liberties and judicial prestige. But resort to the law of conspiracy should be regarded with more apprehension, since it temporarily disguises a greater harm to constitutional principles with a cover of legality. In view of the value of extremist speech to political discourse in a stable, liberal democracy (as opposed to a nation harboring resentment against a humiliating post-war settlement), Jackson's Nuremberg-inspired desire to narrow drastically the scope of constitutionally protected speech detracts from his accomplishments at the War Crimes Trial.[199]

IV. Conclusion

When this negative aspect of the Trial is considered along with the intra-Court conflict engendered by Jackson's involvement, and with the disastrous airing of grievances that was a consequence of his separation from events in this country, one is driven to conclude that the decision to accept the Nuremberg assignment was imprudent. This is not to disregard the significant accomplishments of the Trial or to fail to appreciate Jackson's contributions to this historic event. As a onetime critic of Nuremberg ultimately conceded: "[T]he world . . . has every reason to be profoundly grateful to Mr. Justice Jackson and his associates, who, in the face of enormous practical difficulties and widespread theoretical criticism, persisted until they demonstrated the justice of the *ad hoc* method adopted at Nuremberg."[200] But, in view of the drawbacks of Jackson's involvement, his participation should have been preceded by an act he was unwilling to perform—his resignation from the bench.

This raises the distressing possibility that the benefits accruing from judicial participation in future international trials must be purchased at the cost of the skills of great judicial figures. Indeed, such a policy would at times involve a failure to exploit enriched judicial

---

[198]Shklar, note 10 *supra*, at 215, 218.

[199]See Meiklejohn, Political Freedom (1960); Bollinger, The Tolerant Society (1986).

[200]Wyzanski, note 31 *supra*, at 59.

minds, since extra-judicial participation could occasion jurisprudential improvements like those experienced by Jackson without an offsetting degeneration in other constitutional values. It might be argued, however, that resignation from the bench need not precede judicial involvement in international trials, since intra-Court conflict is not an inevitable consequence of such activities. The motives behind involvement in extra-judicial assignments are not invariably self-serving, and consultations with Court members would help prevent dissonance within the Court.

Yet, there are several considerations that militate against the view that this sort of off-the-bench activity should be tolerated. The diversion of any amount of time and energy from primary judicial obligations warrants concern, given the Court's significant workload. Moreover, a mere impression of improper motivation in the acceptance of an extra-judicial task has troubling implications for judicial prestige. The assignment of questionable motives to participating Justices is a distinct possibility, as charges of political gamesmanship greeted Jackson even before his outburst over losing the Chief Justiceship.[201] Similarly, and as the scholarly assessment of Jackson's post-Nuremberg decisions suggests, the imputation of bias or jurisprudential change to participating Justices seems probable. Finally, and most importantly, there is no guarantee that future international trials will be successful. Nuremberg was a triumph, despite serious legal problems, only because of the profound and unprecedented evil of the Nazi defendants. Few decisions would be as clearly deserved or universally accepted.

[201]See unsigned letter to Harlan F. Stone, headed Princeton, N.J., April 15, 1946, HFSP, Box 75.

PAUL FINKELMAN

JAMES MADISON AND THE BILL OF RIGHTS: A RELUCTANT PATERNITY

In May 1789, when the first Congress was just two months old James Madison indicated his intention to introduce a series of amendments to the Constitution. A month later Madison finally found an opening in the agenda to propose his amendments.[1] He faced opposition from all sides.[2] Former federalist allies, like Fisher Ames and Roger Sherman, dismissed Madison's call for amendments as unnecessary, imprudent, or worse yet, an attempt by Madison to gain popularity.[3] In private correspondence they were even more critical of Madison's proposals.[4]

Paul Finkelman is Visiting Associate Professor of Law, Brooklyn Law School.

AUTHOR'S NOTE: I wish to thank Willi Paul Adams, Kenneth Bowling, Michael Kent Curtis, Peter Hoffer, Ralph Ketcham, Knud Krakau, Sanford Levinson, Pauline Maier, Jack Rakove and Frank Rohmer for their very useful comments on this article. Portions of this paper were read at the Organization of American Historians, the American Society for Legal History, and the colloquium of the John F. Kennedy Institute at the Free University of Berlin.

[1]Speeches of Madison, Annals of Congress, 1st Cong., 1st Sess., (May 4, 1789 and June 8, 1789) 257; 440–469.

[2]William E. Nelson argues that the "Federalists acceded to Antifederalist demands for the protection of personal rights as the price of ratification," Nelson, Reason and Compromise in the Establishment of the Federal Constitution, 1787–1801, 44 Wm. & Mary Q. 477 (3rd ser., 1987). This seems correct only for the ratification conventions, where federalists in Massachusetts, Virginia, and New York voted for recommended amendments after the conventions ratified the Constitution. However, by 1789 many federalists in Congress were no longer willing to support amendments. Only Madison's maneuvering, tenacity, and arguments led them to support the Bill of Rights.

[3]Brant, James Madison: Father of the Constitution, 1787–1800 267–68 (1950).

[4]Bowling, "A Tub to the Whale": The Founding Fathers and the Adoption of the Federal Bill of Rights, 8 J. of the Early Republic 223, 237 (1988).

0-226-09573-8/91/1990-0005$02.00

Many antifederalists were equally unsupportive. Elbridge Gerry, who had refused to sign the Constitution in part because it lacked a bill of rights, was unwilling to support Madison at this time.[5] Aedanus Burke, on the other hand, wanted amendments but not the kind Madison proposed. He thought Madison's were "frothy and full of wind, formed only to please the palate; or they are like a tub thrown out to a whale, to secure the freight of the ship and its peaceable voyage."[6]

Despite this resistance, Madison persisted. Ultimately Congress accepted most of the substance of what Madison suggested.[7] Within five months Congress agreed to twelve amendments, ten of which were ratified by 1791.

For his persistence in the summer of 1789, Madison well deserves his reputation as the father of the Bill of Rights. This may indeed have been "some of his noblest work,"[8] and modern civil libertarians have good reason to claim Madison as one of their own. As Leonard W. Levy has persuasively argued, Madison's "accomplishment in the face of opposition and apathy entitles him to be remembered as 'father of the Bill of Rights' even more than as 'father of the Constitution.'"[9] This article does not challenge the conventional wisdom on this point; rather, it explores the route that Madison took to his well-earned place in the history of liberty.

Despite his eventual support for a bill of rights, Madison had no well thought-out intentions on this subject. Rather, he had well thought-out reservations about a bill of rights. While always sympathetic to the goal of preserving liberty, Madison, even as he introduced the Bill of Rights in the Congress, had little faith in the value

---

[5]In nine recorded votes on the Bill of Rights, Gerry voted against Madison seven times. They voted together, in the majority only on two minor procedural questions which were overwhelmingly defeated. These votes are compiled in Schwartz, 5 The Roots of the Bill of Rights 1116, 1124–25, 1127, 1132, 1137, 1161, 1163 (1971).

[6]Speech of Burke, Annals of Congress, 1st Cong., 1st Sess. (Debate of August 15, 1789) 774. On this issue, see generally Bowling, note 4 *supra*, at 223–51. George Mason thought Madison's proposals were "Milk & Water propositions," while Senator Richard Henry Lee dismissed them as "not similar" to the amendments proposed by the Virginia ratifying conventions. *Id.* at 233.

[7]Madison proposed that "No State shall violate the equal rights of conscience, or the freedom of the press, or the trial by jury trials in criminal cases." This provision passed the House of Representatives but was eventually struck out by the Senate. Schwartz, note 5 *supra*, at 1027, 1156.

[8]Burns, James Madison: Philosopher of the Constitution 15 (1973).

[9]Levy, The Bill of Rights, in 1 Encyclopedia of the American Constitution 115 (Levy, Karst & Mahoney, eds., 1986).

of what he derisively called "parchment barriers."[10] Madison's paternity of the Bill of Rights was a reluctant one that he accepted only after political realities forced him to rethink long-held positions.

Madison's primary purpose in supporting amendments was twofold: to fulfill promises made to his constituents during his campaign for Congress and to undermine opposition to the Constitution. On this latter point Madison argued that the amendments "would have stifled the voice of complaint, and made friends of many who doubted the merits of the constitution."[11]

I. Madison and the Authorship of the Bill of Rights

The amendments Madison introduced in the House of Representatives were rewritten by a committee, amended on the floor, and then altered again by the Senate. The Congress wisely rejected the very structure of Madison's amendments. Madison proposed that the amendments be imbedded into various sections of the Constitution because "He feared that the placement [of the amendments at the end of the Constitution] would lead to ambiguities about how far the original Constitution had been superseded by the amendments."[12] Had Madison's idea been accepted the "Bill of Rights" would not exist as such, although the rights themselves would still be found in the Constitution. Fortunately, Congress accepted Roger Sherman's suggestion that the amendments be added in a series at the end of the Constitution. It is quite likely that the impact of the Bill of Rights on our society would have been seriously diminished if it had not been one coherent body of rights found in one place in the Constitution.

The Senate categorically rejected Madison's favorite proposal—an amendment declaring that "No state shall infringe the right of trial by Jury in criminal cases, nor the rights of conscience, nor the freedom of speech, or of the press." This amendment would have limited the power of the states to undermine religious liberty, freedom of expression, and due process of law.[13] Such an amendment

[10]James Madison to Thomas Jefferson, October 17, 1788, 11 The Papers of James Madison 295–300, quoted at 297 (Rutland ed. 1977) (cited below as Papers of Madison).

[11]Speech of Madison, Annals of Congress, 1st Cong., 1st Sess. (June 8, 1789), 444.

[12]Bowling, note 4 *supra*, at 242.

[13]4 Documentary History of the First Federal Congress of the United States of America: Legislative Histories 39 (Bickford & Veit, eds., 1986). At the Constitutional Convention

would have radically altered the federal structure of the new government.

Though other members were active in the House and Senate debates, Madison was without question the key player in the adoption of the Bill of Rights. Perhaps "the Bill of Rights would be in place whether Madison had been present or not."[14] It would, however, be a different bill of rights and it certainly would not have been ratified by 1791. Madison was, as Jack Rakove has persuasively argued, "almost alone" in the First Congress "in believing that prompt action on amendments was a political necessity."[15] It may be true that "there was too much pressure from George Mason, Thomas Jefferson, Richard Henry Lee and others for the matter simply to have dropped."[16] But many antifederalists were exerting pressure for amendments that most probably would not have been ratified; they were also exerting pressure for a second Convention, which might have undone the work of the 1787 gathering. Without Madison's boundless energy in supporting amendments, despite his ambivalence about their value, strong anti-federalist pressure might have undermined the new government under the Constitution, leading to unforeseen developments. If there was a "framer" and a "father" of the Bill of Rights, it was Madison.

II. The Bill of Rights and the Constitutional Convention

The Constitutional Convention never seriously considered adopting a bill of rights. Near the end of the Convention the issue was discussed briefly and disposed of summarily. At the same time the delegates defeated various proposals for the protection of specific civil liberties, many of which were eventually incorporated into the Bill of Rights.

On August 20, 1787, Charles Pinckney "submitted sundry propo-

---

Madison had tried, and also failed, to incorporate greater limitations on the states by giving Congress the power to overrule state legislation. Hobson, The Negative on State Laws: James Madison, the Constitution, and the Crisis of Republican Government, 36 Wm. & Mary Q. 215 (3rd Ser., 1979). See also Banning, James Madison and the Nationalists, 1780–1783, 40 Wm. & Mary Q. 227 (3rd Ser., 1979), for a discussion of Madison's early nationalism, and Banning, The Hamiltonian Madison, 92 Va. Mag of Hist. & Biog. 7 (1984), for Madison's fear, "As late as 1789" that "the necessary powers of the central government would prove vulnerable to the encroachments by the states."

[14]Rutland, The Trivialization of the Bill of Rights, 31 Wm. & Mary L. Rev 287 (1990).

[15]Rakove, The Madisonian Theory of Rights, 31 Wm. & Mary L. Rev. 245, 246 (1990).

[16]Rutland, note 14 *supra*, at 287.

sitions" to the Convention. While some of Pinckney's propositions ultimately were included in the body of the Constitution, the Committee on Detail ignored his proposals to insure freedom of the press and to prohibit the quartering of troops in private homes. On September 12 the Convention rejected a proposal by Elbridge Gerry that the right to a jury in civil cases be guaranteed by the Constitution.[17]

George Mason, Madison's Virginia colleague, then suggested that the entire Constitution be "prefaced with a Bill of Rights." He thought that "with the aid of the State declarations, a bill might be prepared in a few hours." Roger Sherman argued that this was unnecessary because the Constitution did not repeal the state bills of rights. Mason replied that federal laws would be "paramount to State Bills of Rights." This argument, however correct, had little effect on the Convention, which defeated Mason's motion with all states voting no.[18] Within the Virginia delegation Madison opposed this motion.

The next day advocates of a bill of rights made one last attempt to add protections for basic civil liberties. Gerry once again proposed a guarantee of juries for civil trials, and once again the state delegations unanimously rejected this proposal. Pinckney and Gerry then proposed "that the liberty of the Press should be inviolably observed."[19]

Sherman again argued that under a government of limited powers specific protections of liberty were unnecessary because "The power of Congress does not extend to the Press." Five states were unconvinced, and voted for the proposal.[20] It is possible Madison voted for this motion, because we know Mason and Randolph carried at least one other Virginian within their delegation. But a majority of the state delegations sided with Sherman, defeating the motion to protect "the liberty of the Press."[21]

On Saturday, September 15, 1787, the next-to-the-last day of the Convention, George Mason expressed his reservations about the Constitution. He observed: "There is no Declaration of Rights, and the laws of the general government being paramount to the laws and

---

[17] 2 The Records of the Federal Convention of 1787 587 (Farrand ed. 1966) (cited below as Farrand).

[18] 2 Farrand 587–88.

[19] *Id.* at 5.

[20] Madison recorded the vote as 4 in favor and 7 states opposed. Both the official records and McHenry's notes recorded 5 states in favor and 6 opposed. 2 Farrand 611, 618, 620.

[21] *Id.* at 617–18.

Constitutions of the several States, the Declaration of Rights in the separate States are no security." Mason noted that under this Constitution "the people" were not "secured even the enjoyment of the benefit of the common law."[22]

Mason had other objections to the Constitution. He disliked the commerce power, the treaty-making provisions, the continuation of the African slave trade for *at least* twenty more years,[23] and the power of the President to grant pardons, especially to "those whom he had secretly instigated to commit" crimes and "thereby prevent a discovery of his own guilt."[24] These complaints about the Constitution were magnified by the lack of a bill of rights. Mason feared that the Senate and the President would combine "to accomplish what usurpations they pleased upon the rights and liberties of the people," while the federal judiciary would "absorb and destroy the judiciaries of the several States." He thought the expansive powers of Congress threatened the "security" of "the people for their rights." Without a bill of rights all this was possible. He complained, "There is no declaration of any kind, for preserving the liberty of the press, or the trial by jury in civil causes; nor against the danger of standing armies in time of peace."[25] For these reasons, Mason refused to sign the Constitution.

Another Virginian, Edmund Randolph, also refused to sign. He proposed a second convention to consider amendments, including a bill of rights. Elbridge Gerry of Massachusetts agreed with Mason on many substantive issues, including the dangers posed by the aristocratic nature of the Senate and the centralizing tendencies of the commerce power. He would have been able to "get over all these" defects "if the rights of the Citizens were not rendered insecure" by the virtually unlimited power of Congress under the necessary and proper clause and the lack of a guarantee of jury trials in civil cases.[26] But, without such guarantees, he too refused to sign the Constitution.

---

[22]*Id.* at 637–38.

[23]Finkelman, Slavery and the Constitutional Convention: Making a Covenant with Death, in Beyond Confederation: Origins of the Constitution and American National Identity 218–21 (Beeman, Botein &. Carter, eds., 1987).

[24]2 Farrand 637–38.

[25]*Id.* at 639–40.

[26]*Id.* at 632–33; Hon. Mr. Gerry's Objections to signing the National Constitution, in 2 The Complete Anti-Federalist 6–7 (Storing ed. 1981).

While Mason, Randolph, Gerry, and Pinckney argued for explicit protections of liberty, James Madison remained oddly silent. Madison was one of the most vocal delegates to the Convention. He said something on virtually every issue raised during the summer-long meeting. Why did Madison fail to support his colleagues from Virginia on this major issue? Why, if he was opposed to a bill of rights, did Madison not speak against their proposals?

There is no immediately satisfactory answer to either question. One explanation for Madison's reticence, and indeed for the majority's refusal to add a bill of rights, is a lack of time. The delegates had spent most of the summer discussing the framework of the new government. Only late in their deliberations did some delegates begin to perceive a threat to liberty from the increasingly centralized government. By then it might seem that the delegates had exhausted themselves creating the machinery of government and had neither the time nor the energy to work on a bill of rights.

Certainly by late August, and even more so by mid-September, most of the delegates were "hurrying toward adjournment" and had little patience for further debate.[27] But this explanation, though plausible, is ultimately unsatisfactory.

The first proposal for civil liberties protections came before the Convention on August 20, when Charles Pinckney suggested libertarian additions to the Constitution. This was late in the Convention, but certainly not too late for action. The contrast with the Fugitive Slave Clause,[28] which was for black Americans the antithesis of a bill of rights, is revealing. Charles Pinckney and Pierce Butler introduced this clause on August 28. The Convention adopted it the next day, after almost no debate, even though Americans had virtually no prior experience with the interstate rendition of fugitive slaves. The delegates, then, were clearly capable of swiftly and decisively expanding the Constitution even at the end of the Convention.[29]

The lack of time argument is especially unpersuasive in Madison's case. On September 14, three days before final adjournment, Madison proposed giving Congress two new substantive powers: to grant charters of incorporation and to create a national university.

---

[27] Ketcham, The Dilemma of Bills of Rights in Democratic Government, in The Legacy of George Mason 29 (Pacheco ed. 1983).

[28] U.S. Constitution, Art. IV, §2, cl. 3.

[29] Finkelman, note 23 *supra*, at 219–24.

That day Madison also supported a change in the wording of Article I to discourage standing armies. Clearly Madison was willing to make changes late in the Convention, but a bill of rights was not on his agenda.

The explanation for Madison's silence may be that on this issue he was uncharacteristically ambivalent. On the one hand, as a firm supporter of individual rights and personal freedom, Madison did not oppose the concept of protecting rights. He was, according to one former editor of the Madison papers, "the only one [among the founding fathers] who could be called a civil libertarian by the rigorous standards of the American Civil Liberties Union."[30] As early as 1774 Madison had considered "the possibility that a 'Bill of Rights' might be adopted by Congress and confirmed by the King or Parliament, such that America's liberties would be 'as firmly fixed and defined as those of England were at the revolution.'"[31] Later he played a role in drafting Virginia's Declaration of Rights.[32] As one historian has argued, "No man of his [Madison's] generation had a broader or deeper commitment to the general principles of civil liberty and procedural justice."[33]

On the other hand, for a variety of theoretical, practical, and political reasons, he was uncertain if the new American Constitution ought to have a bill of rights. Thus, Madison avoided the bill of rights debate. While not speaking out on the Convention proposals to protect individual liberty, Madison voted against most of them. During the ratification debates, when forced to take a stand, he opposed a bill of rights, although not always with great conviction. Even when arguing for amendments on the floor of the House, Madison was never fully convinced that a bill of rights was necessary or even desirable. In fact, for nearly two years—from the end of the Convention in 1787 until Congress endorsed the amendments in 1789—Madison consistently accepted the validity of the federalist arguments against a bill of rights.

---

[30]Hobson, James Madison, the Bill of Rights, and the Problem of the States, 31 Wm. & Mary L. Rev. 267, 268 (1990).

[31]Maier, From Resistance to Revolution: Colonial Radicals and the Development of American Opposition to Britain, 1765–1776 245 (1972).

[32]Rutland, James Madison: The Founding Father 11 (1987), points out that Madison proposed a key amendment to Mason's draft of the Virginia Declaration of Rights, changing religious "toleration" to "full and free exercise."

[33]Meyers, The Mind of the Founder: James Madison xxxvii (1973).

III. Reasons for Federalist Opposition to a Bill of Rights

There are five general reasons why Madison, along with most other federalists, opposed the addition of a bill of rights. These men believed one or more of the following propositions about a bill of rights: that it was 1) unnecessary; 2) redundant; 3) useless; 4) actually dangerous to the liberties of the people; and, 5) violative of the principles of republican government embodied in the Constitution.

1). The lack of necessity argument rested on the twin assumptions that the states were the main guarantors of liberty and that the national government under the Constitution lacked power to interfere with basic rights and liberties.

In the Convention Madison's allies argued that state protections of liberty were adequate. James Wilson asserted that one purpose of the states was "to preserve the rights of individuals." Oliver Ellsworth explained that he looked to the state governments "for the preservation of his rights." Roger Sherman argued that "the State Declarations of Rights are not repealed by this Constitution; and being in force are sufficient." He believed that the national legislature might "be safely trusted" not to interfere with the liberties of the people. Madison joined a majority of the delegates in supporting Sherman's position.[34]

Madison also agreed that as a compact for a government of limited powers, the Constitution did not empower the national government to interfere with liberty. After ratification Madison would assert that "the rights in question are reserved by the manner in which the federal powers are granted."[35]

2). Somewhat inconsistent with the argument that the national government could not interfere with liberty was the claim that the Constitution already protected liberty. Although federalists asserted that the Constitution did not need a bill of rights *per se*, they were quick to point out that the document contained many clauses which protected individual liberties and rights.

The Constitution prohibited any "religious test" for office hold-

---

[34] 1 Farrand 354, 492, and 2 Farrand 588. In the debate over a specific protection for a free press Sherman again argued that "The power of Congress does not extend to the Press" and thus the proposal was unnecessary. *Id.* at 618. Here Sherman carried a narrow majority that probably did not include Madison.

[35] Madison to Jefferson, October 17, 1788, 11 Papers of Madison 295–300, quoted at 297.

ing; prohibited government officials from simultaneously holding more than one office; and prohibited the suspension of the writ of habeas corpus except in time of actual invasion or rebellion. Article I prohibited both Congress and the states from adopting *ex post facto* laws and bills of attainder or granting titles of nobility. Article III guaranteed jury trials in criminal cases in the district where the alleged crime took place. Article III also eliminated the old English concepts of treason and constructive treason, by requiring two witnesses to an overt act.

These Constitutional provisions protected many basic liberties and rights. One Madison biographer found "twenty-four elements of a Bill of Rights in a Constitution that is said to contain none."[36] Supporters of the Constitution did not make such a careful count, but they extolled the protections of liberty in the document.

3). A third argument of the federalists conflicted with these first two. Federalists argued that a bill of rights would be useless in stopping the government from trampling on the liberties of the people. Many members of the Convention, including Madison, believed that paper guarantees of basic rights meant very little. During a debate over prohibiting *ex post facto* laws, Daniel Carroll of Maryland and James Wilson argued that "these prohibitions in the State Constitutions have no effect" and thus it was "useless to insert them" in the national constitution.[37] More than a year after the Convention Madison told Jefferson that "experience proves the inefficacy of a bill of rights on those occasions when its controul is most needed. Repeated violations of these parchment barriers have been committed by overbearing majorities in every state." He noted that in Virginia he had "seen the bill of rights violated in every instance where it has been opposed to a popular current." He warned that "restrictions however strongly marked on paper will never be regarded when opposed to the decided sense of the public; and after repeated violations in extraordinary cases, they will lose even their ordinary efficacy."[38]

Madison's views on the inefficacy of "parchment barriers" reflected his fundamental distrust of democratic majorities. In the Vir-

---

[36]Brant, The Bill of Rights: Its Origin and Meaning 12 (1965).

[37]2 Farrand 376.

[38]Madison to Jefferson, October 17, 1788, 11 Papers of Madison 297–99. For similar views by federalists see Letter of Cassius, No. 8, reprinted in Essays on the Constitution of the United States 28 (Ford ed. 1892), and 2 The Debates in the State Conventions on the Adoption of the Federal Constitution 174 (Elliot, ed., 2nd ed., 1836).

ginia legislature Madison had encountered men who "seemed so parochial, so illiberal, so small-minded, and most of them seemed to have only 'a particular interest to serve.' They had no regard for public honor or honesty" and were "reluctant to do anything that might appear unpopular."[39] Such "clods," as historian Gordon Wood has called them,[40] could not be expected to obey the restrictions of a bill of rights.

4). Federalists, including Madison, also argued that a bill of rights might actually be dangerous. This was based on the legal theory that any rights not enumerated in a bill of rights would have been given up. This argument assumed that a complete enumeration of all rights would be impossible. Thus, in defending the Constitution in the Pennsylvania ratifying convention, James Wilson asked who would "be bold enough to undertake to enumerate all the rights of the people?" He thought no one could, but warned that "if the enumeration is not complete, everything not expressly mentioned will be presumed to be purposely omitted." He asserted that members of the Convention considered a bill of rights "not only unnecessary, but improper."[41] Alexander Hamilton made a similar point in *Federalist* 84, arguing that a bill of rights was:[42]

> not only unnecessary in the proposed Constitution, but would even be dangerous. They would contain various exceptions to powers not granted; and, on this very account, would afford a colorable pretext to claim more than were granted.

Madison agreed with this analysis. He told Jefferson if a bill of rights was added to the Constitution it had to "be so framed as not to imply powers not meant to be included in the enumeration."[43]

Madison further worried that a bill of rights might be dangerous because it would not fully secure rights. He believed "that a positive declaration of some of the most essential rights could not be obtained" because he assumed that New Englanders would weaken any attempt to require a separation of church and state. Thus Madison feared that the "rights of Conscience" would be "narrowed much

---

[39]Wood, Interests and Disinterestedness in the Making of the Constitution, in Beyond Confederation, at 74.

[40]*Ibid.*

[41]3 Farrand 144, 161–61.

[42]Hamilton, Federalist 84, in 4 The Papers of Alexander Hamilton 706 (Syrett ed. 1962).

[43]Madison to Jefferson, October 17, 1788, 11 Papers of Madison 297.

more" by a bill of rights than any government would dare do on its own.[44] An incomplete or limited protection of conscience was, in Madison's mind, worse than none at all.

5). Finally, the very notion of a republican government led federalists to argue that a bill of rights was unnecessary. Part of this argument was based on the notion that Congress lacked the power to legislate on the subjects that would be covered by a bill of rights. But this analysis went beyond the concept of a limited government. Oliver Ellsworth, writing as "Landholder," argued that the theory of the Constitution itself precluded the need for a bill of rights. "Landholder" asserted that a bill of rights was something that the people wrested from the king, thus in America a bill of rights was "insignificant since government is considered as originating from the people, and all the power government now has is a grant *from the people*." Similarly, James Wilson argued that "it would have been superfluous and absurd, to have stipulated with a federal body of our own creation, that we should enjoy those privileges, of which we are not divested." James Iredell argued that in England a bill of rights was necessary because of the Crown's "usurpations" of the people's liberties. But, under the new Constitution the people delegated power to the national government, and thus Iredell argued that such usurpations by the national government were impossible. Iredell asserted that under the Constitution the government could no more "impose a King upon America" than "go one step in any other respect beyond the terms of their institution."[45]

The more sophisticated and skeptical Madison understood that a republican government might threaten liberty, but that such threats would not be by a minority attacking a majority. Rather, the threats to liberty were most likely to emanate from the legislature which represented the majority of the people. Madison further doubted that in a republic a bill of rights would have any effect against a determined legislative majority. In the Virginia ratification debates he asserted that "If there were a majority of one sect, a bill of rights would be a poor protection for liberty." Freedom of religion, he argued, was secured by "that multiplicity of sects, which pervades America, and

---

[44]Madison to Jefferson, October 17, 1788, *id.* at 297.

[45]The Landholder, No. VI, reprinted in 3 Documentary History of the Ratification of the Constitution: Ratification by the States: Delaware, New Jersey, Georgia, Connecticut 489 (Jensen ed. 1978); Substance of an Address by James Wilson and Answer to Mr. Mason's Objections to the new Constitution, by Marcus [James Iredell], in Pamphlets on the Constitution 161, 335 (Ford ed. 1888).

which is the best and only security for religious liberty in any society."[46] After Virginia had ratified the Constitution Madison made much the same point to Jefferson:[47]

> Wherever the real power in a Government lies, there is the danger of oppression. In our Governments the real power lies in the majority of the Community, and the invasion of private rights is *chiefly* to be apprehended, not from acts of Government contrary to the sense of its constituents, but from acts in which the Government is the mere instrument of the major number of the constituents.

Madison simply did not believe that a bill of rights could forestall a determined majority which might want to act in ways which would trample on the rights of a minority.

IV. Working for Ratification

Madison left the Philadelphia Convention hopeful that the Constitution would be ratified. He initially did not plan to become involved in the ratification struggle, but soon was drawn into it.[48] Once involved, he became dedicated to two related goals: securing ratification and preventing a second convention to amend the Constitution because he believed such a convention would undermine the Constitution.

Madison was clearly ambivalent about the Constitution. It did not create the strong, consolidated government that he had hoped for. Indeed, "The Constitution Madison expounded and defended as 'Publius' was a pale version of the plan he had carefully worked out before the Philadelphia meeting."[49] He thought the plan was a vast improvement over the Confederation. But, whether he thought it a sufficient improvement is another matter. In urging his friends at home to support the Constitution Madison argued that the Convention had succeeded in "blending a proper stability & energy in the Government with the essential characters of the republican Form" while retaining "a proper line of demarcation between the national

---

[46] Madison in the Virginia ratification convention, reprinted in 11 Papers of Madison 130.

[47] Madison to Jefferson, October 17, 1788, *id.* at 298.

[48] Editorial note, 10 Papers of Madison at 259.

[49] Hobson, The Negative on State Laws: James Madison, the Constitution, and the Crisis of Republican Government, 36 Wm. & Mary Q. 217 (3rd Ser., 1979).

and State authorities."[50] But, this seems more like a political posture than an accurate reflection of Madison's true beliefs.

In more private correspondence he argued that the government created by the Constitution was still too weak. Shortly before the Convention ended he wrote in secret code to Jefferson, who was still in France, that the plan of government "will neither effectually answer its national object nor prevent the local mischiefs which every where excite disgusts agst. the state governments."[51] In late October he still bemoaned the fact that the Convention had rejected his proposal to give Congress a "constitutional negative on the laws of the States."[52]

If Madison really believed that the Convention had created a proper but delicate balance between competing interests, as he wrote his friends in Virginia, then he properly feared amendments which would destroy this balance. Similarly, if Madison really viewed the Constitution as creating too weak a government, as he privately expressed to Jefferson, then he certainly did not want any amendments, including a bill of rights, which would have further weakened the national government.

Opposition to the Constitution formed as soon as the document became public. The most common antifederalist complaint was the lack of a bill of rights. Thus, in defending the Constitution Madison was forced to oppose the call for a bill of rights. To do otherwise would have been to admit that the Constitution had a major defect. Madison could not admit this; along with most federalists, he was firmly convinced that ratification of the Constitution was an all-or-nothing proposition, and an admission of the need for a bill of rights would prevent ratification.

Madison's first test of the issue came in the soon-to-be defunct confederation Congress, which received the work of the Convention. Madison was one of over a dozen signers who were also members of Congress. These "fiery zealots"[53] wanted quick action to send the Constitution on to the states without any changes. In accomplishing this, Madison helped defeat a motion by Richard Henry Lee and Melancton Smith to add a bill of rights to the Constitution. The successful arguments in this brief debate were procedural, focusing on

[50]Madison to Edmund Pendleton, Sept. 20, 1787, 10 Papers of Madison 171.

[51]Madison to Jefferson, September 6, 1787, *id.* at 163–64.

[52]Madison to Jefferson, October 24, 1787, *id.* at 212.

[53]The term is Richard Henry Lee's, and is quoted in Brant, note 3 *supra*, at 161.

the complications that would arise if Congress added its own proposals to the work of the Convention.[54] Here Madison was able to oppose the addition of a bill of rights without having to take any position on its merits.

For the next two months Madison continued to avoid the question of a bill of rights. In mid-October he commented to Washington about the unfair nature of George Mason's attacks on the Constitution, but he did not mention Mason's demand for a bill of rights. When he reported to Edmund Randolph the growing opposition to the Constitution over "the omission of the provisions contended for in favor of the Press, & Juries &c.," Madison again failed to comment on the validity of the argument or to propose a strategy for combating it.[55]

On October 24 Madison sent Jefferson a seventeen page letter, analyzing the strengths and weaknesses of the Constitution. This important document reveals that the Madison "who later became an indefatigable publicist in support of the new Constitution was in fact profoundly disappointed with the results of the convention."[56] Madison's main objection to the final document was the inability of the national government to veto state legislation. Madison feared that majorities within the states would destroy the liberties of minorities. He thought this problem could be prevented by giving the national government the power to overrule the states. In an argument later developed in *Federalist* 10 and 14, Madison declared that "private rights will be more secure under the Guardianship of the General Government than under the State Governments" because the constituency of the national government would be so diverse that no single group would ever control it.[57]

Madison did not think that a majority in the national government might also oppress the people and deny them basic liberties. Thus, he had nothing specific to say about a bill of rights, except to note that George Mason had left Philadelphia "in exceeding ill humour"

---

[54]Madison to George Washington, September 30, 1787, 10 Papers of Madison 179–81.

[55]Madison to Washington, October 18, 1787, *id.* at 196–97; Madison to Edmund Randolph, October 21, 1787, *id.* at 199–200.

[56]Editorial note, to letter of James Madison to Thomas Jefferson, October 24, 1787, *id.* at 205.

[57]James Madison to Thomas Jefferson, October 24, 1787, *id.* at 212. In 1789, when he drafted what became the Bill of Rights Madison attempted to make certain amendments applicable to the states in one last attempt to secure a federal veto over some state legislation. This provision passed the House but was deleted by the Senate.

and that his chief complaint was that he "considers the want of a Bill of Rights as a fatal objection."[58] Madison did not comment on the merits of this position. At this point in his career Madison thought that the national government needed to be strengthened to protect the people from their state governments, but he saw no reason to think that the people needed a bill of rights to be protected from the national government.

V. Defending the Constitution, Opposing a Bill of Rights, and the Federalist Papers

In mid-November 1787 Madison joined Alexander Hamilton in writing *The Federalist*.[59] This was the beginning of his active involvement in the ratification process. As "Publius" Madison began to articulate more fully—and in public—his opposition to a bill of rights.

In his first contribution to the series, the now-classic *Federalist* 10, Madison argued that the greatest danger to liberty in a Republic came from "the violence of faction" which he defined as "a number of citizens, whether amounting to a majority or minority of the whole, who are united and actuated by some common impulse of passion, or of interest, adverse to the rights of other citizens, or to the permanent and aggregated interests of the community."[60] Madison saw no way to eliminate the causes of faction without destroying political liberty itself. But he argued that political factions might be controlled by increasing the size of an electoral district, thus increasing the number and diversity of the electors, so no single interest could actually obtain a majority. "Extend the sphere, and you take in a greater variety of parties and interests; you make it less probable that a majority of the whole will have a common motive to invade the rights of other citizens; or if such a common motive exists, it will be more difficult for all who feel it to discover their own strength, and to act in unison with each other."[61]

---

[58] Madison to Jefferson, October 24, 1787, *id.* at 215.

[59] The editors of the Papers of Madison suggest that Madison was not brought into the project "until the middle of November, perhaps as late as the seventeenth." *Id.* at 261. Ralph Ketcham argues that the collaboration began just after October 10. Ketcham, James Madison: A Biography 239 (1971).

[60] Federalist 10, in 10 Papers of Madison 264. He had of course developed these arguments earlier, in The Vices of the Political System, reprinted in 9 Papers of Madison 350–54.

[61] Federalist 10, in 10 Papers of Madison, at 269.

Under the theory expressed in *Federalist* 10,[62] a bill of rights was unnecessary to protect people from oppressive majorities, because the majorities themselves would typically take the form of unstable coalitions of different groups. As such, they would be unable to threaten the people's liberties. The theory of *Federalist* 10 turned on the informal structure of the government under the Constitution. Competing and diverse interests would neutralize each other, making a bill of rights unnecessary.

In *Federalist* 51 Madison elaborated on how the Constitution's system of checks and balances combined with the diversity of the people to provide formal defenses against one faction taking power and depriving the citizens of their liberty. Madison argued that "If men were angels, no government would be necessary," but, given human nature Madison believed some formal controls were necessary. He thought the people themselves would "no doubt [be] the primary control on the government" but that "auxiliary precautions" were also useful, including the Constitution's aim "to divide and arrange several offices in such a manner that each may be a check on the other." This, Madison argued, would prevent any single branch of government from threatening liberty. Furthermore, the division between the states and the federal government would provide a "double security to the rights of the people."[63]

In *Federalist* 51 Madison again asserted, as he had in *Federalist* 10, that the competing interests caused by diversity of the people was the key to liberty. As long as the [64]

> society itself will be broken into so many parts, interests and classes of citizens, that the rights of individuals or of the minority, will be in little danger from interested combinations of the majority. In a free government, the security for civil rights must be the same as that for religious rights. It consists in the one case in the multiplicity of interests, and in the other, in the multiplicity of sects. The degree of security in both cases will depend on the number of interests and sects.

As Jack Rakove has succinctly phrased it, Madison's theory rested on the notion that "Diversity begets jealousy, and jealousy begets se-

[62]This was a theory of government that Madison had been working on in 1786, when he made Notes on Ancient and Modern Confederacies, and then in the Spring of 1787, when he drafted the memorandum On the Vices of the Political System of the United States. During the Federal Convention of 1787, Madison also argued along the lines later developed in Federalist 10.

[63]Federalist 51, 10 Papers of Madison 477–78.

[64]Federalist 51, *id.* at 478–79.

curity."[65] While not explicitly rejecting the idea of a bill of rights in *Federalist* 51, the implications of his argument are that diversity of interests—not any formal document—would ultimately preserve fundamental rights.

Madison reiterated these points in *Federalist* 57, arguing that the "vigilant and manly spirit which actuates the people of America" would prevent the legislature from usurping its power.[66] Furthermore, ever attuned to turning private interest to the public good, Madison argued that members of the House of Representatives would never betray the liberties of the people because if they did, they would not be reelected. In essence Madison argued in *Federalist* 10, 51, and 57 that the political process, the governmental structures, and the social and demographic diversity of the nation would protect liberty.

In *Federalist* 38 he casually dismissed calls for a bill of rights because the antifederalists could not all agree on what protections of liberty they wanted.[67] Rhetorically asking "Is a bill of rights essential to liberty," he noted the "confederation has no bill of rights."[68] Such arguments were inherently weak. That some antifederalists did not want a bill of rights, or others could not completely agree on its contents, did not diminish the need for one. Madison also well knew that the demand for a bill of rights was a result of the strengthening of the national government by the new Constitution. Thus, it was disingenuous for Madison to argue that the Constitution did not need a bill of rights because the Articles of Confederation lacked one.

In *Federalist* 44 Madison pointed out that the Constitution prohibited the states from passing bills of attainder, *ex post facto* laws, or laws impairing the obligations of contracts, even though such laws were also prohibited in the "declarations prefixed to some of the state constitutions." Here Madison argued that "experience has taught us nevertheless, that additional fences against these dangers ought not to be omitted."[69] Madison did not explain why "additional fences" against the federal government were also not useful.

In *Federalist* 46 he argued that the state governments would prevent the national government from usurping powers not granted in the

---

[65] Rakove, The Madisonian Theory of Rights, 31 Wm. & Mary L. Rev. 245, 259 (1990).

[66] Federalist 57, 10 Papers of Madison 523.

[67] Federalist 38, *id.* at 367–68.

[68] Federalist 38, *id.* at 370.

[69] Federalist 44, *id.* at 421.

Constitution. This implied that the people did not need to fear that their liberties would be taken from them by the national government, and thus, again by implication, that a bill of rights was unnecessary. In *Federalist* 48 he returned to the theory—again by implication—that bills of rights were useless. Here he noted that in Pennsylvania "the constitutional trial by jury had been violated; and powers assumed, which had not been delegated by the constitution."[70] Thus Madison reiterated his belief in the danger and futility of relying on "parchment barriers against the encroaching spirit of power."[71] The same analysis might effectively have shown the potential danger of usurpation of power by the national government under the proposed constitution. But if Madison saw the double-edged nature of his argument, he did not comment on it.

The most direct statement on the bill of rights in *The Federalist* did not come from Madison, but rather from Hamilton, who argued in *Federalist* 84: "Why declare that things shall not be done which there is no power to do? Why, for instance, should it be said that the liberty of the press shall not be restrained, when no power is given by which restrictions may be imposed?"[72] Madison probably subscribed to this position. After all the essays were published, Madison explained that while "the writers are not mutually answerable for all the ideas of each other" the project was carried out "in concert" between the three authors.[73] "In concert" the authors put together a general outline of the project, which probably included some agreement on major issues and strategies. In the absence of evidence to the contrary, it seems reasonable to conclude that Madison did not disagree with Hamilton on this point.

VI. The Private Madison and the Bill of Rights

In his private correspondence during the ratification struggle Madison gave further evidence of his opposition to a bill of rights. This position developed despite pressure from correspondents and friends to recognize the merits of a bill of rights. For George Turber-

70 Federalist 48, *id.* at 459.

71 Federalist 48, *id.* at 456. Madison would use the term "parchment barriers" somewhat later in a direct reference to the bill of rights. Madison to Jefferson, October 17, 1788, 11 Papers of Madison 297–99.

72 Hamilton, Federalist 84, in 4 The Papers of Alexander Hamilton 706.

73 Madison to Jefferson, August 11, 1788, 11 Papers of Madison 227.

ville, a minor Virginia politician, he simply laid out his "powerfull reasons that may be urged agt. the adoption of a Bill of Rights."[74] But to his closest friends, like Washington, Jefferson, and Edmund Pendleton, Madison revealed both his opposition to a bill of rights and his hostility to opponents of the Constitution who demanded such an addition.

Most federalists, including Madison, held their opponents in contempt and did not take seriously their demands for a bill of rights. General Henry Knox believed that antifederalists were "Demagogues and vicious characters." In New England federalists described their opponents as "wicked," "malignant, ignorant, and short-sighted triflers." A federalist in North Carolina referred to his opponents as "a blind stupid set, that wish Damnation to their Country," who were "fools and knaves" opposed to "any man of abilities and virtue." A New Hampshire federalist predicted "that none but *fools*, *blockheads*, and *mad men*" opposed the Constitution. In New York the anonymous "Caesar" thought that the demands for a bill of rights were made by "designing croakers" in order "to frighten the people with ideal bugbears."[75]

Madison also buttressed his opposition to a bill of rights by attacking the integrity and motives of his opponents. He divided Virginia's supporters of amendments into two categories: men like Edmund Randolph and George Mason, who "do not object to the substance of the Governt. but contend for a few additional Guards in favor of the Rights of the States and of the people," and others, led by Patrick Henry, who sought amendments that would "strike at the essence of the System."[76] He believed Henry's group had "disunion assuredly for its object" while disunion was the "real tendency" of all oppo-

---

[74]George Turberville to Madison, April 16, 1788, in *id.* at 23. Madison's letter to Turberville, which contained these "powerful reasons," is now lost, but we can assume that they were a summary of arguments in The Federalist and elsewhere.

[75]Rutland, Ordeal of the Constitution: The Antifederalists and the Ratification Struggle, 1787–1788 34, 73, 269, 216 (1966). Letters of Caesar, II, in Essays on the Constitution 289 (Ford ed. 1892). Ford incorrectly identifies the author of this letter as Alexander Hamilton. See 4 The Papers of Alexander Hamilton 278–79.

[76]Madison to Jefferson, December 9, 1787, 10 Papers of Madison 312. In April Madison modified his analysis, informing Jefferson that Randolph "cannot properly be classed with its [the Constitution's] enemies," while Mason was "growing every day more bitter" and had become "outrageous" in his opposition and would "in the end be thrown by the violence of his passions into the politics of Mr. H______y." Madison to Jefferson, April 23, 1788, 11 Papers of Madison 28–29. When the Virginia convention began Madison happily reported Randolph firmly in the federalist camp, noting that "The Govr. has declared the day of previous amendments past. . . ." Madison to Rufus King, June 4, 1788, *id.* at 76.

nents. Thus Madison felt that there could be "no middle ground" between supporters and opponents of the Constitution.[77]

While Madison conceded that some opposition in Virginia came from "men of intelligence, patriotism, property, and independent circumstances," he thought their grass-roots support was from people "much accustomed to be guided by their rulers." In other words, in Virginia a few demagogues, like Patrick Henry, were misleading the people. In most of the rest of the country the educated elite were "zealously attached to the proposed Constitution." He was particularly pleased that in New England "the men of letters, the principle Off[i]cers of Govt. the Judges & Lawyers, the Clergy, and men of property" almost universally supported the Constitution.[78]

He described the Massachusetts antifederalists as including "scarce a man of respectability." They were a combination of supporters of Shays' Rebellion and "ignorant and jealous men, who had been taught or had fancied that the Convention at Philada. had entered into a conspiracy against the liberties of the people at large, in order to erect an aristocracy for the rich, the *well-born*, and the men of Education." On the other hand, "all the men of abilities, of property, and of influence" supported the Constitution.[79]

Such observations help explain Madison's hostility to amendments. He believed the proponents of amendments were either antinationalists, like Henry, out to destroy the Constitution, or men who lacked "intelligence, patriotism, property, and independent circumstances." They were, in other words, not men who Madison thought should govern the republic. Because Madison believed that all who demanded amendments "threaten shipwreck to our liberty,"[80] he could not admit that any of their points might be valid. No wonder Madison condemned the recommended amendments of the Massachusetts ratifying convention as "a blemish" even though he conceded they were "in the least Offensive form."[81]

---

[77]Madison to Edmund Pendleton, February 21, 1788, 10 Papers of Madison 532–33.

[78]Madison to Jefferson, December 9, 1787, *id.* at 312–13. Madison was "persuaded" that some of those supporting amendments, especially in Virginia, did so "with the most patriotic & virtuous intentions." He conceded that "men equally respectable in every point of character" were on both sides of the issue, but nevertheless believed the opposition in his home state would "either dismember the Union" or injure Virginia's pride and "foresight." Madison to Archibald Stuart, December 14, 1787, *id.* at 325–26.

[79]Madison to Edmund Pendleton, February 21, 1788, *id.* at 532–33; Madison to Jefferson, February 19, 1788, *id.* at 519.

[80]Madison to George Washington, December 14, 1787, *id.* at 327.

[81]Madison to Washington, February 15, 1788, *id.* at 510–11.

Echoing *Federalist* 38, Madison was also contemptuous of the antifederalists because they could not agree on what they wanted.[82] He argued that if the antifederalists "were to enter into an explicit & particular communication with each other, they wd find themselves as much at variance in detail as they are agreed in the general plan of amendments." He believed their only agreement would be on "points of very little substance."[83] Their positions were "as heterogeneous as can be imagined."[84]

That federalists were also "heterogeneous" on many points did not seem to trouble Madison. By the spring of 1788 Madison wanted the Constitution ratified at all costs, and he would work with anyone toward that end and similarly opposed any idea which might undermine that goal.

VII. The Virginia Ratifying Convention

In late February Madison began making plans to return to Virginia to seek election to that state's ratifying convention. Mounting hostility to the Constitution made his presence imperative. By the time Madison left New York the debate over a bill of rights had been altered. The critical change came in Massachusetts.

When the Massachusetts ratifying convention opened in January 1788, an antifederalist majority seemed certain to defeat the Constitution. The convention elected John Hancock, an apparent antifederalist, as its president. A key opposition leader was Samuel Adams, the old revolutionary, who was an important and powerful politician in the Commonwealth, and a man who had been committed to bills of rights since the beginning of the Revolution.[85] Many delegates came to the Boston convention with instructions from their constituents to oppose ratification unless a bill of rights was added to the Constitution.

With opponents of ratification in apparent control, the Massachusetts federalists sought a compromise. They suggested that a series of recommended amendments to the Constitution be sent to Congress along with the convention's ratification. John Hancock was persuaded to present these amendments to the convention. Samuel

[82] Note 62 *supra*.

[83] Madison to Archibald Stuart, December 14, 1787, 10 Papers of Madison 326.

[84] Madison to Edmund Pendleton, February 21, 1788, *id*. at 532–33.

[85] Maier, The Old Revolutionaries: Political Lives in the Age of Samuel Adams 25 (1980).

Adams offered a counter-proposal that the convention actually add a bill of rights to the beginning of the Constitution, and then ratify both. Had this motion been successful, Massachusetts's ratification would have been conditional, and only gone into effect if the other states accepted the Massachusetts amendments. The danger of prior amendments, which is what Samuel Adams wanted, was that each state would propose different amendments and the Constitution would never be ratified.

When his motion for prior amendments was defeated, Adams joined Hancock in supporting ratification with recommended amendments. A few other antifederalists joined as well, and the Constitution squeaked through, by a vote of 187 to 168. A change of only ten votes would have defeated the Constitution in Massachusetts.

The importance of the Massachusetts compromise—ratification with recommended amendments—was not immediately apparent to Madison and his friends. Edmund Randolph thought the Massachusetts amendments were a "paltry snare" which were either "inadmissible," aimed against the Southern states, or "milk & water."[86] Madison thought the ratification in Massachusetts had "almost extinguished" the hopes of the New York antifederalists. He did not think the proposed amendments mattered one way or the other, although he believed they were a "blemish." Madison's attentions were already focused on New Hampshire and Virginia.[87]

In early March Madison left New York for Virginia. For the first time in his public career Madison was forced to campaign for office. On March 22 Madison probably met with Rev. John Leland, an influential Baptist minister who at the time was hostile to the Constitution. Leland and other Baptists feared that the Constitution would undermine religious freedom in the nation. Madison's long record of supporting religious liberty, and his sincere empathy for Leland's concerns, convinced the minister to support Madison for the Virginia convention.[88]

Madison reached Montpelier on March 23, the day before the election for delegates to the Virginia ratification convention. On the 24th

---

[86]Randolph to Madison, February 29, 1788, 10 Papers of Madison 542–43.

[87]Madison to Randolph, Madison to Washington, and Madison to Edmund Pendleton, all on March 3, 1788, *id.* at 554–55; 555–56; 554.

[88]Butterfield, Elder John Leland, Jeffersonian Itinerant, 62 Proceedings of the American Antiquarian Society 183–96 (1952).

Madison overcame his natural shyness to give his first public speech before the voters. He tried to dispel the "absurd and groundless prejudices against the foederal Constitution" that had been growing in his absence. This brief campaign was successful, as he beat his nearest anti-federalist rival by a margin of almost four to one.[89] Madison was pledged to support the Constitution as written. He was not pledged to prior amendments, or any other alterations of the document.

Madison's meeting with Leland was critical to his election campaign, because Madison believed the support of the Baptists was crucial to his electoral success. Indeed, it seems likely that "Madison owed his presence in the Virginia convention to" Leland and other "dissenters whose trust he had earned in the struggle for religious liberty."[90]

The meeting with Leland was also critical for Madison's eventual support for a bill of rights. Until this time Madison dismissed the antifederalist demand for a bill of rights as a smokescreen for defeating the Constitution. In Leland, however, Madison faced a man who wanted to support the Constitution, but sincerely feared that without a bill of rights freedom of religion would be jeopardized under the new government. Madison could not easily dismiss Leland's arguments as politically motivated because they were not. Thus, for the first time Madison was forced to take seriously the bill of rights argument.

The Virginia voters elected a convention that was almost evenly split between federalists and antifederalists. Almost immediately some of Madison's friends urged that the Massachusetts model be applied to Virginia. George Nichols argued it was the only basis on which compromise "can safely take place."[91] Madison agreed. He did not think amendments were a particularly good idea, but he did believe that proposing them as Massachusetts had done, to be considered after ratification, would blunt antifederalist opposition. The Massachusetts plan was "unquestionably the Ultimatum of the foederalists" while conditional ratification or a second convention would "be fatal."[92]

---

[89]Madison to Eliza House Trist, March 25, 1788, 11 Papers of Madison 5–6.

[90]Kukla, A Spectrum of Sentiments: Virginia's Federalists, Antifederalists, and Federalists Who are For Amendments, 1787–1788, 96 Va. Mag. of Hist. & Biog. 282 (1988).

[91]George Nichols to Madison, April 5, 1788, 11 Papers of Madison 8–9.

[92]Madison to George Nichols, April 8, 1788, *id.* at 11–12.

Madison easily saw the practical value of supporting subsequent amendments as a way of obtaining immediate ratification. He told Edmund Randolph he was ready to support them in Virginia. This was perhaps the bridge that could connect strong federalists, like Madison, with more reluctant supporters of the Constitution, like Randolph. Nevertheless Madison remained skeptical about the effectiveness of this tactic. He believed that in Massachusetts the proposed amendments had been directed at popular sentiment, and had actually done little to sway opponents in the ratification convention.[93]

As the Virginia convention approached, Madison's views firmed. There was a real danger that the Virginia convention would endorse conditional ratification based on subsequent amendments or, worse yet, a demand for a second convention. If Virginia adopted either "the Constitution, and the Union will be both endangered."[94] Madison, who had once given lukewarm support to the Constitution, now equated its success with that of the nation itself.

This change was not the result of his changing views of the Constitution. Rather it reflected his realization of the true nature of politics in America. If a second convention came about, Madison feared there would be "little" of the "same spirit of compromise" of the previous summer. Madison expected that at a new convention it would be "easy also for those who have latent views of disunion, to carry them on under the mask of contending for alterations popular in some but inadmissible in other parts of the U. States."[95] Madison could give no quarter to those who wanted fundamental changes in the Constitution, because they would undermine ratification. At the same time, he had to blunt their demand, growing more popular each day, for a bill of rights. Recommended amendments looked better all the time.

In the Virginia convention Madison gave no immediate indication of his new position. Early in the convention he stressed his argument, previously made in *Federalist* 10, that the greatest threat to liberty came from the "majority trampling on the rights of the minority."[96] He also reiterated the argument made by Wilson in the

[93]Madison to Randolph, April 10, 1788, *id.* at 18–19.

[94]Madison to Jefferson, April 23, 1788, *id.* at 28–29.

[95]*Ibid.*

[96]Speech of Madison, June 6, 1788, *id.* at 79.

Pennsylvania convention and by Hamilton in *Federalist* 84 that civil liberties could not be harmed because of the limited nature of the national government. The Congress could create no national religion because "The government has no jurisdiction over it."[97]

Madison then attacked the impracticality of "obtaining previous amendments" to the Constitution. He noted that any amendments Virginia adopted would also have to be submitted to all the other states, which might then submit amendments of their own.[98] This would lead to an endless process that would produce nothing. Significantly, Madison still did not suggest recommended amendments, such as Massachusetts had proposed.

On June 12 Madison argued against a bill of rights because paper guarantees were worth little. Madison asked:[99]

> Is a bill of rights a security for religion? Would the bill of rights in this state exempt the people from paying for the support of one particular sect, if such sect were exclusively established by law? If there were a majority of one sect, a bill of rights would be a poor protection for liberty.

In answering his own questions Madison reiterated his notion that diversity protected liberty. He found that religious liberty was protected by "that multiplicity of sects, which pervades America, and which is the best and only security for religious liberty in any society. For where there is such a variety of sects, there cannot be a majority of any one sect to oppress and persecute the rest."[100] Reminding the Convention that he had always "warmly supported religious freedom," Madison argued that "a variety of sects," not a bill of rights, was the key to religious freedom.[101]

By mid-June Madison privately predicted that opponents of the Constitution would be narrowly defeated in their demand for previous amendments.[102] Confident of ultimate success, for the first time Madison argued against the substance of some rights.

A common antifederalist complaint was that the Constitution did

---

[97]Speech of Madison, June 6, 1788, *id.* at 84.

[98]*Ibid.*

[99]Speech of Madison, June 12, 1788, *id.* at 130.

[100]*Ibid.*

[101]Speech of Madison, June 12, 1788, *id.* at 131.

[102]Madison to Rufus King, June 18, 22, 1788, *id.* at 152, 167. See also, on Madison's confidence, Madison to Hamilton, June 20, 1788, and June 22, 1788, Madison to George Washington, June 23, 1788, and Madison to James Madison, Sr., June 20, 1788, *id.* at 157, 166, 168, 157–58.

not guarantee trials in the district where an alleged crime took place. This complaint would eventually be remedied by the Sixth Amendment. At the Virginia convention Madison argued that such a remedy was unnecessary, and might be decidedly dangerous to the welfare of the nation. He claimed that he would have supported a "provision for a jury from a vicinage" but only if it could be "done with safety." But, Madison argued that in some situations, like a rebellion, a trial "would be impracticable in the county" where the law was violated. Madison noted that even though the jury trial was "sacred" in America, there had nevertheless been numerous "deviations" from it since independence. Madison concluded that the legislature must have "discretion" in setting the rules for trials.[103]

Two days later Madison spoke against ratification with amendments. Now fully expecting to win a vote for ratification, he was also confident the convention would defeat prior amendments. After ratification he was prepared to support "a conciliatory declaration of certain fundamental principles of liberty, in a form not affecting the validity & plentitude of the ratification."[104]

Madison once again argued that previous amendments were impractical and that a bill of rights was unnecessary. The impracticality argument rested on the assumption that a demand for previous amendments by Virginia would lead to similar demands from other states, and require that the ratification process begin again. He then reasserted the long-held federalist position that "every thing not granted" to the federal government by the Constitution "is reserved" to the states or the people. He further argued that "an imperfect enumeration" of rights "is dangerous."[105]

Having dismissed the need for a bill of rights, Madison made one major concession to the opposition. He declared that if Virginia ratified the Constitution, he and other federalists would "freely, fairly and dispassionately consider and investigate your propositions, and endeavour to gratify your wishes." He promised that those amendments which were "not objectionable, or unsafe" could be "subsequently recommended" after ratification. But, he did not admit such amendments might be necessary. Rather, he argued, they would be considered "because they can produce no possible danger,

[103]Speech of Madison, June 20, 1788, *id.* at 164.

[104]Speech of Madison, June 24, 1788, *id.* at 174–75; Madison to Ambrose Madison, June 24, 1788, *id.* at 170–71.

[105]Speech of Madison, June 24, 1788, *id.* at 174–75.

and may gratify some gentlemen's wishes."[106] Thus, even as Madison accepted the idea of amendments, he did so as a matter of political expedience and accommodation, rather than as a matter of conviction.

VIII. Madison, Jefferson and the Bill of Rights: Reconsidering the "Great Collaboration"

While Madison was working for ratification, and fighting against a bill of rights, he was involved in a long-distance correspondence with Thomas Jefferson, who was then America's ambassador in Paris. The two had previously been allied in various political enterprises at the state and national level.[107] Now they disagreed over the importance of a bill of rights.

The conventional historical wisdom is that Jefferson pointed out the importance of a bill of rights "in letters persuading Madison to switch positions."[108] But it is not clear whether Jefferson's letters had any effect on Madison's actions or views. Certainly in the short run they did not, because the distance between the two men, and the long time it took for letters to be exchanged, made it impossible for the letters to have any immediate impact. At first glance, for example, Jefferson's well-known letter of December 20, 1787 seems to be an important criticism of Madison's position.[109] But, Madison did not receive this letter until July, 1788, after Virginia had ratified the Constitution and Madison himself had publicly announced his willingness to support future amendments.

Madison often wrote to Jefferson in code, which allowed him the luxury of great candor in an age when mail delivery was erratic and private letters might fall into the wrong hands. Because of the many months that it took for letters to cross the Atlantic, Madison did not fear that his openness would have adverse political repercussions. Thus, this correspondence tells us what Madison really believed about the bill of rights. The letters confirm that Madison's opposition was not simply tactical, but that he truly opposed the adoption of a bill of rights. This investigation also undermines the view that Jefferson "converted Madison to the cause of adding a Bill of Rights

---

[106] Speech of Madison, June 24, 1788, *id.* at 177.

[107] See generally, Koch, Jefferson and Madison: The Great Collaboration 3–32 (1950).

[108] Levy, note 9 *supra*, at 114.

[109] Jefferson to Madison, December 20, 1787, in 12 Jefferson Papers 438.

to the new federal Constitution."[110] The evidence suggests that Madison was converted to a bill of rights by political necessity rather than logical argument and that the conversion, such as it was, took place before Madison received Jefferson's letter of December 20, 1787 or his other letters urging the addition of a bill of rights.

A. JEFFERSON'S VIEWS

The day after the Convention ended George Washington sent a copy of the Constitution to Thomas Jefferson. In mid-October Benjamin Franklin sent Jefferson an official copy of the document. Finally, on October 24, 1787, Madison sent Jefferson a seventeen page letter and a copy of the Constitution.[111]

In late December, 1787, Jefferson finally received Madison's long letter of October 24th. By this time Jefferson had already seen a copy of the Constitution, and already corresponded with his counterpart in London, John Adams, about the lack of a bill of rights.[112]

Madison's October 24, 1787, letter gave Jefferson a short history of the Convention. Madison was guardedly enthusiastic about the Constitution, but thought it did not go far enough in nationalizing power.[113] Jefferson's thoughtful response, his famous letter of December 20, 1787, reflected quite different concerns about the Constitution. After detailing what he liked about the Constitution, Jefferson turned to "what I do not like."[114]

Jefferson's first complaint was "the omission of a bill of rights providing clearly and without the aid of sophisms for freedom of religion, freedom of the press, protection against standing armies, restriction against monopolies, the eternal and unremitting force of the habeas corpus laws, and trials by jury in all matters of fact triable by the laws of the land. . . ." Jefferson disputed James Wilson's arguments "that a bill of rights was not necessary because all is reserved

---

[110]Levy, Jefferson and Civil Liberties: The Darker Side 3 (1st ed. 1963).

[111]Koch, note 107 *supra*, at 39, states that these men "rushed copies" of the Constitution to Jefferson. This is true for Washington, but not for Franklin and Madison, who sent their letters on October 14 and October 24. Washington to Jefferson, Sept. 18, 1787; Franklin to Jefferson, October 14, 1787; 1787 in 12 The Papers of Thomas Jefferson 149, 236, 270 (Boyd ed. 1955) (cited below as Jefferson Papers). Madison to Jefferson, October 24, 1787, 10 Papers of Madison 205–20.

[112]John Adams to Jefferson, November 10, 1787; Jefferson to Adams, November 13, 1787; Jefferson to Madison, December 20, 1787, all in 12 Jefferson Papers 334, 349, 438.

[113]See text at notes 35–39 *supra*.

[114]Jefferson to Madison, December 20, 1787, 12 Jefferson Papers 441.

in the case of the general government which is not given. . . ."[115] Unbeknownst to Jefferson, Madison had taken more or less the same position as Wilson on this question.[116] Jefferson thought Wilson's argument was "gratis dictum" which was "opposed by strong inferences from the body" of the Constitution. Jefferson argued that "a bill of rights is what the people are entitled to against every government on earth, general or particular, and what no just government should refuse, or rest on inference."[117]

This letter, which is useful for an understanding of Jefferson's views on fundamental rights, had no effect on Madison's actions during ratification, because Madison did not receive it until July, 1788, which was after Virginia had ratified the Constitution and, for tactical reasons, Madison had agreed to support amendments. When Madison answered Jefferson's letter of December 20, 1787, he said nothing about a bill of rights, perhaps because Jefferson's points were already moot.[118] Madison had already agreed to support amendments that were "not objectionable, or unsafe,"[119] not because he had been convinced of their virtues by Jefferson's arguments, but rather because he had accepted the political necessity of them.

On July 31, 1788, Jefferson wrote Madison once again, "rejoic-[ing] at the acceptance of our new constitution by nine states."[120] Jefferson apparently knew about New Hampshire's ratification on June 21, but not about Virginia's (the 10th state) on June 25.[121] Nor did Jefferson know that Madison (without the benefit of Jefferson's letter of December 20, 1787) had supported subsequent amendments. Thus, Jefferson once again urged Madison to support a bill of rights.

The Constitution was "a good canvas, on which some strokes only want retouching." Jefferson's brush would paint a bill of rights that would "go to Juries, Habeas corpus, Standing armies, Printing, Religion & Monopolies." Jefferson argued that "the few cases wherein

---

[115]Jefferson to Madison, December 20, 1787, *id.* at 440.

[116]See text *supra* at III.

[117]Madison to Jefferson, October 24, 1787, 12 Jefferson Papers 270–86; Jefferson to Madison, Paris, December 20, 1787, *id.* at 438, 440.

[118]Madison to Jefferson, July 24, 1788, 11 Papers of Madison 196–98.

[119]Speech of Madison, June 24, 1788, *id.* at 177.

[120]Jefferson to Madison, July 31, 1788, *id.* at 212.

[121]Curiously, from the Jefferson Papers it appears that none of Jefferson's many friends in Virginia bothered to write him after the Virginia convention ratified the Constitution on June 25 or finished its deliberations on the 27th.

these things may do evil, cannot be weighed against the multitude wherein the want of them will do evil." He hoped that "a bill of rights will be formed to guard the people against the federal government, as they are already guarded against their state governments in most instances."[122]

B. MADISON'S VIEWS

In August 1788 Madison sent Jefferson two letters which described the ratification struggles in New York and North Carolina. His focus remained on the adoption of the Constitution, and not on the protection of rights under it. He conceded to Jefferson that the Constitution was not perfect and that "A trial for one year [of the workings of the Constitution] will probably suggest more real amendments than all the antecedent speculations of our most sagacious politicians."[123] This indicates that Madison was more concerned with the mechanics of government under the Constitution than a bill of rights, which he viewed as a tactical issue, rather than one of principle.

In mid-October Madison received Jefferson's letter of July 31, in which the latter strenuously argued for a bill of rights. Madison had never responded to Jefferson's arguments set out in his letter of December 20, 1787. Nor had he responded to Jefferson's public letters, which had continued to "criticise . . . the omission of a bill of rights."[124] Finally, on October 17, 1788, Madison faced the criticism of his friend.

His response showed that after a year of calls for a bill of rights, which included two strong appeals from Jefferson, Madison remained basically unconvinced. Madison claimed that his "own opinion has always been in favor of a bill of rights," but he then repeated the litany of federalist arguments against a bill of rights, including: (1) that it was unnecessary under a government of limited powers; (2) that it could not be complete enough, especially because New Englanders would oppose absolute religious freedom; (3) that the inherent tension between the states and the federal government made a bill

---

[122]Jefferson to Madison, July 31, 1788, 11 Papers of Madison 212, 213.

[123]Madison to Jefferson, August 23, 1788, *id.* at 238–39; see also Madison to Jefferson, August 10, 1788, *id.* at 225. On September 21, and October 8, 1788, Madison again wrote to Jefferson, but did not discuss the substantive questions of a bill of rights. *Id.* at 257–59, 276–77.

[124]Madison to Edmund Randolph, August 2, 1788, *id.* at 215.

of rights unnecessary; (4) that "[r]epeated violations of these parchment barriers" showed that a bill of rights was useless; and (5) that a bill of rights was only needed to protect the people against a monarch, which was not a situation the Americans faced.[125]

Having explained to Jefferson why a bill of rights was unnecessary, Madison offered three reasons why he was now willing to support one. First, he acknowledged that "political truths declared" in a "solemn manner" would "acquire by degrees the character of fundamental maxims of free Government, and as they become incorporated with the national sentiment, counteract the impulses of interest and passion." Second, Madison acknowledged the unlikely event that the government itself might oppress some or even a majority of the people. Although doubtless a depressing scenario for a committed republican, Madison seemed to recognize that even in a republic the elected government might trample on the rights of the people and the people might not immediately resist their own government. Under such circumstances, "a bill of rights will be a good ground for an appeal to the sense of the community." Finally, he conceded a small point to the opposition, noting that perhaps "a succession of artful and ambitious rulers, may by gradual & well-timed advances, finally erect an independent Government on the subversion of liberty," and a bill of rights would be "prudent" "especially when the precaution can do no injury." Not ready to concede too much to the antifederalists (even though they were now thoroughly defeated) Madison immediately added that he saw "no tendency in our governments to danger on that side."[126]

As if he had conceded too much to the opposition, even in this private letter to Jefferson, Madison reiterated his ambivalence about a bill of rights. "Supposing a bill of rights be proper" he wrote, "I am inclined to think that *absolute* restrictions in cases that are doubtful, or where emergencies may overrule them, ought to be avoided."[127] He warned that[128]

> restrictions however strongly marked on paper will never be regarded when opposed to the decided sense of the public; and after repeated violations in extraordinary cases, they will lose even their ordinary efficacy. Should a Rebellion or insurrection alarm

[125]Madison to Jefferson, October 17, 1788, *id.* at 297–98.

[126]Madison to Jefferson, October 17, 1788, *id.* at 298–99.

[127]Madison to Jefferson, October 17, 1788, *id.* at 299.

[128]*Ibid.*

> the people as well as the Government, and a suspension of Hab. Corp. be dictated by the alarm, no written prohibitions on earth would prevent the measure.

Madison's distrust in democracy led him to believe that no legislature would obey either constitutionally or self-imposed limits. The "clods" (as historian Gordon Wood has called them) in the legislature, whether it be state or federal, would do as they pleased.[129]

Well before he received Madison's letter of October 17, 1788, Jefferson made one more plea for a bill of rights. On November 18, 1788, he urged Madison to support a bill of rights, not on ideological or philosophical grounds, but as a matter of practical politics. Jefferson argued that "the minorities [the antifederalists] are too respectable not to be entitled to some sacrifice of opinion in the majority. Especially when a great proportion of them would be contented with a bill of rights."[130] By the time Madison received this letter, in March 1789, he had already adopted this position, and in fact been elected to Congress on the basis of it.[131]

Meanwhile, Madison's letter of October 17, 1788, was delayed even longer than usual for transatlantic correspondence. It did not reach Jefferson until February 1789, and he did not respond until March 15, 1789. In this response Jefferson showed his respect for some of Madison's positions, but continued to argue strenuously for a bill of rights. This letter, however, had little effect on Madison's subsequent conduct—his paternity of the Bill of Rights—because he did not receive it until the end of May. By then Madison had already put Congress on notice of his intention to propose amendments. In response to Jefferson's letter of March 15, Madison wrote that a bill of rights would be introduced into Congress within a week.[132]

IX. Madison Moves Toward His Paternity

Throughout the ratification struggle Madison's opposition to a bill of rights was both tactical and theoretical. In his letter to Jeffer-

---

[129]See text at note 38 *supra*. Wood, Interests and Disinterestedness in the Making of the Constitution, in Beyond Confederation, at 74.

[130]Jefferson to Madison, November 18, 1788, 11 Papers of Madison 353–54.

[131]Madison to Jefferson, March 29, 1789, 12 Papers of Madison 38.

[132]Jefferson to Madison, March 15, 1789; Madison to Jefferson, May 27, 1789, *id.* at 13, 186. Before he received Madison's letter of October 17, Jefferson once more urged his friend to support a bill of rights.

son of October 17, 1788, Madison had detailed his theoretical arguments.[133] His tactical position was one which even Jefferson understood. Simply put, Madison wanted the Constitution ratified without a second convention being called. He felt that even an admission that a bill of rights was necessary might jeopardize this goal, while a concession on prior amendments would certainly have endangered ratification.

Despite his claim in his October 17, 1788, letter that he had "always been in favor of a bill of rights," Madison seems not to have favored one until he introduced his amendments in Congress. Even then, it is not clear that Madison theoretically supported the amendments.

How and why did Madison move to his reluctant paternity? The answers to both questions are tied to the politics of Virginia in 1788–89.

Virginia's ratification of the Constitution was an embarrassing defeat for Patrick Henry. He correctly saw Madison as the chief cause of this outcome. "To humiliate Madison, Henry managed his rejection by the Assembly for a seat in the Senate, referring to him as one 'unworthy of the confidence of the people,' whose election to office 'would terminate in producing rivulets of blood throughout the land.'" In order to "exclude Madison from the House of Representatives as well, Henry, a master of the 'gerrymander' long before that term had been invented, placed Orange County [Madison's home] in a Congressional district otherwise composed of counties considered heavily antifederal."[134] As he had before the ratification convention, Madison was forced to return to Virginia to campaign for office—an activity for which he had little enthusiasm.[135]

Madison arrived home at the end of December, 1788. He faced an uphill election campaign. His opponent was James Monroe, a friend and neighbor, but also a moderate antifederalist who had the support of Patrick Henry and his allies. Henry and his friends had already circulated rumors that Madison opposed any changes in the Constitution, including a bill of rights. Madison was particularly disturbed by allegations that he opposed any amendment protecting religious freedom.

---

[133]Madison to Jefferson, October 17, 1788, 11 Papers of Madison 298–99. See text at note 124 *supra*.

[134]Ketcham, note 59 *supra*, at 275.

[135]Rutland, note 32 *supra*, at 48.

On January 2, 1789, Madison wrote to Rev. George Eve, a leading Baptist minister, to explain his position on the Constitution. As he had a year earlier during the campaign for his election to the ratifying convention, Madison found that Baptist fears about religious liberty were sincere, strongly held, and had to be overcome if he was to win election.

Madison's letter was surprisingly frank for a man seeking votes. He freely admitted his disagreement with Eve; he did not see in the Constitution "those serious dangers which have alarmed many respectable Citizens." Thus while the Constitution was unratified Madison had opposed amendments, because he believed they were "calculated to throw the States into dangerous contentions, and to furnish the secret enemies of the Union with an opportunity of promoting its dissolution." However, with the Constitution ratified he was willing to support "amendments, if pursued with a proper moderation and in a proper mode" because under such circumstances they would "be not only safe, but may well serve the double purpose of satisfying the minds of well meaning opponents, and of providing additional guards in favour of liberty." Madison told Eve that "Under this change of circumstances, it is my sincere opinion that the Constitution ought to be revised, and that the first Congress meeting under it, ought to prepare and recommend to the States . . . provisions for all essential rights, particularly the rights of Conscience in the fullest latitude, the freedom of the press, trials by jury, security against general warrants, &c."[136]

Madison's changing position was partially a function of the calls by his opposition, including Monroe, for a second convention to alter the Constitution. Madison thought a second convention would lead to a disastrous rewriting of the Constitution. With this as a likely alternative, Madison now saw amendments as the best hope for keeping the Constitution more or less as it had been written. Thus, he told Rev. Eve that future amendments were "the safest mode" of changing the Constitution because "The Congress, who will be appointed to execute as well as to amend the Government, will probably be careful not to destroy or endanger it" while a second convention "containing perhaps insidious characters from different parts of America," would "be but too likely to turn every thing into confusion and uncertainty."[137]

---

[136]Madison to George Eve, January 2, 1789, 11 Papers of Madison 404–05.

[137]*Ibid.*

Madison subsequently wrote similar letters to other Virginians, explaining his position on a bill of rights. Two of his letters, which were published at the time, contained his "unequivocal pledge" to work for amendments if elected to Congress.[138] This counterattack turned the tide in his favor. At a meeting of Baptist leaders Rev. Eve defended Madison, reminding his co-religionists that Madison had always supported their interests by fighting for full religious freedom in Virginia.[139] In addition, Madison went to various Baptist meetings, German churches, and numerous courthouses to debate Monroe and explain his new support for amendments. His friends continued to argue his case throughout the district.[140] The campaign paid off with "a resounding federalist victory and remarkable personal tribute to Madison in a district 'rigged' against him."[141]

X. An Ambivalent Advocate

Shortly after his election Madison headed for New York as a Congressman pledged to propose constitutional amendments to protect individual liberty.[142] Although slated to open on March 4, 1789, Congress did not actually begin until April 6, when both houses finally achieved a quorum. When the session finally began a bill of rights was not high on the agenda. Opposition clustered around four different arguments. Some diehard federalists opposed any changes to a Constitution which they thought was beyond improvement. Some antifederalists still hoped for a second convention or substantial amendments that would restructure the new government. They correctly understood that the adoption of a bill of rights would un-

---

[138]Madison to Thomas Mann Randolph, January 13, 1789, later published in the Virginia Independent Chronicle, January 28, 1789; Madison to "A Resident of Spotsylvania County," January 27, 1789, published in Fredericksburg Virginia Herald, January 29, 1789; Benjamin Johnson to Madison, January 19, 1789, 11 Papers of Madison 415–17, 428–29, 423–24. Madison's letter of Randolph was also published in the Virginia Herald and Fredericksburg Advertiser, January 15, 1789, Ketcham, note 59 *supra* at 276, Rutland, note 32 *supra*, at 48.

[139]Ketcham, note 59 *supra*, at 276. See also Rutland, note 32 *supra*, at 48.

[140]Ketcham, note 59 *supra*, at 276–77; see also Rutland, note 32 *supra*. at 48. See also George Nichols to Madison, January 2, 1789, and January 24, 1789; Madison to Washington, January 14, 1789; Henry Lee to Madison, January 14, 1789, 11 Papers of Madison 406–09, 427–28, 417–18, 420–27.

[141]Ketcham, note 59 *supra*, at 277.

[142]Madison was not willing to support "alterations" to the Constitution that would change the fundamental powers of the government or weaken the power of the national government to control the states. See Bowling, note 4 *supra*, at 225–26.

dermine that goal.[143] They viewed the amendments as a "Tub to the Whale," designed to divert antifederalist s from making more substantive changes in the Constitution.[144] Some members of Congress agreed that a bill of rights might be important, but thought there were greater priorities, such as establishing various executive departments, raising revenue, and creating a judiciary. Finally, many in Congress doubtless sympathized with the position expressed by Georgia's James Jackson, who declared that the Constitution was "like a vessel just launched, and lying at the wharf; she is untried, you can hardly discover any one of her properties." Therefore, he argued that amendments should be delayed until this ship of state could be launched and Congress "guided by the experiment."[145]

Madison now believed that amendments ought to be added to the Constitution. He did not think them necessary to preserve liberty—on that point he had not wavered. But he felt a personal obligation to fulfill his campaign promise of supporting amendments. He also hoped that such amendments would remove the fears of many Americans who had opposed the Constitution. Moreover, he believed that Congressional action on a bill of rights would defeat the call for a second convention. Such a convention, he was convinced, would destroy the new Constitution.[146] As he later told Congress, Madison was "unwilling to see a door opened for a reconsideration of the whole structure of the Constitution—for a re-consideration of the principles and the substance of the powers given because I doubt if such a door were opened, we should be very likely to stop at that point which would be safe to the Government itself."[147]

For Madison, then, the bill of rights was now a question of tactics: how could he get the amendments adopted? His "strategy was to seize the initiative for amendments, to use the Federalist majority in the First Congress to finish the unavoidable business of amendments

---

[143]In North Carolina, which had not yet ratified the constitution, Hugh Williamson believed that some antifederalists also held this position. Williamson to Madison, May 24, 1789, 12 Papers of Madison 184.

[144]The phrase comes from Jonathan Swift, "Tale of a Tub" (1704): "Seamen have a custom, when they meet a whale, to fling him out an empty tub by way of amusement, to divert him from laying violent hands upon the ship." Quoted in Bowling, note 4 *supra*, at 223.

[145]I Annals of Congress, 1st Cong. 1st. Sess., 442.

[146]See, for example, Madison to George Eve, January 2, 1789, 11 Papers of Madison 404–05.

[147]Speech of Madison, I Annals of Congress, 1st Cong., 1st Sess. (debate of June 8. 1789), 450.

in such a way as to remove from the national agenda the major Antifederalist objections. . . ."[148]

Even before the session began he sought the advice of sympathetic fellow federalists.[149] After Congress convened Madison's first strategic step was to involve President Washington in the campaign for a bill of rights. At this time Madison was Washington's closest advisor and part time speechwriter. In drafting Washington's first address to the Congress, which also served as Washington's inaugural address, Madison inserted a clause reminding Congress of its duty to consider proposing constitutional amendments in response to the "objections which have been urged against the System, or by the degree of inquietude which has given birth to them." Here Washington declined to make any specific recommendation, but placed his "entire confidence" in the Congress's "discernment and pursuit of the public good." The speech did urge that Congress show "a reverence for the characteristic rights of freemen, and a regard for the public harmony. . . ."[150]

On May 1 Madison proposed that the House send a formal response to the President "assuring him of their disposition to concur in giving effect to every measure which may tend to secure the liberties, promote the harmony, and advance the happiness and prosperity of their country." The House then appointed a committee, chaired by Madison, to draft this reply.[151] On May 5 Madison brought the resolution, which he wrote, to the floor. This resolution included the following paragraph: "The question arising out of the fifth article of the Constitution, [the amendment process] will receive all the attention demanded by its importance; and will, we trust be decided, under the influence of all the considerations to which you allude."[152]

This episode was certainly a coup for Madison. He was able to put into Washington's mouth his own views on the need for a bill of

---

[148]Storing, The Constitution and the Bill of Rights, in Rossum & McDowell (eds.), The American Founding: Politics, Statesmanship, and the Constitution (1981) 32.

[149]Tench Coxe to Madison, March 18 and 24, 1789, Edmund Randolph to Madison, March 26, 1789, 12 Papers of Madison 21, 27, 31.

[150]Address of the President to Congress, April 30, 1789, and Editorial Note, 12 *id.* at 123 & 120. See also 1 Messages and Paper of the Presidents 43–49 (Richardson ed. 1897).

[151]I Annals of Congress, 1st cong., 1st Sess., 242 (May 1, 1789); 12 Papers of Madison 134n.

[152]I Annals of Congress, 1st Cong., 1st Sess., 258 (May 5, 1789); 12 Papers of Madison 132–34. Washington also asked Madison to help him draft a short, formal reply to the House resolution. Washington to Madison, May 5, 1789, reprinted in 30 Writings of George Washington 310, and 310 (Fitzpatrick ed. 1939).

rights. Historian Robert Rutland has suggested that Washington was acting "cautiously"[153] in calling for Congress to act in its own "discernment of the public good." However, it seems more likely that by having Washington ask Congress to act Madison was shrewdly getting the President to endorse amendments without appearing too heavy handed. By writing a speech in which Washington deferred to Congress to work out the details, Madison was not taking any great risk because Madison was already the most effective member of the Congress and was emerging as the "first man" of the House.[154]

Madison then followed this by becoming the prime draftsman of a resolution supporting the speech that he had written for Washington. Through Madison's adroit pen both the President and the House were on record supporting amendments to protect liberty.[155] All Madison had to do now was introduce these amendments and shepherd them through Congress. This, however, was no easy task.

On May 4 Madison told the Congress of his intention to propose amendments later in the month, but on the 25th Madison moved for a postponement. As he explained to Jefferson: "more urgent business" had caused a slight delay, but within a few weeks a "Bill of rights . . . will be proposed."[156]

On June 8 Madison finally had the opportunity to present his amendments. He told the House he was "bound in honor and in duty" to bring the amendments forward. His plan was to "advocate them until they shall be finally adopted or rejected by a constitutional majority of this House."[157] Others in the House wanted a delay, some because they opposed all amendments, some because they thought the Congress had more important work ahead of it. Madison noted that he had already postponed his motion once. In arguing

---

[153]Rutland, The Birth of the Bill of Rights, 1767–1791 198 (1955).

[154]Editorial Note on Madison at the First Session of the First Federal Congress, 12 Papers of Madison 52–53.

[155]Later in the debates Madison produced a letter from Washington in which the President declared he saw "nothing exceptionable in the proposed amendments" and some were "importantly necessary" while others, while not essential were "necessary to quiet the fears of some respectable characters and well meaning Men." Thus, Washington declared his hope they would receive "a favorable reception in both houses" of Congress. Washington to Madison [ca. 31 May 1789], 12 Papers of Madison 191.

[156]I Annals of Congress, 1st Cong., 1st. Sess., 257; 4 Documentary History of the First Federal Congress of the United States of America: Legislative Histories: Amendments to the Constitution Through Foreign Officers Bill 3 (Bickford & Veit, eds., 1986); Madison to Jefferson, May 27, 1789, 12 Papers of Madison 186.

[157]I Annals of Congress, 1st Cong., 1st Sess., 440–41 (Debate of June 8, 1789).

against further postponements, Madison asserted one of his major points in favor of amendments: that "if we continue to postpone from time to time, and refuse to let the subject come into view, it may well occasion suspicions, which, though not well founded, may tend to inflame or prejudice the public mind against our decisions." Madison feared that the "very respectable number of our constituents" who had asked for amendments might conclude that Congress was "not sincere in our desire to incorporate such amendments in the constitution as will secure those rights, which they consider as not sufficiently guarded."[158] Although about to propose amendments, Madison was still not advocating them for their substance. Rather, he argued he had a moral obligation to present them and that it would be politically expedient for Congress to accept them.

Madison's initial speech led the staunch federalist Roger Sherman to urge the House to delay action until it was "a proper time."[159] Madison responded by reiterating the necessity of calming those who feared the new strong central government. He wanted "the opportunity of proving to those who were opposed to" the Constitution that "those who have been friendly to the adoption of this constitution" were also "sincerely devoted to liberty and a Republican Government" and not attempting to "lay the foundation of an aristocracy or despotism." He reminded the House of those who had "apprehensions" that the new government wished to "deprive them of the liberty for which they valiantly fought and honorably bled." He believed that many who had opposed the Constitution were now ready "to join their support to the cause of Federalism, if they were satisfied on this one point." Furthermore, he argued amendments might lure North Carolina and Rhode Island into the union.[160]

While proposing amendments, Madison remained ambivalent about a bill of rights. Madison did not propose a bill of rights as such. Rather, he proposed a series of changes in the main body of the Constitution which would have been scattered throughout the document. Madison noted that his proposal "relates to what may be called

---

[158] *Id.* at 440–44.

[159] *Id.* at 444.

[160] *Id.* at 449. Without knowing that Madison had already introduced amendments, William R. Davie of North Carolina wrote him urging that amendments be adopted before the North Carolina convention, which was scheduled for the following November. Davie to Madison, June 10, 1789, 12 Papers of Madison 210–11. See also George Lee Turberville to Madison, June 16, 1789, *id.* at 222–23, explaining that amendments would "tend very much to satisfy the minds of *those who were really fearful of danger* to the Liberties of their fellow citizens" while undermining those who opposed the Constitution for selfish and narrow reasons.

a bill of rights"[161] but he did not call it that, just as he did not present it as a unified package.

Madison did not argue with passion or even much conviction for his proposal. He admitted that he had "never considered this provision so essential to the federal constitution" that it should have been allowed to impede ratification. But, with the Constitution ratified Madison was willing to concede "that in a certain form and to a certain extent, such a provision was neither improper nor altogether useless."[162]

Madison followed this tepid endorsement of his amendments with a balanced assessment of the pros and cons of a bill of rights. He conceded the virtues of the opposition, but found reasons to counter all their points. Madison's most innovative proposal concerned the vexing problem that "by enumerating particular exceptions of the grant of power, it would disparage those rights which were not placed in that enumeration; and it might follow, by implication, that those rights which were not singled out, were intended to be assigned into the hands of the General Government, and were consequently insecure." He argued that this problem could be "guarded against." He had already done so with a provision which became the ninth amendment.[163]

Madison concluded his opening speech on the bill of rights debate by asking that the House appoint a committee to consider the amendments. He argued that "we should obtain the confidence of our fellow citizens, in proportion as we fortify the rights of the people against the encroachments of the government." To Madison's disappointment, the House referred the amendments to a committee of the whole, thus delaying the process of adoption.[164]

Madison had introduced the amendments because he claimed it "was my duty" to do so.[165] His unstated goal was to convince the nation's moderate antifederalists to support the Constitution. His subsequent correspondence indicates that he believed his strategy

---

[161] I Annals of Congress, 1st Cong., 1st Sess., 453.

[162] *Ibid.*

[163] *Id.* at 456. Madison's original provision read: "The exceptions here or elsewhere in the constitution, made in favor of particular rights, shall not be so construed as to diminish the just importance of other rights retained by the people, or as to enlarge the powers delegated by the constitution; but either as actual limitations of such powers, or as inserted merely for greater caution."

[164] *Id.* at 459.

[165] *Ibid.*

was working. He was certain that the amendments, if adopted, would "be satisfactory to a majority of those who have opposed the Constitution."[166] He was pleased that they were "limited to points which are important in the eyes of many and can be objectionable in those of none." Proudly he noted that "the structure & stamina of the Govt. are as little touched as possible."[167]

Part of Madison's strategy was to avoid controversial political issues so that his amendments would pass as quickly as possible. He thought that "nothing of a controvertible nature ought to he hazarded" in order to avoid a defeat of the amendments. He told Edmund Randolph that he had avoided anything of a "controversial nature" because of the "caprice & discord of opinions" in the House and Senate, which had to approve the amendments by a two-thirds vote, and in the state legislatures, three-fourths of which had to approve the amendments. The amendments had a "twofold object of removing the fears of the discontented and of avoiding all such alterations as would either displease the adverse side, or endanger the success of the measure." In sending them to a North Carolina correspondent he doubtless hoped to push that state toward ratification.[168]

Because the amendments were now in the committee of the whole, Madison had to weigh carefully when he ought to try to bring them up again. Madison's energies, and those of the rest of Congress, were directed at other pending legislation on such matters as the removal power of the President, import duties, western land, and the salaries of congressmen. For the next month most of his correspondence focused on these issues, rather than on the bill of rights. This reflects Madison's low key and deliberate approach to amendments. He had done his "duty" in introducing a bill of rights, and he would continue to fight for the proposal. But, he was not preoccupied with the question.

Tench Coxe, a Philadelphia federalist, agreed with this analysis and happily noted that "the most ardent & irritable among our friends are well pleased" with the amendments, as were "honest" antifederalists. Edmund Randolph, meanwhile, noted that "*strong*

---

[166]Madison to Jefferson, June 13, 1789, 12 Papers of Madison 218.

[167]Madison to Edmund Randolph, June 15, 1789, *id.* at 219.

[168]Madison to Edmund Pendleton, June 21, 1789, Madison to Edmund Randolph, June 15, 1789, and Madison to Samuel Johnston, June 21, 1789, *id.* at 253, 219, 250. See also Madison to Tench Coxe, June 24, 1789, Madison to George Nichols, July 5, 1789, *id.* at 257, 282.

foederalists" in Virginia supported the amendments, while among diehard antifederalists "nothing, nay not even the abolishment of direct taxation would satisfy those, who are most clamorous." Another Virginia friend was pleased the amendments would protect individual liberty "so far as declarations on paper can effect that purpose" while at the same time "leaving unimpaired the great Powers of the government."[169] Hugh Williamson, a leading North Carolina federalist, liked what he saw, but correctly predicted that his state would not ratify the Constitution until after Congress had approved the amendments.[170]

On July 21, during a brief lull in the legislative business, Madison "begged the House to indulge him in the further consideration of amendments." Madison's colleagues were in no mood for another debate in the committee of the whole. Some, like Roger Sherman, opposed any amendments and wanted to end the entire process but a majority voted for a select committee of one member from each state to consider the amendments.[171]

On August 13 the select committee reported back to Congress. For the next eight sessions the House debated the amendments, finally adopting them on August 22. Although active in these debates, Madison did not dominate them.[172] Madison never spoke directly to the merits of a bill of rights but throughout the debates almost always argued for their expediency. Initially he asked if it was "desirable to keep up a division among the people of the United States on a point in which they consider their most essential rights are concerned?" He argued that consideration of the issue would "promote that spirit of urbanity and unanimity which the Government itself stands in need of for its more full support."[173] Later he argued for a particular clause because "it be desired by three important States." Even on the protection of religious liberty—something he fervently supported—Madison would not affirmatively argue for his amendment. He re-

[169]Tench Coxe to Madison, June 18, 1789; Edmund Randolph to Madison, June 30, 1789; and Joseph Jones to Madison, June 24, 1789, *id.* at 239, 273, 258–59. See also Edward Stevens to Madison, June 25, 1789, *id.* at 261.

[170]Hugh Williamson to Madison, July 2, 1789, *id.* at 274–75. See also Benjamin Hawkins to Madison [July] 3, 1789, *id.* at 275.

[171]I Annals of Congress, 1st Cong., 1st Sess. 685–92.

[172]Madison spoke twenty-three times during these debates, while Elbridge Gerry spoke twenty-nine times. Nine other men spoke at least ten times each, for a collective total of 130 times. This is based on a count of speeches in *id.* at 730–808.

[173]*Id.* at 731.

fused to say "Whether the words are necessary or not" arguing only that members "of the State Conventions . . . seemed to entertain an opinion that under the [necessary and proper] clause of the constitution" Congress might "infringe the rights of conscience, and establish a national religion." He consistently "appeal[ed] to the gentlemen who have heard the voice of the country, to those who have attended the debates of the States conventions, whether the amendments now proposed are not those most strenuously required by the opponents to the constitution?"[174]

During the debates over the Constitution many of the antifederalists had reflected "the traditional politics of consensus, the old quest for unanimity, not the new majoritarian politics of the constitution's promoters."[175] Ironically, in the congressional debates over the bill of rights Madison, who was perhaps America's first modern politician, reflected this older notion of politics. He sought reconciliation by giving the antifederalists the protections of liberty that they valued so highly.

Only twice in these debates did Madison seem to speak about the amendments with great enthusiasm. Both brief speeches showed that Madison remained more committed to limiting the powers of the states than to limiting the power of the national government. Thus, he passionately supported a proposal that would have prohibited the states from infringing "the equal right of conscience . . . freedom of speech or the press, . . . [and] the right of trial by jury in criminal cases." Madison thought this was "the most valuable amendment in the whole list."[176] Although the House approved this clause,[177] the Senate did not and thus these rights did not become applicable to the states until after the adoption of the Fourteenth Amendment and its modern development, starting with *Gitlow* v. *New York*.[178] Similarly, Madison strongly and successfully opposed adding the word "expressly" to what became the tenth amendment. Madison thought this would give the states too much power.[179]

---

[174] *Id.* at 746, 758, 775.

[175] P. Maier, note 85 *supra* at 228.

[176] I Annals of Congress, at 783–84.

[177] See note 7 *supra*.

[178] Gitlow v. New York, 268 U.S. 652 (1925).

[179] I Annals of Congress, 1st Cong., 1st Sess., 790.

XI. A Reluctant Paternity and Modern Interpretation

Madison did not enjoy these debates. He wrote to Richard Peters of the "nauseous project of amendments."[180] This phrase has been subject to contradictory interpretations.[181] Jack Rakove has argued that Madison was "probably allud[ing] to the feelings of his colleagues in Congress rather than his own."[182] In another article Rakove has argued that the essence of the "nauseous project" statement was the fact that Madison's support the Bill of Rights was "only for expedient reasons of politics."[183] Robert Rutland, on the other hand, suggests this statement is an "offhand remark" and should not be taken "as a statement of fact." Rutland argues that this statement has been wrongly interpreted to indicate that Madison's support of the amendments was marred by "a tinge of hypocrisy."[184] In this context, Rutland takes exception to Rakove's comments on political expediency.

Rutland is on solid ground in arguing that this statement does not indicate a "tinge of hypocrisy" in Madison's support for the Bill of Rights. Madison, after all, did not think the substance of the amendments was "nauseous." Moreover, even as Madison fought for the Bill of Rights, he never appeared enthusiastic about the proposals. Given his cool and reserved support for the amendments, it would be impossible to consider him hypocritical, even if one were to interpret his "nauseous project" remark to refer to the substance of the amendments. Similarly, Rakove is correct in seeing Madison's support for the Bill of Rights as fundamentally political. Just because it was political does not mean, as Rutland implies, that the support was hypocritical. Here Rutland apparently misread both Madison and Rakove. Madison's support for the amendments was based on a coherent and rational political analysis of the needs of America under

---

180 Madison to Richard Peters, August 19, 1789, 12 Papers of Madison 346.

181 Kenneth Bowling, in A Tub to the Whale, note 4 *supra*, has ignored the phrase altogether, perhaps because it is so distracting, and so easily misunderstood. This analysis is based on Bowling's public comments on an earlier version of this paper at the Organization of American Historians meeting in 1990.

182 Rakove, The Madisonian Theory of Rights, 31 Wm. & Mary L. Rev. 245–46 (1990).

183 Rakove, Mr. Meese, Meet Mr. Madison, The Atlantic Monthly (Dec., 1986), 77, quoted at 84, col. 1.

184 Rutland, The Trivialization of the Bill of Rights, 31 William & Mary L. Rev. 287, 291 (1990).

the Constitution; such a motivation seems hardly an act of hypocrisy.

Rutland is also wrong, I think, in dismissing the statement as is merely an "off hand remark" or a "slip of the pen."[185] The "nauseous" comment was not an isolated one. Madison also described the debates over the amendments as "extremely difficult and fatiguing"[186] and "exceedingly wearisome."[187] What Madison found to be "nauseous," "fatiguing," and "wearisome" was the process of getting the amendments through Congress. No doubt it was. "Madison was sick and tired of the obstructionism of Roger Sherman, Aedanus Burke, William Loughton Smith, James Jackson, and other congressmen who thought the introduction of a bill of rights was a waste of time."[188] Madison probably found this obstructionism particularly distasteful because of his own ambivalence about the goal he sought.

While never actually opposed to the idea of rights, in 1787–89 Madison was never convinced a bill of rights was either necessary or completely harmless. To the end Madison was uncertain about the value of a bill of rights. A few days before the House endorsed the amendments, Madison observed that "we are so deep in them now, that right or wrong some thing must be done." This was hardly the sentiment of an enthusiastic partisan. But, Madison had not become one, even as he supported the addition of a bill of rights. With victory in sight, he could only marshal a series of weak arguments to support his position: a bill of rights was "a thing not improper in itself;" "had no assurances been given" of subsequent amendments the Constitution might not have been ratified; "as an honest man" Madison felt "bound" to support amendments after the Virginia convention; without his promise to support amendments Virginia would have elected antifederalists to Congress; if Madison had not introduced his amendments, opponents of the Constitution would have presented more damaging ones; once the amendments were adopted they "would kill the opposition every where, and by putting an end to the disaffection to the Govt. itself, enable the administration to venture on measures not otherwise safe"; the amendments would head off a second convention; and the amendments were necessary to bring North Carolina into the Union.[189]

[185] *Ibid.* This is also Rutland's terminology.

[186] Madison to Edmund Pendleton, August 21, 1789 12 Papers of Madison 348.

[187] Madison to Edmund Randolph, August 21, 1789, 12 Papers of Madison 348.

[188] Rutland, note 184 *supra*, at 292.

[189] Madison to Richard Peters, August 19, 1789, 12 Papers of Madison 347.

In sum, Madison argued that the bill of rights should be adopted because it might help the country, and could not hurt it. "We have" he told Congress "something to gain, and, if we proceed with caution, nothing to lose."[190]

Despite his ambivalence and misgivings about a bill of rights, Madison fought hard for the amendments. Duty to his constituents, duty to himself as an "honest man," and his keen sense of politics kept him going. But, so too, no doubt, did Madison's libertarian values. Whether opposing amendments during the ratification struggle or giving them lukewarm support in Congress, Madison rarely opposed the idea of protecting basic rights and liberties. He never denied the value of due process, freedom of expression, and religious liberty. If he doubted the value of the amendments, he never doubted the values they stood for. That, in the end, enabled him to support the Bill of Rights, even while uncertain if it was either necessary or prudent. He would, in effect, leave that question up to future generations.

Madison's ambivalence about the Bill of Rights serves to remind the living generation that liberty is ultimately protected, not by parchment barriers, but by the "vigilant . . . spirit which actuates the people of America."[191] The Bill of Rights articulates the goals of that spirit.

---

[190]Speech of Madison, in I Annals of Congress, 1st Cong., 1st Sess., 450 (June 8, 1789).

[191]Federalist 57, in 10 Papers of Madison 523.